PARALEGAL
PRACTICE

and
PROCEDURE

THIRD EDITION

A Practical Guide
for the
Legal Assistant

Deborah E. Larbalestrier

PRENTICE HALL
Englewood Cliffs, New Jersey 07632

Prentice-Hall International (UK) Limited, *London*
Prentice-Hall of Australia Pty. Limited, *Sydney*
Prentice-Hall Canada Inc., *Toronto*
Prentice-Hall Hispanoamericana, S.A., *Mexico*
Prentice-Hall of India Private Limited, *New Delhi*
Prentice-Hall of Japan, Inc., *Tokyo*
Simon & Schuster Asia Pte. Ltd., *Singapore*
Editora Prentice-Hall do Brasil, Ltda., *Rio de Janeiro*

© 1994 by
PRENTICE HALL
Englewood Cliffs, NJ

10   9   8   7   6   5   4   3

Library of Congress Cataloging-in-Publication Data

Larbalestrier, Deborah E., 1934–
    Paralegal practice and procedure : a practical guide for the legal
assistant / Deborah E. Larbalestrier.—3rd ed.
        p.   cm.
    Includes index.
    ISBN 0-13-108572-7 (case).—ISBN 0-13-108564-6 (paper)
    1. Legal assistants—United States—Handbooks, manuals, etc.
2. Legal secretaries—United States—Handbooks, manuals, etc.
I. Title.
KF320.L4L36   1994   94-28860
340'.023'73—dc20   CIP

ISBN 0-13-108572-7   ISBN 0-13-108564-6(PBK)

PRENTICE HALL
Career & Personal Development
Englewood Cliffs, NJ 07632
A Simon & Schuster Company

On the World Wide Web at http://www.phdirect.com

Printed in the United States of America

This book is dedicated to today's legal assistant
and others whose lives I have touched through my efforts
to establish a viable adjunct legal profession,
with the hope that this Third Edition will make their jobs
even easier, thereby making the years of hard work,
devotion, and sacrifice worthwhile.

CONTENTS

Chapter 6 How to State a Cause of Action in a Civil Case   93

Chapter 7   Pretrial Practice and Procedure   118

PREFACE TO THE THIRD EDITION

Since the Second Edition of *Paralegal Practice and Procedure,* new vistas and sites of potential employment have opened up to our profession, again advancing the state of the art of paralegalism.

In recent years, our society has become more litigious, and as a result, the need has grown for more legal services. This need has stimulated and encouraged the increase in the use of paralegals in law offices, bank institutions, corporations, government and generally in any office which has a legal department. Additionally, legal placement agencies and unemployment offices have seen the rise in the call for part-time paralegal assistants as well.

As predicted, the needs of society have drastically changed, and the Bar Association membership has, once again, risen to the task to accept and help assist in the delivery of legal services to the public, by opening opportunities for service to the public by the paraprofessional, i.e., the paralegal professional.

Listed below are some of the new topics covered in the Third Edition, which convey its value as a reference textbook for your office library.

1. On the horizon, state legislatures and bar associations have put into motion bills and proposals for partially licensing paralegals to perform certain tasks heretofore solely performed by licensed attorneys. You will find herein a state-by-state listing of these proposals.

2. This Third Edition of *Paralegal Practice and Procedure* sets forth new job opportunities for the paralegal. Noted and listed in this Edition are some of the new horizons opening up to paralegals today, which set forth tasks not previously envisioned either by the legal community or the paralegal community.

3. Included in this Third Edition is a chapter on legal ethics for paralegals, which discusses the pros and cons of the propriety of "free-
lance" paralegals, "independent contractors" and "paralegal
services" offered directly to the public. Such questions are asked
and answered as, "What is their status?" "What is the extent of their
competency and efficiency?" and, "Is this the unauthorized practice of law?"

4. We also set forth an In-House Training Program for those law offices
which have yet to recognize the feasibility of using the paralegal
within their firms.

5. This program can also be used to promote the valued legal secretary
to the position of a paralegal. Additionally, this In-House Paralegal Program can serve not only to enhance the skills of the current paralegal but can also show the young attorney associate the value of setting
aside his ego and permitting the paralegal to assist him in the practice of his profession.

6. A new chapter in this Edition concerns employer/employee rights,
or Workers' Compensation, with step-by-step procedures for the
preparation of employees' claims resulting from an industrial injury.
You California readers will note that the new laws regarding Workers' Compensation are also included.

7. There is a new chapter on how to set up a business entity from
scratch, step-by-step procedures for preparing the pertinent documents for a corporation, and a discussion of the various types of
stocks as well as their impact on the corporation's tax liability.

8. We have added an introduction to alternative methods of litigation,
including but not limited to arbitration methodology to settle claims
and litigate disputes, with forms and formats to illustrate their use
and to assist the paralegal in preparing these documents for the attorney.

9. There is a major change in the procedure for removing a state court
complaint to the federal court system.

10. Please note that the chapters on state and federal court systems have
been separated to make for easier reading.

11. Also note that there are revised and new sections to the chapters on
contracts; criminal law; evidence; legal research; real estate; and torts.

12. Included in this Third Edition is a new chapter with overview of the law regarding trademarks/protectable business marks, as well as trade secrets and how to draft an unfair competition lawsuit.

13. Additionally, there are step-by-step procedures on how and when to use the computer in obtaining discovery and developing evidence for your attorney, which include legal research, exhibits, and step-by-step procedures for the retrieval process.

For example:

a) The duties of a legal assistant regarding computerized legal procedures in retrieving case-law date and trial preparation.
b) The use of litigation support systems to aid the legal assistant in preparing legal memoranda, briefs, points and authorities, and such other research material as required by the attorney.
c) An overview step-by-step procedure for the usc of information and data-based computer/word processor systems.

> There are many new forms, formats and checklists, as well as new examples and thought-provoking problems to do self-testing,
> AND MUCH, MUCH MORE.

In summary, this Third Edition focuses on the new job opportunities and changes in the duties of paralegals which have occurred because of both the relaxing of the methodology and utilization of paralegals and the change in society's needs.

We hope this Third Edition will be of additional value and assistance to the paralegal in completing the tasks assigned in a more competent and efficient manner.

And if, in your state, the bar associations and/or state legislatures have already licensed you, or may be in the future, to perform certain legal tasks heretofore performable only by attorneys, this book will aid you in ethically performing these new tasks.

Deborah E. Larbalestrier

ACKNOWLEDGMENTS

Many thanks to the following attorneys for their contributions, ideas, and suggestions for making this book more valuable: James H. Kindel, Esq., Kindel & Anderson; Edward B. Mills, Esq., Sole Practitioner; Benjamin S. Seigel, Esq., Katz, Hoyt & Bell; Hugh Slate, Esq., Slate & Leoni; Ron Jeffrey Tasoff, Esq., Tasoff & Tasoff; Arleen Kaiser, Esq. and Teri Cannon, Esq., Dean, School of Law, University of West Los Angeles.

And to the Litigations Support Systems (Los Angeles): Barbara Angelo, Legal Specialist, WANG Laboratories, Inc.; Irwin G. Manley, Esq., Administrator of Information Services, Gibson, Dunn & Crutcher; Don Meyer, Frederick & Associates; Pamela A. Robinson, Librarian, Gibson, Dunn & Crutcher; Roger Rosen, Paralegal, Gibson, Dunn & Crutcher; John B. Watts, Litigations Paralegal, Hahn, Cavier & Leff, Esquires; Frances Longmire, Freelance Paralegal; Phyllis L. Hicks and Doug Carey, Computer/Word Processor Operators, Orthopedic Hospital; Alice Fitzpatrick, Account Executive, Mead Data Central; and Debbie Preheim, President, Southern Nevada Paralegal Training, Inc.

A very special thanks and acknowledgment to Angela Clark, Mari Aranoff and Russell Bartlett, all top-notch legal secretaries; and to all the wonderful people at Private Secretary for their hard work in typing and proofing this manuscript.

PART ONE

GENERAL DUTIES, PRACTICES, AND PROCEDURES

CHAPTER 1

Paralegal Ethics

THE FUTURE OF THE PARALEGAL PROFESSION

What lies ahead for the paralegal profession? Will we be seeing "paralegal" firms in the next decade? Will we be seeing law students and young associates attending paralegal schools to obtain paralegal skills, such as Court procedures, how to draft complaints and answers, etc.? These were questions asked ten years or so ago. They were hard questions then. Today, in 1994, we have some of the answers.

It is now well established that the paralegal profession is here to stay. Law students have been introduced to the training being taught to paralegals; and we do have "paralegal firms or clinics."

But the status of the paralegal profession is still in a state of flux. It is still crystal clear that there is the need for validation of professional achievement. Formal certification of some type may be a benefit to all concerned. The paralegal profession should be willing to demonstrate its concern for accountability to the organized bar, in the same manner and form as the public demands of attorneys. Additionally, this form of ethical procedure would enhance the quality and credibility of its professional conduct.

The major stumbling block to some form of licensing and/or certification is the phrase "practice of law" and what it means.

It can reasonably be assumed that the basis on which the established legal profession determined what constituted the "unauthorized practice of law" has its foundation in the nine Canons of the ABA Model Code of Professional Responsibility.

The "practice of law," as defined by the legal profession, makes no refer-

3

ence to the delivery of legal services to the public. That is to say, it does not specifically say that educated, well-trained and highly experienced laymen could not deliver legal services to the general public. Nor do the Canons make reference to the conduct of lay persons or non-lawyers. Once hired by an attorney, their conduct is presumed and assumed to be on the same standard as that of the attorney for whom they work.

There have been attempts made to establish a Code of Ethics for these non-lawyers. There are several versions circulating in the paralegal community via paralegal organizations throughout the country, but not under one umbrella like the Canons of the ABA for lawyers which are adhered to throughout the country.

As a result, members of the paralegal community must, and for the most part do, rely on their common sense, experience and education to protect themselves, their profession, AND the attorneys and their clients, to insure the integrity and competence of their performance on the job.

WHY THE STUMBLING BLOCK?

As predicted by the U.S. Labor Department back in the late 1980s, the paralegal profession has grown, and is still growing, by leaps and bounds.

This growth was and is predicated upon the new job opportunities which have opened up for the utilization of these paraprofessionals, such as in the military, legal departments of health care organizations and in the police departments of some cities. Add to this the final realization by attorneys of the economic benefits in hiring a well-trained and educated paraprofessional.

And therein rests the problem.

While there are many independent paralegals who are well-trained, educated and with years of experience who just decided to go out on their own for personal reasons, there has also emerged the "legal technician" or "independent paralegal" who it seems is apparently not supervised and/or does not work with attorneys. Some of these individuals have only had "hours" of education, as opposed to "years."

It is alleged that such people are operating unchecked or without credentials throughout the country. Still to be decided by the organized bar is whether or not these lay persons are impostors; if they are practicing law without a license; or if they are bona fide paralegals, and how to control them. This question is still being debated on the floors of various State legislatures and bar association committee meetings (See Table 1).

TABLE 1: STATE-BY-STATE REVIEW REGARDING PARALEGALS*

Alabama

Paralegals in Alabama are looking into drafting legislation to regulate paralegals in the state. Also, Alabama paralegals who work with the Legal Services Corporation are looking into establishing standards for paralegals.

Alaska

The Alaska Supreme Court has adopted a proposed court rule, effective July 15, 1993, which would allow for the award of paralegal fees under the same rule which allows attorney fees.

Arizona

The state bar's UPL Task Force has been examining the issue of UPL in the state. The Task Force, which is drafting new supreme court rules (to be adopted in 1994, if approved), has invited paralegals to provide comments and suggestions concerning the UPL issue from a paralegal's perspective. A bill, newly introduced in the legislature, would make it a crime to engage in the practice of law not consistent with the supreme court rules.

Arkansas

The Arkansas Bar Association has formed a committee to look into regulation and standards of paralegals. The committee will be studying education and credentialing for paralegals.

California

An assembly bill to allow nonlawyers to provide assistance directly to the public died in committee. Another bill is expected to be introduced in the near future. Pursuant to the direction of the state supreme court, a task force was established to look into regulation of paralegals.

Colorado

The state bar association has a committee which is looking at standards for utilization of paralegals.

Connecticut

A company with the name Legal Documentation Co. avoided a charge

---

* Copyright 1993. James Publishing, Inc. Reprinted with permission from *Legal Assistant Today.* For subscription information, call (714) 755-5450.

of UPL by agreeing to remove "Legal" from the company name and changing its name to The Clerical Documentation Co.

Delaware

The Board of UPL of the Supreme Court of Delaware issued an Order in late 1991 stating that, among other duties, paralegals who attend mediation sessions in lieu of attorneys are not engaged in UPL. The Order expands the role of the paralegal in Delaware.

District of Columbia

(Because of its status as a nonstate, the District of Columbia has neither a legislative body nor a state court. It does have paralegals and paralegal associations, which are nevertheless interested in studying regulation and standards.)

Florida

The Florida Bar Association has established a committee to implement the recommendations of its Nonlawyer Practice Committee (formerly known as the Legal Technician Study Committee), formed in 1991 to study legal technician services in Florida and to consider whether some form of regulation should be imposed. Among its recommendations were that the supreme court

impose limited regulation of legal technicians. The new committee has been given two years to study the issue and present its findings.

Georgia

The state bar established a task force which is looking into regulation of traditional paralegals. They anticipate a report in the next year.

Hawaii

Bills were introduced in the state legislature related to defining UPL, which definitions would have limited traditional paralegal activities. The local paralegal association is working with the committee in the legislature on the language of the bill.

Idaho

A UPL case is pending against a former insurance adjuster who is functioning as an insurance adjuster/paralegal. He is involved in negotiating claims to conclusion for insurance companies.

Illinois

Two 1991 bills introduced in the state legislature to regulate nontraditional paralegals died in committee. Although nothing has been introduced yet, at the time of the bill's defeat, its sponsor indicated that he would try again in the future.

Indiana

The NFPA and local paralegal associations were instrumental in persuading the Muncie Bar Association to abandon proposed local court rules which if adopted would have limited paralegal duties in that jurisdiction, particularly with respect to small claims court, to largely clerical activity. A task force established by the supreme court is studying the role of paralegals in providing legal services directly to the public, and the Indiana State Bar Association's House of Delegates recently adopted guidelines for the utilization of paralegal services as a result.

Iowa

The Legal Assistant Committee of the Iowa State Bar Association has been gathering information in an effort to make a recommendation to the bar association on the regulation of paralegals, and members of the local paralegal association have drafted legislation for regulation of traditional paralegals.

Kansas

The state bar has reactivated its UPL committee.

Kentucky

A Kentucky State Supreme Court justice indicated that he will establish a committee to look at regulation of traditional paralegals.

Louisiana

The local paralegal association has expressed its interest in some form of affiliate membership with the bar association, which might involve a discussion of regulation (although such membership is voluntary).

Maine

The Maine Commission of Legal Needs conducted a study on legal needs in Maine. Among its recommendations was that a system of nonlawyers/paralegals based in courthouses and relevant governmental offices be developed to assist people who need help in dealing with forms and procedure, and that licensure guidelines be developed to permit the supervised practice of law by paraprofessionals, including client counseling and court representation in routine legal matters or certain types of cases.

Maryland

A bill, signed by the governor, allows a nonlawyer to represent a landlord or tenant in summary ejection proceedings in the District Court of Maryland. The Maryland State Bar Association has a Special Committee on Paralegals which has as one of its goals to formulate a bar position in the event of future paralegal licensing legislation.

Massachusetts

UPL cases are pending against DocuPrep for preparing forms, etc.

Michigan

Ethical Opinion R1-125 issued, which provides that a paralegal employed by a lawyer may, in the course of such employment, appear and act for a party in an administrative proceeding as authorized by law.

Minnesota

Pursuant to the direction of the state supreme court, the Minnesota State Bar Association has a Paralegal Task Force which recommended that among other things, the bar association should oppose the licensing of independent paralegals to practice without the supervision of an attorney, and the bar association should take steps, through education and cooperative efforts, to increase the utilization of paralegals working under the supervision of attorneys.

Mississippi

House Bill 940, proposing regulation of traditional paralegals, died. It has not been reintroduced, and there are no plans for similar legislation this year.

Missouri

Attorneys responding to a state bar association survey indicated that they saw no need to regulate paralegals in the state. Members of the Missouri Alliance of Paralegal Associations did not actively endorse the pursuit of regulation by the bar. The Barton County Bar Association is conducting a study relating to regulation of paralegals.

Montana

Senate Bill 9, which would allow county commissioners to appoint or authorize nonattorney court assistants to assist civil litigants in certain courts of limited jurisdiction, was introduced. The state bar association formed an ad hoc committee to look into paralegal regulation.

Nebraska

No current activity reported.

Nevada

A committee has been established pursuant to the direction of the supreme court to propose a regulatory program for paralegals. The Judiciary Committee of the State Legislature is expected to review legislation to regulate paralegals. An independent paralegal in Las Vegas was contacted by a member of the legislature and requested to draft a bill for regulation of paralegals.

New Hampshire

The New Hampshire Bar unanimously adopted associate membership status for paralegals. The bar association's Task Force on Regulation is looking specifically at educational standards and regulation of paralegals.

New Jersey

New Jersey has an Unauthorized Practice of Law Committee. The supreme court issued a ruling that it was not UPL for a nontraditional paralegal to deliver services directly to attorneys.

New Mexico

A proposed supreme court rule defines "legal assistant" as well as sets forth the definition of "practice of law." The New Mexico State Bar also has a Work Study Group Subcommittee to study regulation for delivery of legal services by nonlawyers, specifically nontraditional paralegals;

another subgroup of the subcommittee is focusing on paralegal affiliation with the state bar.

New York

A state bar association committee is addressing revising the guidelines for the utilization of paralegals.

North Carolina

The 1980 recommendation of the state bar's Special Committee on Paralegals, that no program of licensure or certification of paralegals be implemented, still stands.

North Dakota

Although there is no supreme court or bar association committee, local paralegal associations have begun to study regulations and standards.

Ohio

The Ohio Supreme Court Task Force has held public hearings; one issue was the regulation of paralegals. Its report is being drafted for presentation to the supreme court.

Oklahoma

The Oklahoma Bar Association has a Legal Assistant Committee, the aim of which is to develop, promote, and present continuing education for the bench and bar on the economics and utilization of legal assistants. There is a house bill pending that defines "legal assistant," and specifies when legal assistant fees are recoverable.

Oregon

A task force, established to determine the need for legal technicians in Oregon, issued a report recommending regulation of nontraditional paralegals. The report was presented to the State Bar House of Delegates and State Supreme Court. In 1991, a bill for regulation of nontraditional paralegals (legal technicians) was introduced in the state legislature, but met strong opposition by the members of the bar and bench.

Pennsylvania

A general licensing bill, House Bill 1401, is still pending.

Rhode Island

Although there is no state bar committee or state court committee studying the issue, local paralegal associations are looking at criteria for practicing paralegals.

South Carolina

The South Carolina Supreme Court issued an order in which the court declined to adopt rules defining the practice of law.

South Dakota

The supreme court adopted Rule 92-5, which sets guidelines for the utilization of traditional paralegals.

Tennessee

The Tennessee Bar Association presented a proposal to the Tennessee Supreme Court whereby nonlawyers would come under the jurisdiction of the Board of Professional Responsibility regarding UPL. A local paralegal association has drafted language, in case it was needed, for legislation to regulate traditional paralegals. There are no plans, however, to introduce it at this time.

Texas

One proposed bill would regulate traditional paralegals who work under the direct supervision of an attorney. A second bill, drafted by the Texas Coalition of Legal Reform, proposes limited legal services by state-certified Providers of Limited Legal Services (POLLS), who would be allowed to provide and sell legally-oriented materials directly to consumers, to provide general instructions on their use, to teach consumers to research their own legal problem by using law libraries, and to provide information on dispute resolution.

Utah

House Bill No. 9, which would allow judges and court commissioners in divorce courts to be provided the services of a law-trained legal assistant to assist in certain duties, was introduced.

Vermont

The Board of Bar Managers appointed an ad hoc committee to research the issue of nonlawyers appearing before magistrates in family court.

Virginia

The State Bar Committee issued an Opinion setting forth specific guidelines for real estate closings, and allows nonlawyers to conduct real estate closings. Local paralegal associations are looking into adopting standards and guidelines for the utilization of legal assistants.

Washington

The Limited Practice Rule for Closing Officers permits non-lawyers who satisfy the limited practice requirements to engage in certain duties for the transfer of real property. The Washington State Bar Association Legal Assistant's Committee is currently studying regulation issues. A pilot program began which provides for facilitators (nonlawyers/paralegals) to be stationed in the county courthouses in several counties to assist pro se litigants with procedural matters relating to their litigation.

West Virginia

The Board of Governors of the West Virginia State Bar has approved a recommendation from its Legal Assistant Committee that the bar association use the ABA model guidelines for the utilization of legal assistants. The board will now look into further use and implementation of the guidelines.

Wisconsin

The state bar reactivated its UPL committee to look at nonlawyers providing services, such as legal software, to the public. The paralegal association in Wisconsin has been working with a lobbyist to draft legislation for traditional and nontraditional paralegals.

Wyoming

The state bar association recently formed a committee to develop guidelines for legal assistants practicing in Wyoming.

It is for these reasons, as well as the recent incidents of paralegal-attorney improprieties that a discussion of ethical considerations is timely. Presented below are some problems which may have occurred during your office day, and which may bear discussing with your immediate supervisor.

For example, have you ever gone on a date with a client of your attorney? Dated a defendant or a defendant's witness? Have you had what you thought was an "innocent" lunch? THINK ABOUT IT: Conflict of interest or not? The next few pages are food for thought.

FACT SITUATIONS

1. A paralegal working for a partner in a law firm was asked by her attorney to transfer her billable hours from one client's case to another's and to bill on a separate case for hours she had not worked at all. She approached the senior partner of the firm, who was also the chair of the State Bar Ethics Committee, and requested to be transferred to another attorney. The senior partner approved her transfer and said he would speak to the partner. Months later the situation was repeated with the partner's new paralegal.

2. In the first month of her new job, while going through some files, a probate paralegal found a case that was five years old and had not been worked on for a long time. It appeared that the Court dates had been repeatedly postponed and the case forgotten. She pointed out the lack of progress on this case to the attorney. The attorney's response was "We'll get to it when we get to it."

3. A paralegal moved from a plaintiff to a defense P.I. firm and was asked to work on the same case. He notified his attorney of the situation and was told to use what he knew.

4. A paralegal received a frantic call from a client in a dissolution case who said she just found out that her husband had cleaned out their joint checking account. The attorney was out of town. The client asked if she should clean out their joint savings account. The paralegal responded "Well, I can't give you legal advice, but if I were you I would do it."

5. A client wearing a surgical collar came into his attorney's office to sign some papers regarding his personal injury case. Later on that day the

paralegal saw the client walking along the street without the collar. She told the attorney and he told her to ignore it.

Which of the following situations does *not* violate any Code of Ethics for Legal Assistants as adopted by The American Paralegal Association?

a) Ralph worked as a clerk in a law office for ten years. He now has his own paralegal consulting firm.

b) Julie works in a law office under a duly qualified attorney. She drafts legal documents.

c) Ralph is a certified legal assistant and consults with business clients, giving them timely advice.

d) All of the above are in violation of professional ethics.

Which of the following situations does *not* violate any Code of Ethics for Legal Assistants as adopted by The American Paralegal Association?

a) As Mrs. Dalton left the office, Sue and Margaret, legal assistants, discussed her previous divorce package and how it wouldn't apply to her current position. They were standing in the receptionist's area at the time.

b) Sue's mother had some legal problems with a real estate closing so Sue, responding to her mother's request, talked to the real estate attorney to learn some of the facts.

c) Margaret's sister needed a divorce so Margaret prepared all the paperwork for her so she could handle her own.

d) All of the above are in violation of professional ethics.

Which of the following situations does *not* violate any Code of Ethics for Legal Assistants as adopted by The American Paralegal Association?

a) Terry asks his friend Mike to stop at the site of an accident so he can give his paralegal business card to the injured driver. The ambulance is on the scene.

b) Terry asks his friend Mike to stop at the site of an accident so he can give his paralegal business card to the injured driver. The ambulance is *not* on the scene.

c) Terry receives a bonus for every client he brings into the law office. Therefore, he places an ad in the local paper for the law firm.

d) All of the above are in violation of professional ethics.

Which of the following situations does *not* violate any Code of Ethics for Legal Assistants as adopted by The American Paralegal Association?

a) Sam Horn works in a law office as a legal assistant, duly qualified and certified. He prints cards saying: "Law Firm of G, L & M, specialists in litigation and general practice; Sam Horn, certified paralegal."

b) Alexandra Day works in a law office as a legal assistant, duly certified. She prints cards saying: "Alex Day, specialist in litigation and general practice."

c) Becky Night works at an insurance company doing legal research as a certified paralegal. Her cards say: "Becky Night, Certified Legal Research Analyst."

d) All of the above are in violation of professional ethics.

THE LEGAL ASSISTANT AS NOTARY PUBLIC: AN ETHICAL DILEMMA

A legal assistant acting as a notary public is playing a double role, which is fraught with pitfalls and possible conflicts of interest.

To illustrate this dilemma, consider the following:

1. As you know, the most important obligation a notary has to the public being served is:

- To judge what acts constitute the practice of law; and
- What acts constitute the practice of a notary public.

2. And further, a notary public is only responsible for:

- Executing and witnessing documents;
- Confirming that the signatures are legal; and
- The truth or authenticity of said signature.

To do anything else subjects a notary to a possible lawsuit or claim.

On the other hand, the duties and role of a legal assistant per se, in general, go far beyond that of a notary public, such as:

- To interview clients—after instruction of attorney;
- The drafting of preliminary and final documents after approval by attorney;
- The conduction of preliminary and final legal research after consultation with the attorney;
- The conduction of investigation of clients and witnesses at the insistence and request of the attorney:
- The necessary and required legwork and follow-up procedures mentioned above and much, much more in some offices.

So that when you put these two professionals into one individual, as a practical day-by-day procedure, separating them within one individual is no easy task. Hence, the legal assistant who acts as a notary public should ask himself/herself the following questions in order to determine whether stepping into that grey area could be construed as the practice of law.

- Should you charge for it? If so, does the fact that you are being paid cause you to be more careful?
- Do you take more time and give more legal information because you are being paid directly?
- If you are doing this merely as a convenience for the office and do not charge, are you less careful since the ultimate responsibility lies with the boss?
- Do you put more time and have the tendency to give legal advice because you are trained in the art, if it is being done as part of your job as a legal assistant?
- Do you take more time and tend to give legal advice because the client is a friend of yours or do you feel sorry for clients who are unfamiliar with American law and language, and hence do not understand?
- Do you notarize a document because you are told to do so by your employer—such as notarizing a buddy's signature or an unknown client's signature, simply because you have been instructed to do so by your employer?

To further underscore the double role of the legal assistant acting as a notary public, consider the following question.

Question: Do paralegals have the notarial problem of having to make decisions and judgments in the course of their work for which there are no instructions? If so, how does a paralegal solve or attempt to solve this problem?

Answer: "Using your head" or "common sense" are the phrases often used by the attorney.

This is particularly true when a legal assistant should have seen that what her attorney instructed her to do was incorrect, and either advised him tactfully, or gone forward and corrected his mistake. Oftentimes, when a legal assistant is left alone, as when the attorney is engaged in trial or is out of the city, he or she is placed in a position to make decisions without instruction. On these occasions, the paralegal uses his best judgment, resulting from the experience of working closely with his employer which enables him to answer the question: He or she solves the problem as the employer would have done had he been on hand to give the instruction. Even then, a paralegal awaits the return of the employer with fear and trepidation, hoping that the right decision has been made.

Note: We have found it to be a better part of valor to have another attorney in the office review any and all documents prepared in the absence of your attorney before the same are filed with the Court.

Compare this to the role of the legal assistant working as a notary public in solving a similar and like problem. The difference is that as a notary you are not required to work under the direct supervision of an attorney; hence your understanding of the law and the particular aspect of a given situation is more vital and crucial. Any decision you make would be final.

EXAMPLE:

In the case of a paralegal, let us suppose that the employer has instructed his legal assistant to prepare a declaration with supporting Memorandum of Points and Authorities to accompany a motion to be filed in Court by Monday and he is leaving the city for the weekend. The legal assistant, therefore, has to review the file, the facts of the case, do the legal research, prepare the document in his absence, and have another attorney in the office sign it on behalf of her employer, since legal assistants cannot sign legal documents which are filed in the Courts. The other attorney, not being familiar with the case, will of course rely heavily on what the legal assistant has done and therefore would go blindly forward and sign the document.

This is a classic case in which a legal assistant must use judgment to make a decision as to what should be incorporated in the Declaration as well as being sure that the Memorandum of Points and Authorities clearly supports the Declaration in order to win the motion.

Compare this to a notary public, who has the discretion to make the decision to notarize or not notarize a document based on what the client has said. Should the decision be to notarize the document, the notary is taking on the responsibility that what has been stated is the truth as to the facts.

Once that has been done, and the same is recorded, it has become final. The notary is taking a risk because the client may or may not be a stranger, but this is a professional judgment based on years of experience and expertise. The notary may or may not have it reviewed by any attorney, since he or she does not work under the direction of an attorney.

CHAPTER 2

In-House Training Program

Purpose

Law firm management, having been convinced of the need and viability of utilizing paralegals, may find that attorneys do not know how to utilize the special skills of a paralegal efficiently; or how much supervision is necessary; or even what tasks a paralegal can or should be able to perform, without infringing upon the practice of law. The purpose of this chapter, therefore, is to set forth tried and proven duties which can be and are being performed by paralegals without infringing upon the attorney's practice of his profession.

This chapter attempts to answer the two remaining problems facing the attorneys, i.e., what and how lay persons should be taught and trained to perform to their optimum; and to remove the doubts and fears of the attorneys as to what legal task a paralegal is capable of performing without encroaching upon the attorneys' bailiwick.

This chapter is also geared to aiding paralegal managers, coordinators, or liaison attorneys in teaching/training lay persons to become paralegals; or, to fine-tune the skills of a currently-practicing paralegal. It is further intended to give these lay individuals the bread-and-butter tools they will need to become viable members of the law firm or team.

Introduction

Let us assume that your office is engaged in defense litigation and that you are representing the insurance carrier for the defendant. Let us assume further that negotiations between the parties have failed and your offices are in receipt of all the documents pertinent, including, but not limited to, the summons and complaint, the report of the incident, investigative reports, statements of all witnesses, and any medical reports on file to date. All these documents pertain to a five-car collision.

Continuing with this hypothesis, let us assume that there are three plaintiffs, i.e., the driver of the car, the registered owner of the car and a passenger. Then let us assume that there were five defendants, all of whom were either drivers or passengers in the respective vehicles.

This is obviously a case requiring analytical ability to determine the right of the parties and, of course, the liability of your client. As such, based on the qualifications and experience of your paralegal as to the theory of law in this type of case, you could give this assignment to him or her for analysis and evaluation.

To determine this, you would of course have to consider client contact. Could this individual, after the initial client-attorney contact, fill out a report with the client which would be sufficient to obtain the necessary information required and the client's cooperation? Does the paralegal have the proper oral and writing skills?

Another factor to be determined is the nature and extent of the legal research. It is the feeling of some offices that paralegals should not be given in-depth legal research projects. Here again, you should look to the experience and know-how of your paralegal. If instructed properly, a paralegal can successfully pursue and complete any legal research project. In the above hypothesis, a paralegal would be looking to the liability exposure of the client and the negligence on the part of plaintiffs, Court rulings and decisions and other similar and like cases, in order to prepare an evaluation memorandum setting forth these findings and case law.

The customary practice in most medium to large offices is to have a senior lead attorney, an associate attorney, law clerk, legal secretary and a paralegal. This being true, in considering the development of a paralegal program or department, you must ask yourself three questions. Can the legal tasks currently being performed by these individuals be delegated to a layman such as a paralegal? Would this delegation be violative of the duties currently being performed by the senior lead and associate attorney? And further, would this delegation deprive the law clerk of the experience he or she will need for future use in a law practice?

For example, if it is a customary practice for the senior lead attorney to be responsible for "rain-making" clients for the offices, is it fair and equitable that he be required to do demanding, routine legal tasks on the cases he brings into the office? Is it economically feasible for the associate attorney, who in most offices is responsible for the trial work of said cases, to be responsible for the mundane, routine tasks necessary to defend the client's position? And, is it good economics and practical to utilize the services of a law clerk to perform these tasks in a slow methodical manner, when an experienced paralegal can do it in a shorter, more efficient, expeditious manner?

Remember, a paralegal has been trained to be analytical, and for this reason could be delegated the responsibility of analyzing said facts and bifurcating the rights of the various parties, plaintiff or defendant. Depending on your office policy relating to client contact, the paralegal should have developed all the oral skills to enable productive client contact. And remember, the paralegal was specifically trained to do legal research. If you are not using the skills of your paralegal in either of the aforementioned categories, your office is wasting a valuable resource.

As we all know, the legal secretary can be considered the most important person on any legal team. Legal secretaries, for the most part, carry the burden for a new case from its inception. They are responsible for calendaring the statutes of limitation as to when an answer is due; when you can file a motion; how many pages you are allowed on your Memorandum of Points and Authorities; summary judgment; cut-off dates for discovery; when and how to file an arbitration; Court practice and procedure. Oftentimes, the legal secretary is performing paralegal tasks.

ESTABLISHING A PARALEGAL PROGRAM

GENERALLY:

The following is submitted as a flexible step-by-step procedure which can be used in establishing an in-house paralegal training program.

One of the prime factors to be considered is the attorney or attorneys who will be working with the paralegal.

1. The attorney(s) should have an understanding as to what a paralegal is all about and what duties the paralegal is capable of performing;

2. The attorney must want to use these special skills;

3. The attorney must be an individual willing to delegate to his paralegal full credit as a valuable member of the legal team;

4. The attorney must be willing to change old habits;

5. The attorney must have an open mind; and

6. The attorney must be willing to recognize the need for a change with the advent of the paralegal into the legal work force.

Cooperation is the key in this area of transition.

There MUST be a "commitment" by the firm. This is the "key element" in the success of an in-house training program. Additionally, the firm must have "long-range goals" in connection with the in-house training program and in the utilization of its paralegal personnel.

USING THE PARALEGAL TO RAISE THE LEVEL OF EFFICIENCY IN THE LAW OFFICE

Many young associates and/or law students find that certain detailed work, capable of being performed by a paralegal, is incompatible with their education and ultimate desire to become partners in a law firm. And, most often, senior partners prefer to use paralegals for detailed, time-consuming work, since it results in a cheaper, more efficient operation and frees up the young associate or law student to do the things for which he or she was trained.

This preference on the part of the senior partner stems from the fact that the average young associate or law student was not taught Court procedures, preparation of Court pleadings, or with whom or where to file said documents once completed. It is accepted that he must learn these things before he can carry his weight in a law office and be considered an integral member of the legal team—unless, of course, he had the good fortune to work as a law clerk during his tenure in law school.

Utilizing the skills of the paralegal to raise the level of efficiency in this regard is feasible and proper. Indeed, the paralegal can act as a liaison between the partner and the young associates since he or she, if trained, can relate to a young associate much better than a young associate can relate to the senior partner. Furthermore, the senior partner does not have the time to train the young associate in areas of Court procedure and format of pleadings, etc.; hence the paralegal can be used as a trainer in helping young associates pick up the fine points of this phase of the practice of law. The use of paralegals would also enable the lawyers to enhance the quality of the substantial work for which they were trained. Finally, there is the important economic benefit to be derived from the utilization of paralegals.

Let me give you an example. You have an attorney who charges fixed dollars per hour. This attorney would be limited to an eight-hour day and probably most of his time would be devoted to one or two—or if you stretch it—maybe three matters.

On the other side of the coin, if the same attorney had a specially-trained paralegal, he could organize the work to be performed on five, six, possibly even seven matters, thus devoting perhaps one or two hours in instruction. By utilizing the paralegal who could perform routine duties and complete the matter, an attorney could charge eight hours at his rate and charge a lesser rate for the effective working time of a paralegal under his supervision. It is well documented that an attorney who takes advantage of the special skills of a well-trained paralegal can accomplish much more on behalf of his client at a lesser expense to his client, and still generate more income for the firm.

CLARIFICATION OF ROLES

From an experienced legal assistant's point of view, we have determined that the role of the attorney is as follows:

1. Pinpointing the abilities and skills of the legal team, i.e., associate, paralegal and legal secretary;

2. Delegating to the team members the tasks the attorney feels, because of their individualized skills, they can perform more efficiently;

3. Instructing each member, together or separately, as to the conclusion desired in the client's matter so that each will understand the integral role his or her tasks play in the overall picture;

4. Reviewing the draft and/or legal memoranda, and giving final approval of the work accomplished by each.

Most important, it should be remembered by support staff that an attorney is a very busy individual, rain-making business for the office, consulting with clients and advocating their claims before the Courts.

THE KEY

As an aid in determining these special skills and the roles to be played by the members of the legal team, we submit the following Request for Admissions:

1. Admit that the law student's course of study is designed to create a class of persons who will be advocates;

2. Admit that the prime assets of an attorney are his education and resulting specialized ability, judgment and analytical skills;

3. Admit that it is the exclusive domain of the attorney to direct the course of the lawsuit for the benefit of his client;

4. Admit that a primary role of the attorney is deciding on a course of action based upon his knowledge of the law and the facts of the particular case;

5. Admit that the foregoing is designed to reach the conclusions desired by a client, in compliance with the appropriate limit of regulations or statutory laws pertinent thereto;

6. Admit that, together with the advocacy role and the realization of a client's desire, the role of the attorney is to direct an expeditious and efficient performance on behalf of his client;

7. Admit that the above and foregoing is "The Practice of Law" as defined by the organized bar; and finally,

8. Admit that the above and foregoing being true, then any task which does not require the exercise of an attorney's prime assets, i.e., specialized ability, judgment and analytical skills, can be performed by a paralegal.

Thus, the role of a senior partner or associate, and perhaps of the law student, would include the following:

1. Determining the facts of the case, or triable issues;

2. Determining the law, rule or regulation applicable to these facts or issues;

3. Applying the law, rule or regulations applicable; and

4. Proceeding therefrom to plan the strategy to be utilized in advocating the client's claim or lawsuit.

QUALITIES TO LOOK FOR IN A PARALEGAL

- an outgoing personality;
- ability to communicate, both verbally and in writing;

- self-reliance;

- ability to create rather than to perform robotically;

- willingness to accept responsibility;

- willingness to follow *orders and directions;*

- understanding thoroughly not only every step in the prosecution of a claim being handled, but also the critical requirement for *the direct supervision of the attorney at all times;*

- specific training in these special skills either through school offerings or in-house training.

EDUCATIONAL BACKGROUND OF PARALEGALS

For the benefit of the attorneys, and for their review and edification, submitted herewith is a brief description of what paralegals learn in school to prepare them to be members of a legal team.

From this course, the attorneys will get a better idea of what legal tasks they can delegate to the paralegal on their team.

In most ABA-accredited paralegal schools, the following course offerings are taught. These courses are normally taught by attorneys with a paralegal assistant.

1. LEGAL THEORY AND PRACTICE, which discusses the nature of the law and the legal system; and Case Analysis, Legal Ethics and Professional Responsibility.

2. LEGAL WRITING, which concerns itself with basic legal vocabulary, writing logically and reading for comprehension.

3. LAW OFFICE ADMINISTRATION, which deals with the organization and function of a law firm, the development of a paralegal program and how to implement same.

4. LEGAL RESEARCH AND WRITING, wherein the paralegal is given certain problems in legal research to become familiar with the law library including Shepardizing, as well as computerized research (Lexis-Westlaw) and preparation of case briefs and other interoffice memoranda.

5. LITIGATION. This particular area of the course offering can also be a specialization. It includes the introduction in the preparation of complaints, answers, demurrers and various other pre-trial motions; points and authorities.

Additionally, the paralegal learns how to set up various files including but not limited to document files, legal research files, evidence files, indexing and cross-referencing documents and charts, etc.

Discovery in this course includes instruction in the five vehicles of discovery which include the analysis and preparation of interrogatories, answers to interrogatories, requests for production of documents, requests for admissions and preparing notices re depositions.

Trial preparation. This phase of a litigation course concerns itself with summarization of depositions, interrogatories, analyzing and abstracting documents from the file, preparing the list of exhibits, preparation of the trial book and preparing the necessary post-trial motions for after trial, such as the notice of appeal, etc.

It should be noted that a paralegal, in taking the above-referenced course, also has the opportunity to specialize in other areas, such as: WILLS; TRUST AND ESTATE PLANNING; PROPERTY (Real Estate); TORTS; FAMILY LAW; CONTRACTS; WORKERS' COMPENSATION; BANKRUPTCY LAW AND PROCEDURE; and PROBATE ADMINISTRATION.

As you can tell from the above listings, the average paralegal course takes at least two to two-and-a-half years to complete, and as such, the paralegal is well-qualified to assist the attorney in the practice of his profession.

TIPS WHEN WORKING WITH YOUR PARALEGAL

If your office is organized into teams, the paralegal should be aware of each member of the team, and be given a synopsis of the case or cases being worked on and their status as well as the role she or he is expected to play therein. Moreover, it is incumbent upon the paralegal to understand the theory of law in the area, either by an overview discussion of it with the attorney or law clerk, or by doing research on her (his) own.

Once this is accomplished, the attorney should review with the paralegal the client interview sheet to acquaint him (her) with the office policy in the area of client-office relationship and procedure; then specifically that which is personal to each attorney, how he or she likes the pleadings handled and the format that each normally uses.

Since the Court now allows printed forms of complaints, interrogatories, answers, etc., the attorney should make the paralegal aware of the availability of these documents and the attorney's preference for them—or against them—in order to utilize the paralegal's time more efficiently. This is mentioned since those paralegals trained as a result of institutional training have been taught to draft pleadings from scratch and create the document as opposed to filling in blank spaces on a printed form.

Throughout all of the above, you should not leave out your **valued legal secretary,** for without her (or him), it would not work. She plays a very important role as a member of the legal team and should be requested and permitted to work closely with the paralegal.

LEGAL TASKS WHICH CAN BE DELEGATED TO A PARALEGAL

Since this is a high-volume litigation office, we submit the following as examples, but not necessarily limited thereto, of areas where a well-trained paralegal can be used:

1. Drafting "bad faith" and/or "demand" letters, which requires a thorough review of the file (See Exhibit A and B);

2. Preparing draft complaints for the approval, correction, etc., of the attorney;

3. Preparing with guidance, a simple answer, such as a general denial;

4. Preparing routine answers to interrogatories, which require the expenditure of a great deal of the attorney's time reviewing the file;

5. Marshalling of interrogatories or requests for admissions, which requires the review and study of a file to produce another time-consuming project;

6. Doing certain simple legal research projects, depending on the skill of the paralegal. (Since we are seeking to have current paralegals trained or refreshed in the use of the Lexis and Westlaw, this job would be very simple and less time-consuming than the hands-on legal research method.);

7. Preparing certain motions which could either be done in final form at the direction of the attorney, or submitted in draft;

8. Drafting of an affidavit for the attorney in support of a motion;

9. Preparing a Memorandum of Points and Authorities in support of a motion; and finally,

10. Doing all of the above, together with the page-lining of depositions, the summary of medical reports, the summary of reporter's transcripts, the indexing of documents, preparation of exhibits and other trial pleadings.

Exhibit "A"

COMPONENT PARTS OF A DEMAND LETTER

This letter must be sent by certified mail, return receipt requested.

1. The first paragraph of your demand letter sets forth the purpose of the letter, i.e., a demand for a settlement.
2. This paragraph deals with the liability of the party to whom the letter is being addressed.
3. Some attorneys would set forth at this point the contentions of the party who is sending the letter and sometimes it will set forth the contentions of the party to whom it is being addressed.
4. This paragraph (which could be more than one) sets forth the injuries of the plaintiff (defendant) and damages sustained.
5. This is normally the conclusion, which could also be a summary of the previous paragraphs, again explaining why the case should be settled at this point for the figure amount offered in the first paragraph. It is suggested, should the occasion arise and you are requested to do a demand letter, that you discuss paragraphs one and five to be sure that the figure amount discussed is correct.

The information for the contents of paragraphs two, three and four can be found in both your correspondence and pleading files.

Exhibit "B"

"BAD FAITH"
EXTRA CONTRACT LIABILITY

DEFINITION: "No showing of evil motives or intentional misconduct is required, but rather a breach of the covenant of good faith and their dealing implied by law in every contract. It gives rise to tort liability."

FIRST PARTY CLAIMS:

1. Claims under life, health and disability policy;
2. Claims for damages to an insured's property, homeowners insurance, commercial casualty policies, etc., third party claims;

3. When a liability insurer refuses to "defend" the insured against the third party's claim despite the obligation to do so;

4. The "third party" case is one in which the "bad faith" cause of action is based on an insurance company's unreasonable handling of, or refusal to settle a third party's claim against the insured under a liability insurance policy.

CHAPTER 3

The Legal Assistant's Effectiveness in the Modern Law Office

Social change and need are the factors that have encouraged the advent and use of the legal assistant (paralegal) over the past decade. These factors include:

1. Trend toward specialization in law by attorneys, with concomitant development of subspecialists;

2. Desire of legal secretaries for professionalism;

3. Recognition of the legal needs of low- and moderate-income families not adequately served under the old system;

4. Rising costs of, and the need to deliver, legal services more efficiently;

5. Desire of the legal profession to respond positively and reduce the loss of additional areas of their practice to accountants, real estate brokers, and banks;

6. Expanded use of small-claims courts, which removes the need for an attorney and crystallizes the use of legal assistants to aid these lay litigants;

7. Upward trend of the use of mediation courts and procedures.

But the most compelling reason for hiring a legal assistant was, and is, economic. The use of a legal assistant has been a great boon to the increase of the gross income of today's law firm, without raising the cost of delivery of legal services to the public. That use has increased the public's ability to afford an attorney when in need of legal advice.

Change in Hiring Practices and Utilization of Legal Assistants

Large law firms are setting up "paralegal series" or levels within their offices not unlike the Civil Service Paralegal Series within the state and federal government agencies, which now have supervising paralegals who delegate duties to other paralegals, overseeing their work prior to submission to the attorney for review, change, and so forth.

Law firms often train new paralegals or paralegal trainees or legal secretaries who wish to become paralegals as a promotion vehicle. Such recognition of the duties and responsibilities of paralegalism not only enhances the prestige of the legal assistant, but increases salaries and gives the legal assistant a feeling of self-fulfillment.

There is an intriguing change in attitude of today's legal assistant. Ten years ago legal assistants were saying that one of the reasons they were far more employable than the young associate was their staying power; they would not leave the law firm to "go out on their own" as is common practice among young associates after a year or two in a law firm.

Today, we find that there are individual paralegals who free-lance their skills, and there are paralegals operating their own "paralegal services" businesses for attorneys on a per-diem or hourly basis or even on a retainer agreement.

Furthermore, we find legal secretarial-services companies advertising for and using these independent paralegal contractors to attract attorney business for their legal secretarial operation.

And, what is more surprising are the recent surveys and researches which indicate that since there are more employable attorneys in the marketplace than there are employing attorneys (according to legal-placement-service agencies), these young attorneys are seeking job opportunities as paralegals, since that is where the jobs are and what the law firms are hiring.

Impact of the Computer Age

Innovative changes in the growing use of computer technology such as the IBM and Xerox word processors, memory typewriters, and research tools such as Lexis and Westlaw to handle complex litigation, repetitive letters and clauses, and corporate documents, to name a few, have radically changed the duties of legal assistants and at the same time have expanded the role and effectiveness of the legal assistant and his or her value to the employer–attorney.

Specifically, these word-processing and computer systems are being used in almost every phase of the law. The word processor, for example, is being used to create or draft and print out form letters and legal documents, for repetitive clauses, to change, insert, and rearrange paragraphs; and to correct words, names, phrases, and mistakes.

And the litigation support systems have become a vital tool in trial preparation, in the discovery process, and in the handling of voluminous documents in complex litigation.

NEW PARALEGALS ENTERING THE PROFESSION

During the peak of the paralegal movement (from about 1968 to 1975), a legal assistant was primarily a legal secretary turned legal assistant after years of legal work experience in a law office or with other law related background. A letter of recommendation from his or her attorney–employer was sufficient for enrollment in a school offering a paralegal course.

Then there were the housewives and mothers re-entering the job market and being trained in-house by their attorney–employers to become paralegals.

Today's would-be legal assistant may come directly from high school either to be trained in-house, or may take a qualifying examination to enter a paralegal school or may even obtain an on the-job training position while attending school.

Furthermore, today's legal assistant can be in an alternative employment plan, or in a new career for retired persons; this may be a job opportunity for individuals seeking to change careers, such as law students, civil-service employees, armed-forces personnel, and the like.

Most amazing is the prison inmate "attorney" seeking formal education to become a paralegal while still incarcerated in a penal institution.

CHANGES IN EDUCATIONAL REQUIREMENTS AND BENEFITS

Ten years ago all a graduating student could hope to receive from a paralegal course was a certificate of completion. Today, a student can receive the following: Bachelor of Science degree in paralegal studies; Paralegal Specialist Certificate; or Legal Assistant Certificate.

To acquire any of these now requires either an AA degree or its equivalent, or a degree from an accredited college with optional acceptance of such degrees in any transfer. Additionally, some schools are requiring a BA degree from an accredited college as an entrance requirement.

Finally, some schools are now setting up programs that would allow high school graduates, with a high grade-point average or a high score on an equivalency test to enroll in a certificate legal assistant program. Some schools are giving credit for secretarial or business work experience. The enrollment requirement is dependent upon the policy of the school as approved by the appropriate government educational agency.

GENERAL DUTIES OF TODAY'S LEGAL ASSISTANTS

Paralegals are playing an active role in delivery of legal services in the various group and prepaid legal plans and legal clinics.

Moreover, their positive effect can be seen in the various law agencies such as state and federal district attorneys' offices, in public defenders' offices, and even in some correctional institutions.

In some parts of the country, paralegals are now being employed by newspapers and consumer advocate organizations and are even holding legislative positions in state governments.

And as mentioned before, the more experienced legal assistants are proliferating as "independent contractors," servicing attorneys on an "as-needed basis" with the assistance of litigation support systems in their homes. Others are opening up their own "offices" with an in-house attorney on staff.

SPECIFIC DUTIES OF TODAY'S LEGAL ASSISTANTS

Some specific examples of the extended use and scope of legal-assistant duties in today's modern law office are:

GENERAL

Conduct interviews with clients to gather background information.

Draft pleadings and documents.

Organize and maintain files.

Index or summarize documents or transcripts.

Prepare client for court hearing.

Update and maintain library materials.

Review legal periodicals and material relevant to particular areas of law.

Maintain calendar or tickler system.

Be responsible for office administration or personnel.

Conduct legal research, including procedural, administrative and case law research.

BANKRUPTCY

Interview client to obtain information for filing petition and schedules.

Confirm amounts owed to creditors and verify dates incurred.

Identify secured and unsecured claims of creditors.

Draft and file petitions, schedules and proofs of claim.

Obtain case information from United States Bankruptcy Court Clerk.

Check UCC filings, real property records and taxes owed.

Identify exempt property.

Maintain contact with client/debtor and verify compliance with instructions to debtors.

Draft, serve and file debtor's monthly financial statements in Chapter 11 cases.

Draft, serve and file complaints in adversary proceedings.

Correspondence with creditors, creditors' committee chair, creditors' committee attorney, trustee and client.

Prepare applications and orders including enforcement of stay, restraining sales, reinstatement of utility service, venue, avoiding liens, approving reaffirmation or redemption and abandonment.

Prepare prefiling letters to creditors.

Draft and file applications and orders to employ professional persons.

Prepare motion to allow claim or objection to claim.

Draft and file attorneys' fee applications.

Attend Section 341(a) meetings and Chapter 13 Plan confirmation hearing.

Maintain log to check off discharge and status of bankruptcy.

BUSINESS

Check availability and reserve corporate name.

Draft and file articles of incorporation.

Complete and file qualification of foreign corporations.

Draft certificates of authority for foreign corporation.

Obtain good standing certificates from Secretary of State.

Draft bylaws, notices and minutes or consents for organization meeting.

Draft subscription agreements, stock certificates, investment letters and banking resolutions.

Draft shareholder agreements, buy-sell agreements, employment agreements and stock option plans.

Complete and file any assumed name certificates.

Draft and file certificates of designation for preferred stock issuances.

Complete and file election by small business corporation and subsequent shareholders' consents to such election.

Complete and file application for employer identification number, workers' compensation, unemployment insurance and employer withholding tax registration.

Complete and file application for appropriate licenses to operate specific businesses, trade name applications, copyright applications and financing statements.

Order minute book, stock book and seal.

Draft and file application for proper licensing when forming professional or special purpose corporation.

Draft response to auditors' information request, prepare for audit.

Complete reporting and compliance requirements for multi-state corporations including qualifying corporation under state law.

Secure licenses and permits, e.g., liquor, sales tax, health department and building permits.

Complete change of agent/address forms.

Prepare and file annual reports.

Maintain a tickler system for annual meetings, payments of bonuses to offices, contribution to pension and profit-sharing plans, exercise of stock options and filing of annual reports.

Draft notices, proxies, affidavits of mailing, agenda, ballots and oaths of judges of election, for annual meeting.

Draft shareholders, and directors' minutes.

Draft written consents in lieu of meetings.

Draft plans and/or resolutions of liquidation or dissolution including required state forms to effect dissolution.

Draft articles of merger and plan of merger.

Draft closing checklists and closing memoranda.

Assist in closing, managing assembly and execution of documents.

Prepare closing files and bound volumes.

Prepare and file financing statements, UCC agreements or amendments.

Obtain consents to assignments, releases, and signatures on consent resolutions.

Draft articles of dissolution.

Conduct due diligence investigation.

Compile and index documents in corporate transactions.

Draft partnership agreements including non-competition assignment of interests, and approval of substituted partner.

Draft certificates of limited partnership.

Draft and file trade name documents.

Draft amendments to partnership agreements, certificates of amendment to certificates of limited partnership and amended trade name documents.

Draft certificates or cancellation of certificates of limited partnership, trade name withdrawals.

Draft business organization federal and state tax returns.

COLLECTIONS

Conduct initial review of documents provided by client.

Investigate public records for assets, including real estate records and prior judgments.

Verify employment.

Draft demand letter to debtor.

Draft summons and complaint.

Draft motions for or in opposition to summary judgment, including memoranda and affidavits in support.

Draft judgment, cost bill, and other supporting pleadings.

Maintain judgment account worksheet to record payments.

Draft notice of demand to pay.

Draft, file and serve documents for judgment debtor examination.

Draft, have issued and serve writ of garnishment, order to release garnishment and writ of execution.

Arrange for indemnity bond for sheriff.

Arrange for posting of notice of sale or publication of notice of sale.

Maintain communication with sheriff re levy on personal property.

Prepare bid and attend sheriff's sale on real property.

Obtain certified copy of judgment transcript.

Transfer judgment transcript to a different court.

Obtain exemplified copy of foreign judgment.

Prepare affidavit for transfer of a foreign judgment.

Register judgment in a different state.

Prepare and file satisfaction of judgment.

CRIMINAL

Prescreen prospective new client.

Assist in initial interview of client with attorney.

Prepare charges or plea for arraignment, make bail arrangements.

Obtain discovery (police reports, search warrant, affidavit).

Draft motion compelling discovery or to produce additional documents.

Analyze case based on discovery; gather information for plea bargaining.

Draft motion for change of venue, demurrer and motion to set aside indictment.

Draft motion to suppress, motion to controvert, motion for civil compromise and motion for diversion.

Draft motion in limine, motion for return of property, motion to postpone trial and motion to disqualify judge.

Prepare for trial, including interview and subpoena witnesses, examine physical evidence, tangible objects, scene of alleged crime, and coordination of outside investigators and experts.

Arrange for diversion, civil compromise and work release.

Draft supplemental memoranda of law and trial memorandum.

Attend conference with prosecutor and pretrial conferences with judge and attorneys.

Draft jury instructions.

Attend and assist at trial.

Draft motion in arrest of judgment, motion for new trial, and motion for release pending new trial/appeal.

Attend conference with client regarding presentence report.

Draft petition for leniency/probation.

Research law regarding appealable issues and draft notice of appeal, assignments of error and arguments.

EMPLOYEE BENEFITS

Draft qualified plan documents, trust agreements, custodial agreements, money purchase, 401(k), stock bonus, defined benefit plans and IRA plans.

Draft amendments and restatements to plans to bring into compliance with new law and regulations.

Draft summary plan description.

Draft deferred compensation plans including nonqualified executive compensation, stock option and medical reimbursement plans.

Draft affiliate adoption statement.

Draft notification of participation, election to participate, beneficiary designation, election out of qualified joint and survivor annuity, application for benefits and election to contribute.

Consult with business managers and actuaries to determine contribution and benefit formulas.

Prepare schedules showing maximized employer contributions.

Draft summary annual report.

Draft benefit statement.

Draft promissory note and salary assignment for participant loans.

Draft board of directors resolutions for plan adoption, adoption of amendments, and fixing contributions.

Prepare and file application for IRS determination letter.

Prepare and file annual report (5500 series and related schedules).

Prepare PBGC premium forms.

Submit descriptive documents to the Department of Labor.

Monitor progress of implementation of new plans and amendments to verify required actions occur on schedule.

Draft plan amendments, qualify amendments with IRS, notice to Department of Labor.

Coordinate general notice mailings to clients about potential impact of new legal developments on plans.

Prepare notices to employees regarding significant changes in plan.

Develop and maintain checklists, sets of model plans, administrative documents and letters and update as new material is developed.

Prepare summary of amendments required by new registration and assemble list of plans requiring such amendments.

Research interpretive questions on prohibited transactions and qualified and nonqualified plans.

Calculate employer contributions and forfeitures and allocate to participant accounts.

Determine valuation adjustments and allocate to participant accounts.

Calculate participant's years of service for eligibility and vesting.

Calculate benefit for terminated participant.

Test plan for discrimination, top-heaviness, or Section 415 limits.

Terminate plans and qualify terminations with IRS and PBGC.

FAMILY LAW

Draft petition for dissolution, summons, waiver of service, affidavit as to children and response.

Draft temporary motions, affidavits and orders.

Draft notice to produce.

Draft property settlement and separation agreements.

Attend initial interview with attorney and client.

Complete domestic relations questionnaire form.

Arrange for service of documents.

Obtain settings for court hearings.

Assist client in preparation of monthly income and expense sheet.

Arrange for appraisers for real property and personal property.

Draft subpoenas and arrange for service.

Schedule expert witness interviews and availability at trial.

Obtain information for discovery, organize, categorize and determine completeness of discovery.

Draft proposed stipulations.

Prepare and record transfer of asset documents.

Draft decree of dissolution, accompanying motions and affidavits.

Draft motion and affidavit for modification.

Draft petition for adoption and consent for adoption.

Draft decree of adoption.

Draft petition for name change.

FORECLOSURE

Order foreclosure report and review with respect to priority of lien holders and parties to be served.

Locate addresses of parties to be served, draft foreclosure complaint and arrange service.

Draft motion, order of default, judgment and decree of foreclosure.

Draft motion and supporting documents for summary judgment.

Draft subpoenas, notices of deposition, requests for production and prepare for trial if necessary.

Draft pre-sale documents to begin execution including writ of execution and Draft Bid Sheet for sale.

Draft post-sale documents including motion confirming sale, directing sheriff to execute deed and writ of assistance.

Draft deed in lieu of foreclosure.

Draft appointment of successor trustee, notice of default and election to sell, and trustee's notice of sale.

Set sale date and docket statutory deadlines to be met.

Record notice of default and appointment of successor trustee.

Prepare, serve and arrange publication of trustee's notice of sale on grantors, occupants, and subsequent lien creditors.

Record all proofs of service, affidavits of mailing and publication prior to sale.

Check for federal tax liens 30 days prior to sale and prepare and serve IRS with notice of nonjudicial sale if necessary.

Prepare memorandum of amount due on sale.

Prepare trustee's deed, certificate of non-military service, and post-sale memorandum. Record deed and certificate.

Appear at time and place set for sale to postpone sale.

Draft and record trustee's deed after sale.

Take possession, satisfy and transmit promissory note and original trust deed to trustee.

INTELLECTUAL PROPERTY

Prepare patent and/or trademark status summary reports.

Docket and/or maintain docket system for due dates for responses, renewals, oppositions, Sections 8 and 15 filings, use affidavits and working requirements.

Docket and/or maintain docket system for payment of patent annuities in foreign counties.

Conduct patent/trademark searches.

Conduct on-line computer information searches of technical literature for patent/trademarks.

Draft trademark registration application, renewal application and registered user agreements.

Draft power of attorney.

Draft copyright applications.

Research procedural matters, case law, and unfair competition matters.

Conduct factual investigation using magazines and trade publications.

Conduct prior art search.

Conduct patent/trademark searches.

Assist in opposition, interference, infringement and related proceedings.

Arrange for visual aids/models/mock-ups for trial use.

Maintain files of new products and invention development.

Review patent filings with engineers.

Draft licenses/agreements regarding proprietary information/technology.

LITIGATION

Draft complaint.

Draft answer and/or other defensive pleadings.

Draft provisional remedy documents including injunctions, TRO's and attachments.

Draft interrogatories, requests for production, requests for admissions.

Prepare summons and service of process.

Draft discovery motions.

Draft response to interrogatories, requests for production, requests for admission.

Locate, interview and obtain witness statements.

Arrange for expert witnesses.

Arrange for outside investigator.

Review documents for response to request for production including screening for relevance and privilege.

Control numbering and history of documents produced and received.

Obtain/examine public records.

Research legislative history.

Prepare and serve subpoena duces tecum.

Schedule deposition and arrange court reporter.

Draft deposition questions and prepare deposition outline.

Prepare witness files.

Prepare witnesses for deposition.

Attend document productions.

Attend depositions.

Index, digest and summarize depositions.

Follow up after depositions for additional information.

Obtain, review and analyze medical records.

Analyze/summarize factual information.

Prepare statistical/factual summaries or chronologies.

Draft affidavits and declarations.

Draft motions for extension of time.

Draft demand letters and subpoenas.

Organize documents and other physical evidence.

Draft legal memoranda and/or briefs including table of cases, statement of facts and appendices.

Check cites and/or Shepardize.

Review briefs for accuracy of factual information.

Identify and prepare potential and expert witnesses.

Draft stipulation for admissibility of exhibits.

Review trial exhibits for evidentiary purposes, relevance and authentication.

Organize trial exhibits.

Prepare trial notebooks.

Prepare trial subpoenas.

Prepare deposition designations.

Prepare documents and testimony to use for impeachment.

Draft pretrial statements and settlement conference memoranda.

Obtain jury list, biographical information on jurors.

Draft jury instructions and voir dire.

Coordinate witness attendance at trial.

Monitor preparation of charts/graphs and other demonstrative evidence for use at trial.

Attend trial, noting developments of the case as well as reactions of jurors, witnesses and opposing counsel during trial.

Maintain list of exhibits as mentioned, offered, admitted or objected to.

Draft cost bill.

Prepare settlement calculations.

Prepare comparative analysis of terms of potential settlement agreements.

Draft settlement documents, including releases and dismissals.

Supervise post-judgment collections.

Draft notice of appeal.

Draft factual information for appeal brief.

Prepare corrections to trial transcript.

Prepare recap or outline of trial transcripts.

Maintain and update form files.

PROBATE AND ESTATE PLANNING

Meet with client and attorney at initial meeting.

Answer questions from personal representative, surviving spouse and other interested parties.

Prepare and maintain a calendar system.

Locate witnesses to will.

Locate and notify heirs and devisees of probate proceeding.

Publish appropriate notices to interested persons.

Order public records including birth, death, and marriage certificates.

Collect information and/or assets for preparation of inventory and tax returns.

Value assets (date of death and alternate valuation date).

Draft inventory, arrange for and attend inventory of safe deposit box.

Handle matters re ancilliary administrations.

Maintain financial records of estate.

Prepare and file claims for insurance proceeds and death benefits.

Prepare disallowance of claims against the estate and monitor claims including court files.

Correspond with debtors and creditors to obtain pertinent information.

Interpret will provisions.

Apply for employer identification number and file notices of fiduciary relationship.

Prepare and transmit necessary papers to transfer/liquidate assets including stock, real estate and motor vehicles.

Prepare preliminary income projection and estimate taxes.

Prepare state inheritance tax return and federal estate tax return.

Prepare individual income tax returns for beneficiaries.

Prepare decedent's final federal and state individual income tax returns.

Draft federal and state gift tax returns.

Prepare state and federal fiduciary income tax returns.

Arrange for tax releases and payment of taxes.

Draft petitions and orders for partial distribution.

Draft accountings.

Assist in audit of tax returns including correspondence, affidavits and statements submitted upon audit.

Draft distribution schedule and closing documents.

Review documents and tax returns in connection with an ancillary proceeding.

Draft tax returns for nonprobate estate.

Collect data for estate planning including current estate plans and assets.

Prepare tax calculations for various estate plans.

Draft wills, codicils, trust agreements and amendments.

Draft documents necessary to fund trusts.

Prepare and record powers of attorney.

Draft court documents for conservatorship.

Draft inventory and accountings for conservatorship.

Draft federal and state tax returns for conservatorship.

Draft antenuptial agreements.

Draft court documents for guardianships.

Make post-mortem tax planning calculations.

PUBLIC BENEFITS

Represent claimants at SSI (Supplementary Security Income) hearings.

Represent claimants at SSD (Social Security Disability) hearings.

Research appropriate Social Security law.

Assist with Medicare waivers and Medicare appeals.

Assist with Social Security overpayment waivers.

Locate medical information.

Review Social Security file and obtain documentation.

Negotiate with landlord and tenant to resolve problems.

Assist with consumer fraud complaints and forward to Consumer Protection Division.

Obtain documentation for unemployment claim.

REAL PROPERTY

Draft subdivision, condominium and timeshare registrations for in-state and out-of-state registrations.

Draft registrations of recreational subdivisions for federal registrations.

Organize recording procedures for large-scale recording and prepare draft of opinion letters.

Prepare transaction books.

Perform financial calculations (amortization, present and future value, discounting, APR).

Maintain current records regarding CPI, APR, Federal Reserve rate and residential/commercial interest rates.

Draft Truth-in-Lending Disclosure statements.

Draft and review permits.

Draft and review easements.

Review surveys and run out legal descriptions to calculate acreage/square footage, locate easements and determine actuary and adequacy of descriptions.

Draft trust, warranty, bargain and sale and other deeds.

Draft notes, mortgages and contracts of sale.

Draft leases, assignments, extensions, amendments.

Draft purchase and sale agreements, letters of intent, earnest money agreements and addenda.

Draft UCC filing, continuations, amendments, extensions, and terminations.

Draft security agreements.

Order and review title reports including review of underlying encumbrances and exceptions and endorsement requests.

Draft escrow instructions and preliminary closing statements.

Review closing statements and documents prepared by escrow officer.

Review loan pay off documentation and coordinate disbursement of loan proceeds.

Prepare closing memoranda and organize/manage complex closings.

Analyze conveyance, security and lease documents.

Review BLM and county records to determine validity of hard rock mineral claims.

Review and analyze abstracts of title and chain of title to draft title opinions.

Obtain lien waivers and certificates of completion for new construction.

Check and review zoning and comprehensive plan designations; obtain letters on designation as closing requirement.

Obtain and analyze appraisal information based on market, income and cost approaches.

Obtain canceled note, deed of trust, releases and recorded original documents.

Review title policy, insurance policy, closing statement and other closing documents after closing and request corrections/revisions.

Perform/order UCC and litigation searches at county or state level.

Obtain real and personal property tax information for proration and in preparation for appeals to Board of Equalization and Department of Revenue.

Research state laws relating to conveyancing, recording and financial statements.

Maintain current zoning ordinances, comprehensive plans, real estate-related form file, and computer databases.

Research county records to develop abstracts of title.

SECURITIES/MUNICIPAL BONDS

Draft registration statement, prospectus offering memoranda and amendments.

Organize filing of registration statement including coordinating with printer, assembling appropriate copies and preparing transmittal letters.

Monitor distribution of offering memoranda.

Draft 1934 Act reports.

Draft questionnaire for officers, directors and principal shareholders.

Draft promissory notes, underwriting agreements, trust indentures and bond purchase agreements.

Obtain CVSIP number, NASDAQ, Standard and Poor's and Moody's Securities Manual listings.

Draft Blue Sky memoranda and applications for exemption.

Draft legal investment survey.

Draft Blue Sky registration.

Draft and file applications for registration including uniform consent to service of process, powers of attorney, and uniform form of corporate resolutions.

Notify state securities administrators of SEC effectiveness.

Draft and file dealer and/or salesmen registration documents.

Perfect securities or dealer exemptions.

Prepare memoranda on the availability of exemptions.

Research and prepare documents for after-market trading exemptions.

Draft and file documents for registering broker/dealers and/or salesmen with NASD, SEC and state securities commissions.

Draft and file documents for renewing or withdrawing the registration of broker/dealers with salesmen.

Qualify dealer corporations where applicable.

Draft portions of Forms 3, 4, 8, 8-K, 10, 10-K, 10-Q, 13D and 13G.

Prepare drafts of proxy and proxy statements.

Prepare "inside trading" precautionary memo to employees.

Prepare stock exchange listing application.

Draft and file Form 144 and related documentation.

Draft exhibits to private placement memorandum including offeree questionnaire and subscription Agreement.

Prepare and file notice of sale of securities.

Prepare and file for tax shelter registration numbers.

Draft lease agreement, loan agreement, agreement of sale, facilities financing agreement ordinance or contracts.

Draft indenture.

Draft security agreements (deed, guaranty, mortgages).

Review bond purchase agreement or underwriting agreement.

Draft summaries of documents for use in preparing preliminary official statement and official statement.

Coordinate with underwriter the accuracy of the statements.

Finalize basic documents and distribute for execution.

Draft petition and complaint, notice to the public, notice to the district attorney, rule nisi, answers and validation order.

Draft necessary resolutions authorizing the issuance of the bonds.

Calculate debt borrowing base, debt service for financing bond issue refunding studies and conventional mortgage payout schedules.

Prepare exhibits to pleadings and resolutions.

Send bond form to printer.

Proof first galley of the bonds and check manufacturing schedule, coupon amounts and CVSIP numbers.

Check bonds at time of closing and read bond numbered 1.

Draft closing papers for issuer including authorizing resolutions, authentication order to trustee, incumbency certificate, nonarbitrage certificates and CVSIP numbers.

Draft company authorizing resolutions and officers' certificates.

Prepare tax election (if applicable) and arrange for appropriate filing.

Draft recording certificate.

Draft financing statements.

Attend closing, checking all certificates and opinions, insurance policies, legal descriptions.

Compile the closing transcript.

WORKERS' COMPENSATION

Obtain copy of accident report.

Prepare LS-203 and LS-18 forms and transmit to Department of Labor.

Draft request for hearing or response.

Draft application to schedule date or reply, motion to postpone or response, and demand for documents.

Draft trial brief.

Organize medical reports, schedule doctor appointments and meetings and interview doctors.

Organize correspondence with attorneys and doctors.

Request employer medical mileage reimbursement.

Prepare narrative case evaluation.

Supervise compliance with demand for documents.

Evaluate disability utilizing WCB rules and guidelines.

Prepare exhibit list.

Check average weekly wage calculations.

Draft settlement papers and negotiate settlement.

Draft petition for review (WCB).

Draft petition for judicial review.

Draft statement of case.

Draft issue and fact section of appellate brief.

Draft motion for reconsideration.

Draft affidavit regarding attorney's fees.

Brief new case law and analyze WCB and judicial trends.

CIVIL SERVICE PARALEGAL
(EXAMPLES OF TRAINING PROGRAM AND DUTIES PERFORMABLE)

A. The United States Department of Labor, Office of the Solicitor, instituted its Legal Assistant (Paralegal Specialist) Program in late 1973 to provide an opportunity to its support staff for advancement on the job.

Preliminary training was conducted in Washington, D.C., consisting of:

1. Attendance at a local college or university to take a course in the particular law of the department;

2. Attendance at special seminars and training sessions in the area of the law of the department coupled with on-the-job training at the completion thereof.

Step-by-step training procedure:

a. First year: required completion of three units of study at an accredited college or university in an allied subject. As a practical matter, most applicants for promotion in this area took and completed six units of an allied subject.

b. Thereafter, a six- to twelve-month inservice training program (and probation) conducted and supervised by a senior staff attorney.

c. Duties assigned and delegated as the individual progressed in aptitude and the learning process of the procedure of the Office of the Solicitor.

Duties performed:

a. Drafting of pleadings and discovery of a complex nature (complaints, interrogatories, settlements, judgments, etc.);

b. Review of investigative files, preparing case analyses (noting factual and legal issues), recommendations to attorney for review;

c. Assisting in trial preparation:

   (1) Interview witnesses with attorney (and on occasion, without the attorney);

   (2) prepare notes of interview;

   (3) read, review, index and summarize depositions;

   (4) prepare judges' bench books of exhibits to be offered into evidence;

   (5) prepare trial books for use by attorney during trial;

   (6) assist during trial by taking notes of direct and cross-examination of witness testimony;

   (7) compile notes for attorney's use in preparing closing argument;

   (8) obtain necessary case precedents necessary to support argument advanced by attorney;

   (9) pay witness fees;

   (10) assist attorney in preparation of post-trial documents;

   (11) assist in Settlement Conference by taking notes of discussion;

   (12) prepare draft of settlement agreement with stipulations.

   (NOTE: to perform any and all of the above legal tasks requires that your legal assistant be familiar with all legal and factual issues of the case and have a thorough knowledge of all pleadings filed.)

d. Assist in drafting briefs where the legal issue is a common, recurring and relatively non-complex matter.

B. The Office of the State Appellate Defender (Chicago, IL), the state agency created by the State Appellate Defender Act (IL Rev. Stat. Ch. 38, sec. 208).

   The principle function of the Office of the State Appellate Defender is to represent indigent persons on appeal in criminal cases when appointed by the (in this instance) Illinois Supreme Court, the Appellate Court or the Circuit Court.

To provide for this legal representation, the State Appellate Defender has offices in each of the five Appellate Court districts of Illinois: Chicago, Elgin, Ottawa, Springfield and Mt. Vernon.

In addition to the appellate services rendered by the agency, the Office of the State Appellate Defender sponsors ongoing training programs for new employees of the office, in addition to distributing educational material to new attorneys of the agency.[1]

A paralegal working in one of the aforementioned district offices would have the following duties:

1. Initial "ground work" before the Record on Appeal is obtained from the Appellate Court such as:

   a. Appearing in the trial Court for appointment of counsel;

   b. Appearing in the trial Court for substitution of counsel;

   c. Appearing at the appeal compliance check date call before the Chief Judge;

   d. Acting as communicating agent between the Direct Appointment clients and Non-Client (those who are requesting counsel on appeal);

   e. Preparing documents to be submitted to the Circuit Court;

   f. Preparing and filing Notices of Appeal.

PUBLIC SECTOR PARALEGAL SERIES, TRAINING AND JOB DESCRIPTION:

SENIOR CITIZENS ADVOCATE CENTER
JOB DESCRIPTION

A. POSITION TITLE: Para-professional

B. SPECIFIC DUTIES:

   1. Interview clients and prepare necessary intake forms.

---

[1] Adapted from printed revised material of the State of Illinois.

2. Conduct investigations.

3. Screen cases for relevance and importance.

4. Dispose of some controversies through negotiations with adverse parties.

5. Assist in the preparation of case pleadings.

6. Maintain statistical and other appropriate records.

7. Perform appropriate legal research and prepare necessary legal documents for clients.

8. Complete all cases and other work, and close out files.

9. See that all files and records for each client are kept up to date.

10. Meet and work with senior citizens' clubs and organizations.

11. Make referrals for clients to appropriate agencies for legal and non-legal purposes.

12. Attend staff meetings of Senior Citizens Advocate Center.

13. Advocate senior citizens' concerns and activities.

14. Plan new activities and programs for and with senior citizens.

C. SUPERVISOR DUTIES:

1. The para-professional will be directly responsible to the Attorney in the Advocate Center.

2. Inform senior citizens and organizations of their legal rights and assist the Attorney in community legal education.

3. Prepare any evaluations required by the Attorney.

D. QUALITIES:

1. The ability to work with senior citizens.

2. An appreciation for and understanding of the problems of senior citizens.

3. Ability to communicate and work closely with individuals and groups.

4. Ability to operate efficiently in a law practice.

E. QUALIFICATIONS:

1. Graduation from high school or equivalency. (If not attained, sixty days will be given to make arrangements for same.)

2. Experience or additional education or training, in the area of senior citizens' matters.

3. Ability to prepare letters, pleadings, legal memoranda, etc., necessary in cases.

4. Ability to read and understand legal publications necessary to cases.

5. Ability to collect and compile demonstrative evidence for cases.

F. SALARY RANGE:

The salary is $6,000 to $9,500 per year.

THE FUTURE OF LEGAL ASSISTANTS

In the 1970s the use of lay people to assist attorneys in the practice of their profession was a concept; a whisper; an experiment in the law firm and a pilot program in the universities and colleges throughout the country.

The 1980s saw the paralegal profession become a reality. It then set its sights on respectability. It fought for recognition as a true, viable, adjunct legal profession and for some form of licensing or certification.

In the 1980s, paralegals branched out on their own to serve the public as freelance paralegals, in some instances working directly with the public. Others became independent contractors working for attorneys away from the law office setting, in their own office or at home. Those paralegals, still working within the law office framework, complained of "burn out," lack of recognition and acceptance by attorneys as professionals, and the undereducated paralegals invading their work force.

In the 1980s the U. S. Bureau of Labor statistics reported that the paralegal profession was the fastest growing profession in the country and predicted that the number of paralegals coming into the work force would double by 1995.

In the 1990s the need for improved, updated education and training of these lay persons is essential. Certification or licensing is needed in order to separate and identify the legal technician, the undereducated and the highly educated paralegal so that the hiring public will know the duties that can be performed by each segment of the profession. This certification will give the attorney a clearer picture of what the members of this newest legal profession are equipped to do and thereby insure the continued future success and expansion of the paralegal profession.

CHAPTER 4

What the Legal Assistant Should Know About the Court Systems and Court Procedures

THE COURT SYSTEM

Together with a general knowledge of the law, you as a legal assistant should have a better-than-average working knowledge of the courts and how they operate. You should know the location, jurisdiction, and venue of all the courts of the city, county, and federal district where you are working. In addition, you should have some knowledge of both the state and federal appellate courts to which cases arising out of and tried in your area may be appealed.

You should be familiar with the rules of procedure for all the courts in which your law office files lawsuits. The rules vary for criminal and civil cases. There are usually special rules for probate and guardianship and summary procedure. Every law office must have and use a copy of the appropriate court rules of procedure.

The names and addresses of the courthouses, the judges, and the court officials are usually available in local bar association publications or directories furnished by local banks or title companies.

Knowledge of the courts and their official rules can be a timesaver in preparing, filing, amending, and obtaining copies of court documents.

This chapter gives you much of the essential information about the court systems in our country, their jurisdiction and venue, and some practical points and procedures for handling and performing the tasks assigned to you in the course of a day in your law office.

Court systems are created by the federal or state constitutions and, in specific instances, by statutes. The courts operate pursuant to rules of court established by general order of an appropriate court. A local court may also have specific local rules to supplement the general rules. Rules regulate the forms of pleading, time and manner of filing and serving, and other procedural matters.

To determine the jurisdiction of the court, check the constitution or statute which created it. To determine procedure, check the appropriate "court rules." Check state appellate cases which have interpreted the rules, the statutes, and the state constitution.

The word "court" has many meanings. Primarily, it refers to the persons assembled under authority of law at a designated place for the administration of justice.

The persons so assembled are the judge or judges, clerks, marshall, bailiff, court reporter, jurors, and attorneys, all of whom constitute a body of the government. However, it is not necessary that all of the above named individuals be present to constitute a "court," for court is frequently held without a jury.

The word court also refers to the judge or judges themselves as distinguished from the counsel or jury. Thus we have the expression, "In the opinion of the court," or "May it please the court." In this sense the word is written without a capital because it is personified when it stands for the judge.

Furthermore, the word court is used occasionally to refer to the judge's chambers, or the hall or place where the court is being held. Thus, a spectator is present at court in the courtroom, but the defendant is in court because he is a part of the assembly.

STATE COURTS

APPELLATE COURTS

Each state has at least two courts of appeal. Appellate courts may also have some original jurisdiction.

1. The highest court in a state is usually called the supreme court. One of the exceptions to this is the New York Court of Appeals, which is the name of the highest court in the State of New York. The highest court of any state is a court of record and usually has both appellate and original jurisdiction given to it by the state constitution. The original jurisdiction does not include the trial of civil or criminal cases. It may include original jurisdiction of writs of habeas corpus, writs of mandamus, and writs or prohibition, although such writs are also obtainable originally in lower courts of the state.

The highest court in a state may hear direct appeals designated by the state constitution or statute, and it may exercise discretionary appeal by what is sometimes called *certiorari* to a lower appellate court. The highest court will not usually grant a writ of *certiorari* or discretionary appeal unless there is a conflict of decisions in the lower appellate courts of the state or the question of one involving substantial public interest.

2. *Intermediate appellate courts* in a state court system may be called district court(s) of appeal, superior court(s), special court(s) of appeal, and similar names. Depending on the size and population of the state, it may be divided into a number of appellate districts, and the appellate court may hold regular sessions in all districts or may hold special sessions in each district at various times.

For example, in California, there are three districts, with three justices in each district. Regular sessions are held. Appeals from the superior court, which is a trial court in California, go to the district court of appeals.

The names of both the trial courts and the appellate courts vary from state to state, but the principle is the same. The first appeal from the trial court is usually taken to the intermediate appellate court. Its decision is final, unless the highest court in the state decides to grant a discretionary review or certiorari.

TRIAL COURTS

Each state has trial courts of record that have jurisdiction over criminal and civil matters in each county or judicial district (as in Idaho). The courts are located within the county or district. These trial courts are variously named circuit court, county court, common pleas court, or superior court, among other names.

In addition to the trial courts of general jurisdiction in each county, most counties have special courts that handle particular matters such as probate, juvenile cases, and criminal cases. In some states, such special matters are handled by divisions of the trial court (probate division, criminal division, and so forth).

Each county of a state has lower courts that are not considered courts of record where minor disputes may be heard without a jury (magistrate's court and justice of the peace).

A county usually has two basic trial courts where jurisdiction depends on the amount of money in controversy, the nature of the dispute, or the seriousness of a criminal charge.

In California, for example, there are principally two trial courts, superior and municipal (comparable to common pleas court and county court in Pennsylvania and circuit court and county court in Florida).

1. *Superior Courts:* The superior courts (or court with the same jurisdiction) are the trial courts of general jurisdiction in the judicial system. They have original jurisdiction in all cases and proceedings not otherwise provided for and hear appeals from decisions in the municipal, justice, and small claims courts. (Compare Pennsylvania common pleas courts, Florida circuit courts, and Idaho district courts for similar jurisdiction.)

The state constitution permits the legislature to establish appellate departments of this court in counties having municipal courts. In California, for example, each county has one superior court, and the number of judges is fixed by the state legislature, varying according to the population. Superior court judges serve six-year terms and are elected at the general election on a nonpartisan ballot by the voters of the county. Vacancies are filled by the governor. Superior court judges are required to be attorneys, admitted to the practice of law for at least five years immediately preceding election or appointment.

2. *Municipal Courts:* In California the municipal court has jurisdiction in civil cases where the amount is $25,000 or less and have jurisdiction over misdemeanor criminal cases; a magistrate conducts preliminary hearings in felony cases. The municipal courts also exercise small-claims jurisdiction. (Compare Pennsylvania county courts, Florida county courts, and magistrates division of district courts in Idaho, for similar jurisdiction.)

The judges are elected for six-year terms on a nonpartisan ballot by the voters in the judicial district in which the court is located. Vacancies are filled by the governor, the same as superior courts. Municipal court judges are also required to be attorneys admitted to the practice of law for at least five years immediately preceding election or appointment.

3. *Small Claims Courts:* The small claims is the lowest trial court of record and is consumer-oriented. In California, attorneys cannot appear in this court on behalf of a litigant; only the parties involved in the action are permitted. In some states, attorneys are permitted to appear in small claims court but are not required to present a claim.

Appeals from small claims court are usually taken to the highest court in the county or district. (Compare the circuit court in Florida, and the superior court in California. Check your state's statute creating the small claims court.)

Small claims are usually heard before the judge, without a jury. In some states a jury trial can be demanded in a small claims court if the party deposits a required sum of money with the court.

The following is a practical checklist for proceeding with a claim in a state small claim court.

CHECKLIST FOR SMALL CLAIMS COURT

1. Determine the full legal name and address of the person or persons being sued (not a post office box number). This will help determine where the small claim must be filed (venue).

2. Go to the clerk of the small claims court, which is normally part of the county or district court or located in the same building, and fill out the form given.

3. Pay the appropriate filing fee.

4. Arrange for the subpoena or order to be served on the defendant (but not the plaintiff). In some jurisdictions, the plaintiff or the clerk may authorize someone to personally serve the order on the defendant. The subpoena or order will contain the trial date.

5. While waiting for the trial, gather all important documents and have them ready. Contact all potential witnesses and arrange for them to come to the courthouse on the day of the trial or obtain a subpoena from the clerk of the small claims court for any witness who will not come voluntarily. If an interpreter is needed, find out if one is available at the small claims court or if one can be secured through the higher trial court. In some states the higher trial courts have translators available. Otherwise, the plaintiff should bring his own interpreter.

6. Go to the court building early on the day of the trial and ask the clerk *where* your case is being heard. When you get to the courtroom, check the calendar and see that your case is listed.

7. When giving his testimony, the plaintiff should present only the facts, no editorializing or emotion. He must be brief. He should submit all papers and documents that may help his case.

8. If the plaintiff wins, he may ask the defendant courteously for the money awarded him in the judgment.

9. If the plaintiff has difficulty in collecting his money, he should ask the clerk to assist him in obtaining same.

10. In California, the plaintiff is not allowed to appeal if he loses, unless he is ordered to pay as a result of a counterclaim the defendant has filed against him. In some states, either party may appeal from a small claims judgment. Check the state statute creating the court and local court rules to determine the right and time for appeal.

Most states have lower trial courts which are not courts of record. For example: In California justice courts have jurisdiction in civil cases involving minimal amounts and minor criminal cases. Justice court judges, sitting as magistrates, also conduct preliminary hearings in felony cases. Judges of justice courts are elected to six-year terms. Vacancies are filled by the Board of Supervisors (or a similar body in other states). They must either have passed a qualifying examination given by the Judicial Council or must have been admitted to practice law. (Comparable are justice of the peace courts and magistrate's courts in other states where the justice of the peace or magistrate may be elected or appointed.)

SPECIAL COURTS

In addition to the regular trial courts here described, a state may have special courts located in each county or court district to handle particular matters, such as probate, juvenile cases, or criminal cases. In some states these specific matters are handled in divisions of the regular trial court.

EXAMPLE:

A probate court (also called orphan's court or surrogate court in some jurisdictions or the probate division of the higher trial court) would have jurisdiction over the probate of wills and administration of a deceased person's estate and the guardianship of minors and incompetents.

A criminal court (also called quarter sessions or oyer and terminer or the criminal division of the trial court which has jurisdiction of the particular crime) would hear criminal cases with or without a jury and sentence the defendant(s) if found guilty. The defendant in a criminal case is entitled to a jury trial unless he waives it. In most states, the higher county trial court hears felony charges and the lower county trial court hears misdemeanors.

A juvenile court (sometimes a division of surrogate court) would have original exclusive jurisdiction of minor children who are alleged to be neglected, dependent, or delinquent (which includes truancy in some states). Some states allow the removal of cases involving serious crimes alleged against juveniles to the regular criminal court for trial and sentencing.

Large cities in a state may have special courts, such as the Philadelphia Municipal Court and the Pittsburgh Magistrates Court in Pennsylvania.

Some states have special courts which have both original and appellate jurisdiction in regard to claims against the state. An example is the Commonwealth Court of Pennsylvania, which has exclusive jurisdiction of such claims and has jurisdiction concurrent with the common pleas courts of others.

JURISDICTION OF COURTS

The laws of the United States provide that certain causes of action must be brought in court and have provided a set of guidelines to aid the courts and attorneys in determining in which court an action may be brought. These rules and regulations are called first "jurisdiction" and then "venue." A court may have jurisdiction but not venue, but it cannot have venue without jurisdiction.

Jurisdiction is required in every kind of judicial action. It is the power of a court to hear a particular cause and to tender a binding decision as to the cause before it.

To hear and determine a cause the court must have *in personam* jurisdiction (of the person) and *in rem* jurisdiction (of the subject matter) involved in the dispute.

In personam jurisdiction (not to be confused with *in propria persona,* which is the term used when a plaintiff or defendant acts as his own attorney) means the court has jurisdiction over the defendant(s). Each defendant must be served with notice of the lawsuit in the manner prescribed by the law.

In rem jurisdiction means that the court has jurisdiction over the subject matter in controversy. Service of process may be constructive (by advertising) or by substitution (as where a secretary of state is authorized by statute to accept service for an out-of-state motorist involved in an accident in the state, or where the Insurance Commission of the state is authorized by statute to accept service of a subpoena for an action against an insurance company registered to sell insurance in the state). Examples of jurisdiction are:

> A magistrate's court has jurisdiction over a traffic violation but cannot hear and determine a case for first degree murder;
>
> *or*
>
> A county court may not have jurisdiction over a claim for damages that exceed $5,000;
>
> *or*

An action for damages caused by an automobile collision cannot be brought in a probate court. The probate court does not have jurisdiction;

or

A foreclosure proceeding dealing with real property can be brought in the county where the property is located even though the mortgagor resides elsewhere, so long as he is served with process in accordance with the law.

or

A court has no jurisdiction if the required service of process has not been made.

Jurisdiction of a court may be "original" or "appellate." The state trial courts have original jurisdiction, except for some appeals from inferior trial courts and administrative agencies. Many state statutes require such appeals to be heard *de novo* (trial over again).

After a case has been tried and decided in a court of original jurisdiction, it may be brought into a higher court having appellate jurisdiction for review of the lower court decision—usually on a question of law. Appellate courts have original jurisdiction over some matters, as discussed earlier.

While jurisdiction refers to the power of the court to hear the subject matter and render a judgment concerning it, venue refers to the proper place for the trial of the particular action.

Jurisdiction of the case is determined by the allegations of fact and the prayer of the complaint. The complaint limits what the court can award by way of damages or other relief sought.

Under the new rules, however, monetary amounts may or may not be listed or prayed for. You should check with your attorney when it comes to the inclusion as to whether or not a monetary amount should be included in the prayer. (Be sure to check your local codes.)

VENUE OF COURTS

Venue refers to the correct (or incorrect) place for the trial of the particular action (city, county, and so forth) where more than one court has jurisdiction of the subject matter of the case. Venue is regulated by statute and/or rules of court.

A motion (request) for change of venue may be made when:

1. The action was filed in a county other than the residence of an individual defendant or the principal place of business of a corporate defendant

2. There is prejudice of the judge which can be arbitrarily challenged once in some states (this is the basis for a motion to rescue in some states)

3. A fair trial cannot be had for various other reasons, such as pretrial publicity

4. The substantial inconvenience of producing witnesses and records

5. The ends of justice would be best served by a change of venue for some other statutory reason

The statutes in many states provide for a change of venue on some or all of the preceding grounds and others. Even where there are grounds for change of venue a judge has some reasonable discretion to grant or deny such a motion.

In California, a Notice of Motion for Change of Venue will take care of some errors regarding jurisdiction. If the motion for change of venue is on the ground of the wrong court, then there must be a Declaration of Merits, as well as the motion itself, and it must be made at the time the answer or demurrer is filed.

If the motion for change of venue is based upon the convenience of witnesses, then a Declaration of Merits is not necessary. In most jurisdictions, a Motion for Change of Venue is a "speaking motion," which is a written motion containing specific allegations of fact and law which will be argued by the attorney for the movant at the hearing of the motion. Check your state statute (code) and local court rules for change of venue grounds and procedure in your area.

STATE COURT PRACTICE AND PROCEDURE

The following sample practices and procedures are those used in the State of California and are submitted here by way of example only. The forms and names of pleadings or motions described in this section may differ from state to state, but the caveats and suggestions given in this section are appropriate and applicable to practice and procedure in all state courts.

State court proceedings are conducted for and on behalf of the litigants by attorneys duly licensed to practice in the state where the case is being heard, with few exceptions. Under certain circumstances, it is permissible for a litigant to represent himself in court. Such an appearance by the litigant is called a *pro se appearance,* or it is said that the litigant is appearing *in propria persona.* Courts generally frown on this procedure and encourage parties wishing to follow this practice to obtain the advice and counsel of a licensed attorney before they proceed by self-representation. Advice of counsel is often needed before filing in small claims court, even though the appearance of counsel in the small claims court is not required and may not be permitted.*

Certain court documents or papers must be filed in the office of the clerk of the court to start the legal proceeding and to bring it to its final conclusion. These "court papers" consist of a series of written statements of the claims and defenses of the parties to the lawsuit. The written statements that are required (as opposed to permitted) to be filed before a lawsuit (action) is "at issue" (ready to be tried before the court) are called " pleadings." Other court papers or documents that may be filed in addition to or in lieu of pleadings are "motions," "notices," "stipulations," "requests for admissions," other "discovery" documents, as well as court "orders" when signed by the court.

An "action" is commenced when the first pleading is filed with the clerk of the court by the person bringing the action.

Generally, the person who brings the suit is called a "plaintiff." He makes a written statement setting forth the facts which are the basis for his suit. This court paper or written statement is called a "complaint." In certain courts and jurisdictions this written statement is called a "declaration" or "petition." It is the first court paper filed in the office of the clerk of the court to begin the action.

A "summons" or its equivalent, which is a notice that a legal action has been started, is then issued by the clerk of the court and served with a copy of the complaint upon the person against whom the legal action is being brought. That person is called a "defendant."

The defendant answers the complaint, defending himself against the allegations contained in the complaint by filing a written "answer" in which he admits or denies the facts stated by the plaintiff in the complaint, and may allege further facts which constitute "new matter" in the form of "affirmative defenses" or a "counterclaim."

After the defendant files an answer, the plaintiff may or may not be required to file a "reply" (replication), depending on the rules of court for that particular court.

---

* See Small Claims Court, page 57.

Instead of filing an answer to a complaint, a defendant may file and argue written motions or demurrers objecting to the complaint on legal grounds. For the purpose of such a motion, the facts alleged in the complaint are considered to be true but not admitted by the defendant. If such a preliminary motion of the defendant is denied by the court, the defendant must file an answer, and the case proceeds as herein described.

Most state courts as well as federal courts allow all parties to seek relevant evidence for use in the trial of the case by formal rules of "discovery." These procedures are governed by the rules applicable to the court where the case is filed. They include "depositions," "interrogatories," and "requests to produce," among others. Any or all of these formal methods of discovery may be used before the trial in addition to any informal investigation of the facts.

When all pleadings have been filed, all pretrial motions disposed of by order of court or withdrawal of the motion and all pretrial discovery completed, the case is ready for trial. It is "at issue."

When the case is tried, it is submitted to a court and jury or to a court without a jury (nonjury trial) for a final decision. In a jury trial, the judge decides questions of law, and the jury decides questions of fact. In a nonjury trial, the judge decides questions of both law and fact.

PLEADINGS AND MOTIONS

In preparing pleadings and motions, the name and location of the court (including the name of the division of the court), the names of the parties, and a place for inserting the case number to be assigned by the clerk of the court must be typed as the heading of the document. That information is called the "caption" or "title" of the case. The caption or title must be typed on all "court papers" to be filed in the case, including orders to be signed by the judge.

Be sure that the name of the court and the names of the parties are correct. Use complete individual names and exact registered corporate names. If a party is not suing or being sued in his individual capacity, indicate the proper capacity.

EXAMPLES

John Doe, Trustee for Richard Roe

or

John Doe and Richard Roe d/b/a
Doe Plumbing Supplies

The foregoing examples are for use in so-called adversary proceedings. In probate and in cases where an action is brought on behalf of or against another person or group, the caption of the case may not contain the names of all parties.

EXAMPLES

IN RE:
ESTATE OF JOHN DOE, deceased

or

STATE ex rel. DOE vs. ROE

A. Summons and Complaints

The "summons" is not a pleading. It is the notice of the filing of the first pleading, and it is an instruction to the defendant to answer the pleading (complaint) or be subject to judgment by default.

The filing of the complaint with the clerk of the court sets a litigation matter into motion. A copy of the complaint must be served on a defendant in accordance with applicable law to give the court personal jurisdiction over that named defendant.

A copy of the complaint is served with the summons by the sheriff or other process server (where permitted by rules of court). After service, the server files a "return of service" showing where and when the defendant was served. A copy of the return of service is usually mailed to the office of the plaintiff's attorney's.

Caveat: When a complaint is filed, the legal assistant or other person assigned to the office calendar should set an appropriate date for checking on whether the complaint has been served if a return of service is not received before that date. Check local rules as to availability of further attempts to serve and possibly better address instructions, and so forth. The defendant(s) does not have to answer the complaint until he is served. For more details on preparation and service of summons, see Chapter 5.

After the defendant is duly served, the defendant must take affirmative action or the plaintiff will obtain a judgment by default against the defendant in a *civil* case. The defendant must respond to the complaint.

The defendant may respond by filing a pleading or an appropriate motion.

The most common responses of a defendant(s) are discussed in B. and C. in this section.

B. General Demurrer (*Motion to Dismiss*)

The general demurrer or motion to dismiss attacks the whole complaint or some alleged cause of action or count contained in the complaint on the basis that a cause of action has not been stated. It may be filed in lieu of an answer within the time allowed for filing an answer (see C.).

Some defenses to a cause of action must be grounds for filing a general demurrer, or motion to dismiss if the defenses appear on the face of the complaint. Those defenses, among others, are:

1. Statute of limitations
2. Laches
3. Standing to sue
4. Res judicata
5. Illegality in a contract action
6. Contributory negligence of assumption of risk in a tort action

The filing of a demurrer or motion to dismiss tolls the time for filing an answer.

Caution: Some other pretrial motions do not toll the time for filing a responsive pleading.

GENERAL DEMURRER*

The complaint does not state facts sufficient to constitute a cause of action.

or

The first cause of action does not state facts sufficient to state a cause of action.

or

The complaint does not state facts sufficient to constitute a cause of action in that the alleged cause of action is barred by the Statute of Limitations (or you can state any other defenses appearing on the face of the complaint).

---

* Demurrers are not used in some states. Under the Federal Rules of Civil Procedure, and under many state court rules of civil procedure, a demurrer is called a Motion to Dismiss. The motion to dismiss must state the grounds for dismissal with some particularity.

It is wise to prepare a law memorandum in support of a general demurrer or motion to dismiss if the grounds are not obvious.

C. Answer and Counterclaim

Unlike the motion to dismiss or general demurrer discussed in A., which are motions, the answer of a defendant(s) is a pleading.

The answer is the first pleading required of the defendant in response to the complaint filed by the plaintiff.

The answer admits or denies the facts alleged in the complaint. Facts showing that the defendant has an affirmative defense to the complaint are also alleged in the answer or such defenses are considered to be waived. See A., where the facts showing an affirmative defense available to the defendant appear on the face of the complaint.

If the affirmative defenses are pleaded in the answer, the facts are stated under the heading Affirmative Defenses following a paragraph-by-paragraph (numbered as the paragraphs of the complaint that are being answered are numbered) admission or denial of the plaintiff's statement of facts in the complaint.

A counterclaim may be pleaded in the defendant's answer or in a separate document with the same caption of the case. See also C., where a "cross-complaint" is used instead of a counterclaim in California.

The counterclaim must state a valid cause of action, just as the original complaint must state a valid cause of action. See Chapter 5.

In addition to his answer and whether or not the answer contained a counterclaim or a counterclaim was separately filed, the defendant may feel that he has a cause of action against a co-defendant or against a person not party to the plaintiff's action, which other cause of action arises out of the facts alleged by the plaintiff. If so, he may want to file a cross-complaint as discussed in E. or a "third-party complaint" as discussed in F.

D. Reply (Replication)

The reply or replication is a pleading by which the plaintiff responds to the answer filed by the defendant. It is necessary in case of certain allegations in the answer, but it is usually not required. Check with your attorney as to whether a reply is necessary when you receive the answer from the defendant's attorney. This is important. If a reply is required, there is a time limit for filing it. Check the court rules of civil procedure. The time is usually the same as the time for the defendant to file his answer to the complaint.

E. Cross-Complaint

A cross-complaint is a separate document, in a separate cover and designated or titled as a cross-complaint.

In some jurisdictions, it may be part of the answer and therefore may be entitled Answer and Cross-Complaint. You are cautioned to check your local courts for this procedure. In some state courts and in the federal courts there is a provision in the rules of pleading for a cross-complaint and for a third-party complaint.

In any event, in California a cross-complaint is considered a separate independent action and may join new and additional parties and may be filed with or without the answer—and in an extreme case—whether an answer is filed or not. Talk to your attorney about this latter procedure.

Caution: The latter procedure is a dangerous procedure since a cross-complaint in and of itself does not deny any of the facts alleged in the plaintiff's complaint. Failure to deny the plaintiff's allegations automatically admits them as set forth in the plaintiff's complaint. As a practical matter, cross-complaints are usually filed and served with the answer to the complaint. A cross-complaint may be filed and served after the time for filing and served after the time for filing the answer has expired, but it is dangerous to put off the preparation and filing of the cross-complaint. In doing so, you *may* overlook the time for filing the answer and end up in default.

The cross-complaint must state a cause of action against the cross-defendant. For rules of pleading, see Chapter 6. The rules of pleading applicable to drafting a complaint apply to drafting a cross-complaint.

F. Third-Party Complaint

In many state jurisdictions, a cross-complaint is filed by a plaintiff against another plaintiff(s) or it is filed by a defendant against another defendant(s). That is also the procedure in the federal trial courts. The cross-complaint may be indemnity or liability arising out of the facts alleged by the plaintiff in the complaint.

A third-party complaint brings a new party into the cause of action. A third-party complaint is filed by a defendant when he believes a person not made party to the action by the plaintiff, is responsible directly to the plaintiff for the facts alleged in the complaint; or is liable over to the defendant by way of indemnity; or is jointly liable with the defendant if the defendant is liable to the plaintiff; or is liable to the defendant in any other way on the facts alleged by the plaintiff.

In California, the cross-complaint seems to serve the purpose of both a cross-complaint between plaintiffs or defendants and a third-party complaint to bring in a new party.

The third-party complaint must state a cause of action against the third-party defendant. For drafting, see Chapter 6. The rules of pleading applicable to drafting a complaint apply to drafting a third-party complaint.

G. Amended and Supplemental Pleadings

Sometime during the course of civil litigation it will be necessary for you to amend your pleadings, or in the alternative, to file a supplemental pleading upon the discovery of new evidence of information material to the case. Court rules allow certain amendments without leave of court. There is usually a time limit on such an amendment. Pleadings may also be amended by stipulation between the parties or upon motion to the court for leave to amend.

EXAMPLES

1. Where you have, subsequent to filing your summons and complaint, discovered the name of a necessary party–defendant previously described and designated as a "Doe";

2. Where you may have incorrectly spelled the name of a defendant such as "Schmidt," when it should have been "Smith"; or

3. Where you have omitted alleging facts necessary to state the cause of action.

The time limit for amendments as of course (without stipulation of the parties or order of court) is usually before a responsive pleading, which includes a demurrer or motion to dismiss, if filed.

Amended pleadings should be so designated in the title of the pleading which follows the caption of the case.

EXAMPLES

AMENDED COMPLAINT

or

SECOND AMENDED COMPLAINT

or

AMENDED ANSWER

In most states, if an attorney or party *has entered his appearance in the case,* an amended pleading can be filed and a copy served on the attorney.

In such instance, it is not necessary to prepare a new summons or to have the amended pleading served personally on the adverse party.

If an "amended complaint" is filed before the answer to the original complaint is *due*, it may be wise to have the amended complaint served with an alias summons (or its equivalent in your state) to lay the groundwork for a default judgment if the defendant does not appear or fails to file an answer or other responsive pleading. You want your default against the right defendant on the right cause of action.

H. Pretrial Motions

The "demurrer" or "motion to dismiss" (see B.) is one of the pretrial motions.

A "motion to strike," a "motion for judgment on the pleadings," and a "motion for summary judgment" are also generally used before trial.

These motions should be used only when you are sure that you have valid grounds for the motion. The motions should not be used as a delaying tactic, but they are often so used.

Note that the filing of the foregoing motions, except motion to dismiss, does not toll or extend the time within which the movant is required to file a responsive pleading. For this reason, be sure to flag the statute of limitations on your file and your follow-up procedure to avoid a default being taken against your office or should you want to take a default against the opposing counsel.

The parties making and opposing a motion for summary judgment are permitted to file affidavits in support of their arguments. If an affidavit is filed, a counter-affidavit should be filed to show that there is a genuine issue of material fact in order to defeat the motion.

Grounds for the motions must be stated in the motions. A law memorandum in support of the motion may be indicated. The motion will be argued by the attorneys at a hearing on the motion.

I. Post-Trial Motions

Post-trial motions include "motion for new trial," "motion for judgment n.o.v." (notwithstanding the verdict), and "motion to set aside judgment," among other post-trial motions most frequently used. Court rules of civil procedure govern the content and time for making these motions.

Grounds for the motion must be stated in the motion. It is generally wise to prepare a law memorandum in support of the post-trial motion. The motion will be argued by the attorneys at a hearing on the motion.

CHAPTER 5

What the Legal Assistant Should Know About Federal Court Practice and Procedure

FEDERAL COURTS

The United States is a federal government, and as such is charged with the responsibility of preserving the governments and laws of the fifty states. It is therefore not unreasonable to state that in its attempt to define or bring into proper relationship the laws of the various states, problems of conflict of laws will arise. We will not discuss this problem and mention it only to give you a broad understanding of the meaning and import of the federal court system.

The federal court system was provided for in Article III of the Constitution of the United States. That Article established one supreme court and such other inferior federal courts as Congress "may from time to time ordain and establish."

As a result of the federal Constitution and acts of Congress, the regular federal court system today consists of the following courts:

FEDERAL COURT SYSTEM

A. *The United States Supreme Court*

1. The *final arbiter* of law in American Jurisprudence.

2. Decisions can really *only* be reversed by the Court itself, or by Congressional legislation.

3. *It may* have *some* "original" jurisdiction in some state/federal disputes, as well as "diplomatic" matters, BUT—

   The thrust of the Court's work is in the *"appellate"* area.

B. *United States Circuit Courts of Appeal*

Under authority of Article III of the U.S. Constitution and Judiciary Act of 1789, there are 11 Federal Judicial Circuits. (See 28 U.S.C.A., Section 41.)

C. *Federal District Courts:* This is the "first level trial" network in the Federal Court system. Approximately 92 districts. Each state has one— New York, Texas and California have four.

In addition to the regular federal courts in the system, there are special federal courts created by Congress from time to time. At the present time, the following are special federal courts:

1. United States Court of Appeals for the Federal Circuit (formerly U.S. Court of Claims and United States Court of Customs and Patent Appeals)

2. United States Claims Court (has trial jurisdiction for cases formerly triable in the former U.S. Court of Claims)

3. United States Court of International Trade (formerly the Customs Court)

4. The Tax Court of the United States (formerly known as United States Board of Tax Appeals)

5. United States Court of Military Appeals

6. District of Columbia Superior Court and District of Columbia Court of Appeals, which have jurisdiction of local district matters

7. District Bankruptcy Courts, which are associated with the federal district courts throughout the states, territories, and the District of Columbia for the purpose of hearing and administering federal bankruptcy laws. Appeals from the district bankruptcy courts are taken to *bankruptcy* appellate panels of the U.S. Court of Appeals for the federal circuit in which the district bankruptcy court is located.

THE SUPREME COURT OF THE UNITED STATES

The United States Supreme Court is the ultimate authority for the interpretation of federal law and constitutional law as it affects both the federal and all state government actions. It has both appellate and original jurisdiction. It may grant discretionary review (*certiorari*) of cases from the United States Court of Appeals of the various United States judicial circuits.

The Supreme Court is located in the Supreme Court Building, 1 First Street NE, Washington, D.C. 20543.

UNITED STATES COURTS OF APPEAL

These twelve courts are located in each of the present eleven United States judicial circuits plus the District of Columbia circuit. Every state and territory of the United States (including Guam and Puerto Rico) belongs to one of the eleven judicial circuits.

Appellate jurisdiction includes appeals from the United States District Courts and various federal administrative and regulatory agencies. The rules of procedure for the United States Circuit Courts of Appeals are promulgated by the United States Supreme Court and supplemented by rules made by each circuit for its courts. Check both sets of rules before you proceed with a federal appeal. Follow them exactly or the right to appeal may be lost.

The United States judicial circuits and the states and territories that belong to each circuit are as follows:

District of Columbia	District of Columbia
First	Maine, New Hampshire, Massachusetts, Rhode Island, and Puerto Rico
Second	Vermont, Connecticut, and New York
Third	New Jersey, Pennsylvania, Delaware, and the Virgin Islands
Fourth	Maryland, West Virginia, Virginia, North Carolina, and South Carolina
Fifth	Mississippi, Louisiana, and Texas
Sixth	Ohio, Michigan, Kentucky, and Tennessee
Seventh	Indiana, Illinois, and Wisconsin
Eighth	Minnesota, Iowa, Missouri, Arkansas, Nebraska, North Dakota, and South Dakota
Ninth	California, Oregon, Nevada, Montana, Washington, Idaho, Arizona, Alaska, Hawaii, territories of Guam, and Northern Mariana Islands
Tenth	Colorado, Wyoming, Utah, Kansas, Oklahoma, and New Mexico
Eleventh	Alabama, Georgia, and Florida

Compare federal judicial circuits to federal judicial districts discussed in the following section.

UNITED STATES DISTRICT COURTS

The United States district courts are courts of original jurisdiction and are federal trial courts located in every state and territory of the United States and in the District of Columbia.

In addition to their jurisdiction to hear cases involving federal law, these courts also have jurisdiction to hear some state matters if the dispute is between citizens of different states and the amount in controversy exceeds a certain statutory amount. Under such circumstances, a case started in a state court may be "removed" from the state court to the federal district court, if approved by the federal court on a statutory "petition for removal." After removal to the federal district court, the court will apply the substantive law of the state where the cause of action arose but will apply the federal rules of civil procedure to the case after it is removed—ref. Federal Rule of Civil Procedures 81 (c). The district court may also review some decisions of some federal agencies.

Some less populated states have just one federal judicial district in the state. The following is a chart of the federal judicial districts:

Alabama (Northern, Middle, Southern)

Alaska

Arizona

Arkansas (Eastern, Western)

California (Northern, Eastern, Central, Southern)

Colorado

Connecticut

Delaware

District of Columbia

Florida (Northern, Middle, Southern)

Georgia (Northern, Middle, Southern)

Guam

Hawaii

Idaho

Illinois (Northern, Central, Southern)

Indiana (Northern, Southern)

Iowa (Northern, Southern)

Kansas

Kentucky (Eastern, Western)

Louisiana (Eastern, Middle, Western)

Maine

Maryland

Massachusetts

Michigan (Eastern, Western)

Minnesota

Mississippi (Northern, Southern, Eastern, Western)

Montana

Nebraska

Nevada

New Hampshire

New Jersey

New Mexico

New York (Northern, Southern, Eastern, Western)

North Carolina (Eastern, Middle, Western)

North Dakota

Northern Mariana Islands

Ohio (Northern, Southern)

Oklahoma (Northern, Eastern, Western)

Oregon

Pennsylvania (Eastern, Middle, Western)

Puerto Rico

Rhode Island

South Carolina

South Dakota

Tennessee (Eastern, Middle, Western)

Texas (Northern, Southern, Eastern, Western)

Utah

Vermont

Virgin Islands

Virginia (Eastern, Western)

Washington (Eastern, Western)

West Virginia (Northern, Southern)

Wisconsin (Eastern, Western)

Wyoming

In each federal district, with the exception of Guam and the Northern Mariana Islands, there is at least one federal bankruptcy court. Puerto Rico has two federal bankruptcy courts, and the Virgin Islands district has one.

In addition to the foregoing regular federal courts, various special federal courts are created and done away with by Congress from time to time.

The following section describes some of those special federal courts, tells how and for what purpose they were created and what court rules of procedure apply to practice before those courts.

SPECIAL FEDERAL COURTS

The special federal courts were created by Acts of Congress at various times. The jurisdiction of a special court is determined by the statute that created it. An easy reference guide to congressional acts (called federal statutes) is the United States Code Annotated. It is a multivolume set of law books that contains the text of all federal statutes with pocket parts in the back of each book updating it yearly. Citations to that reference set are given in the following list of special federal courts so that you may check jurisdiction:

1. *United States Court of Appeals for the Federal Circuit.* See 28 U.S.C.A. 1338, 28 U.S.C.A. 1346, 15 U.S.C.A. 1071, 19 U.S.C.A. 1337, 28 U.S.C.A. 1295. See also this court's special rules supplementing the Federal Rules of Appellate Procedure.

2. *United States Claims Court.* See 28 U.S.C.A. 2503, 28 U.S.C.A. 2522. See also Contract Disputes Act of 1978, para. 10 (a) (1). Court prescribes its own rules.

3. *United States Court of International Trade.* See 28 U.S.C.A. 1582, 28 U.S.C.A. 2631-2647. See also Customs Court Act of 1980, Tariff Act of 1930, Trade Act of 1974, Trade Agreements Act of 1979. The proce-

dural rules are in accordance with the statute, 28 U.S.C.A. 2631-2647, as amended.

4. *The Tax Court of the United States.* See 26 U.S.C.A. 7601 and 26 U.S.C.A. 7453. The procedural rules for the tax court follow 27 U.S.C.A. 7453.

5. *United States Court of Military Appeals.* See 10 U.S.C.A. 867 and the All Writs Act, 28 U.S.C.A. 1651.

6. *The District of Columbia Superior Court and the District of Columbia Court of Appeals* both have jurisdiction of local District of Columbia matters. These courts are in addition to the regular federal district and circuit courts for the District of Columbia, which are also located in the district. The local jurisdiction was transferred from the federal district court to these additional courts by an Act of Congress called Court Reform and Criminal Procedure Act of 1970.

FEDERAL COURT PRACTICE AND PROCEDURE

GENERAL JURISDICTION

The district courts in the federal court system have original jurisdiction of actions involving a "federal question" (such as breach of a federal statute or regulation or a violation of the provisions of the Constitution of the United States) and of all criminal actions where the defendant is charged with a federal crime (a crime defined by Act of Congress). Some examples of federal questions or issues are admiralty, maritime, or prize cases; poor bankruptcy proceedings; interstate commerce and antitrust suits; patent, copyright, trademarks, and unfair competition lawsuits under federal acts; civil rights cases based on federal statutes or the Constitution of the United States; and those claims arising out of and under the federal labor acts.

Special federal courts are courts of "limited jurisdiction" and as a general proposition of law you must spell out, with statutory specificity, the authority of the court to hear the matter. These courts were created by federal statute.

Note: Failure to state and prove facts establishing jurisdiction may subject your claim to an automatic rejection at any given point of the proceeding up to and including the appellate hearing. As the legal assistant, therefore, you should read the United States Code, Title 28, Sections 1331 and 1332 and the citations for special federal courts. These U.S. Code sections set forth the conditions under which a case can be filed in federal courts and are the statutory authority giving the federal court jurisdiction to hear and determine the claim. See the annotated statutes to find cases interpreting the Act, such as 28 U.S.C.A. 1331 and 1332.

PRACTICE AND PROCEDURE—GENERAL RULES

Federal courts apply "procedural rules" under the Federal Rules of Civil Procedure. The "substantive law" will be the law of the State where the incident occurred. *NOTE:* A MUST—The federal courts must have "subject matter jurisdiction."

Federal questions are those matters "arising under" the Constitution, such as: a federal statute; a federal/administrative regulation; or an international treaty; and all violations of the Federal Criminal Code.

Types of Jurisdictions Under Federal Rules of Civil Procedure

A. Concurrent Jurisdiction (Diversity): joint jurisdiction with the State Court, at the discretion of Congress, "When a case can be properly tried in either a federal or a state court." State Court, based on state law involved; minimum contact; or in Federal Court, based on diversity of citizenship.

Diversity of citizenship must include the following:

(a) citizens of two different states;

(b) the complaint must meet the jurisdictional amount, which is *not* required in a federal question case, i.e., $50,000.00.

B. Subject Matter Jurisdiction: These are the types of cases which the court may legitimately hear and decide, such as Municipal Court limit; Superior Court limit; subject matter; bankruptcy, criminal, and so forth.

C. Jurisdiction Over the Person (in Personam) falls into two categories and can be based on:

1. Over the person; any person(s) who resides within the jurisdictional area served by the court; or,

2. The Long-Arm Statutes (public policy):

(a) conducting business within the forum area;

(b) committing a tort within the forum area;

(c) insuring persons or property located within the forum; and

(d) entering a contract that will be performed within the forum area.

D. In Rem Jurisdiction Over Property of the defendant within the forum area or any assets of the defendant which can be attached or garnished within the court's jurisdiction.

E. Exclusive Jurisdiction or cases which can only be tried in a particular court or, if only a particular type of court can hear and determine a case, such as "bankruptcy" and "cases having the United States as a party."

F. Prudent Jurisdiction is where a case or problem has both a federal and a state claim.

G. Appellate Jurisdiction goes beyond the trial stage; and,

H. Original Jurisdiction.

Step-by-Step Procedure in Commencing A Federal Court Action: Pleading Stage

I. File a complaint: no technical language needed—just "tell a story."

In the Federal court—emphasis is placed on "the trial," rather than "forms" needed to "get to trial." As opposed to the State Court—where one is required to use a particular and exact form of pleading.

Service of Process

A. The clerk will issue "a summons" on the defendant or his/her agent.

B. U.S. Marshal serves this package.

C. Pre-trial Motions

    1. *Motion to Dismiss*

        a) Not sufficient to state a cause of action;

        b) Denying jurisdiction of the Court; or

        c) Other—

            If granted—the case is dismissed.

            If dismissed "without prejudice," the plaintiff *can refile* in the proper Court; or amend the complaint.

            If dismissed "with prejudice," the plaintiff *cannot* amend or refile.

    2. *Motion for a More Definite Statement,* which is asking for more "specific statements" (special demurrer)

    3. *Motion to Strike,* which is merely asking the Court to strike from the complaint matters (facts) which are not "germane" to the case.

4. *Motion for General Demurrer:* this motion admits to all allegations but denies that these allegations state a cause of action. If granted, the case is dismissed.

    THEN

5. *Answer*

6. Counterclaim against the plaintiff cross-claim against a third party. Plaintiff MUST file a "reply" to the *counterclaim.*

Pleading Stage

    A. Motion for Judgment on the pleadings;

       and

    B. Motion for Summary Judgment.

These can be filed by either party *after* all other pleadings have been resolved. The summary judgment is granted as a "matter of law."

Discovery Stage: Five types of discovery.

    A. Deposition;

    B. Interrogatories;

    C. Demand for Production of Documents;

    D. Physical/Mental Examination; and

    E. Request for Admissions.

THREE MAJOR METHODS FOR RESOLVING LEGAL CONTROVERSIES

Alternatives to Trial:

A. *Negotiation:* concerns itself with discussions or conferences between the parties, seeking to establish the final form of future proceedings; or a settlement of the controversy.

    1. It is a *"mutual agreement";*

    2. It is *informal;* and

    3. It is simple.

Drawback: it is *"not binding"* upon the parties.

As opposed to:

B. *Mediation:* where the matter is referred to a *third* party, who will attempt to reconcile the differences between the parties and attempt to settle it, through compromise ("win some, lose some"). Give each party "a portion of what that party is seeking." In some circumstances, the mediation is a "factfinder" who will then issue a conclusion based on the facts as he or she understands them.

C. *Arbitration:* This vehicle is used by referring the controversy to a third party chosen by the litigants or one provided by law, whichever is applicable. Here, to avoid going to trial, the result is "an award," the "final resolution" of the controversy. Arbitration is often mandated by law or provided for in an agreement. Hence, you have two types of arbitration:

1. *Compulsory;* and

2. *Voluntary.*

PROCEDURE FOR REMOVAL OF A STATE COURT ACTION TO THE FEDERAL COURT SYSTEM

1. Prepare the notice for removal. Be reminded that where the State Court requires a "fact pleading," Federal Courts require only notice pleadings, i.e., pleadings which contain a brief statement of the facts to satisfy the State rules.

Be sure in your statement that you include the jurisdiction of the federal law giving you the eligibility to file the action in the Federal Court system. An example of this would be the constitutional requirement that the claim arises under federal law thereby creating a cause of action for the plaintiff; as well as the diversity of citizenship.

2. Serve a copy of the Notice of Removal with the Federal Clerk together with all pleadings and any State Court orders that were filed in the State Court. You might check with the Federal Court Clerk to determine if a filing fee is required. This is peculiar to each District Court.

3. Please be advised that you no longer need to obtain from any insurance company a bond to cover costs incurred in this removal process.

4. Give prompt notice to the State Court that you have removed the case to the Federal Court system.

PLEASE NOTE that you should file your answer to the pleading (complaint) or the Notice of Removal in the State Court *before* the 30-day Statute of Limitation has passed. Otherwise, a default judgment can be taken against the client.

5. Thereafter, be sure to notify all parties of the Notice of Removal to Federal Court. Be sure that each and every plaintiff, if more than one, is also notified.

6. As the legal assistant, it will be your job to check the file to determine if any State Court orders were rendered during the course of the proceeding. If so, please advise the attorney so that he can in turn advise as to whether or not to seek Federal Court changes in the orders.

7. Be reminded, or take note, that the removed case does not have to be repleaded in the Federal District Court.

PLEADINGS AND MOTIONS

In some state courts you have what are commonly called "common law pleadings" or "code pleading," which, in effect, means that everything has to be stated in legal "words of art." Many state courts have adopted modern court rules of civil procedure, as well as modern court rules of criminal procedure. Most of these modern state court rules are similar in content to the Federal Rules of Civil Procedure. The trend today is to get away from long technical pleadings and instead submit a plain, simple statement of the facts or defenses to a claim. This is primarily true in the federal court system. Facts sufficing to allege a "cause of action" must be stated after facts that show jurisdiction of the court. Pleadings are simple pleadings in the federal system and all you have to do is notify the defending party generally what is being alleged against him— ref. Federal Rules of Civil Procedure, Title III, Rules 7 through 16, particularly Rule 8(a).

Note: Check local district court rules for size of paper to be used for pleadings and motions.

A. Summons and Complaint

The "summons" and a copy of the complaint are normally served on the defendant by a United States Marshall to start the action.* Should you wish someone other than a marshal to serve the summons and complaint, you must obtain authority from the clerk of the court to do so. This is done by applying to the court clerk with a printed form entitled Request for Personal Service. This is

---

* Ref. Summons and Complaint in a state court action on page 65.

merely a formality as the clerk simply signs and stamps the document— ref. Federal Rules of Civil Procedure 4(c).

Practical hint: Service on minors must be made on the guardian *ad litem,* or agent, appointed by the court: state law determines—ref. F. R.C.P. 4(d)(2) and F. R.C.P. 17(c).

Upon completion of the service of process you should immediately cause the proof of service of the summons and complaint to be filed with the court. Though this procedure is optional, we have found it to be a practical extra step as documents have a way of being misplaced or lost. Should a question arise as to proper service, having the original on file with the court is your best protection and proof.

B. Answer

After service of the summons and complaint, the defendant has twenty days in which to file a responsive pleading, unless otherwise extended by the court or excepted under Federal Rules of Civil Procedure 12(a). Defenses must be appropriately pleaded or they are waived, with few exceptions.

An answer to be filed by the U.S. attorney or other officer or agency of the government has sixty days in which to file a responsive pleading—ref. F. R.C.P. 12(a).

Basically, the answer is the same as that prepared and filed in a state court that has adopted modern court rules of civil procedure. As in a state court answer, you have to admit or deny part of a paragraph, or you can specifically deny part or generally deny part of a paragraph, and so forth. But here too it is deemed admitted if you do not do one or the other.

A cautionary measure: Note that a denial for lack of information sufficient to form a belief as to the jurisdictional facts is an appropriate challenge and puts the burden of proof on the plaintiff.

Just as in a state court that has adopted modern court rules of civil procedure, "affirmative defenses" should be pleaded in the answer to a federal court complaint—ref. F. R.C.P. 8(c).

Under F. R.C.P. 12(b), you can put certain defenses in your answer, or make a motion to dismiss based upon the following defenses:

1. Lack of jurisdiction of the subject matter.
2. Lack of jurisdiction over the person.

3. Improper venue.

4. Insufficiency of process—meaning that the summons and complaint was improperly issued—ref. F. R.C.P. 4(a) and (b).

5. Insufficiency of service of process of summons—meaning that the summons was incorrectly served. In some state courts, such as California, a "motion to quash" is used to raise this question—ref. F. R.C.P. 4(c) through (i).

6. Failure to state a claim upon which relief can be granted. This would be the same as a general demurrer in some state court actions or a motion to dismiss for failure to state a cause of action in other state courts (see Chapter 6).

7. Failure to join an indispensable party. This is important, because even though they are not a party to the action, if they were not brought in as a party–defendant (or party–plaintiff) complete relief could not be given to the parties privy to the lawsuit. Remember that when this party is brought in, you must consider the problems of venue, service of process, and diversity jurisdiction.

Some defenses cannot be waived. They are as follows:

1. Lack of subject matter. (See statute creating the federal court.)

2. Failure to state a claim upon which relief can be granted. (See Chapter 6.)

3. Failure to join an indispensable party. (See F. R.C.P. 19 and compare F. R.C.P. 20 covering permissive joinder of parties and F. R.C.P. 21 covering the right to add or drop parties.)

The defenses that cannot be waived are defenses that concern the jurisdiction of the court. If a court has no jurisdiction it has no power and its judgment is void.

Other affirmative defenses as defined in F. R.C.P. 7(c) must be pleaded or they are waived.

Note: The Statute of Limitations, contrary to some popular opinion, is an affirmative defense that must be pleaded or it is waived.

C. Counterclaim

The counterclaim is the pleading filed by a defendant against a plaintiff in the action that states facts that show the defendant also has a legal claim against the plaintiff: See Chapter 6, "How to State a Cause of Action." Sections (a) through (f) of the Federal Rules of Civil Procedure govern Counterclaims.

Compulsory Counterclaim. The compulsory counterclaim is the claim of defendant arising out of the transaction that is the subject matter of plaintiff's action. It must be brought or you have automatically waived the right of the client to bring it. You do not have to show independent jurisdiction in the federal court. The plaintiff has to file and serve a reply to this counterclaim within twenty days of receipt thereof—ref. F. R.C.P. 13(a) and 13(c).

Permissive Counterclaim. The permissive counterclaim is the claim of defendant for any other claim he may have against the plaintiff. Such claim need not be alleged or alluded to in the original complaint. Such claim does not have to arise out of the same transaction—ref. F. R.C.P. 13(b) and 13(c).

Counterclaims maturing or acquired after pleading are covered in F. R.C.P. 13(e). See F. R.C.P. 13(f) for an omitted counterclaim.

D. Cross Claims

A "cross claim" arises between parties on the same side of a lawsuit. Cross-claims are always *permissive.* The test for a cross claim is that the claim must arise out of the transaction or occurrence that is the subject of the pending lawsuit—ref. F. R.C.P. 13(g) and (i).

An example of a cross claim in a defendant-against-defendant situation may be under the theory of indemnification, that is, the defendant claims that the other defendant has agreed to hold him harmless against any claim by the plaintiff in the matter.

After the cross claim has been served, the defending party has twenty days in which to file his answer (sixty days for the United States Attorney). You do not have to plead facts showing jurisdiction in your cross claim.

E. Third-Party Complaint

Rule 14(a) of the Federal Rules of Civil Procedure (F.R.C.P.) applies to the bringing in of a third party by a defendant in a federal lawsuit. Section (b) of that Rule applies to bringing in of a third party by a plaintiff. All rules regarding pleadings and procedure in this section on federal practice and procedure apply to the third-party plaintiffs and defendants whether they were brought in by the original plaintiff or the original defendant.

A third-party complaint is filed by a defending party to bring in an outside party he feels is really the person liable for the plaintiff's complaint or the defendant's counterclaim. When your attorney brings in a third party in his client's case, you must have a summons issued and personally served on the new party with a copy of the third-party complaint (which will have a copy of the *original* complaint attached). See F. R.C.P. 14(c) as to third-party practice as it applies to admiralty and maritime court.

The new third-party defendant and you as the third-party plaintiff will then follow the federal practice and procedures as given herein for the original plaintiffs and defendants.

Note: A third-party complaint may be filed without leave of court if it is filed not later than ten days after the original defendant's answer is filed. Otherwise, defendant (third-party plaintiff) must get an "order of court" permitting him to file the third-party complaint—ref. F. R.C.P. 14(a).

F. Amended and Supplemental Pleadings

You can amend your original pleading without permission of the court, as long as it is done *before* the defendant files his answer. There is a leeway of about twenty days. Thereafter, you have to prepare a motion for leave to amend. The defendant, of course, would have to file an amended answer if you are granted permission to amend the complaint—ref. F. R.C.P. 15(a).

If a defendant files a motion to dismiss or other preliminary motion objecting to the complaint, the court will usually give you leave to amend the complaint if it grants the motion. See G., titled Pretrial Motions.

The procedure for filing an amended pleading at your request after the defendant has filed his answer is basically the same as in a state court proceeding. You make your regular motion to amend the pleading and attach a copy of the proposed pleading as an exhibit. The judge may want to see what you have amended to determine whether or not to grant your motion.

Check your local federal district court rule to determine whether you must retype the entire amended complaint and refile it after leave to amend is granted.

G. Pretrial Motions

A pretrial motion must be in writing and must state the grounds for the motion with particularity. The motion may be written together with a written notice of hearing on the motion, depending on the local federal district court rules and customs—ref. F. R.C.P. 7(b). Filing of the pretrial motions that are prescribed in Federal Rules of Civil Procedure 12 extend the time for filing an answer until ten days after the court's order on the motion.

1. *Motion for a More Definite Statement.* If this motion is granted and it is not obeyed within ten days after notice of the order, or such other time as the court may direct, the court may at its discretion strike the pleading or make such other order as it deems just. The motion is used where a pleading is so vague or ambiguous that a party could not reasonably respond to it in a required responsive pleading. The key word is reasonably. Pleading does not require perfect clarity.

If a motion for more definite statement is granted and the plaintiff obeys the order by filing an amended complaint, the defendant (movant) has ten days from the date the amended complaint is filed to file his answer.

2. *Motion to Strike*—F. R.C.P. 2 (f). This motion is made before responding to a pleading within twenty days after service of the pleading; as a result of this motion the court may order stricken from any pleading any redundant, immaterial, impertinent, or scandalous matter. In some state courts a motion to strike does not expand the time for filing an answer.

3. *Motion for Judgment on the Pleadings*—F. R.C.P. 12(c) of the Federal Rules of Civil Procedure. This motion may be made after the pleadings are closed, but within a time that will not delay the trial of the action.

Caution: This is a dangerous motion, in that if matters outside of the pleadings are presented and admitted into evidence by the court, the motion can be treated as a summary judgment and can be disposed of such as provided in Rule 56. Of course, should this occur, all parties are given notice and a reasonable time within which to present materials pertinent to such a motion by Rule 56.

4. *Motion for Summary Judgment*—F. R.C.P. 56. This motion will be granted if there are no genuine issues as to any material fact and the moving party is entitled to a judgment as a matter of law. As in the state court system, this motion is normally made after the completion of all discovery. And, similarly, you can obtain a partial summary judgment under federal practice procedures, as in the state court system, to narrow the triable issues of fact.

The purpose of this motion is, primarily, to achieve a quick, final resolution of a dispute when there is no real necessity for a trial. If this appears on the face of the pleadings, a motion for summary judgment is proper.

Under Rule 56 of the Federal Rules of Civil Procedure, the parties making and opposing a motion for summary judgment are required, if such affidavits are available. The court may also consider depositions and sworn answers to interrogatories filed in the case.

When the attorney wishes to proceed with any of the preceding motions, a legal assistant should (1) carefully review the file; (2) reread the deposition(s) or the summary digest of the depositions; (3) reread answers to interrogatories and requests for admissions; (4) read the applicable code sections; (5) check the law applicable to the facts; and (6) then draft the appropriate motion to be reviewed by the attorney before filing.

Note: One can also file a motion for partial summary judgment under Rule 56(c) for liability alone despite the fact that the amount of the liability is still in dispute. This is often easier to obtain than final summary judgment.

PROCEDURE FOR FILING MOTIONS

1. In the federal district court file written motions and notices of hearing thereon not later than five days before the date set for the hearing on the motion—ref. F. R.C.P. 6(d).

2. That notice gives opposing counsel seven days from receipt of service of the motion to file his memorandum of law and/or affidavits in opposing the motion. Service by mail is complete upon mailing. Ref. F. R.C.P. 5(b).

Practical hint: A law memorandum in support of a motion or opposing a motion is not required by the Federal Rules of Civil Procedures. However, a law memorandum makes your position clearer and saves time for the court. Your task, as the legal assistant to prepare a law memorandum is clear, overt, and measurable, particularly if the legal issues raised by the motion are complex or not obviously in your favor.

Your local federal court rules may require filing the original and one copy (or duplicate originals). Federal courts will now accept a photocopy if it is legible. Check these matters with the clerk of your local federal court before proceeding.

On the motion for the production of document, if the list is too long or if there is controversy as to the need for certain documents requested, the court clerk will send out an order requiring the parties to meet and decide on what documents should be produced. The parties usually have two weeks to perform or reply to this request. It may be your task to review the documents with your attorney and help draft the joint statement with opposing counsel or her/his assistant.

DISCOVERY PROCEDURES

Discovery in civil cases in the federal courts is governed by the Federal Rules of Civil Procedure 26 through 27. That part of the rules is Title V Depositions and Discovery.

A legal assistant may be required to:

1. Set depositions dates by notice. See F.R.C.P. 27(2).
2. Send out sets of written interrogatories. See F.R.C.P. 33.
3. Request production of documents and things and for entry upon land for inspection and other purposes. See F.R.C.P. 34.
4. Prepare to take a physical or mental examination of a defendant. See F.R.C.P. 35.
5. Send out a set of requests for admissions. See F.R.C.P. 36.

The scope of federal court discovery is quite broad in that any matter not privileged, which is relevant to the subject matter, is discoverable. You can utilize any of the preceding vehicles as much as you want, whenever you want. And, most important, there is no thirty-day rule that all discovery should be completed before trial, as in some court rules.

As a legal assistant you should be able to draft some of the discovery documents, subject to review by your attorney. Protection from improper and unduly burdensome discovery can be obtained by order of the federal court in which the action is filed or where a deposition is being taken—ref. F.R.C.P. 26(c).

A. Depositions

Depositions are usually taken after the complaint is filed. In certain circumstances they are allowed before the action. See F.R.C.P. 27.

Depositions have to be noticed by a party–litigant in the action, but you can take the deposition of anybody by giving reasonable notice whether or not the person to be deposed is a party to the action. If you want documents produced at the deposition you should describe them with particularity in a *subpoena duces tecum* to a nonparty or in the notice to a party.

If you are not sure of the name or the identity of the custodian of records of a corporate or government defendant, merely describe in your *subpoena duces tecum* or notice the subject matter of the deposition and clearly state which pertinent documents you wish presented at the deposition. Thereafter, it is incumbent upon the corporation or government entity to designate a person to come to the deposition with the proper documents.

A transcript of the deposition must be filed with the court clerk immediately after it has been reviewed and signed by the party deposed.

During a regular deposition all the attorneys will ask any question they want that is within the general scope of discovery. The federal rule, and some state rules, also allow depositions to be taken on specified questions only. See F.R.C.P. 31. As a legal assistant you should be able to draft these questions subject to review by your attorney. See F. R.C.P. 26(c) for Protective Order and F. R.C.P. 37 for Motion to Compel discovery.

B. Interrogatories

As in the state court system, you can only serve interrogatories on party-litigants in a federal court action. Though urged, but not generally followed in state courts, in preparing written answers to a set of interrogatories for filing in the federal court, you must type the answer to the interrogatory being answered just below the question.

EXAMPLE

Interrogatory 1. What was the date of the accident?

Answer: July 30, 19___.

Interrogatory 2. What was the time and place of accident?

Answer: On or about 12:15 P.M. at the intersection of Doheny and Olympic Boulevards, Los Angeles, CA.

Interrogatories in a civil case in federal court are governed by Rule 33 of the Federal Rules of Civil Procedure. Some of the provisions relating to interrogatories are:

1. Interrogatories may be filed and served any time after commencement of the action.
2. And, unless extended by the court, the time within which to answer a set of interrogatories is thirty days—F.R.C.P. 6(e). If they are served by

mail, you get an extra three days. An extension of time other than this must be obtained by stipulation of the parties approved by the court or by order of court on motion of a party—ref. F. R.C.P. 6(b) and (d). One exception is where interrogatories are filed so quickly that forty-five days have not passed since the filing of the complaint—ref. F. R.C.P. 33(a).

3. If your attorney has any objections to the interrogatories, he has thirty days after service within which to file the objections or answer the interrogatories. Note that these objections are prepared for his signature, *not* that of the client.

4. If a party fails to answer or object to interrogatories that were served on him by you, your attorney may file a Motion to Compel Further Answers. This can be done at any time, as opposed to the procedure for objection to interrogatories. See F. R.C.P. 37.

C. Requests for Admission

"Requests for admission" can be served any time after commencement of the action. The party to whom the request for admission is directed has thirty days to respond per F. R.C.P. 36(a), unless forty-five days have not passed since service of the complaint and summons on him. For example, if plaintiff wants to serve a request early, say ten days after the filing and service of the summons and complaint, the party to whom the request is directed has thirty-five days to respond.

FEDERAL MULTI-DISTRICT LITIGATION

The concept of federal multi-district litigation was created and is governed by statute. See 28 U.S.C. 4207. The statute creates a federal judicial panel and prescribes the rules for its jurisdiction and proceedings.

A multi-district claim may be held before the statutory Judicial Panel on Multi-District Litigation, the members of which are appointed by the chief justice of the United States.

STEP-BY-STEP PROCEDURE FOR FILING A MULTI-DISTRICT LITIGATION CLAIM

1. Prepare an original and required copies of each document: the claim or summons and complaint, motion for transfer, and a proof of service or notice of opposition pursuant to Rules 9–11 of 28 U.S.C. 4207.

2. These documents should then be submitted for filing with the clerk of the panel, either by mailing or personal delivery to:

Clerk of the Panel
Judicial Panel of Multi-District Litigation
1030–15th Street, N.W.
320 Executive Building
Washington, D.C. 20005

Note: No document should be left with or mailed to a judge of the panel.

3. Thereafter the clerk of the panel, as in state and other federal court actions, places the date of filing on all documents filed.

4. Copies of motions for transfer of claims or actions, pursuant to 28 U.S.C. Section 1407, should be filed in each district court where an action is pending that will be affected by the motion.

5. Copies of motion for remand, pursuant to 28 U.S.C. Section 1407, should be filed in the district court in which any action affected by the motion is pending.

6. Within ten days of filing of a motion to transfer, an order to show cause (or conditional transfer order), will be issued by the panel. Each litigant or his attorney must give the clerk of the panel, in writing, the name and address of the attorney designated by that litigant to receive service of process and other documents relating to the case being heard by the judicial panel of multi-district litigation.

Note: Only one attorney shall represent a party-litigant, and any party-litigant not represented shall be served any and all pleadings by mailing to his last known address.

7. In connection with number 6 here, the clerk of the panel shall provide all counsel and party–litigants not represented by counsel with a Panel Service List of names and addresses of the designated attorneys and the parties they represent and the names and addresses of the parties not represented by counsel.

8. See Rule 7 of 28 U.S.C. Section 1407, as to the practice and procedure for filing motions in Multi-District Litigation Panel.

9. See Rules 9 and 10 of 28 U.S.C. Section 1407, regarding conditions and provisions for the practice and procedure relating to "tag-along actions."

Note: As the legal assistant you should be aware of Federal Court Rule changes as follows: (1) mandatory initial pre-discovery disclosure of witnesses and documents; and mandatory pre-trial disclosures; (2) mandatory meetings among counsel before any discovery; (3) substantial expansion of expert witnesses; and (4) limitations on the numbers of interrogatories and depositions.

CHAPTER 6

How to State a Cause of Action in a Civil Case

WHAT IS A CAUSE OF ACTION?

A cause of action is the legal or equitable right to recover damages or other claimed relief in a court action. The statement or allegation of the facts sufficient to support or deny that relief from the court are stated in pleadings prepared in accordance with the rules of court in which the legal action alleging the cause of action is filed.

The right to bring a legal action in any court is the right to seek judicial relief for the cause of action in the "jurisdiction" of the court in which a legal action is filed.

The facts alleged in the pleadings must be proved or admitted before the plaintiff in the cause of action can recover.

It might be noted at this point that some rules differ from the federal rules in that they require the complaint to state facts sufficient to state a cause of action, whereas the federal court uses the word "claim"—F. R.D.P. 8(a).

WHAT ARE THE ELEMENTS OF A CAUSE OF ACTION?

To recover damages or other relief from a court, you must allege (state) facts in a complaint that, if proved at the trial, would entitle the plaintiff to a final judgment after trial of the case.

The legal elements of a cause of action are found in case law, statutes, and government regulations.

Damages are recovered in an action "at law." Other relief may be obtained in an action "in equity."

The factual elements of the cause of action must be stated in the complaint.

The legal elements of the cause of action are argued by the attorney to the court and explained by the court to the jury in the trial of the case.

During the initial interview with the client (in some offices this is done by the legal assistant), the attorney will hear the basic facts relating to the client's problem. From those facts, he will decide, as a matter of law, whether the client has a cause of action over which some court has jurisdiction. See Chapter 4 for court systems and procedures.

Note: Before the attorney can decide the foregoing, he may require the legal assistant to interview the client further to get additional facts, documents, and other information which is necessary to decide whether the client does have a cause of action. The attorney or the legal assistant may also do some preliminary legal research to determine whether the client has a "case which will stand up in court" (cause of action). See Chapter 7, "Pretrial Practice and Procedure and Chapter 8," and Chapter 8, "Legal Research Tools."

To state a cause of action in a pleading, the facts which show the right of the plaintiff to recover must be stated in numbered paragraphs. The first paragraphs state facts that show the court's jurisdiction of the subject matter and of the parties. The following paragraphs state the facts in logical (chronological) order, showing that the client has a right to recover for legal reasons.

The facts are as important as the law in stating a cause of action. The facts stated in a pleading must show that the defendant had a legal duty to the plaintiff which he breached without legal excuse. A legal excuse for breaching a legal duty to the plaintiff under the facts stated by the plaintiff in his complaint is called an affirmative defense. The defendant's affirmative defense(s) consists of facts alleged by defendant in his answer that, if proved at the trial, show that plaintiff is not entitled to recover even if he suffered injury inflicted by the defendant because the defendant's actions were legally excused. See Chapter 4 for court procedures.

EXAMPLE

AB, while driving to work, ran a red light and hit CD's vehicle from the rear, causing personal injuries to CD. In this instance. CD has a legal right to recover against AB, since AB violated a statute prohibiting drivers of automobiles to run red lights.

As a result of violating the state statute, AB intruded upon CD's right to safe driving on the highway, causing CD personal injury and resultant damage to CD's vehicle.

AB had a duty to obey the law, and in not obeying the law, breached his duty to CD, giving rise to a good cause of action for personal injuries and property damage. It would be up to the courts to determine the extent of the damage being sought, thereby giving CD the relief prayed. If the facts of the accident are different, AB may have an affirmative defense.

EXAMPLE

AB was making an illegal left turn from the right lane when CD hit the side of the car being driven by AB because CD was exceeding the speed limit.

In the second example, both parties violated their respective duties to obey the law. If the complaint filed states that CD struck the side of the other car because CD was exceeding the speed limit or committing other violations it may state a cause of action against CD. But, if CD, in his answer, alleges that AB was making an illegal left turn from the right lane, CD has stated an affirmative defense to the cause of action stated by AB. That affirmative defense is "contributory negligence" or "comparative negligence," depending on the law of the state where the accident happened.

BASIC CAUSES OF ACTION AT LAW

Causes of court actions at law are divided into two basic categories that are important to determine in which court the legal action should or must be filed:

A. Local Actions

Local actions usually include those actions dealing with real property. Examples are: quiet title action; action to gain possession of real property; foreclosure of a trust deed or mortgage; or any other action to determine an interest in real property.

EXAMPLE

Where two or more owners seek a division of a piece of real property for purposes of a sale, but cannot agree how to divide it, or who is entitled to what size share. This is a typical partition suit.

or

Where a person claims by adverse possession against the present owner of a piece of property. An action in ejectment or an action to quiet title may be appropriate. Both actions are called "real actions."

"Local actions" must be brought in the county where the property is located or where the local action arose.

"Transitory actions" are actions that can be tried anywhere the defendant can be found and served with process. In a transitory action the substantive law of the place where, for example, the accident took place is applied. The court hearing the case follows its own procedural law.

B. Transitory Actions

"Transitory actions," on the other hand, deal with personal injury, with personal property, and with breach of contract. These actions may be filed in the county where at least one of the defendants resides.

Typical transitory actions may be filed as follows: A personal injury may be filed in either the county where the accident occurred or in the county where the defendant lives; a breach of contract action may be filed in any county where one of the defendants lives or where the contract was entered into, or in the county where the contract was to be performed or substantially performed.

State statutes may prescribe "venue" (as opposed to jurisdiction) for bringing transitory actions, particularly where corporations are involved. Check state venue statutes and see the Chapter 4 discussion of venue under court procedures.

BASIC CAUSES OF ACTION IN EQUITY

In most civil cases, the party–litigants suffering harm are seeking money awards to alleviate their loss and/or pain and suffering. Though this would appear to be the norm, there are times when a "money damage award" will not and does not, make the individual whole. In such event he may file a complaint in equity. These courts hearing a case in equity can make an order to prevent irreparable injury and give relief where a court of law will not or cannot. A court hearing an equity case may order the return or delivery of property or the performing or refraining from doing some other act.

Courts of equity consider the equitable rights of both parties. They weigh what is and what is not fair. For example, issuance of an injunction is not a matter of right but rests in the discretion of the court, which will consider whether greater injury will result to defendant from granting the injunction than would be caused to plaintiff by refusing the injunction.

The most important prerequisites to filing an action in equity are as follows:

1. The plaintiff does not have an adequate remedy at law.
2. The plaintiff is suffering, or is about to suffer, an irreparable harm.

A plaintiff may be entitled to equitable relief if he does not have a remedy at law. Therefore, if a money award alone will satisfy the damages caused, do not file your lawsuit in a court of equity. You do not have a cause of action in equity in such case.

Another consideration of the equity courts may be whether the court decree, if ordered, will be feasible to enforce.

In an equity case, the court hears the case without a jury. The court makes findings of both fact and law as the basis for its final order. The court may, in some cases, allow a jury to hear a certain factual phase of the case if the judge believes it would be necessary, on his own motion or on the motion of a party to the case.

The basic relief that an equity court may give, if the plaintiff states a cause of action entitling him to equitable relief, may be one or more of the following: injunction, specific performance, rescission, or reformation.

INJUNCTION

An "injunction" is an order of court directing a party to a cause of action in equity to do some act or to refrain from doing some act.

EXAMPLES

A "mandatory injunction order" requires that the act be performed.

A "negative injunction order" requires the defendant to refrain from doing the acts specified in the order.

and

A "preliminary injunction" may be granted before or during a trial.

A "permanent injunction" may be granted after the hearing and may be made a part of the final order of the court in the case.

SPECIFIC PERFORMANCE

This is the usual equitable remedy available to a plaintiff in cases arising from contractual relationship. The overriding consideration is still whether the legal remedy (money damages) is adequate, and furthermore, whether the consideration bargained for is unique and thereby irreplaceable. This is the court's decision.

EXAMPLES

The court may order the defendant to execute a deed for real property to the plaintiff where defendant had agreed to sell to the plaintiff but has since refused to sell without any legal excuse (affirmative defense).

or

Let us assume that the client's complaint for specific performance is based on a personal service contract wherein the defendant, when promising to perform a unique service for plaintiff, had either expressly or impliedly promised not to perform this service for anyone else. This is called a "negative covenant" or promise and thus, by enjoining the breach of this negative covenant, the court has indirectly ordered specific performance of the contract. The defendant may not perform for anyone else at the time and/or place where he had agreed to perform for plaintiff.

Such negative covenants arise most often in the fields of entertainment, television, or motion-picture production.

RESCISSION

"Rescission" is an equitable remedy whereby plaintiff seeks to avoid the existence of a contract.

The primary consideration of rescission is whether the grounds for rescission occurred *at* or *before* the time the contract was entered into by the parties.

The usual basis for a complaint for rescission are:

1. Mistake (the facts constituting the mistake must be stated) in the complaint
2. Misrepresentation or fraud (the facts constituting the fraud must be stated in the complaint)

A "bilateral mistake" of fact by each party that is material to the contract is one that goes to the very essence of the contract.

In the case of a "unilateral mistake," the courts will not order a rescission of a contract for a unilateral mistake unless the nonmistaken party knows, or should have known, of the mistaken party's mistake. The court will, however, grant an equitable rescission for a unilateral mistake not known by the defendant if the degree of hardship incurred by plaintiff by having to perform the contract outweighs the expectancies of the defendant. To do otherwise, it is felt, would be unjust enrichment.

Fraud that induced the making of the contract that plaintiff desires to rescind must be pleaded in the complaint with specificity. That means that the misrepresentations must be stated and the other fraudulent actions must be described in some detail (evidentiary facts need not be pleaded).

Where acts of fraud are alleged, it must also be stated that the plaintiff had a right to rely on those acts or misrepresentations and that plaintiff *did rely* on them.

Note: When drafting a complaint in equity for rescission, get all the facts you must allege to comply with that pleading requirement. You cannot just state that defendant committed "fraud." That is the legal conclusion that the attorney has to prove by introducing evidence of the facts you allege.

REFORMATION

"Reformation" is the equitable remedy for reforming or changing a written contract by decree to conform to the original intent of the parties. This occurs when the writing does not state exactly what the parties meant it to state.

The difference between reformation and rescission is that in rescission there is a finding that no original, valid contract existed, as it was entered into only because of a mistake, misrepresentation, or fraud.

In reformation there is a valid original contract that simply does not conform to the true intent of the parties.

To state the cause of action, the complaint must allege the facts of the contract as written and the actions or events that show what the parties *both* intended.

WHO ARE THE PARTIES TO A CAUSE OF ACTION?

There are basically two parties to any lawsuit in a civil action: the moving party, which is the plaintiff who initiated the action, and the defender or defendant against whom the action is being brought.

A plaintiff can be any person or legal entity that has a legal, legitimate grievance against another; be this an executor, administrator, trustee, relator, conservator, guardian or guardian *ad litem,* or other person who is acting for another—ref. F. R.C.P. 17(a). A plaintiff is usually represented by a lawyer, but he may act in *propria persona* (in his own behalf as in the "do-it-yourself divorce" or in a small claims court). Every plaintiff must follow the rules of court that apply to his cause of action.

Situations and circumstances may arise in these civil actions where each of the parties here described may play double or identical roles. This occasion may arise when the defendant here referred to files a cross-complaint, thereby becoming both a defendant and a cross-complainant in the same action, wherein he is seeking affirmative relief based on the allegations of fact contained in plaintiff's complaint.

The plaintiff above referred to would then be plaintiff and cross-defendant, and must respond to the allegations in the cross-complaint.

Another person or legal entity may enter into this same lawsuit as an "intervenor," a third or outside party privy to the subject matter and facts seeking relief; or arising out of the same transaction he may be brought into the lawsuit by one of the present parties. These additions of parties would be done by court motion establishing them as a necessary or permissive party to the action, or it could be done by stipulation between the parties—ref. F. R.C.P. 17 through 25.

Other names given to a plaintiff or defendant in an action before the courts are petitioner, declarant, or relator.

EXAMPLE

A party seeking a dissolution of marriage (divorce) or of a writ of mandamus, or writ of prohibition, or writ of *habeas corpus* as used in criminal cases, or writ of review, which is the appeal vehicle used in industrial cases, is called a "petitioner" instead of a plaintiff.

The defendant in the preceding actions is called a "respondent," but some states may still refer to such defending party as defendant.

The moving party in appellate procedures is called an "appellate" and the defending party may be called either a respondent or an appellee, since the policy as to this name designation varies from state to state, or may be interchangeable.

By whatever name, the moving party must state a cause of action.

JOINDER OF PARTIES

In a lawsuit the question of who or what constitutes an "indispensable," or a "conditionally necessary party," or a "compulsory joinder," or a "permissive joinder" is a matter of legal interpretation and argument. As such, it is a continuing dispute among the judiciary and attorneys. If the question is raised by any of the parties, your attorney has to make a court appearance on a motion. If your attorney raises the question, it would be necessary for you to prepare the appropriate notice and motion with accompanying affidavits and case authority. Or in lieu thereof, prepare a demurrer (if applicable in your state). Either method will allow your attorney to go to court and argue his point. Copies of these documents are to be served on opposing counsel, as court rules require.

A. Compulsory Joinder

Compulsory joinder is applicable if a court determines a party to be "materially interested" and the absence of such party will cause substantial prejudice to the court and all other parties concerned. See your local court rule comparable to F. R.C.P. 19.

B. Permissive Joinder

Permissive joinder allows persons to join in the action if they allege facts entitling them to relief on some ground of privity to the original transaction that is the subject of the lawsuit. See your local court rule comparable to F. R.C.P. 20.

WHO MUST STATE THE CAUSE OF ACTION?

In order to succeed in a legal action, the plaintiff or petitioner must have the "capacity to sue." The person who has the legal capacity to sue states the cause of action in the complaint or petition.

EXAMPLES

1. An incompetent does not have the capacity to sue in his own name. An incompetent is a person who has been "adjudged" legally incompetent by a court. Incompetency and ignorance or inefficiency are not synonymous.

2. A minor does not have the capacity to sue in his own name. It should be noted that the age of majority is now eighteen in many states (conforming to the new voting age), but the age of majority is still higher in some states.

3. A corporation does not have the capacity to sue in most states unless it is duly registered as a domestic corporation or registered as a foreign corporation doing business in the state.

PRACTICAL DUTIES OF THE LEGAL ASSISTANT IN DETERMINING AND CREATING CAPACITY TO SUE

A. Minor or Incompetent

Before filing a complaint for a minor or incompetent, the lack of capacity to sue must be cured. The duty of the legal assistant would be to draft the petition for appointment of a guardian *ad litem* for the minor or appointment of a conservator or guardian for the senile or incompetent. This petition should be prepared and signed by the parties at the time of drafting.

Failure to have a guardian appointed does not deprive the court of jurisdiction over the person and estate. A guardian has the same power as the person he represents with an exception: Any compromise or settlement or satisfaction of judgment must be approved by the court. Check your local state statutes in this regard.

If a "guardian of the property" (to be distinguished from a "guardian of the person") has been appointed by the court that adjudged the person incompetent, that guardian has the capacity to sue on behalf of the incompetent "ward" in any other action. That guardian may be an individual or a corporation (such as a bank that is authorized to conduct trust business). It is not necessary to file a petition for a new appointment in the present cause of action.

Note: State the facts and date of appointment of that guardian in the complaint or petition that is filed after the facts alleging jurisdiction are stated and before the facts alleging the cause of action. The same pleading procedure applies where another court has formerly appointed a guardian of the property of a minor plaintiff.

B. Corporation

As you know, a corporation is considered to be a legal entity with full power to sue or be sued. Foreign corporations (those not incorporated in your state) have similar or like rights to sue or be sued. But if a corporation has not registered to do business in a state, it may not have the right to bring a lawsuit, though it may have the right to defend against a lawsuit. The important thing to determine, therefore, is whether the plaintiff corporation has complied with the state regulations relating to incorporation and/or registration of a foreign corporation to do business in the state where it is bringing the action.

A "de jure corporation" is a corporation formed in compliance with the rules and regulations of applicable state law.

A "de facto corporation" is an organization that exercises corporate powers and franchises under color of law, absent compliance with the rules and regulations of state law for forming or continuing as de jure corporation. The elements necessary for a *de facto* corporation are as follows:

1. A valid law that encompasses the assumed rights,
2. An attempt on the part of the organizers to incorporate under such law, and
3. Overt exercise of these purported powers.

The effect of omission to comply with state registration statutes and whether or not a *de facto* corporation may be created without filing articles of incorporation depends on the terms of state statutes that govern incorporation. Those statutes vary from state to state.

Note: The importance of checking the exact corporate status of a corporation before allowing it to file as a plaintiff is that its existence as a legal entity may be challenged by the defendant and a counterclaim of the defendant against the individual incorporators or stockholders may be asserted. Also check the corporate status of all defendants you are suing. Get and *use* the *exact* registered corporate name and corporate status. A judgment against a defendant with an inaccurate corporate name may cause serious problems in collecting the judgment.

Also note that even if the corporation cures the registration defect(s) after the lawsuit is filed, its right to sue or defend may not be retroactive in some states. This problem is especially critical if the statute of limitations will soon run out on the corporation's claim.

C. Partnership or Business Using Assumed Name

A partnership may sue in its partnership name or in the names of all the general partners.

Note: If a partnership's name is a fictitious name, the name must have been registered or filed under the Fictitious Names Act in the state where it does business. Check the state statute for registration requirements. For a "limited" partnership, see the state statute. Failure to register the fictitious name creates problems similar to those discussed here as to failure to properly register a corporation.

An individual may do business under an assumed or fictitious name. For immediate clarity and under most court rules, the caption of a legal action may name "John Doe d/b/a Atlas Plumbing Supplies" as plaintiff. Instead of that, the plaintiff's real name alone may be used as plaintiff, but it should be alleged in the body of the complaint, following *either caption,* that "the plaintiff was doing business as Atlas Plumbing at all times pertinent to the complaint."

See the foregoing note regarding registration of a fictitious partnership name. The same law and caution applies to an individual person doing business under an assumed or fictitious name.

D. Government Entity

A government entity may have a cause of action in a court against another government entity or against an individual or against any other defendant.

When a government entity is the plaintiff, it may use its own name as plaintiff or it may, under certain statutes, bring an action on behalf of someone else.

EXAMPLES

1. Criminal case charging a federal crime or violation of federal law *United States* v. *John Doe.*

2. Criminal case charging a state crime or violation of state law *State of Florida* v. *John Doe.*

3. Case by one state against another state *State of West Virginia* v. *Commonwealth of Pennsylvania.*

4. Case by a state, on behalf of an individual, for violation of a consumer protection statute, environmental protection statute, or other protective statute, based on information, *State of New York* EX REL. *John Doe* v. *ABC Corporation.*

Where your attorney's client has a cause of action against a government entity as the defendant the "doctrine of sovereign immunity" must be considered before filing the legal action.

As a general rule, in the absence of statutory authority or consent, the doctrine of sovereign immunity exempts federal and state agencies and their political subdivisions from liability resulting from injury or damage arising out of their exercise of government duties that would include construction in public streets, highways, and the like. It should be noted that "consent statutes" have not received nationwide acceptance and furthermore that a dispute still exists as to whether this type of immunity exempts municipalities in general.

By way of example as to how these consent statutes work, under California law before you can bring a lawsuit naming one of the preceding entities as a defendant, you must first obtain its permission (or consent) by filing a petition or claim for damages. This petition or claim is either a printed form or typewritten document, depending on the entity involved. Within the document you set forth the facts of the case which justify naming it as the defendant which includes, but is not necessarily limited to, the following:

1. How the incident occurred,

2. An estimate of the damages caused, and

3. The extent of the injuries received.

The statutory procedure for filing this type of claim is found in the statutes or code of your state. Consent statutes that waive sovereign immunity usually contain instruction *on whom, where,* and *when* to serve the complaint. After the complaint is filed in the appropriate court, the rules of that court govern the proceedings. Some consent statutes set maximum limits for recovery against the government entity. Some of these statutes allow recovery of a judgment higher than the statutory limit but require an action of the state legislature to authorize payment of the additional judgment amount in excess of the statutory monetary limit.

For example, in California the following is a practical step-by-step procedure for filing a claim against a municipality or other California government entity. The procedure is representative of presuit claim procedures in other jurisdictions that require *formal* presentation of the claim before filing a legal action in an appropriate court.

CALIFORNIA STEP-BY-STEP PROCEDURE

1. You have one hundred days in which to file a claim after the date of the accident or incident.

2. Thereafter, you have a forty-five-day waiting period after which the claim is deemed rejected.

3. You then have a six-month period in which you must file a lawsuit or be forever barred from being an action to prosecute the claim.

Note: All the above statutory limitations should be checked with your local state statutes so as not to jeopardize the claim.

4. The first step is to file the claim, which is normally a printed form secured from the particular municipality or entity.

5. (Or if the client is late in obtaining the services of your attorney, then obtain an Application for Leave to Present a Late Claim).

6. This latter document should be accompanied by a Notice of Petition for Relief from Governmental Restrictions and Order That Suit May Be Filed, a declaration in support thereof, and a copy of the proposed claim.

7. Your office will receive notification of the hearing on this request. If the petition is approved, prepare the order, file the original and copy with the court clerk, and serve a copy on the Board of Supervisors. If the board does not object, the judge will sign the original order and return a conformed copy within a two-week period. You thereafter have thirty days in which to file your complaint.

Note: All the above documentation should be sent by certified or registered mail, return receipt requested.

PLEADING A CAUSE OF ACTION

The cause of action must be stated in the complaint or petition that will be filed in court by the plaintiff or petitioner to commence the action.

The form, filing, and service of the complaint or petition are governed by the court rules of the court in which the complaint or petition is to be filed. The content of the complaint depends upon the nature of the plaintiff's claim.

WHAT TO INCORPORATE IN THE COMPLAINT

What is a complaint? A complaint, in civil practice (as opposed to a criminal complaint) is the first pleading of a plaintiff. It is a concise statement of the facts constituting the cause of action. Each material allegation of fact must be stated distinctly and be separately numbered.

The purpose of a complaint is to give the defendant information of all material facts upon which the plaintiff relies to support his demand for legal relief.

As indicated above, the information submitted in a complaint is a clear, precise, and accurate presentation of the transaction between the parties and a statement of the plaintiff's grievance.

The complaint must contain certain "ultimate facts." It need not contain "evidentiary facts," which may be necessary to prove the ultimate facts. This is particularly true in federal court complaints. The complaint should not state conclusions of law—ref. F.R.C.P. 7 and 8 and your comparable state court rules.

The courts have established certain rules, as follows:

- An ultimate fact is an "action" or "event" that may be proved by presenting "evidentiary facts" leading to that ultimate fact.
- A "conclusion of fact" is an expected consequence inferred from a given set of facts.
- A "law" is a "principle" that determines whether a particular action or event is legal or illegal in the jurisdiction where the action or event occurs.
- A "conclusion of law" is a statement that certain actions or events comply with or violate a law.

EXAMPLE

1. A speed limit is a law.
2. The defendant was driving his automobile at a rate in excess of seventy miles an hour.
3. Testimony that defendant's car was going more than seventy miles an hour and a picture of car tire marks on the pavement on the road at the scene of the accident are evidentiary facts of the ultimate fact that defendant was traveling seventy miles an hour at the time of impact.
4. A statement that the defendant's driving at seventy miles an hour was a violation of his legal duty to plaintiff is a conclusion of law.
5. Whether a photograph of the car tire tracks is admissible in evidence at the trial is a conclusion of law.

Some conclusions of fact may be stated in a complaint as ultimate facts. They are: malice, intent, knowledge, and comparable state court rules.

Allegations of fact in the complaint should normally be based on and stated as "actual knowledge."

Where actual knowledge can not be obtained by reasonable investigation, material facts may be stated on information and belief:

EXAMPLE

Let us examine the case of Mary Pitts, hospital nurse, who wants to file a slander suit against her former employer, XYZ Hospital. In her complaint, she will claim defamation of character resulting from a publication of defamatory remarks.

The publication in this instance could have been a memorandum circulated throughout the hospital, or a letter of recommendation to a prospective new employer containing defamatory remarks, thereby causing Mary Pitts to be denied the new employment.

In the ordinary course of events, Mary Pitts would not have been present when the publication was disseminated. She might not know the exact words used in the letter. She would of necessity have to allege "on information and belief," the ultimate fact of the publication and its content since she would not have had direct or personal knowledge of the same.

This type of hearsay allegation is often necessary within the medical malpractice area of the law or in an equity action for an accounting. In a medical malpractice action, the party bringing the suit must rely on the opinions of others—medical experts—since the average layman knows nothing about medical practice and procedures. So any allegation made as to wrongs committed or injury suffered by way of medical malfeasance, negligence, and so forth, would have to be on information and belief, or the lack of it.

In the preceding examples, it is important to note that the moving party has neither actual nor constructive knowledge of the facts alleged. (Constructive knowledge is information that one is presumed to know generally since it is a matter of public record.)

The wording for the type of allegations described here would be "Plaintiff is informed and believes, and based upon such information and belief, alleges . . . ," or "Plaintiff does not possess sufficient information to allege ultimate facts, as the only source of information is in the sole custody and control of the defendant, but plaintiff believes that. . . ."

A. Stating More than One Cause of Action in the Complaint

Separate claims in a complaint are alleged in separate "counts."

A plaintiff may have one or more legal claims based on the same set of facts. The claims may be alternative *or* cumulative. Each such claim must be stated in a separate count.

In drafting a complaint, all causes of action arising out of the same set of facts must be pleaded, or the ones not pleaded are "waived." Other unrelated claims may also be pleaded against the opposing party, but they are not waived if not pleaded—ref. F. R.C.P. 18.

Each count is numbered as one, two, three, or Count 1, Count 2, and so forth. The consecutive numbering of the paragraphs in each count does not begin with one in each count.

EXAMPLE

Paragraph 9 may be the first paragraph in Count 2 but is still numbered 9 in the plaintiff's claim for relief or recovery of damages.

EXAMPLE

Count 1—Negligence; Count 2—Intentional Tort, and so forth might be included in a complaint to recover damages for personal injuries.

B. Incorporating Facts in the Complaint by Reference

Exhibits incorporated in the complaint. In lawsuits based on a written instrument, most courts permit the parties to attach a true copy of the document to the complaint as an "exhibit." The exhibit is then incorporated into the complaint by reference to it in one of the numbered paragraphs of the complaint.

EXAMPLE

Plaintiff and defendant entered into a written contract on January 17, 19—, a copy of which is attached hereto as Exhibit "A" and made a part hereof by reference as though fully set forth in *haec verba*.

Note: Be doubly sure that all allegations in the complaint referring to the attached document(s) are a word-by-word, line-by-line exact quotation, since the slightest deviation may subject your complaint, or that portion of it, to a motion to dismiss (demurrer). In such a case, the document controls. The allegations that inaccurately describe the exhibit documents may be subject to Motion to Strike.

Allegations from other counts incorporated in the complaint. The facts alleged in one count contained in a complaint may be incorporated by reference in other counts in facts, which must be specifically alleged in a new count.

A safety measure: Here again, you must be careful that you are realleging *all* the proper factual allegations to state a cause of action in the new count and not limiting yourself to the allegations pertinent only to the first count.

EXAMPLE

Count 1—Negligence. Count 2—Intentional Tort or punitive damages: Plaintiff incorporates herein by reference all of the allegations contained in Paragraphs 1, 2, 3, 4, and 5 of its First Cause of Action (Count 1) as though the same were fully set forth herein.

The conduct of the defendant was intentional, willful and wanton and in complete disregard for the right of . . . and so forth.

C. Defenses Appearing on the Face of the Complaint

As the purpose of any complaint or petition filed in behalf of the plaintiff is to present his legal claim to the court, it should not contain or set forth any possible defenses to the allegations contained herein. In other words, do not do the work of the defendant or educate him. However, the facts alleged must be true and complete enough to state a cause of action.

Defenses, such as the Statute of Limitations and the Statute of Frauds, even if they appear on the face of the complaint, must be responded to by the defendant. He may file an answer or file a countercomplaint.

DRAFTING THE COMPLAINT

We now know what a complaint is, the purpose of a complaint, and the types of facts and allegations to be incorporated therein. Now we can proceed to place them in proper order and to come up with a final product.

The following will be explained in an elementary fashion for the benefit of those persons who have not heretofore been required to actually draft a complaint and follow through with the procedures involved therein.

Basically, legal documents filed with the court are on legal-size paper with a printed margin.

A. Caption

Representative: In upper left-hand corner place the attorney's name, address, telephone number, and representative capacity (attorney for plaintiff or defendant, and so forth) in some states. In other states that information appears at the end of the complaint.

Name of court: At or on about line 8 (depending on your local court procedure and rules) the name of the court is centered in all capital letters. In some states the court's name appears to the right of center at the top of the complaint.

EXAMPLE

THE SUPERIOR COURT FOR THE STATE OF CALIFORNIA,

COUNTY OF LOS ANGELES

or

IN THE CIRCUIT COURT
OF THE FIFTH JUDICIAL
COUNTY, FLORIDA

Parties to the Action: To the left, at or about line 11, are first the name(s) of the plaintiff(s); below, in the middle, is the word versus or an abbreviation thereof "v" or "vs." After the abbreviation and directly below the name of the plaintiff(s) is the name of the defendant(s).

Filing Information and Title: To the right, on or at line 11, type a space for the court case number and directly below this type the title of the document.

EXAMPLE

Complaint for Breach of Contract

Note: In some courts, the title of the document is typed in all capital letters in the center immediately below the other caption information.

B. Body of the Complaint

The introductory paragraph of the complaint identifies the plaintiff and is not numbered. After the introductory paragraph you incorporate the knowledge gained in the prior section of this chapter as it relates to the inclusion or exclusion of ultimate or evidentiary facts or pleading conclusions of law that may be demurrable or factual conclusions that may be accepted. As a result, the body of a complaint is normally divided into the following five categories:

1. Fictitious name or Doe clause
2. Jurisdiction of the court over the subject matter
3. Agency clause (if your court rules require it)
4. Allegations (statements) of ultimate facts that show that plaintiff has a cause of action
5. Prayer

If applicable, attach any of the following exhibits:

1. The verification (if your court rules require it or the attorney desires it);
2. Proof of certificate of mailing.

Proof of certificate of mailing is normally at the bottom of the document and signed by the secretary responsible for mailing the complaint if it can be served by mail. Ordinarily, the complaint must be served personally with a summons. In that case a certificate of mailing is not typed on the document.

First Paragraph—Fictitious Name or Doe Clause: The purpose of this clause is to enable the moving party to file his complaint against and serve an unknown or undiscovered defendant prior to the running of the Statute of Limitations. The moving party must allege this ignorance in the complaint as a separate allegation, otherwise he is forever barred to join such defendant in the lawsuit. The allegation is made in a separate "numbered" paragraph.

SPECIMEN FICTITIOUS NAME CLAUSE

The true names or capacities, whether individual, corporate, associate, or otherwise, and defendantship of defendants DOES I through ___, inclusive, are unknown at the time of the filing of this complaint to plaintiff, who therefore sues said defendants by such fictitious names and will ask leave of court to amend this complaint to show their true names or capacities and defendantship when the same have been ascertained. Plaintiff is informed and believes, and based upon such information and belief, alleges that each defendant designated herein as a DOE was responsible, negligently or in some other actionable manner, for the events and happenings referred to herein that proximately caused injury to plaintiff as hereinafter alleged.

Second Paragraph—Jurisdiction of the Court Over the Subject Matter: This is a separate numbered paragraph that sets forth the authority of the court to hear and determine the controversy.

Note that there is a statement when setting forth the jurisdiction over individuals and an alternative one for corporate entities.

SAMPLE CLAUSES

INDIVIDUAL RESIDENCE REQUIREMENT:

2. Plaintiff is now, and at all times herein mentioned has been, a resident of the County of _____, State of _____.

CORPORATION RESIDENCE REQUIREMENT:

2. Defendant is now, and at all times herein mentioned has been, a corporation duly organized and existing under and by virtue of the laws of the State of _____.

or

Defendant is now, and at all times herein mentioned, a corporation duly organized and existing under and by virtue of the laws of the State of Delaware and licensed and authorized to do business in the State of _____, having its principal office in the City and County of _____.

Third Paragraph—Agency Clause: The purpose of this paragraph is to pinpoint the responsibility for the wrong or injury committed by defendant and anyone else whose name and/or capacity you may not know at the time of filing the complaint.

A further purpose is to anticipate that, that individual may have been part of a larger entity, and since you do not know this for a fact, you include a Doe as an agent to accommodate the unknown individual or entity.

EXAMPLE

John Greu and Does I and II, and each of them.

To allege or state a possible agency relationship between the parties, including course and scope of employment together with, consent and permission "of each of them," the following sample clauses may be used.

SAMPLE AGENCY CLAUSE

At all times herein mentioned, defendant, and each of them, was the agent, servant, and employee of each remaining defendant and was at all times herein mentioned acting within the course, scope, and authority of said agency, service, and employment.

SAMPLE PERMISSION CLAUSE

Plaintiff is informed and believes, and thereon alleges that at all times herein mentioned, defendant, and each of them, was driving the subject vehicle with the consent, permission, and knowledge of each of the other remaining defendants.

Fourth and Following Paragraphs—Allegations of Ultimate Facts That Gave Rise to the Cause of Action and Resulting Damages: In these paragraphs you spell out in detail, with specificity and in chronological order, the events and happenings that led to the wrong or breach of duty and the resulting damage caused thereby.

Note: You may want to read this entire chapter before drafting the complaint. In these paragraphs state the date, place (and time if applicable), the actions and events creating defendant's negligence or his breach of contract, and reliance on statements or acts of defendant, and any other factual elements of the cause of action.

Each of the foregoing should be separately stated in separate, distinctly numbered paragraphs. *Never* lump them in one paragraph.

SAMPLE SEPARATE PARAGRAPHS

1. At all times herein mentioned _____ Street, at or near its intersection with _____, was a public street and highway in the County of _____, State of _____.

2. On or about _____ plaintiff _____ was operating his automobile in an _____ direction on _____ street in the County and State aforesaid.

3. At said time and place, defendants, and each of them, so negligently managed, operated, and controlled their said motor vehicle in a ____ direction along and their vehicle to collide with [the rear, broadside, etc.] plaintiff's automobile, thereby proximately causing severe and serious physical injuries to plaintiff, all to his damage in the sum of ____ ($____).

Note: These are the paragraphs wherein you establish the situs, place the defendant at the scene of the incident, and spell out the negligent acts of the defendant that caused injury, irreparable harm, breach of contract, wrongful death, and so forth, and "general damages."

If "special" or "consequential" damages were suffered, the facts causing those damages should also be set out in separate paragraphs.

Last Paragraph of Each Count in Complaint—Prayer: This is a statement of the relief, damages, restitution, or other action by the court that is requested by the plaintiff.

SAMPLE PRAYER IN A COMPLAINT FOR SPECIAL DAMAGES

WHEREFORE, plaintiff prays for judgment against defendant, and each of them, as follows:

1. General damages in the sum of $_____;

2. For sums incurred and to be incurred for [medical treatment, etc.; repairs; maintenance; delays in construction, etc.] in conformity to proof;

3. Loss of income incurred and to be incurred [from rents, loss of ability to work, etc.] in conformity to proof;

4. Loss of sums incurred to repair automobile, building, etc.

5. [Optional: punitive damages, exemplary damages; special damages, etc.]

6. Costs of suits;

7. For such other and further relief as to the court seems just and proper in the premises.

or

(For General Damages)

WHEREFORE, plaintiff demands judgment against the defendant for damages in excess of five thousand dollars ($5,000) [or the lowest jurisdictional amount for the trial court in which the legal action will be filed] plus costs of this proceeding and interest [where applicable].

Signature: Complaints in civil actions require the signatures of both the attorney and the plaintiff(s) in some jurisdictions. In other jurisdictions, the signature of the attorney alone is sufficient. In some jurisdictions a petition to a special court may require the petitioner's signature or verification and a complaint to the regular trial court may not. Check your local court rules to determine what signatures are required.

Verification of Complaint: Simply stated, a "verification" is a statement that follows the complaint that is dated and signed by the plaintiff, who declares thereby (in some states under penalty of perjury) that to the best of his knowledge and belief everything contained in the answer or complaint is true and correct. Check local court rules for need for verification of a complaint.

After drafting the complaint, prepare a summons for each defendant. The summons is a separate document that is served on *each* defendant with a copy of the complaint.

PROCEDURE FOR FILING THE COMPLAINT

1. Prepare original complaint to file with the court, one copy to be served on each defendant named (with extra copies for the Does) and one office copy.
2. If the same is to be verified, either
   a. Have client come in to review the document and then sign, or
   b. Mail a copy along with the original to client for signature.

Practical hint: It has been our experience that it is best to have the clients come in, since they invariably have questions that are easier to answer face to face as opposed to over the telephone. Also, this removes the possibility of losing the original or having it marred by coffee or a child's play in the home of the plaintiff or answering defendant. Furthermore, most laymen have difficulty in signing a document in the right place or fail to date it, both of which are of great importance. Otherwise, you merely have to return it to the client for one or the other reason, or both. For proper execution, having them come into the office saves time, particularly if you have a Statute of Limitations problem.

3. After the foregoing has been accomplished, prepare and attach a copy of the summons to each copy of the complaint with a paper clip, except on the copies that are attached permanently with a staple.
4. File the original complaint, with appropriate filing fee in the office of the clerk of the court and have the original summons issued. You should check the filing fee with the appropriate court clerk since filing fees vary from county to county and state to state.

5. Have a copy of the summons and complaint served on each defendant. If service is to be made on a minor or incompetent, you not only bring the action in the name of the guardian *ad litem* who was appointed by the court, but you serve it upon the named guardian *ad litem.* This does not obviate the necessity for naming the minor or incompetent in the caption of the lawsuit. It merely means he is not served with the service of process. See Chapter 7 for manner of service.

Note: Of prime importance here is the notation of the date and time on which the foregoing was filed for each defendant. The reason: All summonses and complaints must be served within a certain period or a plaintiff may be forever barred from serving any unserved defendant or prosecuting the claim of plaintiff. You should check your local court rules in this regard.

The service of process is your activity of the case. A case can be dismissed for lack of activity thereon. Should this happen, your attorney can and must appear in court to show cause why the matter should not be dismissed. Your duty in this regard is to systematically audit your attorney's active files and keep them updated to guard against this possibility. Failure to do this brings on malpractice lawsuits and increases malpractice insurance rates and premiums. State laws do vary as to the legal consequences of failure to serve a summons properly.

6. When the sheriff or process server (See Chapter 4 on court procedure) files his "return of service" of the complaint and summons, check it to see that the defendant was served. Then make a notation of the date of service on your office calendar so that a "default judgment" can be prepared if the defendant does not file an answer by the answer date stated in the summons.

The following chapter deals with pretrial court proceedings after the complaint and summons have been served.

CHAPTER 7

Pretrial Practice and Procedure

CHRONOLOGY OF PRETRIAL PRACTICE AND PROCEDURE

Pretrial practice and procedure is governed by rules of court, usually promulgated by the highest court in the state.

Many state courts have adopted court rules of civil procedure similar to the Rules of Civil Procedure adopted by the federal courts.

Reference to the federal civil rules will be made in this book by using the initials, F.R.C.P., and the number of the federal rule. Check your comparable state rule in your state court rules. Also check local state court rules that may supplement the general state court rules but cannot do away with them.

In Chapter 6, "How to State a Cause of Action in a Civil Case" the proper drafting of a complaint was covered.

The first court procedure in a civil action (whether at law or in equity) is to file the complaint in the office of the clerk of the court where the lawsuit is to be heard or tried. That is called "commencement of the action."

Representative court procedures are discussed in more or less chronological order in the sections of Chapters 4 and 5 entitled State Court Practice and Procedure and Federal Court Practice and Procedure.

In this chapter you will find more details and practical hints for preparing, filing, and serving court papers.

SERVICE OF PROCESS (CIVIL)

A lawsuit cannot be tried until the complaint is "served" on all the defendants who are to be bound by the final judgment. If any defendant is not served, he does not have to do anything in a court case even though he is named as a defendant in the "caption" of the case—ref. F.R.C.P. 4 and state statute providing for "constructive" or "substituted" service in certain cases instead of "personal service."

The case can proceed against other defendants who have been served, if the one(s) not served is not a "necessary party" (as opposed to a "permissive party")—ref. F.R.C.P. 19 and 20. The case cannot proceed unless all necessary parties have been served.

The service may be by personal service of process or substituted service (as by advertising a notice of the action in the local newspaper a required number of times), *depending on the nature of the case.*

EXAMPLE

A "local action" affecting real property located in the county where the action is brought can be served by constructive service if the defendant cannot be found after diligent search. Most courts require that an Affidavit of Diligent Search be filed with the clerk of the court before constructive service is binding.

or

A state statute may provide that the secretary of state or other state official may be served with a complaint filed against an out-of-state motorist for an automobile accident that happened in the state. The sheriff in the county where the office of the state official is located serves (usually two) copies of the complaint on the official, who then notifies the defendant by mail of the action.

SUMMONS

A. Purpose and Use of Summons

What is a summons? A summons is a court printed form that is used to give notice to a defendant of an action pending against him in the court that issues it.

The summons is that printed notice from the court, prepared by you and signed by the clerk of the court or his deputy, directing the sheriff or marshal or other lawfully appointed person to personally serve the defendant (or an adult member of his household or other person designated or allowed by statute to accept service) with the notice that an action has been filed against the defendant in the court named in the summons.

The summons contains the number of days or a certain day before which the defendant must appear or answer or otherwise plead in response to the complaint (a copy of the complaint is served with the summons).

The name of the court in which the defendant must appear (such as small claims court) or respond to by a pleading or motion appears in the captions of both the summons and the complaint.

If a defendant fails to answer or otherwise plead or appear within the specified time limit shown on the face of the summons, the plaintiff can file a motion and secure a default judgment.

EXAMPLE

In a California state court, you should file a Request for Entry of Default Judgment with the court, in duplicate, together with the original summons and proof of service. (This is on the reverse side of the summons.) These documents should be accompanied with an Affidavit of Nonmilitary Service and Memorandum of Costs.

Most summonses have a thirty days' returnable period. In California state court, the exceptions are: summons on a partition suit, summons on unlawful detainer action, summons on action against a judgment debtor, and a family law complaint.

When the time allowed for serving an original summons has expired because it was not served, you may want to apply for an "alias summons," or you may be able to use constructive service as described earlier.

Note: An alias summons is a duplicate of the initial summons issued by the court; that is, you merely cause the original summons to be retyped with the *same* caption, parties, and court case number with the addition of the word "alias" placed just preceding the word summons. This document is then submitted to the court with a request that it be issued and be resigned by the deputy clerk and dated. This is the procedure followed should the initial original summons be lost, misplaced, damaged, prematurely filed with the court for safekeeping, or not served within the allotted time as described earlier. An affidavit setting forth the circumstances under which one of these occurred should accompany your request for issuance of an alias summons.

B. Preparation of a Summons

The heading and caption on the summons should be *exactly* the same as on the complaint. The exception to this rule applies when you have a long list of defendants, in which case it is usually permissible to list them either up to and including the name of the defendant you want served, or just the first-named defendant followed by the phrase "et al." In either case the name of the defendant plus anyone you want served must appear on the body of the summons (spelled and complete, as it is in the caption of the complaint).

In some states where unknown defendants can be sued as Does, as in California, put the Doe names in the caption of the summons even though a summons cannot be presently served on them. In the body of the Doe summons, type the following notation:

> You are hereby served in the within action as the person named herein as "Doe I."

In all states, the name of the defendant plus the name of any person who is allowed by law to accept substituted service for him individually or for a corporation must appear in the body of the summons. Only the defendant's name appears in the caption of the summons. Where a resident agent or registered agent is to be served as a substitute for service on a corporation as its principal office, the name in the body of the summons might be:

> Richard Roe, as registered agent for ABC Corporation, a Florida corporation. (Give the registered agent's address if it is not the same as the corporation's address.)

or

> John Doe, Insurance Commissioner for the State of Florida
> Tallahassee, Florida

for

> XYZ Casualty Insurance Company

> (Give the correct home office address for the insurance company even though it is out of state)

By preparing a summons accurately and in accordance with the rules for personal service or substituted service, the legal assistant can save her attorney valuable time and money.

When the attorney says "sue this corporation" the following preliminary steps *must* be taken:

1. Get a status report from the department of state in the state where you believe the corporation is incorporated or from your department of state if it is a domestic corporation.
2. Read the status report to get the name and address of the registered agent for service of process of a domestic corporation.
3. If it is a foreign corporation, check with your department of state to see if it is "registered" to do business in your state; and, if so, who is its resident agent for service of process.
4. In all the preceding cases get *and use* the *exact registered corporate* name in the summons and complaint captions.

If you are not 100 percent sure of your own client's exact registered corporate name, it is wise to check so you will use its correct name as plaintiff in the caption of the summons and the complaint.

If you are preparing a summons for an individual who does business under a fictitious or assumed name, you may just use his individual name in the summons, but if the claim is for a contract or activity conducted by him in the fictitious name, use both in the summons and in the complaint.

EXAMPLE

John Doe d/b/a Atlas Plumbing Supplies

C. Proof of Service of Summons and Complaint

If a sheriff, marshal, constable, or individual makes the service, he must file a certificate or affidavit of service that is often on the reverse side of the summons or may be on a separate printed form or one that has been typed up. Or, in lieu of proof of service one may file a written admission or acknowledgment of service by the defendant. Any typed form must contain the complete caption of the case and court number heretofore assigned, and signed (and notarized if out-of-state), or declared under penalty of perjury.

D. Appearance of Defendant

If a defendant or an attorney for the defendant files an "appearance" in the case or files any responsive pleading in the case, that is proof that the defendant was served or had notice of the case, unless it is a special appearance to object to service only.

If the appearance is general, the defendant must comply with the rules of court in responding to the pleadings from then on or he may suffer a default judgment. A defendant cannot waive jurisdiction, but he may waive "service of process" by his actions in defending a case. In some courts the defendant's attorney may file a "special appearance" for the purpose of attacking jurisdiction or service of process only but the special appearance should be drafted by the attorney. *Do not use a general appearance form for this purpose.*

USE OF RESPONSIVE PLEADINGS

A defendant may respond to a complaint by filing an answer or a motion objecting to the complaint. See Chapter 4 on court procedures.

ANSWER AND COUNTERCLAIM

A. Purpose of Answer and Counterclaim

The defendant's answer, with or without affirmative defenses, plays a vital role in raising "issues" of fact in the pending litigation. The defendant does this by denying the truth of at least some "material allegations of the complaint" or by pleading an affirmative defense to the allegations contained in the complaint. The defendant is not required to answer evidentiary facts or conclusions of law, but he should deny them to play it safe. He may deny by stating that he "has no knowledge."

The attorney may want you to prepare a "motion to strike" those facts and/or other allegations—ref. F.R.C.P. 12(f).

Caution: Under the federal rules, the filing of a motion to strike tolls the time for filing a responsive pleading. In some state courts, the motion to strike does not toll the time unless a "motion for more definite statement" or "motion to dismiss" is also filed. Check your state court rules comparable to F.R.C.P. 12 (a) through (h) on this point.

A counterclaim may or may not be included in the defendant's answer. See Chapter 4, the sections on State Court Practice and Procedure and Federal Court Practice and Procedure.

If a counterclaim is to be filed for your attorney's client, you may type a separate document with the caption of the case and title it cause of action against the plaintiff. See Chapter 6, "How to State a Cause of Action in a Civil Case."

An alternative is to include the counterclaim in the answer following the affirmative defenses, if any.

Caution: If your office represents the plaintiff and the defendant files a counterclaim against him, you must respond as the counter-defendant. Prepare an answer to counterclaim, using the same principles discussed in this section for filing an answer to the original complaint.

The defendant may or may not allege facts in his answer to show that he has an affirmative defense, but he may do so. If he does not plead an affirmative defense, he waives it—ref. F.R.C.P. 8(c).

The Most Common Affirmative Defenses

1. Accord and satisfaction
2. Arbitration and award
3. Assumption of risk
4. Contributory negligence
5. Comparative negligence (in states where that defense in a negligence case is available)
6. Discharge in bankruptcy
7. Duress
8. Estoppel
9. Failure of consideration
10. Fraud
11. Illegality
12. Injury by a fellow servant
13. Laches
14. License
15. Payment
16. Release
17. *Res judicata*
18. Statute of frauds

19. Statute of limitations
20. Waiver

In addition to the common affirmative defenses listed, most of which can be pleaded in an action at law, there are certain affirmative defenses peculiar to equity. One of them is the "doctrine of unclean hands." This doctrine stems from the common law and stands for the proposition that he who seeks equity, must do equity. A court of equity will carefully scrutinize the conduct of the plaintiff in determining whether equitable relief should be granted.

This doctrine operated under the general concepts of:

1. Balancing the damages and injuries;
2. Hardship on the defendant or third party as opposed to the rights of the plaintiff; and
3. Fairness to all parties.

In an action at law, the statute of limitations (statutory time for that particular type of claim has run) is an affirmative defense.

In an action in equity the court may consider the statutory time limitations but will not necessarily enforce it or require its application.

Equity does not concern itself with the "passage of time," but with the effect of the passage of time on the rights of the defendant.

If the defendant can convince the court that though the statute of limitations has not run, the plaintiff has "unreasonably delayed" in filing the action to the prejudice of defendant's rights, plaintiff may be barred.

This defense of "laches" thus serves to shorten the statute of limitations and may prevent the moving party from asserting his claim for some particular equitable relief.

If the defendant, in his answer, does include facts tending to show an affirmative defense, a "reply" by plaintiff may not be required, but if it is allowed without order of court, many attorneys like to play it safe by filing a reply by plaintiff denying the factual allegations made in the affirmative defense paragraphs of the defendant's answer—ref. F.R.C.P. 7, which does not allow a reply to be filed in such case except by order of the court. Check your state court rule which describes the pleadings allowed in its courts.

Special courts, such as probate and juvenile courts, may have different rules for pleading. See other chapters of this book for special court procedures.

B. Drafting Answer and Counterclaim

An answer must be filed within the prescribed time (usually thirty days) after the summons and copy of complaint are served on the defendant, unless a preliminary motion objecting to the complaint has been filed.

If a counterclaim is to be filed it may be included in numbered paragraphs in the answer (which may or may not include affirmative defenses). Most court rules allow a counterclaim or cross-complaint to be filed in a separate document with the same caption.

Whether the counterclaim is so included or it is drafted as a separate document, the counterclaim must state a cause of action against the plaintiff/counterdefendant or it will be subject to the same preliminary motions as a complaint. See Chapter 6, "How to State a Cause of Action in a Civil Case."

The answer itself, including affirmative defenses, if any, should be drafted in accordance with the court rules of the court in which it is to be filed. For filing an answer in federal courts, see F.R.C.P. 7(a)(c) and 8(b), (c), and (d). Your state court will have comparable or similar rules.

The first step in drafting an answer is the meticulous reading of the complaint that you are answering. The second is to decide what allegations must be admitted and what allegations must be denied in the answer.

Note: We have found it a good practice to note your denials and admissions in the margin of the complaint for quick review, recounting, and rechecking with your boss. It also makes it easier to decide on your affirmative defenses to the complaint.

It may be necessary to talk to the client about the facts alleged to determine whether they can be admitted or denied. Certain harmless facts may be admitted.

If harmful facts must be admitted because they are true, the attorney may want to settle the case or the defendant may have an affirmative defense to those facts.

In denying or admitting facts alleged in the complaint, it may help you to understand the types of admissions or denials that can be made in and by an answer.

If no answer is filed, the facts in the complaint are admitted. Any facts that are not denied in the answer are admitted. Facts admitted in the answer are admitted for all purposes in the lawsuit. Some court rules treat a general denial as no answer and as an admission. Other court rules allow a general denial.

The federal court rules and many state court rules treat a statement of "without knowledge or information to form a belief as to the truth of paragraph" (the corresponding paragraph in the complaint) as a denial.

In most courts any numbered paragraph of the complaint may be admitted in part and denied in part in an identically numbered paragraph in the answer (qualified denial).

Denials are sometimes categorized as "general denials," "qualified general denials," and "specific denials."

Note: The key in answering a complaint is you must either deny or admit each allegation. Failure to do either as to any allegation is considered an admission as to the truth of the allegations so omitted.

A general denial is a simple, uncomplicated, one-sentence denial of all the allegations in a complaint, but it is not recommended.

EXAMPLE

This answering defendant denies each and every allegation contained in the complaint, and the whole thereof.

In some states the defendant may take advantage of this type of denial only if he can do so in good faith. That is, have a *bona fide* reason for denial.

If the reason is not *bona fide,* the general denial is treated as an admission.

A qualified general denial is a combination of admission of particular allegations and a general denial of a particular paragraph of a complaint.

EXAMPLES

In answer to Paragraph IV, defendant admits that he has his principal place of business in Los Angeles, California, but denies each and every other allegation contained in said paragraph.

or

In answer to the allegations contained in Paragraph IV, this answering defendant admits the allegations beginning on line 12, on page 4, with the word "herein," and denies each and every other allegation contained in said Paragraph IV.

A specific denial is a denial of each paragraph of the complaint. Some paragraphs may be admitted.

EXAMPLE

Paragraph I is denied.

Paragraph II is *admitted.*

Paragraph III is denied.

(and so forth, for each paragraph)

Any of these types of denial may be made on "information and belief" or on "lack of information and belief."

EXAMPLE OF DENIAL ON INFORMATION AND BELIEF

In answering Paragraph IV, this answering defendant is informed and believes that the allegations contained herein are untrue and, based upon such information and belief, denies generally and specifically the truth of each and every allegation contained in Paragraph IV.

Note that since this denial is based upon information and belief, it is in the conjunctive, and neither "information" alone nor "belief" alone will suffice—you have to have both to successfully resist a special demurrer or comparable motion, as either used alone is not a denial.

EXAMPLE OF DENIAL BASED ON LACK OF INFORMATION AND BELIEF

In answering Paragraph IV, this answering defendant has no information or belief on the subject sufficient to enable him to answer the allegations contained herein, and based upon such lack of information and belief, denies generally and specifically, conjunctively and disjunctively, each and every allegation contained in Paragraph IV.

A denial will fail if there is an unauthorized use of the denial allegation based on information and belief or the lack of it, or if the denial contains a negative pregnant or is in the conjunctive as set forth earlier.

While the use of the denial mechanism based on information and belief seems a likely or easy way to go, it is primarily used where the defendant cannot honestly deny or admit with any certainty any of the allegations for one reason or another. (Your attorney can help you here since these facts will no doubt be brought out in the initial client-attorney interview, so check with him.)

If the defendant, in truth or in fact has knowledge or can obtain the knowledge required by the allegation, a denial on information and belief or lack of information and belief will not stand and will probably be subject to a motion to strike. So, though the defendant may not have personal knowledge, if the subject matter is of public record it is presumed that the defendant has constructive knowledge, making his denial or lack of information and belief invalid and a sham since he had a means of acquiring the knowledge.

The third step in drafting an answer is to determine whether your client has an affirmative defense(s).

Note: An interview with the defendant after he has also read the complaint is a *must.* The attorney and/or the legal assistant may ask the client the questions and get the documents from the client that are necessary for the attorney to decide whether one or more affirmative defenses should be pleaded in the answer. At this interview, the client should also be questioned about facts that might be the basis for a counterclaim against the plaintiff or the bringing in of a "third-party defendant" or a "cross-defendant."

Some examples of pleading affirmative defenses follow:

AFFIRMATIVE DEFENSE (PAYMENT)

1. Before commencement of this action, defendant discharged plaintiff's claim by payment of the amount claimed.

or

AFFIRMATIVE DEFENSE (STATUTE OF FRAUDS)

1. The agreement alleged in the complaint was not in writing and signed by the defendant or by any person authorized to act for the defendant.

2. The agreement was alleged to be a lease for more than one (1) year, to-wit, five (5) years.

3. The statutes of this state require a lease for more than one (1) year to be in writing.

or

AFFIRMATIVE DEFENSE (RELEASE)

1. On November 1, 19—, and after plaintiff's claim in this action accrued, plaintiff released defendant from that claim by a written release, a copy of which is attached hereto, made part hereof and marked Exhibit A.

Note: Photocopy the written release. Attach a photocopy to each copy of the answer. Put the original in the evidence file for use at trial.

The fourth step is to decide whether a counterclaim (or cross-complaint in California) should be included or filed separately. The decision to file a counterclaim, cross-complaint, or third-party complaint may be postponed, but the answer or motion objecting to the complaint *must* be filed now. When all the facts are gathered and the decisions are made as here described, and it has been decided that an answer is to be filed, the actual drafting of the answer begins.

C. Filing and Serving Answer and Counterclaim

The answer must be drafted, typed, filed, and served within the time prescribed by the applicable "court rules" (10, 15, 20 or 30 days in various states and types of cases), if no demurrer or motion objecting to the complaint is filed.

The section following this one discusses motions that may be filed in lieu of an answer, among others. Chapter 4 also has some suggestions on this matter in the sections on court procedure.

Note: The time allowed by court rules in any state for filing an answer is not much time for accomplishing all the tasks and decisions described in Drafting Answer and Counterclaim. Sometimes a client fails to bring in a complaint served on him until several days after the service.

In any case, regardless of the client's delay, he will expect your attorney to make a proper legal response on his behalf. It may be necessary for you to arrange for an extension of the time for filing an answer by calling the office of opposing counsel.

If you are able to get opposing counsel to agree to the extension of time (because your attorney is out of town or trying another case, or the like), it is wise, and sometimes necessary to confirm the extension of time.

We have found it a very good idea to make an original and copy of this confirming letter, with the following phrase at the bottom adjacent to the signature line:

"I AGREE TO THE ABOVE EXTENSION"

_____   _____

(date)

There follows a space for the signature of opposing counsel and a line for the date, as indicated here.

Sometimes the opposing counsel forgets he gave you an extension, or his secretary may have forgotten to tell him, or he forgot to write you a confirming letter, or she may have misfiled it. It happens.

It is strongly urged that you develop an index register or docket calendar for the posting of follow-ups. This will enable you to keep on top of your own time and important dates. A five-to-seven day follow-up is best.

See Chapters 4 and 5 under state and federal court procedures for further general tips and warnings as to the preparation and filing of an answer or alternative motions.

You must file the original of the answer and/or counterclaim in the office of the clerk of the court and must also mail copies of the document (including any attached exhibits) to all the parties to the action who have entered an appearance in the case.

Note: In some multiple-party cases, the court may excuse sending copies to every party if the expense and time would be too burdensome. Such excuse requires a written order of the court.

When the answer is filed, the plaintiff may or may not have to reply under your court rules (see Chapter 4 on court procedures). In any case, use your office calendar or index to note that the client file should be pulled on a certain future date if nothing happens in the meantime.

Note: If a client file "sleeps," some court rules allow dismissal for want of prosecution after a certain period of inactivity on the case. See the court rules for a time at which this drastic action can be taken in your court. *But,* index your case file to be pulled long before that. Index the file to be pulled a short time after the next pleading from opposing counsel is required.

At the time of filing the answer and/or counterclaim with the clerk of court, you must also mail or deliver copies of same (including copies of the exhibits attached and incorporated in the original answer and/or complaint) to counsel for each party to the lawsuit that has entered on appearance in the lawsuit, as well as on opposing counsel (unless there are so many parties that the court has made an order limiting this usual requirement).

D. Pretrial Motions Concerning Pleadings

Court rules govern the form and time for filing certain common pretrial motions. A pretrial motion is a request to the court that must be written. It is usually signed by the attorney, not by the client.

Most court rules require the "grounds" (reasons for the motion to be stated with "particularity" as to law and/or fact, as applicable) in the motion. The attorneys for the parties argue the motion at a "hearing."

1. A Motion to Dismiss. This motion is filed for reasons similar to those stated in a demurrer to the complaint, which is still used in some states.

Under the federal court rule, F.R.C.P. 12(b), and many state court rules a motion to dismiss (demurrer) may raise the following defenses:

a. Lack of jurisdiction of subject matter

b. Lack of jurisdiction over the person

c. Improper venue

d. Insufficiency of process

e. Insufficiency of service of process

f. Failure to state a claim upon which relief can be granted (or failure to state facts sufficient to constitute a cause of action)

In some states one may also move to dismiss or demur to a complaint on the basis of an affirmative defense *if* the facts constituting that affirmative defense appear on the face of the complaint.

In some states a general demurrer or special demurrer is used instead of a motion to dismiss or motion to strike or motion for more definite statement. See Rule 12(b) of the Federal Rules of Civil Procedure for the use of these motions instead of demurrer.

In California, where demurrers are used, the following discussion may be helpful to illustrate what can be accomplished be it either motion to dismiss or demurrer, depending on the form used in your jurisdiction.

In California, the general demurrer attacks and tests the sufficiency of the whole complaint, stating that the complaint does not state a cause of action or that an answer does not state facts sufficient to state a defense. It has the effect of asking the court to search the whole complaint or answer and counterclaim for the failure or defective allegation of essential facts to state a cause of action or defense. In the instance of a general demurrer, the defendant need not plead specific defects.

In California, a special demurrer serves the purpose of a motion for more definite statement, a motion to strike or a motion to dismiss for affirmative defenses appearing on the face of the complaint. The one most often appearing on the face of a complaint is the "statute of limitations." This defense is prohibitive to the recovery of damages arising out of a valid cause of action, unless the claim was filed within the statutory time period, that is, personal injury, one year from the date of the accident; property damage, three years from the date of the accident; malpractice, one year from the date first recognized, and so on. This defense is usually pleaded in the answer as an affirmative defense.

Another commonly used defense is that of *res judicata* which is self-explanatory—"the thing has been decided." This is a rule of law that bars the relitigation of the same cause of action between the same parties. You can raise this defense, if not discernible on the face of the complaint, in your answer to referring to the judgment rendered in the prior action.

Contrary to the rule for stating the general demurrer, in utilizing a "special demurrer," you must point out with specificity the defect in the pleading where other than a failure to state a cause of action is the issue. For example, defect as to form, which means a cause of action exists but there are curable detects in setting forth the cause of action, may be subject to a special demurrer, comparable to a motion to strike in other jurisdictions.

A special demurrer or a motion to strike is important, since unless it is raised by way of a demurrer or motion, the defendant waives his right to object to a "defect in form." Only the right to raise "defects in substance" can be raised at a later time during the course of the proceeding.

A special demurrer may be filed to force a plaintiff to state facts in the complaint, which if set forth would afford the defendant the opportunity to file a general demurrer. That is comparable to a motion for more definite statement in other states and the federal courts.

A motion for more definite statement or a special demurrer for the purpose of getting more essential facts might state:

> It cannot be ascertained from the complaint herein whether the contract on which the alleged cause of action is founded and referred to is written or oral.

2. Motion to Strike. This motion is made to get the court to strike all parts or all of a pleading that is defective in form.

The motion to strike does not mean that the stricken pleading or part is removed from the court record. It is just "ignored" from this point on.

The words used in the federal court rules and in many court rules providing for a motion to strike use the words: "insufficient defense" or any redundant, immaterial, impertinent, or scandalous matter—ref. F. R.C.P. 12(f). The meaning of these words, except the word "impertinent," is for the most part the common meaning of the word. Impertinent, as used in the court rule, means the matter should not be in the pleading as a matter of form as, for example, it is superfluous or unintelligible as stated or not appropriate because it is irrelevant to the cause of action or defense.

A motion to strike an answer because it "does not state a sufficient defense" serves the same purpose that a motion to dismiss a complaint for failure to state a claim or cause of action serves. It was noted earlier that a general demurrer can be used for either of those purposes in the State of California or states where demurrers rather than motions are used to object to pleadings.

As a general rule, a motion to strike goes to the other matters of irrelevancy, redundancy, or sham.

For example, if in your state your attorney is not automatically entitled to receive attorney's fees when filing a complaint unless (1) there is a contract or (2) there is something in the codes that permits attorney's fees, and you nevertheless included such a request in your prayer without alleging this authority, the defendant can file a motion to strike that portion of the prayer of the complaint as both immaterial and impertinent.

Another common example of the use of the motion to strike is when the plaintiff's complaint asks for punitive damages, since a claim for punitive damages prayed for and not stricken may allow the plaintiff to inquire into the wealth of the defendant later on unless a "protective order" is sought and obtained.

The motion to strike can be effectively utilized against a pleading. If a complaint is verified and defendant files a general denial, plaintiff can file a motion to strike the answer on the ground that it is not a verified answer. Conversely, if someone other than the party to the action verifies the complaint, defendant can make a motion to strike the improper verification.

3. Motion to Compel. This motion is normally used when either party fails or refuses to answer interrogatories or requests for admissions. The moving party simply files a motion requesting the court to "compel" the opposing party to answer and to apply sanctions, which are normally penalties in the form of a monetary award if the party fails to answer as ordered. Another sanction the court may impose is to dismiss a complaint or strike an answer of the party who fails to comply with the order.

4. Motion to Quash Service of Summons. This is another common type of motion whereby if there is no jurisdiction of the court over the subject matter, you attack this deficiency by filing a special demurrer or motion to dismiss; but if there is no jurisdiction of the court over the person, you may file a "motion to quash" service of summons. This is known as a "special appearance" and is only used to attach jurisdiction of the court over the person. This motion to quash must be accompanied by points and authorities to support your contentions; then it is up to the court. Any other type of appearance, that is, another motion, demurrer, answer, and so forth, by a defendant may create jurisdiction. In other words, if you plan to file a motion to quash, you cannot turn around and file any other type of pleading in the case, for to do so is to subject the client to the complete jurisdiction of the court in most states. In some states, the question of jurisdiction and other defenses may be raised in a motion to dismiss without that problem if the question of ineffective service is resolved in favor of the movant.

5. *Motion for Judgment on the Pleadings.* This motion cannot be made until the required pleadings in the case have all been filed and the case is "at issue." At issue means ready to be tried but not that the case has been set for trial.

A "motion for judgment on the pleadings" can be brought at any time before the trial of the action. Most court rules do provide that the motion must be made within such time as not to delay the trial.

This is a noticed motion that should be accompanied by a memorandum of points and authorities and in California, a declaration by your attorney in support thereof. You should include in his declaration what order is being requested and the basis of your request. In other words, give the court a good, valid reason and sufficient facts for granting the motion and resultant order.

In all jurisdictions, it is advisable to prepare a law memorandum in support of the motion if your attorney represents the movant or opposing the motion if he is not.

6. *Motion for Summary Judgment.* In the legal community the "motion for summary judgment" is considered the most devastating. To the attorney who makes the motion and wins, it is also the sweetest victory. The key: the word judgment by way of a motion. In other words, you are making a motion requesting the court to grant you a judgment against the opposition "without benefit of trial" of the issues.

In the federal courts and in many states this motion may be filed any time after the expiration of twenty days after the complaint was filed.

Either party can make a motion for summary judgment alleging "no triable issue of facts" or "no genuine issue of material fact," for if there is only a question of law left for determination, questions of law can be decided by a judge. Courts should and do take this motion very seriously. It is a final judgment which cannot be appealed.

You should know that a motion for partial summary judgment can be filed as to a cause of action or count in some courts. It does not have to be filed against the entire complaint in some jurisdiction.

EXAMPLE

If in your request for admissions you have received an admission that a contract did in fact exist, that the plaintiff did in fact comply with all the terms of the contract, and that the defendant did in fact breach the contract, you could file for a summary judgment as to liability and remove that issue of liability from the trial of the action. The issue that remains to be tried is the amount of the damages.

As with all motions heretofore discussed, a law memorandum of supporting case authority and statutes, if any, in support of your motion should be prepared. In California, a declaration for the signature of your attorney (or at his direction, for the client) setting forth the basis for the motion should be prepared. The content of this declaration is the ammunition for your summary judgment. Your attorney can win or lose his motion on the declaration alone. Hence, it should state, succinctly and in chronological sequence, the facts of the case to aid the court in reaching its decision in your favor, that is, that there are no triable issues as to any material fact to be determined and that the moving party is entitled to a judgment as a matter of law.

In the federal courts, supporting and opposing "affidavits" are required to support or oppose a motion for summary judgment—ref. F.R.C.P. 56.

In many state courts, affidavits may or may not be required. Some states permit but do not require affidavits.

In some states that require or permit affidavits, the "affiant" (person who is making the affidavit) signs a statement of facts by him from his own knowledge (not heresay). The statement must be sworn before and also signed by a notary public (or other person authorized by state law in the state where the affidavit is made to take oaths). In most states, the affidavit may be made by a party or a nonparty.

EXAMPLE

In California, a contractor must be licensed to practice his trade. Let us say for argument that the plaintiff is a contractor who does not have a license, yet has been practicing his trade. As a result of a dispute with the owner of the property for whom he is building a garage, he has filed a complaint for breach of contract and for damages.

Thereafter, the defendant files his answer to the complaint and as a result of discovery determines that plaintiff was not a licensed contractor. He can then file a motion for summary judgment on the ground that plaintiff was not a licensed contractor at the time of entering into the contract and, furthermore, that plaintiff had not, since and during the pendency of the action, secured a license to practice his trade as required by the laws of the State of California.

In this connection, you should be sure to obtain a certified document from the proper state authority that indicates that the plaintiff was not a licensed contractor, nor had he applied for such license, and so forth. This could cause a summary judgment victory for your attorney.

A step-by-step procedure for preparing for summary judgment is as follows:

After discussing the file and reviewing the complaint of the plaintiff with your attorney who represents the defendant, it is determined that the case has no merit, or that there is no defense to it, you may prepare the necessary documentation to support your motion for summary judgment. The documents to be prepared are:

1. Notice of motion and motion (motion for summary judgment and notice of hearing)
2. Declaration of your attorney or client, or both (affidavit[s] of facts with necessary exhibits attached and incorporated by reference into the affidavit)
3. Memorandum of points and authorities in support of summary judgment (law memorandum in support of summary judgment)
4. If you have had responses to requests for admissions or answers to interrogatories or a deposition, appropriate excerpts or copies of these should be attached or referred to in your declaration, or in the alternative request that the court take judicial notice thereof.

Make sure that declaration(s) or affidavit(s) are signed before a notary. The foregoing package should be filed, and copies of everything in the package must be served on opposing counsel at least ten days prior to the date upon which the motion is set for hearing.

Caution: Note that the filing of this motion does not toll or extend the time within which opposing counsel is required to file a responsive pleading. Be sure, therefore, to flag the regular responsive pleading date on your file and your "come-up" calendar to avoid a default being taken against your office or should you want to take a default against opposing counsel.

It is extremely difficult for attorneys to obtain a summary judgment since it, in essence, prevents the losing party from cross-examining witnesses.

If there is a question about even *one* fact material to the cause of action, a court cannot lawfully grant a summary judgment. Immaterial or irrelevant facts will not be undisputed to get a summary judgment.

MISCELLANEOUS PRETRIAL MOTIONS

In addition to the pretrial motions described earlier that are often lengthy, requiring both tact and law reasons for the motion to be stated with particularity in the motion as written, there are innumerable pretrial requests that can be made by written motion. Some may be heard *ex parte* (only movant's attorney present). Your attorney will tell you when he needs such motions.

The caption of *all* motions is the regular caption of the case in which the motion is filed.

The nature of the motion is usually stated under the caption as the title in all caps, as:

MOTION FOR CONTINUANCE, MOTION FOR TRANSFER, MOTION TO DISMISS, MOTION TO STRIKE, OR MOTION TO DISMISS THIRD-PARTY COMPLAINT (and so forth).

The written motion is filed with the clerk of the court, and a copy of the motion is mailed or delivered to opposing counsel (or all parties, as the case may be). *Be sure to make a copy of the motions for your office file!*

If the motion requires a hearing, a "notice of hearing" may be sent with the copy of the motion or may be made part of it, or the motion may be filed and a hearing date obtained later. Check your attorney's desires and the court rules in this matter.

PART TWO

GENERAL TRIAL PREPARATION

❧ CHAPTER 8 ❧

Legal Research Tools

This chapter will reintroduce you to the basic traditional tools of legal research, as well as to the most recent, the computerized tools of legal research. It will discuss what they are, how to use them, and will furnish examples of their finished product.

There are many companies involved in supplying computerized tools of legal research, such as Aspen, Auto-Cite®, DCD, Flite, Juris, Wang, and Westlaw.

COMPUTERIZED TOOLS OF LEGAL RESEARCH

The traditional manual legal research approach appears to be fading into the sunset as the number-one way in which to accomplish research projects, though there are still some attorneys and paralegals who feel more comfortable using the traditional method of checking *Shepard's Citations* case law. They get self-satisfaction from holding in their hands books that contain their cases. They still like to work with papers, tablets, or cards; this, despite the fact that computer research methods make for faster retrieval, more accuracy, and greater scope of scan and depth of material available in completing a research project.

And, as we all know, there is always a problem in a law office and there are always emergencies when briefs have to be filed right away. This requires quick numerical citation checking, such as that found in *Shepard's Citations* to determine if the cases are on point and up to date. But there are things one can get by using Auto-Cite®, for example, that you cannot get any other way.

THE LEXIS (SYSTEM)

Using the Lexis (system) automatic-citing segment to verify case law and cases takes about one half hour whereas if you were to do it by the traditional method, it would take you four to six hours. This being true, and since it is your job as a paralegal to be productive, this type of litigation support system helps you to do more.

Understandably, attorneys may be wary of these computerized legal support- and word-processing systems because there is less personal creativity on their part. But, with the paralegal, personal judgment and analysis are still a necessary part of these computerized approaches to legal research. In line with this thought, when legal problems arise that send you to a computerized system to check the case, if you do not use it fully or regularly you may lose your ability to use it effectively.

By way of example, using the Lexis system for illustration, some of the following steps might be of assistance to the research expert. Initially, the researcher must take care to modify his thinking in terms of the concept utilized by this computer. We all know that different judges express the same concept in different ways. The computer, however, stresses these legal expressions under the same generalized categories. As the researcher, you are the expert in the area the moment you sit down at a Lexis computer.

But, before you reach the status of expert, you must train your mind away from the traditional form of research. Unlike traditional research, there are no intermediary steps such as digests, indexes, or headnotes. You simply enter words or phrases. With Lexis you can be as specific as you like, or as general as you like. With Lexis you immediately go to the cases containing your terms.

Just as important, before you can describe yourself as an "expert," you have to learn how to interact with the computer.

A. Structure of Lexis

1. Concordance (Lexis). Lexis does not read cases. The way the system operates is that every single word and every single case is given what Lexis calls "an address" and those addresses are combined on a list that is called a concordance.

Now, let us say you wish to search for cases in which the word "contract" appears. Every occurrence of the word contract is assigned a number describing the document in which it is listed and the word position in that document. This is then put on a "concordance" list.

Then let us say you enter the word "breach." The word breach is handled in the same manner as the word contract.

The computer thereafter pulls on these two lists, starts to cross-match them, and comes up with cases with both words in them. It would therefore bring up all cases dealing with contracts and breach, or breach of contract.

2. Libraries (Lexis). Lexis is a whole-text search retrieval system provided by Mead Data Central. All the documents in the system are grouped into libraries.

The General Federal Library contains such source material as the federal case law, federal register, code of federal regulations; Supreme Court briefs; and the United States Code.

The state library contains case law from all fifty states.

Specialized federal libraries encompass case law commercial regulatory materials in such areas as tax, securities, trade regulations, and so forth.

Lexis also includes the law of France and England in its data base.

Nexis contains newspapers, wire services, business magazines, and newsletters. It supplies information about legal issues not necessarily limited to case-law reporters, for example, the amounts of money awarded in settlements of newsworthy cases.

B. Use of Lexis

1. Words. One of the things about the Lexis computer you should be aware of is that it does not do any thinking, it just carries out your request exactly as you put it in. *You have to understand what it understands from your information.* It is basically a word system, so you have to understand what it understands to be a word.

To the Lexis computer, a word is any character or group of characters with a space on either side. Plural and possessive forms are automatically retrieved.

Variations in words can be retrieved by using an (!) at the end of a word. For example: "Educate!" will retrieve "educate" as well as "educational."

Tip: Lexis searches for individual words, not phrases. You should therefore avoid unnecessary words. For example: Xerox Corporation; instead of putting in the entire phrase "Xerox Corporation," you should simply put in the word Xerox. This is done so that Lexis does not have to search for every occurrence of the word "corporation."

Once you have decided on the words that are necessary for your request, it becomes equally necessary for you to figure out how they should appear and how close together or in what relationship they should appear in the case in order to have meaning to you.

2. Connectors. This is where the "connectors" come in. Although there are about eight connectors in the system that allow you to add or exclude terms, there are only three that are used most of the time, and those are "or," "and," and "w/n."

Hence to search for say, "freedom of the press," or "free speech and censorship," you might enter "free! w/15 speech or press and censor!"

3. Segment Searches. Documents in Lexis are broken down into "segments," such as "date" segments, "court" segments, "name" segments, "counsel" segments, and so forth.

> Example: Let us say you want to find the Bakke case on Lexis. You would tell Lexis you only want to see cases where the word "Bakke" appears as a party to the action. To do this you would enter the name (Bakke) and ask the computer to find this word only in the "name segments." In this example, the parenthesis triggers the segment search. Absent the parenthesis, what you would get from the computer would be the phrase "Name Bakke."

> or

> Example: You want to look for the opinions of a particular judge on the subject of, say, sex discrimination. You would enter the following: "Sex/3 discrimination and written by (Pfaelzer)" in the "court segments."

4. Case Citations by Name. Lexis does not analyze the material, but it does take you directly to any case mentioning the case you are citing. For example: A search for "Ernst w/15 Hochfelder" would find all cases citing that landmark case, including slip opinions.

5. Case Citations by Number. Shepard's is available on Lexis in much the same format as the manual Shepard's appears. By entering a case number citation, you retrieve a list of case number citations citing your case number, including Shepard's treatment and analysis abbreviations of those cases.

MECHANICAL CHECKLIST FOR USING LEXIS

a. *Signing-on:* The first thing you do to get access to the computer's memory is to type your ID number and press the transmission key.

b. Then you put in any of the pertinent client information for billing purposes.

c. *Library-file selection:* Then you pick the library and file of your choice.

d. *Search:* At this point, which is the first level, you enter your request. All cases in the chosen library and file, which contain your search terms, will be retrieved. **Note:** You can do your search either by individual state or by all states at the same time. From this list you may pick the case or cases you feel appropriate for your needs.

e. *Modify:* At the second level you can then modify or refine your request by adding new terms. **Note:** Any number of levels can be used in this procedure.

f. *Display:* Cases can be viewed in "full," that is, every word displayed. KWIC which is an abbreviated display of your terms in context or Cite, which is a list of retrieved cases.

g. *Print:* After all the above has been accomplished to your satisfaction you can then request a print-out. (See Figure 8.1.)

Figure 8.1. Sample Print-out Request

```
MAIL-IT OPTION TAKEN: OCTOBER 1, 1985
                          IDENTIFICATION: 38542

YOUR CLIENT:   ADMNI FOR RANDALL
    LIBRARY:   CAL
       FILE:   CASES

YOUR REQUEST AT THE TIME THIS MAIL-IT WAS INITIATED:
RAPE AND BIRD

NUMBER OF DOCUMENTS THAT SATISFY YOUR REQUEST
THROUGH:
    LEVEL 1...    60

LEVEL   1 PRINTED

OUTPUT FORMAT: CITE
```

Summary

Remember, the computer contains raw material, that is, the full text of cases as written by judges. To this end, your problem analysis must be performed *prior* to seeking retrieval of applicable information for your project.

Computerized research can greatly speed up and simplify the research process. At the present time, it is to be used in conjunction with manual methods for current, complete, and comprehensive results.

RECAPITULATION OF THE THOUGHT PROCESS AND MECHANICAL PROCEDURES IN USING THE LEXIS

A. Develop your legal problem.

B. Develop the words for your research in the language you think the court might have used.

C. Once you have identified the words, choose the ones that would most likely express your ideas to get the answers you required.

D. When you have accomplished the above, it is time to "sign on" to the Lexis terminal. Recall that your first act in this process is to transmit your I.D. number and then press the "transmit" key.

E. Thereafter, you should type and transmit the name of the client and/or business account number, whichever is applicable for billing the client.

F. The first thing to appear on the Lexis screen will be a list of the available libraries in the Lexis terminal. Choose the library appropriate for your research project.

G. It is now time for you to enter your request into the Lexis. Experience has taught us that it is a better part of valor to enter your ideas one at a time. And, as you will recall, these are called "levels." (See Figure 8.2.) It is at this point that you would type and transmit the words and connectors that express your first idea.

Note: Lexis does the search and will give you the number of the cases it has found, from which you can modify your request or you can at this point review the cases retrieved.

H. You can review the cases that are found; or you may want to add words or connectors identifying your second idea. The Lexis will ask for the modification you request, while at the same time displaying the previous level and

Figure 8.2. Sample Portion of Lexis Level 1 Display

Services of Mead Data Central

LEVEL 1 - 60 CASES

45. BERNARD P. CALHOUN, Petitioner, v. THE SUPERIOR COURT OF SANDIEGO COUNTY et al., Respondents., Supreme Court of California in Bank, 46 C.2d 18, Dec. 30, 1955

46. THE PEOPLE, Respondent, v. FRANK E. TALLMAN, Appellant., Supreme Court of California in Bank, 27 C.2d 209, Nov. 9, 1945

47. THE PEOPLE, Plaintiff and Respondent, v. RUDY SAVALA, Defendant and Appellant., Third Dist., 116 C.A.3d 41, Feb. 20, 1981, As modified Feb. 23, 1981; Hg. den. May 13 and 15, 1981.

48. THE PEOPLE, Plaintiff and Respondent, v. DANIEL BETTS, Defendant and Appellant., Second Dist., Div. Two., 110 C.A.3d 225, Sept. 15, 1980.

49. In re DANIEL CAUDILLO on Habeas Corpus., Second Dist., Div. One., 89 C.A.3d 333, Feb. 9, 1979; Hg. granted May 24, 1979 (See 26 C.3d 623)

50. DAVIS DUDLEY, Petitioner, v. THE SUPERIOR COURT OF LOS ANGELES COUNTY, Respondent; THE PEOPLE, Real Party in Interest., Second Dist., Div. Four., 36 C.A.3d 977, Jan. 24, 1974

51. In re DORIAN C. JONES on Habeas Corpus., First Dist., Div. Three., 35 C.A.3d 531, Nov. 21, 1973

52. THE PEOPLE, Plaintiff and Respondent, v. MELVIN CLARK, Defendant and Appellant., Fourth Dist., Div. One., 30 C.A.3d 549, Jan. 17, 1973

53. THE PEOPLE, Plaintiff and Respondent, v. JOSEPH RODRIGUEZ SALDANA, Defendant and Appellant., First Dist., Div. Two., 233 C.A.2d 24, Mar. 16, 1965

54. THE PEOPLE, Plaintiff and Respondent, v. THOMAS NORMAN LINDSAY, Defendant and Appellant., First Dist., Div. One., 227 C.A.2d 482, May 27, 1964

55. DELBERT ARTHUR MULKEY, Petitioner, v. THE SUPERIOR COURT OF VENTURA COUNTY, Respondent; THE PEOPLE, Real Party in Interest., Second Dist., Div. Two., 220 C.A.2d 817, Oct. 2, 1963

56. THE PEOPLE, Plaintiff and Respondent, v. RAYMOND ALVARADO OLIVAS, Defendant and Appellant., Second Dist., Div. One., 214 C.A.2d 472, Mar. 26, 1963

57. THE PEOPLE, Respondent, v. JESSE LOPEZ AVELAR, Appellant., Second Dist., Div. Two, 193 C.A.2d 631, July 10, 1961

58. THE PEOPLE, Respondent, v. THOMAS JULIUS TOPHIA, Appellant., Second Dist., Div. One, 167 C.A.2d 39, Jan. 9, 1959

59. THE PEOPLE, Respondent, v. ARVIE DEAN HENRY, Appellant., Second Dist., Div. Three, 142 C.A.2d 114, June 7, 1956

60. THE PEOPLE, Respondent, v. ELEAZAR SMITH, Appellant., Appellate Department, Superior Court, Los Angeles, 161 C.A.2d Supp. 860, June 23, 1958

LEXIS NEXIS LEXIS NEXIS

the number of cases retrieved. It is here that you can request a new level of your search.

Note: This type of process, going from level to level, can be performed over and over again, that is, requesting different levels or more refinement of previous levels.

I. The next step in your process thereafter would be to review the case or cases, that the Lexis has found. Lexis will put the full text of the case on the screen. You can then read the case, and having finished reading the first case, you can press the "next case" key, and Lexis will display the next case in order.

J. Or, if you are satisfied with the case you have found, you can push the "next page" key and Lexis will display the next page of the case you are reading that you feel is on point.

Note: During your research it is possible to read the entire case on Lexis by merely pressing the "full" key.

K. Finally, to be sure that the cases you have found on Lexis are still the law as of the date you have researched them, you can use the Auto-Cite capability on the Lexis to check the status of the case or cases in which your case is cited.

WESTLAW SYSTEM

Westlaw is a computer system owned and operated by the West Publishing Company. Its libraries cover regional and state opinions of state and federal courts throughout the country. The cases herein have headnotes of paragraphs that represent the opinions of the courts and use the language of the court as fully as possible. In doing research with Westlaw, the following searches may be utilized:

A. Search by fact words, and problems;

B. Search by known name of case;

C. Search by key number; and

D. Search by citations of the case.

For example, when entering a search via a "fact word," you can use either complete sentences or just a descriptive word. In the language of the Westlaw computer system, this is known as "natural language." In using this methodology, the computer will find and printout any and all documents that contain any of the words or sentences used in your request, with certain limitations as to the word identification, that is, pronouns, prepositions, and so forth (see Figure 8.3).

Figure 8.3. Westlaw Search: Copy of the Print-out from the University of Florida Terminal.

A COMPUTERIZED LEGAL SEARCH SYSTEM
PRESENTED AND OWNED BY
WEST PUBLISHING COMPANY
CONTAINING COPYRIGHTED MATERIAL FROM 1961-1976

AVAILABLE 8AM - 8PM, CENTRAL DAYLIGHT TIME
MONDAY-FRIDAY
+ + SYSTEM NOT AVAILABLE MONDAY, JULY 5, 1976 + +
PLEASE TYPE YOUR PASSWORD AND PUSH ENTER:

THE FOLLOWING FILES ARE AVAILABLE

THE FEDERAL FILES COVERING CASES REPORTED FROM 1961
THRU JUNE 30, 1974 ARE:
SCT..... SUPREME COURT REPORTER
FED..... FEDERAL REPORTER
FS ..... FEDERAL SUPPLEMENT AND FEDERAL RULES
       DECISIONS

COPYRIGHT 1961-1974 WEST PUBLISHING CO.

THE STATE COURT FILES COVERING CASES REPORTED FROM
1967-1974 ARE:
ATL..... ATLANTIC REPORTER WHICH COVERS THE STATES
       OF CONN., DEL., D.C., ME., MD., N.H., N.J.,
       PA., R.I., AND VT.
CRP..... <u>CALIFORNIA REPORTER WHICH COVERS ALL
       CALIFORNIA COURTS.</u>
NE ..... NORTH EASTERN REPORTER WHICH COVERS THE
       STATES OF ILL., IND., MASS., N.Y., AND OHIO
NW ..... NORTH WESTERN REPORTER WHICH COVERS THE
       STATES OF IOWA, MICH., MINN., NEB., N.D.,
       S.D., AND WISC.

PLEASE TYPE FILE IDENTIFIER, OR PUSH ENTER FOR MORE
INFORMATION.

AUTO-CITE® (SYSTEM)

Auto-Cite® is a service of Lawyer's Co-Operative Publishing Company, which provides a case verification or cite-checking service. It is a data base of federal and state citations that allows the user to verify spelling, full party names, parallel cites (appellate history of a case), and specifically, the accuracy of legal citations in briefs and other legal writings before they are submitted to the court or opposing counsel. (See Figure 8.4.)

Anyone using the Auto-Cite® system should be familiar with the specific abbreviations used by Auto-Cite® (similar to the *Shepard's* system).

JURIS

This computer was developed by the Department of Justice in cooperation with West Publishing Company for use by the Department of Justice only.

Figure 8.4. Auto-Cite® Sample Session

```
98 ARIZ 18
        State v. Miranda (1965) 98 Ariz 18, 401, P2d 721, revd 384 US
436, 16 L Ed 694, 86 S Ct 1602, 10 Ohio Misc 9, 36 Ohio Ops
2d 237, 10 ALR3d 974.
        Rosenstiel v Rosenstiel (1964) 43 Misc 2d 462, 251 NYS2d 565,
vacated 21 App Div 2d 635, 253 NYS2d 206, affd 16 NY2d 64, 262
NYS2d 86, 209 NE2d 709 13 ALR3d 1401, cert den 384· US 971, 16
L Ed 2d 682, 86 S Ct 1861.
269 So2d 190
NO CASE STARTS ON THE PAGE GIVEN, PAGE REQUESTED
IS WITHIN DECISION OF
        W.T. Grant Co. v Mitchell (1972) 263 La 627, 269 So 2d 186,
affd 416 US 600, 40 L Ed 2d 406, 94 S Ct 1895.
222 App Div 166
        Palsgraf v Long I. R. Co. (1927) 222 App Div 166, 225 NYS
412, revd 248 NY339, 162 NE99, 59 ALR 1253, reh den 249 NY
511, 164 NE 564, 59 ALR 1263.
127 CA2ds 828
        Judson Pacific-Murphy, Inc. v Thew Shovel Co. (1954) 127 Cal
App 2d Supp 828, 275 P2d 841 (ovrld Fentress v Van Etta Motors
157 Cal App 2d Supp 863, 323 P2d 227 (disapproved Sabella v
Wisler 59 Cal 2d 21, 27 Cal Rptr 689, 377 P2d 889).
23 TCt 126
        Joslyn v Commissioner (1954) 23 T Ct 126 (A), affd in part and
revd in part (CA7) 230 F2d 871.
326 FSupp. 1159
        Cohen v Chesterfield County School Board (1971, DC Va) 326 F
Supp 1159, af (CA4 Va) 467 f2d 262, op withdrawn by order of ct
and revd (CA4 Va) 474 F2 395, revd 414 US 632, 39 L Ed 52,
94 S Ct 791.
```

FLITE

This is another full-text computer system, which is used by the United States Department of Defense, by way of the Air Force. (The word FLITE stands for Federal Legal Information Through Electronics.)

It is available only to Department of Defense personnel, and the data therein includes such information as the United States Code, Court of Claim's Decisions, Defense Department International Law Materials, and Court Material Reports.

TRADITIONAL TOOLS OF LEGAL RESEARCH

Some law firms have extensive private law libraries. Even a solo practitioner must have a modest law library, even if it must be in wall shelves in his office.

Most counties or courts have a law library open to attorneys and sometimes to the general public.

The traditional tools of legal research are the books and multivolume sets of case reports, statutes, and legal forms contained in those libraries.

There are primarily four basic methods of legal research, using those books:

1. Topical approach
2. Descriptive word approach
3. Table of cases or statutes
4. Words and phrases

The tools of legal research are divided into two basic categories:

1. Primary sources; and
2. Secondary sources.

PRIMARY SOURCES USED IN LEGAL RESEARCH

A. Statutory Law

This includes enactments of a state legislature (state statutes) or of the United States Congress (federal statutes).

Rules and regulations of administrative agencies created by those statutes often supplement or implement the statutory law.

Your sources for determining applicable statutory law are:

1. "Sessions laws" or "public acts or codes," are officially printed by each state and by Congress after each legislative session. They are usually printed chronologically, but some states also print an official code that contains the laws in topical order. The federal official code of laws passed by Congress is called the United States Code. It is arranged alphabetically by topic.

2. "Annotated statutes" are privately printed statutes in codified form that contain the actual text of the statutes, plus comments and citations to court cases that have interpreted the particular section of the statute under which the case citation (and brief summary of the point of law) is printed.

For example, the United States Code Annotated (U.S.C.A.) has fifty titles, from Agriculture to War. The U.S.C.S. (United States Code Supplement, formerly Federal Case Annotated) is similarly arranged.

Note: In citing a statute in a brief, most court rules require that the official code rather than the annotated code be used. There is no problem, as the annotated statute follows the same number as that used in the official code. For example, you can just change U.S.C.A. or U.S.C.S. to U.S.C. (United States Code) in your brief if you are using the very practical and helpful U.S.C.A. or U.S.C.S. in your research. The same applies if you are using the state code annotated.

B. Case Law

"Case law" consists of written court opinions (usually appellate courts). Case law often interprets statutes. Otherwise, the case law is creating the "common law" in its jurisdiction. This latter function is called "creating legal precedent." Lower courts in a jurisdiction are bound by the legal precedent set by the appellate court.

Your sources for case law are:

1. "The State Reports," if your state has official state reports. The cases for one state are printed in chronological order in consecutively numbered volumes by that state.

2. "The National Reporter System" (West Publishing Company). All state cases are printed in more or less chronological order in consecutively numbered volumes, grouping decisions of several states in reporting units of the system, such as:

GEOGRAPHICAL

Pacific Reporter

Atlantic Reporter

California Reporter

New York Reporter

North East Reporter

North West Reporter

Southern Reporter

South Western Reporter

All federal cases are reported in consecutively numbered volumes, grouping decisions of various levels and types of federal courts, in:

Supreme Court Reporter

Federal Court Reporter

Federal Supplement

A legal research manual in a colorful pamphlet form titled "West's Law Finder," published by West Publishing Co., St. Paul, Minnesota, is a must for a paralegal to understand doing any legal research and particularly where he is using cases reported in a regional reporter. Two pages from that pamphlet are reprinted in this book with the permission of West Publishing Company. (See Figure 8.5.)
3. Unofficial selected case reports.

Annotated Case Reports: The "American Law Reports." These books contain only selected cases from all the states and contain opinions of judges, briefs of counsel, and discussion and reasoning of the law applicable to the case before the bar, and a summary of the decisions reached. (See Figure 8.6 on page 155.)

The most important segment of A.L.R. of benefit to the researcher is not the published case in point, but the annotated part that follows the case. The annotation is a detailed analysis of the practical point of law in the published case, as that point of law is dealt with nationwide. The annotation thus becomes a handy tool enabling the researcher to see, in a relatively short period of time, the various ways individual state codes and courts treat problems identical with those arising in sister states. The annotation, composed by lawyers

Figure 8.5. Sample Case Report. A decision of the Supreme Court of Ohio as reported in the advance sheet of North Eastern Reporter.

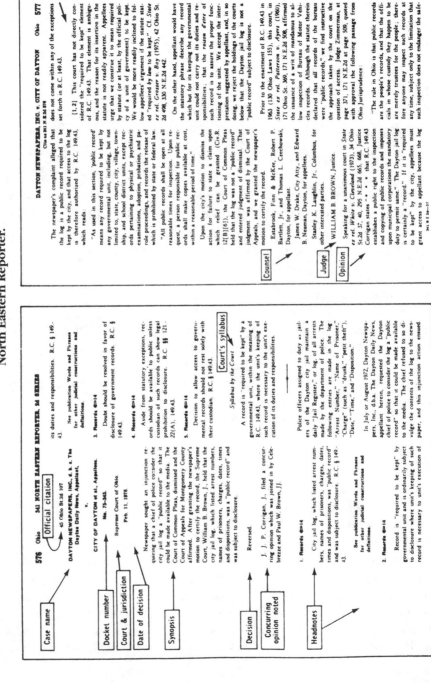

Figure 8.6. Sample Law Digest. A page from Federal Practice Digest 2d, showing *Roe* v. *Wade* under key number Abortion 1.

1 ABORTION

1 F P D 2d —30

For later cases see same Topic and Key Number in Pocket Part

U.S.Tex. 1973. Prior to approximately the end of the first trimester of pregnancy the attending physician in consultation with his patient is free to determine, without regulation by state, that in his medical judgment the patient's pregnancy should be terminated, and if that decision is reached such judgment may be effectuated by an abortion without interference by the state.

Roe v. Wade, 93 S.Ct. 705, 410 U.S. 113, 35 L.Ed.2d 147, rehearing denied 93 S.Ct. 1409, 410 U.S. 959, 35 L.Ed.2d 694.

From and after approximately the end of the first trimester of pregnancy a state may regulate abortion procedure to extent that the regulation reasonably relates to preservation and protection of maternal health.

Roe v. Wade, 93 S.Ct. 705, 410 U.S. 113, 35 L.Ed.2d 147, rehearing denied 93 S.Ct. 1409, 410 U.S. 959, 35 L.Ed.2d 694.

If state is interested in protecting fetal life after viability it may go so far as to proscribe abortion during that period except when necessary to preserve the life or the health of the mother.

Roe v. Wade, 93 S.Ct. 705, 410 U.S. 113, 35 L.Ed.2d 147, rehearing denied 93 S.Ct. 1409, 410 U.S. 959, 35 L.Ed.2d 694.

State criminal abortion laws like Texas statutes making it a crime to procure or attempt an abortion except when on medical advice for purpose of saving life of the mother regardless of stage of pregnancy violate due process clause of Fourteenth Amendment protecting right to privacy against state action. U.S.C.A.Const. Amend. 14; Vernon's Ann.Tex P.C. arts. 1191–1194, 1196.

Roe v. Wade, 93 S.Ct. 705, 410 U.S. 113, 35 L.Ed.2d 147, rehearing denied 93 S.Ct. 1409, 410 U.S. 959, 35 L.Ed.2d 694.

State in regulating abortion procedures may define "physician" as a physician currently licensed by State and may proscribe any abortion by a person who is not a physician as so defined.

Roe v. Wade, 93 S.Ct. 705, 410 U.S. 113, 35 L.Ed.2d 147, rehearing denied 93 S.Ct. 1409, 410 U.S. 959, 35 L.Ed.2d 694.

C.A.Fla. 1975. The fundamental right to an abortion applies to minors as well as adults. U.S.C.A.Const. Amends. 1, 14.

Poe v. Gerstein, 517 F.2d 787.

Portion of Florida abortion statute requiring consent of parent, custodian or legal guardian if pregnant woman is under 18 years of age and unmarried could not be justified by state interests in preventing illicit sexual conduct among minors, protecting minors from their own improvidence, fostering parental control, and supporting the family as a social unit, and thus such consent requirement was unconstitutional. West's F.S.A. §§ 381.382, 458.22(3), 744.13, 827.06; U.S.C.A.Const. Amends. 1, 14.

Poe v. Gerstein, 517 F.2d 787.

Fundamental right to abortion could not be abridged on the basis of compelling state interests, where, inter alia, the statute in question was not "necessary" to achievement of such interests or was unlikely to achieve them. West's F.S.A. § 458.22(3).

Poe v. Gerstein, 517 F.2d 787.

State's societal interest in marriage relationship was not sufficiently "compelling" to justify Florida statute precluding abortion without the written consent of husband if pregnant woman was married, unless husband was voluntarily living apart from his wife. West's F.S.A. § 458.22(3).

Poe v. Gerstein, 517 F.2d 787.

Florida statute precluding abortion without consent of husband if pregnant woman was married and husband was not voluntarily living apart from her could not be justified by state's interest in protecting the husband's rights with respect to the fetus and with respect to the procreation potential of his marriage, and said statute was unconstitutional as infringement on woman's fundamental right to abortion. West's F.S.A. § 458.22(3).

Poe v. Gerstein, 517 F.2d 787.

C.A.Ill. 1974. It is not until from and after the first trimester of pregnancy that a state may regulate abortions by regulations reasonably related to the preservation and protection of maternal health.

Friendship Medical Center, Ltd. v. Chicago Bd. of Health, 505 F.2d 1141, certiorari denied 95 S.Ct. 1438.

Any general health regulations which would apply to first trimester abortions must be limited so as to give effect to a woman's fundamental right of privacy.

Friendship Medical Center, Ltd. v. Chicago Bd. of Health, 505 F.2d 1141, certiorari denied 95 S.Ct. 1438.

C.A.Minn. 1974. Absent compelling circumstances of state interest, regulation of certain fundamental rights, including abortion, is unconstitutional.

Nyberg v. City of Virginia, 495 F.2d 1342, certiorari denied 95 S.Ct. 169, 419 U.S. 891, 42 L.Ed.2d 136.

Where state fails to take cognizance of separate trimesters of pregnancy in its regulation of abortion procedures, the regulation is overbroad and invalid.

Nyberg v. City of Virginia, 495 F.2d 1342, certiorari denied 95 S.Ct. 169, 419 U.S. 891, 42 L.Ed.2d 136.

For cited U.S.C.A. sections and legislative history

employed by Lawyer's Co-operative Publishing Company, is the second authority, the published case itself being the primary authority.

Along with the mail volumes of the basic ALR series, you will find means of updating the case in point in the Bluebook or Supplemental decisions, the Late Case Service and the Pocket Parts. Methods of getting into the system initially include the Quick Index volumes to A.L.R. and the A.L.R. decisions cited in court opinions or even in your opponent's brief or in legal treatises.

Although the American Law Report is not the only annotated selective law report extant, it is a popular tool used by researchers desiring annotations. Check your office or local law library for other annotated selective series.

The American Law Report is broken down as follows:

A.L.R. First Series

A.L.R. 2d

A.L.R. 3d

A.L.R. Fed.

C. Constitutions

The primary authority that limits statutory law made by Congress or by any state is the Constitution of the United States. The various constitutions of the several states may limit the authority of the state's legislature, in addition to but not in derogation of the United States Constitution. Often, as in California, there will exist an annotated edition of the state constitution, for example; the West California Code, in which court decisions interpreting or construing the various provisions of a constitution are set forth in greater or less detail.

The United States Code Annotated contains the text of the United States Constitution and citations to federal cases that interpret it or construe it.

SECONDARY SOURCES USED IN LEGAL RESEARCH

These are the unofficial but authoritative literature consisting of encyclopedias, periodicals, restatements of the law, treatises, and so forth. They are the indexes to primary authority.

The jumping-off point for a successful research project, therefore, would most likely be a major secondary source. Hence, this source should be kept current by replacing the supplements that arrive in your office in the form of loose-leaf pages or pocket parts immediately. Failure to do this may place you in a position of developing a memorandum of law with old decisions. See Updating Citations on page 158.

These sources are written in text form and as a general rule are only persuasive in nature and are not binding upon the courts. They are used primarily to find cases cited in the footnotes to the text and to refresh your memory on the general law involved in the case which is being researched. If no cases are cited in the text and none can be found, the secondary source may be cited and quoted in your law memorandum or brief. In some cases the court may use the quotation as the basis for reaching its decision.

Of these secondary sources, the most commonly used are the encyclopedias which provide you with detailed summaries of existing law with citations, together with leading cases. The most common of these are:

1. *Corpus Juris Secundum*

2. *American Jurisprudence* updated to *American Jurisprudence Second (Am. Jur. 2d)* and

3. Individual state encyclopedias, such as *California Jurisprudence, Florida Jurisprudence 2d (Fla. Jur. 2d),* etc.

OTHER LEGAL RESEARCH SOURCES

To superficially compare state laws you can look to the following sources:

1. "The Council of State Governments or Legislative Research Checklist." Copies of these can be obtained by writing to The Council of State Governments, Iron Works Pike, Lexington, Kentucky 40505.

2. "Aspen Computerized Law Index," 4415 Fifth Avenue, Pittsburgh, Pennsylvania 15213.

3. "Martindale-Hubbell Law Directory," Martindale-Hubbell, Inc., Summit, New Jersey 07901. Volume VII of this set normally gives an overview look at the law of each of the fifty states plus the District of Columbia, Puerto Rico, and the Virgin Islands.

Other legal research sources which may produce a "case in point" are the law review articles found in law school journals put out by the various law schools throughout the country.

Law review articles which cite or discuss a particular case or statute may be found by checking your case in the appropriate *Shepard's Citations*. See the discussion which follows.

UPDATING LEGAL RESEARCH BY USE OF SHEPARD'S CITATIONS

For the "official" word on how to bring a case, statute, or other citation up to date, you refer to the "How to Use Shepard's Citations" or "The Para-Legal" and the "Lawyer's Library," booklets published by Shepard's Citations, Inc.

Shepard's Citations are printed in red bound volumes for each case reporting systems unit. Paperbound supplements are published on a monthly or quarterly basis, depending on the activity in a state or the federal courts covered by the bound volume. The supplements are later incorporated into updated pamphlets or volumes.

The scope of the various available *Shepard's Citations* includes citations of cases and statute; it covers federal, state, local government, municipalities, and administrative agencies, as well as citations to materials from legal publications and articles.

If you have the numerical citation to a case (even if you do not have its name) you can update it in *Shepard's Citations*.

A list of numerical citations to other cases, articles, and so forth, is given under each case or statute if it has been cited elsewhere.

If you are checking a court decision in *Shepard's Citations*, you will find in the list of numerical citations under your numerically cited case, the history of your case and the treatment of your case by other courts since it was decided.

Read the cases listed that appear to be on your point and *repeat* the procedure for each of them you intend to cite in your law memorandum or brief.

The history of your case is abbreviated as follows:

a . . . . affirmed

cc . . . . . . connected case

D . . . . . . Dismissed

M . . . . . . Modified

r . . . . reversed

s . . . . same case

S . . . . Superseded

v . . . . vacated

US cert den

US cert dis

US reh den

US reh dis

The treatment of your case is abbreviated as follows:

c . . . . criticized
d . . . . . . distinguished
e . . . . . . explained
f . . . . . . followed
h . . . . . . harmonized
j . . . . dissenting opinion
L . . . . . . Limited
O . . . . . . Overruled
p . . . . . . parallel
q . . . . . . questioned
v . . . . . . vacated

Note: It is not necessary for you to memorize the lists shown here, as the same list of abbreviations appears in the form pages of every volume of *Shepard's Citations.* As a practical matter and time-saver you will probably want to remember a few of the abbreviations and their meanings.

Figure 8.7 is a sample page from *Shepard's Citations* illustrating the use of the foregoing abbreviations.

UNIFORM SYSTEM OF CITATION

You have completed your legal research by using computer tools or traditional tools.

You are preparing a law memorandum or legal brief that will contain "citations" to primary or secondary sources of law.

Your appellate court rules may have specific instructions and samples of the form in which it wants cases cited in an "appellate brief." Local courts may or may not have similar instructions for citing legal authorities in a law memorandum.

You usually cannot go wrong if you follow *Uniform System of Citation.* That book is a valuable yet inexpensive ring-bound paperback book printed and distributed by The Harvard Law Review Association, Gannett House, Cambridge, Massachusetts 02138.

In addition to the form for the citation itself to federal and state statutes and cases and to law periodicals, depending on the research source, the book gives uniform and accepted rules for introducing and using the citations in the text of the brief and in any footnote.

The book has an exhaustive index to both instructions for citing cases and examples of citations.

Getting into the habit of using the prescribed forms for citation will take a legal assistant one step closer to perfection. The attorney will love it.

Figure 8.7. Shepard's Case Citation

GREYHOUND v. SUPERIOR COURT OF CALIFORNIA
56 Cal 2d @ 355

(Shepard's)

Treatment of Case:	(f)	194 A2d @ 190 (46)
(d)	244 A2d @ 591 (6)		200 A2d @ 789 (47)
	244 A2d @ 591 (33)		194 A2d @ 190 (56)
			202 A2d @ 240 (65)
			202 A2d @ 243 (69)

Treatment of Case:
(d) 244 A2d @ 591 (6)
     244 A2d @ 591 (33)

(e) 60 C2d @ 730 (1)
     205 A2d @ 370 (15)
     205 A2d @ 370 (16)
     58 C2d @ 171 (42)
     205 A2d @ 368 (46)
     205 A2d @ 371 (71)
     205 A2d @ 371 (72)
     58 C2d @ 177 (76)
     205 A2d @ 377 (79)
     218 A2d @ 440 (79)

(f) 194 A2d @ 190 (46)
     200 A2d @ 789 (47)
     194 A2d @ 190 (56)
     202 A2d @ 240 (65)
     202 A2d @ 243 (69)

Cited in: American Law Review and Stanford Law Review; Pacific Reporter, Federal Statutes; Harvard Law Journal, Journal of Bar Association, Dowling & Ryland's English Bail Court Reports, South Carolina Law Reports, Paine's United States Circuit Court Reports and New York Law (Review or Record).

You would therefore have to look up each reference where the case was cited to determine if the decision reached therein was overturned, sustained, superseded, etc.

You would follow the Shepardizing procedure for every reference cited until you were satisfied that:

1) The case was on point;

2) The case was not on point;

3) That the decision had been overruled or affirmed by subsequent decisions or

4) As a means of finding more cases on the same issue..

Simply put, the art of shepardizing is merely the way you confirm or disaffirm the law as it stands at the point in time you wish to use it—and how it got there. And further, that the point of law your attorney is planning to use has not been vacated or superseded (or other like ruling) by a decision reached in the appellate courts.

Writing Effectively

Writing is a difficult skill to develop. Most people are intimidated by the written word since, unlike the spoken word, it has permanency. Moreover, to develop your skill requires constant practice, practice and more practice. Most of us lack the ability to express ideas in writing and this expression is essential, if not mandatory, to professional success.

Hence, emphasis will be given to your thought processes; the fundamentals of legal vocabulary, grammar, punctuation; proper citation form; writing logically and effective reading for comprehension.

Any journalistic student will tell you that there are five "W" questions that should be answered in any writing project. They are: WHO, WHAT, WHY, WHEN AND WHERE. Never assume that answers will come later.

When you are given a writing assignment, the first thing you must determine, or clearly understand, is the purpose for the document. You must ask yourself exactly what it is you want from the Court. Do you want the Court to grant or deny a Motion? Do you want the attorney to settle the case? Do you want to persuade the attorney that he is in a "no-win" situation? Do you want the Appellate Court to rule in your favor? Do you want to appease the anxieties of the client? All of these are affected by your writing skills, or lack thereof.

Once you have determined the purpose of the project, then think it through and decide upon the message to be transmitted.

Your writing must be clear and concise. Avoid ambiguities. Avoid superfluous words. Avoid being verbose. Use lead-in words and phrases that make the ideas flow smoothly and carry over to the next paragraph. In the art, these are called transition phrases or connector words.

Do not twist facts. Do not omit unfavorable facts or inflate some and hide others.

Finally, remember your research helps you to get the facts straight, to verify sources and to prepare your contentions. Notetaking during research is critical to that process. The tried and proven method for notetaking is the use of index cards which can be and are then later organized according to your particular headings. When these initial steps, i.e., notetaking, organization of cards and other preparation are complete, the writing can begin.

In the above connection, three basic elements for every composition (be it a Demand Letter, Memorandum of Law, Memorandum of Points and Authorities, or a Brief) are as follows:

- The Introduction. This could also be called Statement of Facts; nevertheless it is the beginning of the composition. This paragraph should capture the reader's interest immediately.
- The Body. This part consists of your ideas and the support for these ideas. In your Memorandum of Law or Memorandum of Points and Authorities or Brief, this would be called a "Contention" or a "Statement of the Law" upon which your attorney is basing his argument. Then you would add the legal support or authority for the contention.
- The Conclusion. Some attorneys call this a "Summary," as this is just what it is. Your conclusion merely recapitulates your contentions and statutory authorities in a summary format. It gives the Courts the reason why they should or should not grant the Motion.

These are skills which can be learned through training and practice. A good command of the English language is vital, and more than a passing knowledge of legal terminology is mandatory.

THE LEGAL MEMORANDUM

The purpose of a legal memorandum is to inform your attorney or other members of the law firm of the status of the law, giving both sides of the question. You may make a recommendation, if possible, and if not, then be sure to so state. If the law is clear on the issue raised, a conclusion is proper.

You should allow at least three or four hours for the preparation and completion of a legal memorandum, unless the problem is filled with complexities. Then several days of concentrated, uninterrupted research will be necessary. In other words, when given a legal research problem, give yourself time to get acclimated to the task and for complete understanding. Do not be afraid to ask questions as you are being instructed. Most attorneys prefer that you ask the questions prior to commencement of the job, rather than during the performance and certainly not after completion. To do otherwise, causes irritation. To follow the former shows alertness and humility.

As an aid to taking notes we suggest you develop abbreviations of the words often used by your attorney. This will be of extreme value in discussing the assignment and later in reading and making notes about the cases. For example:

pltf. = plaintiff

triangle mark for defendant

bfp = bona fide purchaser

c/p = community property

x = comp-cross-complaint or cross-complaint

PI = personal injury

comp case = workmen's compensation

S/L = Statute of Limitations

S/F = Statute of Frauds

and so on.

In drafting the legal memorandum we suggest the following:

1. Develop an approach by using an outline or chart. This will enable you to clearly understand not only what it is your attorney wants, but it will help you determine what method you should use to get the desired result.

2. Pick out the phrase or theory that clearly sets forth the proposition or issue you want to support. Follow the procedure outlined above in the section on Shepardizing, and start reading the cases which come closest to the issue or problem involved—and of course, those that are in opposition to your case. It is always good to know what opposing counsel will have up his sleeve. This extra effort and foresight on your part will be appreciated.

When attacking the legal research project, your point of reference is the applicable state code, i.e., penal code, civil code probate code, etc. These sources will normally point you in the right direction. In proceeding with your research, it is *fatal* to overlook or forget to check the supplements to the codes (or pocket parts as they are commonly called); or the advance sheets published by the appellate court system.

As you read, make notes on 3 x 5 cards or a legal tablet made especially for that purpose, noting the key points raised leaning towards the issues of your case. For easy referral always note the book, the volume, page number, paragraph and section of each case read and to be re-read.

The easiest way to do this is to look at the headings of each case on the "front or fact sheet" of the case (sometimes called the "table of contents"). These two sections of the case will tell you if the case is for or against your proposition; if so, to what extent, alleviating the necessity of your having to read the case in its entirety.

Should the case be on target, Shepardize it again. Failure to do so may cause your attorney to walk into court and get mud on his face if the case has been overruled or superseded by another more recent decision.

NINE GUIDELINES FOR PREPARING THE LEGAL MEMORANDUM

After you have completed your Shepardization of the cases you feel cover your points, read them again, and again for accuracy of citation and applicability. Then prepare your legal memorandum, paying particular attention to the following:

1) In citing a case, always place the official reports first, but also give the unofficial report citations;

For example, in California we would cite a case as follows:

People v. *Gould* (1971), 54CA2d 621; 7 Cal Rptr 273; 354 P2d 30 Cal—being the official reports, and the unofficial reports being California Reporter (Cal Rptr) and the Pacific Reporter (P) which includes nine other states outside of California.

2) When copying a statute and you find that certain portions of the statute are underlined in the Code book, *do not* underline when you quote the statute. The line under the words is not part of the statute. It merely tells the reader that those words are new to the statute. The same applies to the asterisk found in the text of a statute quoted in a code. The asterisk shows the reader that the statute has recently been amended by way of deletions of words. The asterisks are not part of the statute.

3) In setting off quotations, citations, etc., indent on both paragraphs for the single space. Do not use quotation marks when indenting.

4) If citing old cases, say so and explain the connection and purpose for the reference to them.

5) One of the greatest pitfalls in citing cases is the use of the words *supra, infra* and *ibid.* Know them, their meaning and use them properly.

Supra (always underlined) means that which came before;

Infra (always underlined) means that which comes later; and

Ibid (always underlined) means on the same page; or in the same book.

6) In your discussion use strong phrases such as "it appears that the bulk of authority" or, "the bulk of case authority states that"; or "the law is clear," etc. Don't be frightened. Let your attorney know you have done your homework.

7) Be relevant; never forget the case you are discussing. Always "tie-in" your case law and authority with the subject matter of your legal memorandum. In other words, do not lose sight of your objective and ramble.

8) In your conclusion, list or refer to or even incorporate your leading citations, and

9) Make it readable, interesting and *brief.*

Thereafter, sit down with your attorney and discuss what you have done, explain your thinking in reaching your conclusion. Make your discussion practical, not argumentative. Have both sides of the issue, with supporting authority, well in mind. These things will aid your attorney in making a legal determination as to strategy. You are not the final authority—just his sounding board.

CHAPTER 9

Pretrial Discovery

PURPOSE AND LIMITS OF DISCOVERY

In addition to informal investigation of facts before trial by the attorney and his support staff, as dramatically illustrated by Perry Mason and Della Street, there are formal methods for discovery of facts set forth in the rules of civil procedure of the federal courts and many state courts. Those formal rules are explored in this chapter.

As a general proposition, parties to a lawsuit may utilize the vehicles of discovery to obtain facts regarding any issue pertinent to the claim or claims of a plaintiff or defenses of a defendant that are not privileged.

This means that it can be any matter adjunct to a claim of the defendant or defense of a claim by the defendant. This discovery by either or both parties can relate to documents, books, objects, and the identity and whereabouts of individuals who may have information relevant and material to the lawsuit.

The law is clear that even though the matter revealed through the vehicles of discovery may not be admissible at the time of trial, the discovery process can go forward along that line if the materials sought appear reasonably calculated to lead to the discovery of admissible evidence.

The nature and extent of allowable discovery in state court systems is controlled by statutes court rules and case law interpreting them. The reference source books for these statutes are your state code or statutes, including your "evidence code," if any, your state rules of civil procedures, and your local rules of court, all of which can be found in your office or local law library.

Discovery in the federal court system is governed by the Federal Rules of Civil Practice and federal cases interpreting the rules. These rules can be found either in your office library or the local law library.

West Publishing Company publishes a desk book containing reprints of court rules for many states. The desk book also contains the federal court rules for the federal district courts in the state, among other information.

Most multivolume annotated statutes have one or more volumes giving the text of the related court rules with case annotations to the rules to show how the court interprets the rules.

THE FIVE WHY'S OF DISCOVERY

1. To obtain additional factual information at the least expense to the client.

2. To negate and avoid "surprise" documentary evidence or witnesses at the time of trial and to share the results of any investigation to aid settlement of a case.

3. To reduce triable issues, thereby shortening the duration of the trial.

4. To preserve evidence or testimony of witnesses.

5. To get a preview of opposing counsel's case.

The philosophy of the discovery process is that all actions before the courts should be tried on facts as opposed to the wit and showmanship of an attorney. Formal discovery is a search for truth based on those facts.

Many state court rules follow the Federal Rules of Civil Practice, although these rules are not binding on state practice. They do, however, act as a guide and are persuasive in interpreting state court rules of procedure.

EXAMPLE

When Rule 33 of the Federal Rules of Civil Procedure was amended to correct the abuse of discovery in the use of interrogatories, many states picked up this more humane and timesaving procedure to elicit information via the written question.

The recent amendment to the Federal Rules of Civil Procedure, Rule 26, has also brought about major changes in the discovery process that many states have not adopted. This Rule 26 provides for the creation of a "discovery conference,"* wherein the judge presiding will set up an orderly plan for discovery when the party–litigants, through their attorneys, cannot agree to the implementation of such a discovery plan. Should this happen (or when it happens), the judge can issue an order targeting the issues for discovery, the time schedule for implementation of the discovery, as well as the restrictions in the discovery process and the amount of money that can be expended for its implementation.

It is, therefore, incumbent upon you as the legal assistant to be aware and have a full working knowledge of the new changes in the law affecting discovery as it relates to your employer's practice and as a result of the duties performable by you. And in addition, you must be cognizant of and knowledgeable in the use of litigation support systems in the discovery process (see Chapter 8, "Legal Research Tools") and whether these discovery print-outs are admissible into evidence at the time of trial. (See Chapter 10, "Admissibility and Use of Evidence.")

There are certain time limits on discovery. Under the most normal of situations, time is always of the essence in a law office. But trial preparation has greater time restrictions. In most states, absent a stipulation between the parties, all discovery has to be completed within a thirty-day period prior to the date of trial. (You should check your local statutes and codes to determine the applicability of this limitation.) The purpose of this time period is to close all discovery proceedings to give the parties time to prepare for the actual trial of the case.

It is for this and other reasons that you as the legal assistant should start your discovery process immediately upon receipt of an answer, or upon service of the answer. In most states you can serve Interrogatories and Requests for Admissions twenty days after receipt of the answer, as well as schedule a deposition.

Court rules also provide time limits for answering interrogatories and responding to "requests for admissions" or "requests to produce."

---

* Rule 26(f)—Discovery Conference: At any time after commencement of an action the court may direct the attorneys for the parties to appear before it for a conference on the subject of discovery. The court shall do so upon motion by the attorney for any party if the motion includes (1) a statement of issues as they appear; (2) a proposed plan and schedule of discovery; (3) any limitations proposed to be placed on discovery; and (4) a statement showing that the attorney making the motion has made a reasonable effort to reach agreement with opposing attorneys on the matters set forth in the motion. Each party and his attorney are under a duty to participate in good faith in the framing of a discovery plan if a plan is proposed by the attorney for any party. Notice of the motion shall be served on all parties. Objections and/or additions to the matter set forth in the motion shall be served not later than ten days after service of the motion. See Federal Rules of Civil Practice, pages 66 and 75, U.S. Code Title 28.

TYPES OF DISCOVERY

There are basically six vehicles or devices of discovery:

1. Interrogatories—written questions;
2. Depositions—oral examination and cross examination of a witness (mini-trial solutions);
3. Production of Documents—motion;
4. Physical and Psychological Exam—motion;
5. Request for Admissions—written statement of fact filed and served by one party;
6. Request for Production of Stationary Objects—motion.

The exception to the right of discovery by any of the foregoing methods are:

1. "Privileged Information" is not subject to the discovery process. That is the information received by way of one-on-one conversation or that communicated by written statement (letters, telegrams, and so forth) between client–attorney, husband–wife, doctor–patient, clergyman–parishioner, and the like, as provided in state statutes or case law "rules of evidence."

2. "Nonprivileged Information," which is not subject to the discovery process, consists of statements from a witness or party or documents that are not reasonably calculated to lead to the discovery of admissible evidence.

3. The "work product" of your attorney. Therefore, in answer to an interrogatory or request for admissions involving that, you can acknowledge or admit having such a statement, but it would be necessary for opposing counsel to file a motion for production and copy or inspection to secure the same, even though the work product is not an attorney-client communication.

Note: Ask your attorney if you are in doubt as to whether you should supply information contained in your office case file.

INTERROGATORIES

Interrogatories are typewritten questions that are submitted to another party to the case. That party must answer the questions in writing and sign under oath. Interrogatories cannot be submitted to a person who is not a party to the case.

Depositions, unlike interrogatories, may be taken of anyone who may have knowledge of facts relevant to the case, even though he (or a corporation) is not a party to the case.

A. Use of Interrogatories

Developing interrogatories is a matter of reasoning. That is to say, you must first determine what it is you are attempting to accomplish and what information you are seeking to obtain from the answers to the questions. You will hope that true answers will be admissions of fact you are attempting to secure to remove triable issues of fact. Ask yourself, "Will these questions and/or requested statements obtain the desired result?" If your answer is "yes," then you are on the right track.

Now, with your word processor (or other type of computer machine for litigation support), the canned, voluminous sets of interrogatories and requests for admissions (as used by many large law firms, inhouse corporate attorneys, and so on) can now be customized by you to fit the current situation as well as individual litigants. This can now be done easily and quickly simply by rearranging paragraphs, words, phrases, and/or by the addition of words, phrases, paragraphs, and so forth.

B. Drafting Interrogatories

The principles applied in plaintiff interrogatories are the same for both defendant and plaintiff's case. <u>Interrogatories</u> may be served on plaintiff any time <u>after the complaint is filed.</u> They may be served on any party <u>after he is served.</u>

Sample procedure for drafting interrogatories <u>after</u> *plaintiff's complaint has been filed.* The defendant has filed an answer. Your office may or may not have taken the deposition of the defendant. Your attorney wants to pin down certain facts with specificity. You are given the task of developing a set of interrogatories to be propounded to the defendant. What do you do?

a. You look to the complaint to determine the contentions of the plaintiff, and the alleged wrongs committed by the defendant. Then you look to the answer of the defendant, together with the affirmative defenses claimed by the defendant. It is at this point, if your office has established a computer litigation system, that you can retrieve the complaint and/or answer for review and search for those issues pertinent to the request of your attorney either by head-notes, subject search, or full text review. This, of course, depends on the system your office has established.

b. Once you have reviewed your retrieval information and know the information you want as discussed in A above, Use of Interrogatories, you are ready to develop your interrogatories. Your retrieval system or the office library may contain more or less standard and lengthy forms for the questions usually asked in a particular type of case.

c. Read the canned interrogatories and delete any not applicable to your particular case. Modify the ones that do apply. Add original questions about particular matters you need to discover in your case.

d. You should attempt to draft your interrogatory as single direct question, phrased to clearly inform the receiver what it is you want to know. The interrogatory can be divided into as many subdivisions as you like to make it more intelligible and easier to answer.

e. The first paragraph of the set of interrogatories would be the boiler-plate notice paragraph stating statutory or court rules basis under which the interrogatories are being propounded.

EXAMPLE

Plaintiff, pursuant to Sections _____ and _____ of the Code of Civil Procedure, requests that the following interrogatories be answered, under oath, separately and fully, within thirty (30) days by defendant (or plaintiff whichever is applicable).

The trend now is to have a paragraph in the notice of interrogatory before you start the interrogatory, spelling out the definitions of words, phrases, and so forth, and the scope of the questions so as to avoid any misunderstanding of what is being asked and thereby insuring responsive answers. Hence, you should include a paragraph or paragraphs as follows:

EXAMPLE

In answering these interrogatories, you are required to not only furnish such information as you know of your own personal knowledge, but information which is in the possession of your attorneys, investigators, insurance carriers, or anyone else acting on your behalf or their behalf.

or

It is intended by these interrogatories to elicit information not only within your own knowledge but obtainable by you . . .

and

If you cannot answer the following interrogatories in full, after exercising due diligence to secure the information to do so, so state, and answer to the extent possible, specifying your inability to answer the remainder, and stating whatever information or knowledge you have concerning the unanswered portions.

f. The first several interrogatories of course, would be directed to personal data, that is, name, address, telephone number, occupation or business, and address and telephone number of same (all depending on the nature of the lawsuit), and this could include medical information and educational background. Then comes the meat of the purpose of the interrogatories.

EXAMPLE

Let us say, it is an action for breach of contract for the purchase and sale of a piece of real property and the plaintiff is attempting to secure the return of his deposit, claiming that he was unable to secure the loan, or that the application for credit was refused; and furthermore, that his demand for the return of his deposit has been rejected by defendant.

It has been our experience that having the factual contentions in front of you (on a tablet) makes for easier referral in following your thoughts in developing interrogatories. In the above example, you want to establish the demand of the plaintiff *and* the refusal by the defendant, among other things.

Your interrogatories on that point may be drafted as follows:

Interrogatory No. 5: Did plaintiff pay deposit described in the contract, a copy of which is attached to the complaint filed in this action? If so,

    a. Amount?
    b. When paid?
    c. To whom was it paid?

Interrogatory No. 6: Did plaintiff ever demand return of his deposit? If so, when did he demand the return of the deposit?

Interrogatory No. 7: Was the demand (or demands) made in writing or orally?

    a. If in writing, to whom was the demand(s) addressed?
    b. If orally, to whom was it made?

Interrogatory No. 8: Under what circumstances was the demand(s) made? Describe in detail.

Interrogatory No. 9:

    a. If the demand(s) was rejected, by whom was it rejected?
    b. Upon what authority did this individual reject the demand?
    c. What is the name, address, telephone number, and capacity of the person rejecting the demand?
    d. State the basis of the rejection setting forth with particularity, each and every fact relating to the rejection.

Interrogatory No. 10:

    a. At the time of the rejection, were there other persons present?
    b. If your answer to (a) above is in the affirmative, list the names and addresses of each and every such person present and their interest in the subject matter of this complaint.

There is no limit to the number of interrogatories you may include in a set of interrogatories. There is no limit on the number of sets of interrogatories you may serve so long as they are not redundant or used for harassment.*

An example of the introduction to a second set of interrogatories is given on page (174).

Interrogatory No. 1 (or Interrogatory No. 11): In some jurisdictions, the Interrogatory numbering continues from the last one rather than starting each set with No. 1.)

---

*In California, the new Civil Discovery Act, effective July 1, 1987, has now limited the number of interrogatories and requests for admissions which can be propounded.

Attorney for Plaintiff

SUPERIOR COURT OF THE STATE OF CALIFORNIA
FOR THE COUNTY OF LOS ANGELES

_____ ,	) NO.
	)
	) PLAINTIFF'S SECOND SET OF
Plaintiff,	) INTERROGATORIES TO
VS.	) DEFENDANT
	)
_____ ,	)
Defendant	)
_____	)

TO DEFENDANT _____, AND ITS ATTORNEYS OF RECORD:

Plaintiff _____ requests that pursuant Section of the Code of Civil Procedure each of the following second set of interrogatories be answered fully, separately, and under oath within thirty days by defendant _____.

The definitions in the first set of interrogatories to said defendant and the exhibits attached hereto are each incorporated herein by reference as if fully set forth.

g. In typing the interrogatories most court rules require that sufficient space be left after each question to permit the answer to be typed immediately following each question.

C. Answering Interrogatories

The principles are the same for answering the interrogatories propounded to either the plaintiff or the defendant, except for the time difference referred to hereafter.

In all jurisdictions that permit interrogatories, the answers must be verified or sworn to.

In some jurisdictions the original of the answers to interrogatories is filed in court and a copy of the answers is sent to all the parties. In other jurisdictions the original and a copy is returned to the attorney who submitted the interrogatories to your client. *Check your court rule.* See F.R.C.P. 33(a) as an example of procedure.

Sample Procedure for Answering Interrogatories. Interrogatories to be answered by your attorney's client are received in the mail or by delivery. They must be fully answered or objected to within the time limit prescribed by your rule of civil procedure (usually thirty days but not more than forty-five days from the date the summons and complaint was served on a defendant if the interrogatories are directed to the defendant). See F.R.C.P. 33(a) for an example of this rule.

a. You put the *due date* for the answers on the official calendar.

b. You read the interrogatories and determine whether any of the questions can be answered from documents your client has already provided.

c. You photocopy the interrogatories and mail them to the client with an explanatory letter or have the client come into the office to answer the questions. Ask the client to write the answers in the spaces provided, where practical.

d. After having obtained the answers to the set of interrogatories from the client, either by way of an interview or through the mail, the legal assistant's role is one of review and rewording (rewording should not change the *content* of the answer). You do this by comparing the answers given with the factual, supporting documentation in the file and by making follow-up telephone calls to the client or other source of the client's information (such as his bookkeeper or tax accountant). It is also wise to compare the answers to any answers formerly given by the client in a deposition to avoid inconsistency.

Precautionary measure: Any deviation between the answers submitted by the client and the documents in your file, as well as any unanswered questions should be called to the attention of the attorney.

If any questions are improper (irrelevant, invasion of privacy, harassment, and the like) consult the attorney. He may want to object to a particular interrogatory rather than answer it. If the question is objected to, the reason for the objection should be briefly stated instead of an answer *or* a motion for a protective order may be required as provided in F.R.C.P. 26(c). Most states that have modern rules of civil procedure have a similar provision.

e. If there is no objection to an interrogatory it must be answered completely to avoid a motion to compel by counsel when he receives the answers—ref. F. R.C.P. 37.

f. Type the client's answers in the space provided following each interrogatory. If there is not enough space for the complete answer, type it in a separate paper to be attached to the answers. Type "Reference to the attached sheet" in the space provided for the answer.

g. Have the client read and sign the typed answers or the verification. Where the rules require the answer to be sworn to, make sure the notary has signed.

h. Prepare the notice of filing or the notice of answer to interrogatories (as your court rule requires). The caption appears at the top of the notice and the typed and signed answers to interrogatories are attached.

i. File the original answers and send copy of notice of filing with a copy of the answers to all parties *or* file the notice of answers to interrogatories and send a copy of the notice and a copy of the answers to all parties (depending on your court rule as discussed earlier).

REQUESTS FOR ADMISSION

As you progress through the discovery procedures, it will become increasingly apparent that certain items in the litigation are not disputed and other items may be admitted prior to the trial of the action, pursuant to court rules allowing requests for admissions to be made by either party.

These undisputed facts could conceivably be grounds for either a partial summary or final summary judgment, or they may be the basis for a document called "Requests for Admissions."

A. Use of Requests for Admissions

In any event, despite the fact that some of the facts stated in the complaint may be undisputed, if they are an integral part of the defense planned by your attorney, you should attempt to pinpoint and document them to avoid having to argue them at the time of trial.

Or you may be sure of some evidentiary facts that you know are true but may be easier to prove by admission, rather than by formal proof at trial.

Sometimes opposing counsel will "stipulate" (agree without argument or motion) as to the truth of such facts. Most often, he will not.

In a formal effort to obtain an admission that opposing counsel refuses to stipulate, you may prepare and file a document entitled Requests for Admissions, Ref. F. R.C.P. 36.

This vehicle of discovery, like the Summary Judgment, is considered to be one of the most devastating in the litigation procedure, since opposing counsel has only four choices: to admit the matter; to deny the matter; to refuse to admit or deny the matter (it is admitted with a certain time limit, usually thirty days if it is not denied or objected to); or to object.

If he admits the matter, it is a judicial admission and admissible into evidence; if he denies the matter, the moving party can make a motion requiring opposing counsel to pay the costs of proving the matter if it is proved at the time of trial. If opposing counsel neither wants to admit or deny the matter, he is required by law to respond. He must convince the court, by formal objection in the form of a motion, that he has made a reasonable investigation before he is allowed such a response. If he objects, he has to prove the objection is based on lack of personal knowledge, and this is hard to do if he has raised it in the complaint.

B. Time for Filing and Responding to Requests for Admissions

If a request for admissions is served on your attorney, you must act immediately. He *must* read it. He *must* do something or the facts and application of the law to the facts (if included in the request) are admitted.

This document can be filed and served on opposing counsel any time after service of the summons or after an appearance of opposing counsel in the action.

Your local Civil Code Procedure or court rule of civil procedure provides a return date for the answer or objection. Under most court and code rules, the failure to object or to file a written denial constitutes an admission as described here.

C. Drafting Requests for Admissions

The following examples for requests for admissions are based on the case example given on page 178 under paragraph f.:

SAMPLE OPENING PARAGRAPH

With reference to the set of requests for admissions served upon you herewith for each request that you deny, explain fully all facts upon which such denial is based, including, but not limited to, specific acts or concrete possibilities or examples of situations. Mere conclusions or speculations or erroneous rumors without basis of fact are not sufficient answers.

Request for Admission No. 1: Admit that you entered into the agreement with plaintiff on January 27, 19—, for the purchase of the subject real property, which agreement appears on Exhibit A to the complaint filed in this action.

Request for Admission No. 2: Admit that plaintiff applied to the First National Bank for the loan described in the agreement and that he signed the necessary preliminary documents, as required by law to approve his application for a loan covering the balance of the purchase price of said real property.

Request for Admission No. 3: Admit that the First National Bank refused to make the loan described in Admission No. 2 to the plaintiff.

Request for Admission No. 4: Admit that plaintiff's ability to secure the loan was a condition precedent to the agreement described in Admission No. 1.

Request for Admission No. 5: Admit that you had an attorney review the aforementioned agreement prior to your execution thereof.

Request for Admission No. 6: Admit that plaintiff's first demand for the return of his deposit was made on or about February 27, 19—.

Request for Admission No. 7: Admit that plaintiff showed you a copy of his application for loan and the written denial of the loan by the First National Bank at the time he made his first demand described in Admission No. 6.

Request for Admission No. 8: Admit that the date on the written denial of loan by the First National Bank was February 25, 19—.

The Code provides for failure to respond within the time allowed provided that the same must be deemed admitted. But this warning must be included in the request for admissions. Thereafter, if they fail to respond, send out a registered letter or a certified letter that your office is deeming the answers to be admitted based upon that code section. This method is a *must*. (Check your local codes to see if this is applicable in your state.)

Note: What should you do with a request for admission when in doubt? When in doubt: deny. These are life and death matters, and we have found that it is a better part of valor to deny them rather than admit them. Otherwise, check with your boss to see if he, in his strategy, wants to admit some of them.

DEPOSITIONS

A deposition is an oral examination and cross-examination of any person (not necessarily a party) who may have information *or* evidence relative to the issues of fact in a legal action.

What distinguishes a deposition from the other types of discovery is the fact that it is the only vehicle of discovery that permits you to take the testimony of an individual who is not a party to the action.

The testimony is taken out of court at a convenient location (usually the office of the attorney who demands the deposition). The testimony is taken under oath administered by the qualified person designated to record (and usually transcribe) the deposition.

A. Setting the Deposition

1. *The deposition of an individual can be taken:*

   a. Upon oral examination (F. R.C.P. 30) or;

   b. Upon written questions (F. R.C.P. 31). The most common is the oral examination. This deposition is the only vehicle of discovery that parallels open court testimony. It includes cross-examination. It is for this reason that some people call it a "mini-trial."

2. *A deposition may be demanded and held:*

   a. By any party in the action;

   b. At any time after the service of the summons and complaint until the case is set for trial;

   c. Against any party (by motion) or nonparty (by subpoena);

   d. Without an order of court.

3. *The deposition of a nonparty witness may be taken:*

   a. By issuance and service of a subpoena showing the time and place of the deposition for taking his testimony. He need not bring documents unless the subpoena *states* that documents are required.

   b. By issuance and service of a *subpoena duces tecum* for production of documents at the time of the taking of the deposition. That is the form of subpoena that requires the witness to bring documents described generally or specifically in the *subpoena duces tecum.*

4. *Practical tips in setting the deposition are:*

   a. Deposition of corporate entities that are parties to the action. To take the deposition of a corporate entity, you need only serve the notice of taking the deposition on the attorney representing the corporation if it is party to the action, just as you do in the case of an individual party.

b. Geographical limitations, for which you should check the applicable court rules or state code of civil procedure to determine the restrictions for taking the deposition of a nonparty who resides in the state. In California, for example, a deposition can be taken only in the county of residence of a nonparty or more than 75 miles from his place of residence. When setting the deposition of such a nonparty, you would serve the subpoena on him requiring him to appear at a designated time and place in his required geographical area.

You would have to obtain special permission from your local trial court requesting the sister state court to issue a subpoena directing the attendance of the individual at the deposition.

To save time and money the deposition on written questions referred to may be used when a nonparty witness is out of state and submitted to the court reporter where witness resides, who thereafter reads the questions to the witness and transcribes the answers—ref. F. R.C.P. 31.

In any and all events, the moving party has the full responsibility for sending to the court all transcripts of depositions and making all the arrangements as to place of deposition and obtaining the transcript of the proceedings.

c. Demand or request, which means that appearance at a deposition may be demanded by the attorney who wants to take the deposition. It may be arranged by request followed by a confirming letter and/or written stipulation that is filed with the court. There are times when you should demand rather than request. To demand the taking of a deposition you will prepare a notice of taking deposition or a subpoena for deposition. This latter procedure is done either to protect your office (or client) to ensure that the defendant will be present if he or his attorney have been uncooperative (which happens), or to make it more convenient for your attorney's scheduled office appointments or court appearances. In using this latter procedure, an arbitrary date is picked at your convenience, usually ten days' notice away from the date upon which you have set the deposition.

Step-by-Step Procedure: For example, if you want the deposition to be held on June 21, you should prepare and mail out your notice prior to, but no later than, June 10, with proof of mailing.

Concurrently with filing your notice, you should arrange for a court reporter to be present at the time and place set in the notice. It is best to confirm this by a letter or other appropriate writing addressed to the reporting agency or reporter.

> d. Deposing nonparty witnesses, from whom you *must* take the deposition to preserve their testimony, since you cannot send interrogatories to nonparty witnesses, as you can to parties to the action. This procedure is a little more complicated than for disposing witnesses who are parties.

KEY MEASURES FOR DEPOSING NONPARTY LITIGANTS

1. First, you must prepare and have issued a subpoena for deposition (*subpoena duces tecum* if you are seeking the testimony plus records, documents, and so forth), which is served on the proposed witness with the date of the deposition thereon.

2. Then, you also prepare, file, and serve the notice of taking deposition of the witness. This notice is served on all parties, keeping in mind the time restriction heretofore mentioned.

3. The sticky part here is the date. Before you send the notice to all parties, *you must first know that the witness has been served.* If for any reason he is not served within the time allowed to complete your ten-day notice to the opposing party, you must reset the date to allow for the service of the notice to all parties. This can be difficult, especially if the witness knows you are trying to serve him and is avoiding service.

4. After the preceding procedure has been followed, the procedure for taking the deposition of a nonparty witness is the same as that for taking the deposition of a party witness.

5. Those who can attend a deposition during these proceedings are only the attorneys for both or all parties, the person who is to be deposed, any other interested party–litigant, and a court reporter. This proceeding is normally held in the offices of the attorney for either party. It is not a public proceeding even though it resembles a mini-trial.

B. Summarizing a Deposition

The Purpose of Summarizing. Summarizing a deposition or making a digest of the facts elicited from the testimony given in a deposition is used as a tool by your attorney before and at the trial of a lawsuit to:

1. Make voluminous testimony more manageable (condensing it);

2. Verify crucial or disputed facts in a case, that is, how fast was the defendant driving, or how many drinks did defendant have, and so forth;

3. Provide the attorney a quick index of testimony;

4. Facilitate the attorney's direct and cross-examination of the witness who gave the deposition while that witness is on the stand during trial;

5. Aid the attorney to quickly detect inconsistent testimony. This is important if she wants to impeach or discredit a witness during the course of examination or cross-examination;

6. Lay the foundation for a motion to produce or for requests for admissions during the discovery process;

7. Pinpoint questions of fact that should be further developed by interrogatories or further deposition.

SUGGESTED GUIDELINES IN PREPARING A DEPOSITION SUMMARY

1. Listen carefully to instructions from your attorney and take notes of the points she wants verified.

2. Determine the foregoing in specifics and establish why it is important.

3. Read through the entire deposition in a cursory way attempting to spot testimony regarding these points. (If time permits, note the page and line where you spotted the testimony and any apparent inconsistencies.)

4. If possible (or applicable) read the deposition of another material witness for comparison, noting the page and line of any statement made relative to the points in issue which either confirm or contradict particular statements of the witness.

5. Reread the deposition which you are summarizing slowly and carefully to get the overall context of the subject matter clearly in mind, paying particular attention to the conversations before and after each point or issue raised.

6. Once again, make brief notations of your findings relating to the inconsistencies, including line(s) and page(s) involved.

7. Read two to five pages ahead of yourself to allow the testimony to fall into place and/or make sense to you. Do not dive head-on into reading, attempting to digest it all at once—this is fatal.

8. Since the first few pages (normally) are preliminary statements of identification laying the foundation for the actual testimony, you can pass over them, and should.

9. If applicable, or as an aid to the attorney, draw a schematic map or diagram or chart to help explain.

10. Ignore the "objections" made by the attorneys while taking of the deposition.

11. Write a brief, more or less chronological narrative of what the witness testified to (if possible).

12. Make a list of lines and page numbers where particular answers were important to a point in issue (state the point).

EXAMPLE

Demand for return of deposit made:

Page 25	Line 20
Page 46	Line 13

Credit application a condition of the contract:

Page 49	Line 12
Page 66	Line 14

13. Have the information from Steps 3, 4, 6, 9, 11 and 14 typed. That is your digest. Attach it to the applicable deposition and give it to your attorney. *Keep your digest brief. You are supposed to be saving him or her time.*

PREPARING YOUR SUMMARIES

Since a major part of your job is summarization of Medical Reports, Depositions, Interrogatory Responses, Request for Admissions and perhaps Responses to a Request for Production of Documents, it is appropriate that we discuss in some detail the manner in which and the approach to prepare these summaries.

While it can be argued that there is no black and white way, or set rule, for developing a summary, there are some basics which you can adhere to . . . a skeleton if you will.

A summary (like a brief) is what the word says. If you are given a transcript which contains 1000 pages, turning in to the attorney a 500-page summary is out of the question. The same is true of a Deposition. So how do we reduce it? **That is the question**. We submit the following tried and proven methodology:

TRANSCRIPTS:

1. When given an assignment by your attorney, be sure you understand just what it is the attorney is seeking, i.e., inconsistency in testimony; rulings of the Court on objections, etc.

2. Cursorily review the first ten pages or so of the transcript, to get a feel of it. If the transcript is short, quickly review the entire document before commencing your summary.

3. Hone into only those things which are germane to the subject about which your attorney is concerned. I caution you not to think for your attorney; and do not interpret what the witness stated under oath. If necessary, to make the point, quote verbatim what the witness or client or defendant stated.

4. **DO NOT** paraphrase a statement made by a defendant. Paralegals do not make judgments as to what should be included in a summary; this is for the attorney alone. If you feel that something has been stated or emphasized which would be a benefit to the attorney, it is suggested that you make a side note on a separate sheet of paper of this fact.

DEPOSITIONS:

1. First, determine if the attorney wants a Page/Line Summary; a Narration Summary; or just a Summary;

2. If he wants a Page/Line, determine if he wants a Page/Line of a thought or question;

3. Or, if he wants each page paged/lined regardless of what the testimony is about. This would be, more or less, a verbatim page/line; and

4. Here again, determine the needs of the attorney, what he wants pinpointed and emphasized and use your best judgment as to whether or not each

and every word should be included in the Page/Line, since you do not want to return a 25-page Page/Line on a 65-page Deposition.

INTERROGATORY/REQUEST FOR ADMISSIONS:

Summarizing these discovery documents can be the most difficult of the legal tasks assigned, in that you **MUST** set forth the answer of the respondent as stated. **DO NOT PARAPHRASE IT OR STATE WHAT YOU ASSUMED THEY MEANT TO SAY.** If you feel that there is an inconsistency in the answers, note or flag it for your attorney's attention.

When doing these types of summaries, you should have the questions and statements, as well as the answers, before you. You should attempt to include the question or statement in the Summary of your Responses so that your attorney will know what was being asked and answered.

MEDICAL REPORTS:

These are the easiest summaries to do since, unless otherwise requested, the only thing you are looking for is past history of a pre-existing injury; or an injury similar to the one before the Bar and the corresponding treatments including drugs. Remember, the attorneys have medical experts to read and analyze these medical records explain what they mean. This is not your job.

The bottom line to all of this is to keep your Summary and Page/Lines **brief.** That is what a Page/Line and Summary is all about. If your attorney wanted to read a 65-page Deposition or a 400-page transcript, he would not need you.

Figure 9.1

MEMORANDUM

```
TO:      FILE
FROM:    NW/DEL
DATE:    March 23, 19__
CASE:
```

PAGE/LINE SUMMARY OF THE DEPOSITION OF
_____, VOLUME _____
TAKEN ON WEDNESDAY, FEBRUARY 10, 19__

PAGE/LINE   SUMMARY
6/10 - 13/23   Admonishment to the witness regarding deposition procedures.

13/24 - 16/8   The witness' attention was directed to Exhibit 211, the Complaint on file; and was specifically asked about Paragraph 7 therein. The witness did not know _____ nor had he ever met _____ , nor did he know what _____ looked like or his involvement in the investigation.

16/9 - 18/7   The witness was referred to Paragraph 8 of said Complaint and indicated that he did not know _____ ; had never met _____ ; could not identify him or had any conversations about a _____. The witness further stated that he did not know _____ , had never met _____ ; would not be able to identify him, nor had he had any conversations with anyone about _____ . The witness stated that he met _____ on September 12, 1983, as he was the person who interviewed him. He denied seeing Mr. _____ since that day or having any contact with him or discussing him with anyone.

_____ vs. _____
Depo. of _____ , Volume _____
March 23, 19____
Page Two

PAGE/LINE   SUMMARY
18/7 - 22/12   The witness' attention was directed to Paragraph 11 of the Complaint, and asked who made the oral contract of employment with him, to which the witness replied, _____, and indicated she was the only one who had said something to him which indicated that he had made an oral contract of employment.

The witness did not recall the certain express contractual terms and conditions under which he was employed.

22/13 - 27/6   Referring the witness to Lines 17-20 of Paragraph 11 of the Complaint, referring to express memoranda, oral representations and promises by _____ management, the witness indicated, "I don't recall specifically."

The witness admitted that there was a handbook, but he was not certain if these oral representations and promises were there; or if the handbook set forth the terms and conditions of his employment. The witness indicated that he did not feel he was bound by the provisions in the handbook.

The witness had no knowledge of the policies other than those in the personnel policy book; nor could he recall any other memoranda which he understood set forth the terms and conditions of his employment at

_____ .

27/8 - 31/5   Directing the witness' attention to Paragraph 12 regarding termination from employment except for good cause, the witness stated that he was told this by his boss, _____ . The witness stated that this was discussed a few times; that Mr. _____ had told him that if he did his work and did a good job, there would be no reason for terminating him; that he would have a job for life and indicated this on two different occasions.

PRODUCTION OF DOCUMENTS AND THINGS

If other discovery is to be effective and your attorney is to be successful in the trial of the action, he must be aware of the existence of any pertinent documentation relevant to the subject matter of the lawsuit. In some cases, copies are sufficient, such as copies of medical reports supplied by a hospital (usually for a fee for copying).

Your client may know of the existence of such documents and who might have custody of them. (Question the client about this.) Or you may discover the existence of such documents during other discovery, such as during a deposition or in an answer to an interrogatory.

These documents could have been discovered by you when receiving the answers to the interrogatories heretofore received; and/or through reviewing, summarizing, or digesting the various depositions. If so discovered, you can move for their production, copying, and inspection through the use of a notice or request to produce, compelling a party to produce relevant documents for inspection. You may also force a party–litigant or nonparty to permit inspection of tangible evidence such as machinery, real property, and the like.

The preceding section on deposition described an alternative to a motion or request to produce.

A notice or request to produce does not usually have to state reasons for the production. If the notice or request is attacked by a motion for a protective order made by opposing counsel, then reasons must be given. See F. R.C.P. 26(c).

The federal court rules and many state rules do not require that reasons be stated in the notice or request to produce—Ref. F. R.C.P. 34. The request must list the items to be inspected either by individual item or by category and must describe the item or category with reasonable particularity.

In California, the notice must be accompanied by an affidavit and declaration, which must include the following in a succinct statement:

1. The specific items requested, described in enough minute detail to make it easy for the custodian of records (or other authorized personnel) to identify and obtain them.

2. A detailed description of each of the documents or things and why they are material to your case and how the production thereof is relevant and necessary;

3. Other supporting facts as to why the discovery should be permitted; and,

4. It must state that the documents requested are under the exclusive control and possession of the person being noticed or requested to produce.

The request or notice to produce can be used to inspect stationary objects or objects too big or heavy to move, such as machinery or a large number of stored items, as well as documents.

Real estate may also be inspected in response to a request to produce.

Sample language for drafting a request for production of documents and things and real property under the Federal Rule of Civil Procedure 34 follows:

SAMPLE REQUEST TO PRODUCE BOTH DOCUMENTS AND THINGS AND TO INSPECT REAL ESTATE
(Type Caption of the Case and the title REQUEST TO PRODUCE)

Pursuant to Federal Rule of Civil Procedure 34, plaintiff, _____ , requests defendant, _____ , to respond within thirty (30) days to the following requests:

1. That defendant produce and permit plaintiff to inspect and to copy each of the following documents:

 (Here should be listed the documents, either individually or by category, a succinct, clear description of each.)

 (Also here should be stated the time, place and manner of making the inspection and other related acts.)

2. That defendant produce and permit plaintiff to inspect and to copy, test, or sample each of the following objects:

 (Here should be listed the objects, either individually or by category with a clear, succinct description of each object.)

 (Here again, you should state the time, place and manner of making the inspection and other related acts.)

3. That defendant permit plaintiff to enter (describe property to be entered) and to inspect and photograph, test or sample (briefly describe that portion of the real property and objects to be inspected).

 (Here, again, you should set forth the time, the place and the manner of making the inspection and any other related acts.

___(Signature)_____
Attorney for Plaintiff
Address

CERTIFICATE OF SERVICE (on the parties)

_____
Attorney for Plaintiff

Have the attorney sign the request and the certificate of service. File the original of the request to produce and mail copies of it to the party to whom it is directed. Most court rules require that copies must be mailed to all parties (unless excused by court order and when the parties are numerous).

PHYSICAL AND MENTAL EXAMINATION

A notice and motion for physical and mental examination of a party is used primarily in personal injury, medical practice, and workmen's compensation litigation, since it is in these types of lawsuits and claims that the mental and physical condition of a litigant becomes an issue.

Those matters are also an issue in a proceeding for appointment of a guardianship for an alleged incompetent, but special court rules apply in such proceeding.

As a legal assistant you will know of an expert in the medical field pertinent to the injury who can and may be used prior to and at the time of trial. Opposing counsel may want to, and normally does, use his own medical expert. Opposing counsel will prepare and file the motion in such case. Or the attorneys for both sides may agree to use the same doctor. The person to be examined must also agree or it will be necessary to get a court order for the examination.

Once the examining physician has been agreed upon by the parties, or the court has made an order, the moving party usually makes the appointment with the doctor for the party. The moving party is usually the defendant's attorney, and the party to be examined is usually the plaintiff or claimant.

The procedure for forcing the physical or mental examination of a party in a federal court action is provided in the Federal Rule of Civil Procedure 35.

In both state and federal courts good cause must be shown for requiring the examination, which is obviously an invasion of privacy if it has not been consented to by the party to be examined even if his consent could be implied by filing a lawsuit claiming physical or mental injury.

Therefore, if it is determined by your attorney that a physical examination is desired, it can be obtained by making a motion, on notice as prescribed by law, to be served on all the parties. In California, this motion, too, should be accompanied by a declaration stating the reason for the request (the showing of good cause) and a memo of points and authorities in support thereof.

The physician performing the examination is required to submit a detailed, narrative report, which in a workmen's compensation case is to be served on all parties and in a personal injury or medical malpractice case mailed, upon request, to the party examined. The party being examined may submit any previous medical reports and x-rays for the use and benefit of said physician.

Note: Even if the physician files a report, you can still take his deposition. As a general rule the purpose of this type of motion for a physical or mental examination is to secure a copy of the doctor's findings and conclusions after examination where the defendant believes that the injuries complained of or sustained by plaintiff are not as severe as indicated.

As a plaintiff legal assistant you should be aware that your client must comply with any order of court for a physical or mental examination. He has also waived the doctor-patient privilege in this circumstance, and opposing counsel has a right to see the medical report.

ORGANIZING THE MEDICAL RECORD*

A large stack of medical records looks like a forbidding mass of scrawled handwriting and endless paper. You will find that in the copying process pages sometimes become mixed up. A copy service will usually number stamp the bottom of the page, so you have another frame of reference even if the pages are out of order. Many times the copying is very poor making reading the record almost impossible. If erasures in the record are suspect, the original may have to be examined.

The secret to any task of this nature is organization. Not only will being organized make the report on the hospital records clearer, it will let you know, before starting the attack on the records, whether you possess every record you need, or whether you will have to complete the record by requesting the missing portions.

In tackling any record you may want to get a clear picture of what it is about by reading the legible portions first and the scribbles next. Paper post-it notes serve well to mark pages and passages as you begin the task.

The separate sections, for example, the doctor's orders, can then be chronologically summarized. The summary of each section should correlate when completed to give the total picture of each day spent at the hospital. If there are any discrepancies they should be detectable when the summaries are compared in their chronological sequences.

Medications ordered should be listed, and noted whether they were ordered and given or ordered and not given. Time of medicating could be very impor-

---

A Guide to Medical Records by Arleen Kaizer, esq., page 57 and pages 63–66. Published by OMA Enterprises, Inc., Las Vegas, Nevada 89109. Used with permission.

tant, but realize that with the problem of contemporaneous charting, the time the medication is listed as given (usually when on medical rounds) is an approximation in most cases.

Allergies should be singled out on any charting so mistakes are avoided. If there was more than one hospitalization on the patient, check to see if the allergy to be avoided is the same.

An entire case can turn on the meaning of an abbreviation. When requesting documents from a hospital, be sure to request their manual for documenting medical records and their list of approved abbreviations.

When your summary of each day and stage of treatment is completed, the history of the patient and what was done to the patient should become clear.

Ownership of Records

In general, hospitals own their records. Physician's records belong to the physician. But this does not mean the patient does not have the right to review these records.

How Errors Are Made

Because of stressful working conditions, each and every department in a hospital has the possibility of making one or more errors daily. For example, just follow the route of the drug distribution system in a hospital.

Procedure	*Possible Errors*
1. Doctor orders meds for patient.	Medication inappropriate to treat illness; Prescription may be ambiguous or written incorrectly; Patient may be given meds or wrong dose of right meds.
2. Nurse incorrectly transcribes the doctor's orders.	
3. Drug ordered but not given.	
4. Extra-dose error.	
5. Wrong time error.	
6. Wrong delivery mode.	Delivery mode includes: Oral Sublingual (beneath the tongue)

Procedure	*Possible Errors*
	Intranasal
	Inhalation therapy
	Intracutaneous
	IM
	IV
	Intra-arterial
	Intracardiac
	Intrathecal
	Rectal
	Vaginal
	Topical

Ask, What Happened?

Ask yourself why do we have this case? What type of case is this? It will save you much time in reading medical records if you know the degree of scrutiny expected by the litigation involved. For example, if the hospital, doctor, and/or dental records are in the file because of treatment given after a hit-and-run, the information that is most relevant would be diagnosis, the type of treatment given, was there a trip to the emergency room or was the client/patient hospitalized for any length of time?

Document the time and expense involved, type of treatment and if there is any outpatient charting to be done and kept elsewhere in the hospital. Did the injured take any medication? Did he/she use recreational drugs? Was he/she working with machinery? Or did the patient have severe allergies?

FREEDOM OF INFORMATION ACT

Products Liability

In a products liability case involving a pharmaceutical you may also have to subpoena the pharmacy records, including the record of buying the medication and information as to lot and batch. More technical information will be needed to assist the expert witness. Begin thinking of what material you may want to request to assist you in the case.

The address to request information of public record is:

Freedom of Information Staff, FDA
Room 12 A-16
5600 Fisher Lane; Rockville, Maryland 20857

Medical Malpractice

It is understood that the strictest scrutiny of hospital records will be necessary for a medical malpractice case. This process will demand several readings of the record to re-create the picture as it was at the time of injury. Careful examination of the record could also tell you if there is a malpractice or not. But do not rely on the strictest scrutiny alone. Keep in mind all the factors that have to be discovered to show malpractice, and above all use common sense.

If your office has a computer that you can program to extract information, you can assemble it page by page and then retrieve it by department and have each department summary at hand.

WHAT ELSE ARE YOU LOOKING FOR?

The extent of injury/disability is corroborated by objective medical findings.

Objective	*Subjective*
Examiner can observe, by sight, touch, sound (scar, atrophied limb)	Determination of the existence of a condition depends solely upon patient's response (headache)

- When a claim is based on totally subjective complaints, see if the client is consistent. Lack of consistency suggests fabrication.
- Is there a pattern? Is there evidence of normal progressive healing?
- If diagnosis is based solely on patient history and subjective complaints, there is no actual medical corroboration of injury or disability.
- Objective language should always be used in the chart. A note that says a patient uses excessive pain medication, without an indication of an actual amount of pain medication and which medication is taken may be subject to dispute.

ORGANIZATION IS THE SECRET

- Find out what type of case you are working on. Keep in mind the problems of proof you will have to face sometime in this case. Ascertain what degree of scrutiny is expected of you.

- Chronological order for all departments in the medical file reconstructs what was being done and any improvement or lack of improvement. Make certain there are no pages or major portions missing. If there are records missing, ask why and find them.

- If the handwriting is driving you mad, read the legible parts first, mark the rest with post-it or colored paper clips, then fill in the blanks.

- Remember, each section of the chart should correlate with the other sections of the chart.

- Dental records are the easiest of medical records to read. Before beginning, familiarize yourself with a chart of the teeth and the numerical significance given to each tooth to identify it.

- If a case requires the records of the administrative portion of the hospital, be sure and get the hospital procedures as guidelines. If the hospital is one of the defendants, do not forget to get the corporate guidelines, find out which services are contracted for (*i.e.,* janitorial etc.), insurance coverage, etc.

- Records from a doctor's office may not be as extensive as the hospital records, but may be just as revealing in preparing your case. Sometimes a doctor will write the amount he is going to charge the patient somewhere on the page with his diagnosis. This could be extremely damaging in certain cases.

- At times, a doctor writes his uncertainty into the record noting some symptoms and then adding "other problems" opening the door for an accusation of incompetence.

- If the words "ordered a thorough workup" are in the record without any indication of what was ordered and what the doctor considers a thorough workup, the rest of the chart will be a big guessing game as it will be hard to surmise what was done and what was or was not found. This can make the doctor culpable for "padding" the bill if unnecessary tests are included in this workup.

- If a prescription record must be obtained from a local pharmacy, do not just be satisfied with the computer printout you may receive. When filled, the front of the prescription becomes a legal document. This front side should reveal name of patient, address, phone, age (sometimes), name of drug, amount, directions, refill instructions and signature of doctor; and for controlled substances, federal narcotics number of physician.

- The pharmacist may write the price on the front. But, the back of the prescription which may reveal information about what transpired; number of refills given; whether generic was dispensed; if the store was short in stock and how many were dispensed; if compounding was necessary, the amount of ingredients compounded, etc. Be certain to check both sides.

- If medical records are from another state or part of the country, there may be some difference in abbreviations and meanings. If this is the case then you need to have the hospital manual listing the meanings and abbreviations which are part of staff protocol.

- Sometimes the writing will be absolutely impossible to decipher. Don't frustrate yourself by fixing on those words. They may or may not eventually be read. Just try to do your best on all the other parts of the record.

RECORDS SEPARATE FROM PATIENT MEDICAL RECORD

There are other types of medical records you may or may not require for your case, which will not be in the hospital record. They will not be in the doctor's office records either. Some of them may be the consulting physician's office records on your patient, the visiting nurse records, school nurse or employment infirmary records.

If you have a problem with medical equipment or a medical device, you will need maintenance records, request forms, engineering preventive maintenance records, manufacturer's guidelines for maintenance, lot, batch and serial numbers of equipment.

Since a hospital has policy manuals for everything it does, it is best initially to subpoena a list of the table of contents of the hospital's manuals and then request the manuals which apply to your case. Hospital policies are evidence of the standard of care.

Some courts are beginning to recognize that strict liability can be applied to a hospital when mechanical and administrative services are considered separate from medical service, eliminating the sales/service dichotomy.*

Johnson v. *Sears Roebuck*, 355 F. Supp 1065 (1973) *Berg v. U.S.*, 806 F. 2nd 978 (1986) (hospital negligent in maintaining equipment and training staff): *Rose v. Hakim*, 506 F. 2nd 806, 335 F. Supp 1221, (1971) (strict liability applied to hospital for use of defective machinery).

You may need every clue to have all the pieces of the puzzle fall into place. Above all, if you are convinced the answer is somewhere in these hieroglyphics, keep looking, you will find it. If what you are seeking is not in the medical records, other sources to inspect are:

- Hospital Bylaws
- Department Protocols
- Risk Management Records
- Procedure Manuals for each Department
- JCAHO (Joint Commission on Accreditation of Healthcare Organizations) Manual*
- State Licensing Requirements
- Federal Requirements

Lawyers have their own language as doctors have their own language. While medical terms are Latin and Greek in their origin, it is hoped this guide will make them understandable.

DISCOVERY ENFORCEMENT ORDERS (SANCTIONS)

A. The Deposition

Court rules provide for enforcement of deposition discovery where a party-litigant has noticed a deposition or sent out a set of interrogatories requiring the adverse party to attend the deposition or answer the interrogatories. Should the defending party fail to respond to either, the moving party may make an application to the court requesting the court to do so.

If a party fails to show up for his deposition, the court on written motion of a party may:

1. Strike all or portions of any pleading heretofore filed by the defendant;
2. Dismiss the complaint or portions thereof;
3. Enter a judgment by default against the defendant and in favor of plaintiff;

Darling v. *Charleston Community Memorial Hospital,* 33 Ill. 2d 326, 211 N.E. 2d 253 (1965) (JCAHO standards admisssible as evidence of proof of the standard of care).

4. Grant such other and further relief as to the court seems just and proper, including but not limited to attorney's fees;

5. For federal court rule see F.R.C.P. 37(d).

The only recourse open to a moving party when a nonparty witness fails to appear for the taking of his deposition is a "motion for contempt of court." This is proper since, if you recall, a nonparty witness has to be subpoenaed to attend a deposition, and therefore his failure or refusal to comply with the subpoena is in contempt of court.

During a deposition, a witness who has appeared for the deposition and is being deposed may refuse to answer one or more questions, or an attorney may object to certain questions but allow his client to answer.

If the client refuses to answer or his attorney does not allow him to answer, opposing counsel has a right to apply to the court for an "order to compel" the answer—ref. F.R.C.P. 37(a), as well as file a motion for sanctions for failure to comply with the courts order to compel.

B. Interrogatories or Requests to Produce

Answers to interrogatories and responses to requests to produce (as well as answers given to depositions) are useful to your attorney not only at the time of the trial of the action, but in nailing down the contentions of the parties and the testimony of prospective witnesses before the trial. For that reason the court rules providing for compelling a party to answer interrogatories and respond to requests to produce are important to him.

Hence, if the defending party fails to respond to any question (such as, in answering, he has admitted that he has expert witnesses or that he plans to call such witnesses, but he has failed to give you the requested names and addresses of those expert witnesses), you are in a position to make a motion to compel the party to give the names and addresses, or otherwise completely answer particular questions.

HOW TO DETERMINE WHEN TO COMPEL

Review the answers to interrogatories submitted when they are received to determine if the answers are adequate, the answers are responsive, and the answers are complete.

If any of the foregoing are applicable, then you would prepare a motion to compel further answer (accompanied by the declaration of your attorney in California), which motion or declaration should include the following:

1. The areas in which the answers were inadequate;

2. The areas in which the answers were incomplete;

3. The areas in which the answers were not responsive.

With reference to items 1, 2, and 3, include the number of the interrogatory that you claim is objectionable, or the page and line at which it is found, or quote the interrogatory itself.

4. Then request the court to impose sanctions for the failure of defendant to comply if the party fails to complete the particular interrogatories in accordance with the court's order to compel. See F.R. C.P. 37.

The court may grant a motion to compel further answers, adding a monetary sanction plus attorney's fees and court costs to be paid if the party does not comply as ordered. However, if the argument of opposing counsel as to why the interrogatories were not fully or completely answered is more convincing, the court will deny the motion. If the court finds that your attorney's reasons were not well founded, it must require your attorney to pay the costs of court involved.

Note: Written motions under A., The Deposition, and B., Interrogatories or Requests to Produce, discussed earlier, contain the caption of the case at the top and are titled MOTION TO COMPEL.

DISCOVERY PROTECTIVE ORDERS

The use of discovery vehicles can be and sometimes are abused by attorneys on behalf of the party–litigants. For this reason "discovery rules" provide a means for protecting the recipient of the abuse, by way of protective orders.

These orders are obtained by applying to the court, by written motion and notice of hearing of relief from discovery that is abusive or improper. Though the courts have extensive power in this regard, the burden of proving that the discovery requested or demanded is abusive or improper is on the moving party. He must show "good cause" why the court should intervene and prevent or stop the discovery being requested or demanded.

A. What Is Good Cause for Protection?

Some of the grounds you can use in the motion for protective order or your attorney's declaration in support of the motion for a protective order, are:

1. The discovery category is too broad, or is irrelevant;
2. The discovery requested has been received and is presently in the possession or under the control of defendant (plaintiff);
3. Further discovery would be harassment, time-consuming, expensive, and/or would work undue hardship on defendant (plaintiff), and;
4. Further discovery would unnecessarily delay trial because of party's delay in seeking that discovery.
5. If it is a motion for a protective order relating to a medical examination the ground could be: that it would be dangerous to both the health and welfare of the client; but if it is allowed, that it be restricted to one examination for the benefit of all parties in the action, and so forth.

After a protective order is obtained, the other party may prepare and serve new interrogatories or requests and/or take further deposition asking different questions that do not violate the court's "protective order."

Some protective orders protect against part of a discovery document and allow and require answer or response to other parts.

EXAMPLE

A request to produce in a negligence action where punitive damages are not alleged includes copies of defendant's income tax. Plaintiff's income tax returns may be relevant where loss of wages is an element of damages.

FEDERAL RULES OF CIVIL PROCEDURE GOVERNING THE USE OF LSS IN THE DISCOVERY PROCESS IN COMPLEX LITIGATION

You must be familiar with and thoroughly understand the applicability of the federal and state rules of computerized litigation support systems. Computer data may be used in the discovery process to the advantage of your employer. It has been established through case law that in some instances it may hinder the discovery process or prevent the use of the computer print-outs as evidence at the time of trial.

To this end, note that the use of computerized information in complex litigation is generally governed by Rules of Evidence 26 through 37, and Rules 44 and 45 of the Federal Rules of Civil Procedure, or by your state evidence code, or your court rules (and/or civil practice law).

For an informative book on the use of computer evidence and procedures, see *Computer Law: Evidence and Procedure* by David Bender, published by Matthew Bender & Co., Inc., New York.

CHAPTER 10

Admissibility and Use of Evidence

THEORY AND CONCEPT OF EVIDENCE

The legal assistant should have a thorough working knowledge and understanding of the *basic* rules of evidence that govern the admissibility or inadmissibility of facts, documents, testimony, and so forth. That basic knowledge will help develop evidence through discovery procedures when the legal assistant is aiding the attorney in preparing for trial. This chapter will be addressed only to those elements of evidence relevant to the duties performable by a legal assistant in an on-the-job situation.

In addition, because of the overwhelming increase in the use of computers in both legal research and fact gathering, the effect and use of computer evidence will also be discussed and samples will be shown relating to the admissibility of computer data as well as testimony or more traditional documentary evidence.

In this connection, the legal assistant must know what rules affect the admissibility or inadmissibility of traditional evidence, as well as what those rules provide in regard to the admissibility, inadmissibility, or acceptability of that evidence. Computer printouts and expert testimony explaining the programming and operation of computers is often relevant in modern complex litigation.

Facts are the backbone of any case. Evidence is the means used to prove an ultimate fact. Evidentiary facts are the bits and pieces of fact presented to a court during the trial for the purpose of proving the ultimate facts necessary to allow the plaintiff to recover or the defendant to prevail in the case.

The rules of evidence are contained in statutes or codes and in the case law interpreting those statutes or codes.

The rules of evidence are designed to do the following:

1. Set up a series of rules by which the court can referee court procedure, or if you like, by which a lawsuit can be tried;

2. More important, to insure that whatever testimony is received and presented to the court, oral or documentary, is trustworthy, reliable, and relevant information.

Evidence is anything offered to prove the existence or nonexistence of a fact. It may be oral testimony, writings, photographs, charts, and the like.

What are some of the elements of admissible evidence?

1. Must be relevant to the issues;

2. Must be something that can be perceived;

3. Must tend to prove or disprove a relevant fact;

4. Must be useful to the trier of fact in rendering a decision as to the truth of the ultimate fact that is sought to be proved by the offered evidentiary fact.

TYPES OF EVIDENCE

DOCUMENTARY EVIDENCE

Documents can be authenticated (admissible at trial) in several ways.

A. Exemplified or Certified Documents

A document that is regular on its face is the best type of evidence. It is a presumption of law that it is the genuine document. This type of document may be a public document of one type or another such as a deed, a birth certificate, or a death certificate with an official seal stamp thereon.

Since it is well known that documentary evidence often has much more impact on a jury than oral testimony of a witness, the legal assistant has the double duty and responsibility to see that all documents to be used as evidence by the attorney are: (1) gathered together in one place and (2) are exemplified or certified by the proper authority if necessary to make it admissible without testimony of the custodian of the public record.

EXAMPLES

A. By attestation of the clerk of the court, with the seal of the court affixed; or the officer in whose custody the record is legally kept under seal of his office. *A* is "certification."

B. By a certificate of the chief judge or presiding magistrate of the court, to the effect that the person so attesting the record is the clerk of the court; or that he is the officer in whose custody the record is required by law to be kept; and that his signature to the attestation is genuine. *B* is "exemplification."

C. By notarization before a duly licensed notary public, etc. *C* is "notarization."

If opposing counsel does not or may not agree to stipulate to the admissibility of a certified copy of a document, it is best for the legal assistant to obtain an exemplified copy, unless the document is part of the record in a case or other situation where the court can take judicial notice of it.

B. Judicial Notice of Documents

The court, at the trial, may take "judicial notice" of certain public documents, such as the documents in the files of its own or other courts in the state where it is located. Check the rules of evidence in your jurisdiction for judicial notice.

Some court rules require that a written request for judicial notice be filed before trial. If so, prepare it for that document.

As a practical matter, it is wise also to get a certified copy, which may or may not be admissible but is a convenient way of learning the exact contents to the document that the court is judicially noticing.

C. Authenticated by Testimony

At or during the trial of the action, the attorney has to lay the foundation for the introduction of a document that is not exemplified or judicially noticed or stipulated to be authentic before he can prove that the document is what he alleges it to be and means what he claims it to mean.

Take, for example, a promissory note. The attorney has to satisfy the court that it is the duly executed promissory note entered into between the parties. He can do this by several different means:

1. One of the parties can testify to the fact that the promissory note was executed in his presence;

2. One of the parties can give testimony as to his signature on the document;

3. A third party, as a notary or other subscribing witness, can identify the document by testifying that it was signed in his presence.

EXAMPLE

Q: Mr. Brown, I show you this paper and ask you if you recognize it?
A: Yes.
Q: Did you see anyone sign it?
A: Yes.
Q: Who signed it?
A: The defendant, John Jones.
Q: When did he sign it?
A: On October 15, 19—.
Q: After that paper was signed by the defendant, what did he do with it?
A: He gave it to me.
Q: Has it been in your possession since then?
A: Yes.

The document would then be offered into evidence.

DEMONSTRATIVE EVIDENCE

"Demonstrative evidence" is evidence that can be exhibited or shown to the court. It must be relevant and is marked as an exhibit for the party who produces it.

Before and during the trial, the legal assistant may have to keep track of the whereabouts of the demonstrative evidence for the attorney. This type of evidence may be physical or scientific demonstrations or a photograph, chart, or graph.

TESTIMONY

Testimony is the oral response to oral questions asked by the attorneys during the trial. The answers must be statements of fact, not opinion, unless the witness has been qualified as an expert on the given subject.

To qualify a witness as an expert, the attorney may introduce at the trial any or all of several criteria as the qualifying groundwork: education; experience; recognition by associations and organizations in the field; and/or authorship of publications on the subject.

The proposed expert usually testifies to these. His statements are taken as true unless they are objected to by opposing counsel.

Note: When arranging for calling an expert witness who has not testified as a witness in court before, it is best to explain to him before the trial that he should have this information immediately available, preferably in writing to refresh his recollection at the time of trial.

Opposing counsel may want to stipulate that he is an expert or he may not.

A review of the two following cases will demonstrate the importance of the testimony of an expert witness in the trial of a case. See *Perma Research and Development Co. v. Singer Co.* 542 F2d 111, 6 C.L.S.R. 98 (2d Cir. 1976), *cert. denied,* 429 U.S. 987 (1976) and *Perry* v. *Allegheny Airlines, Inc.,* 489 F2d 1349 (2d Cir. 1974).

The first case is a case in which computer evidence was used to form an opinion and as demonstrative evidence.

In the Perma Research and Development Co. case, the plaintiff's expert witnesses constructed a computer-based mathematical simulation of an automobile skid device. The expert opinion of one was based on data from a simulated formula that he had fed into the computer. A dissenting opinion was filed in that case.

The other case did not involve computer evidence but the damages were the subject of an expert-witness opinion.

In the Perry case, which was a wrongful death case, decedent's superior and an executive of his employer's compensation testified about decedent's salary, prospects for promotion, and future earnings with or without promotion. Based on those figures, an expert economist testified that the net present value of the economic loss caused by the death was $535,000 assuming stated inflation and interest rates. The admission of the expert testimony was sustained on appeal.

CIRCUMSTANTIAL EVIDENCE

"Circumstantial evidence" is indirect evidence. It proves the circumstances surrounding the fact rather than the fact itself. Circumstantial evidence may consist of any type of evidence, as documentary demonstrative or testimony.

But, as in admitting direct evidence of a fact, the circumstantial evidence must be of some probative value. It must tend to prove that the main fact is true because it creates a reasonable factual inference that the main fact is true.

EXAMPLE

"Testimony" that a defendant in a criminal case was seen running away from the house where someone was killed a few minutes after the killing occurred.

and

demonstrative evidence that his clothes were stained with blood immediately afterwards, and so forth.

If you must prove a case by circumstantial evidence you must be sure the evidence you offer would lead a reasonable person to infer that the ultimate fact you are trying to prove is true. You may have to probe more than one circumstantial fact. An example of trying to use computer evidence as circumstantial evidence failed in the case of *Ruppelius* v. *Continental Gas Co.*, 426 F2d 760, 6 C.L.S.R. 632 (9th Cir. 1970).

In that case, plaintiff had the burden of proving that the death of her husband, killed when his car crashed, was not suicide. A computer print-out, duly certified as true copies of official Arizona Highway Patrol Accident Frequency Reports for the vicinity of the incident, for the year in question and the six prior years, was offered in evidence in support of the proposed exhibit. He stated that according to the exhibit there were six accidents in the vicinity for the year in question and four or five for each of the previous years. The incident in question was described on the proposed exhibit as "Fatigue Vehicle Ran Off Hwy." There were no witnesses to the incident, and no officer purported to know its cause. Plaintiff's attempt to prove the death accidental through this circumstantial evidence failed.

In the Ruppelius case, the plaintiff did not offer to show that other accidents referred to on the exhibit were even remotely similar to the Ruppelius incident. The computer record did not show the conditions existing at the site at the time of any other accident, nor the circumstances. The appellate court in the Ruppelius case held that the trial court had not abused its discretion in determining that the probative value of the proposed exhibit was outweighed by its undue consumption of time and potential for "distraction."

Note: The reason the computer print-out was inadmissible was not because it was a computer print-out but because it contained incomplete data that was not supplemented by other evidence. The other evidence could also have been circumstantial, as described in the Ruppelius case, in which a computer print-out was used as circumstantial evidence. It must be realized that a computer print-out may also be used as direct evidence, demonstrative evidence, or as the basis for testimonial evidence. Figure 10.1 illustrates the use of computers and computer print-outs as different types of evidence.

COMPUTERS AND PRINT-OUTS AS EVIDENCE

It is becoming more obvious that the use of computer print-outs as evidence have replaced many of the traditional types of records once used as evidence,

Figure 10.1 Examples of Various Types of Computer Evidence

		DIRECT	CIRCUMSTANTIAL
Testimonial		Testimony that a computer program in question, if executed properly by the hardware, and operating on the data allegedly input, could not cause the incorrect output in question.	Testimony that in the particular circumstances in suit, the probability of software failure is 1,000 times higher than the probability of hardware failure, where the fact in issue is which of these two types of failure was responsible for incorrect output.
Tangible	Writing	A facilities management contract offered to prove the obligations of the parties, where that is in issue.	Print-out of accounts printed out by the same computer at about the same time as the account in issue, offered to show patent inconsistencies of the type alleged to be in the account in issue.
	Record	Records printed out in the regular course of business and offered to prove the status of a party's account, where that is in issue.	A user log showing that at particular times, two alleged price-fixing conspirators were simultaneously on-line to a time-sharing system.
	Demonstrative	A magnetic tape offered to prove that it was defective and responsible for the incorrect output in suit, where an issue is determination of the responsibility for the error.	Magnetic tapes offered to show inherent structural defects, where the issue is whether a tape in the same shipment was defective.

Figure 10.1 Examples of Various Types of Computer Evidence (cont.)

	DIRECT	CIRCUMSTANTIAL
Experiment	A showing in court that a particular portable console functions properly as to input and printout, where such functioning is in issue.	A showing that a portable console inherently functions improperly as to input and output, where the proper functioning of an allegedly identical unit is in issue.
View	A showing at a computer facility that a particular tape drive functions properly, where such functioning is in issue.	A showing that a tape drive inherently functions improperly, where the functioning of an allegedly identical unit is in issue.

such as paper documents, books, permanent, original records of various and sundry types, many of which have been put on microfilm or magnetic tape and now have been placed into a computer program. So far, so good.

The problem arises, however, when there is a need to retrieve some of the materials stored. If what comes up on the screen and on the print-out is inaccurate or defective in some detail, there is a problem of proof.

Practical tip: If your attorney is going to use a computer print-out as evidence at the trial, be sure to get the print-out early enough to check its contents before it has to be offered. It may need legitimate correction or addition by the person who prepared it or by its present custodian.

The court may have to determine if the print-out is a true copy of the original document or a true understanding of the parties; or whether it is sufficient to be considered the original, which could be admitted into evidence to the satisfaction of all parties. See discussion of Best Evidence Rule in this chapter.

What one seems to forget is that the computer is still, after all, a machine. Most of the errors that occur are a result of human error. People write the programs, prepare the data, place this data in the machine; and operate the machine for the retrieval of documents needed or required.

It is for this reason that you are urged to carefully check out your own office computer before you use it; check the computer print-out to determine if it is correct before you submit it to your attorney or mail it to anyone. A computer will give you what it thinks you meant based on what was put into it, rather than what you may have meant.

If you find an error in your own print-out, it is suggested that you rerun your command or request it on another computer of the same model and type as your own to verify the data on the print-out, if another is available.

RULES OF EVIDENCE

It is generally stated that all evidence that is relevant is admissible in evidence unless it is excepted by the rules of evidence applicable in the court where the case is being tried. Federal law takes that position. See 28 U.S.C.A. 402. Those rules containing those exceptions appear in the statutes and case law as discussed earlier in this chapter.

The following is just a brief review of some of the exceptions and exceptions to exceptions found in the various state and federal evidence codes.

BEST EVIDENCE RULE

Secondary evidence is inadmissible if the "best evidence" is available. For example, the best evidence of a written document is the original of the signed contract, deed, note, and so forth.

There are exceptions where the document has been lost or destroyed or otherwise unavailable for production.

Exceptions to Best Evidence Rule

There was a federal case that involved computer lists as best evidence when supporting documents had been destroyed in the course of implementing U.S. Army policy to destroy such papers after two years. It was a court of claims case against the federal government, where the government counterclaimed for damages, relying on "computer billing lists contained in its own books and records"—ref. *Schiavone-Chase Corp.* v. *United States*, 553 F2d 658 (Ct. Cl. 1977).

PAROLE EVIDENCE RULE

"Parole (oral) evidence" is not admissible to alter or vary the terms of a written instrument. This is a rule of substantive law and concerns itself with proving contested issues involving the content of a written instrument introduced in evidence at the time of trial. The writing is considered to contain all the terms of the parties; therefore, no other evidence of the contents can be produced.

Exceptions to Parole Evidence Rule

1. If there is a mistake or imperfection in the writing and this imperfection is alleged by a statement to that effect in the pleadings; or
2. Where the validity of the writing is the fact in dispute;
3. Where the writing is patently ambiguous but definite enough to be enforceable.

Check your state code and case law to determine which, if any or all, of the foregoing are exceptions to the parole evidence rule in your state.

HEARSAY RULE

"Hearsay evidence" is not generally admissible even though it may be relevant to the case. Hearsay evidence consists of out-of-court statements made by someone other than the "declarant" (the one testifying at the trial or hearing). If the declarant is asked to testify to such statements, opposing counsel will object. If the witness gives testimony as to such statements, a verbal motion to strike may be granted.

Hearsay testimony is understandably presumed to be unreliable. An example is the childhood game of "Gossip."

Exceptions to Hearsay Rule

Exceptions to the hearsay rule are based on the fact that certain hearsay may be reliable because of the circumstances under which the statement was made or written by someone other than the witness. Some examples are:

1. Excited utterance by another at the time of the accident or event (no time to think or scheme during the *res gestae);*
2. Statement for purposes of medical diagnosis or treatment made by patient to doctor where the patient has waived the doctor-patient privilege and the doctor is testifying or the medical report containing patient's statements is put in evidence.

3. Business records kept in the ordinary course of business, even though the witness did not make the entries at the time.

4. Records of vital statistics to prove the fact of birth, marriage, death, causes, and so forth;

5. Absence of public record or entry to prove that none was made;

6. Records of religious organizations to prove a birth or death;

7. Marriage, baptismal, or similar certificates;

8. Family records such as notations of significant family incidents in the family Bible;

9. Statements in ancient documents;

10. Market reports and commercial publications to prove a business trend or other business fact;

11. Reputation in the community concerning boundaries or general history of the community, where that is a relevant issue;

12. Reputation in the community, where that is a relevant issue.

For a better understanding and explanation of the exceptions to the hearsay rule as well as other exceptions, we refer you to the Federal Evidence Code 28 U.S.C.A. 802 including the federal case law following that section of the United States Code in that annotated volume.

RELEVANT EVIDENCE

"Relevant evidence" is evidence having a tendency to make the existence of any fact that is of consequence to the determination of the action more probable or less probable than it would be without the evidence. See Section 401 of the Federal Evidence Code 28 U.S.C.A. 401.

Since a legal assistant will be dealing with the facts of a case and doing the legal research to support the theory and strategy for the attorney, we will deal at some length with illustrative ways in which allegations should and can be supported by the weight of evidence. To do this we shall use a hypothetical case and address ourselves to it for clarity.

Assuming we have alleged negligence on the part of the defendant, the matters to be considered when trying to find evidence of that negligent conduct on the part of a defendant may be as follows:

1. That the conduct of defendant fell below the standard of care of an ordinary prudent man;

2. That there was a violation of a statute;

3. That defendant failed to perform a duty other than one prescribed by statute;

4. That by defendant's failure to perform reasonably and with ordinary care a duty that he volunteered to perform proximately caused plaintiff's injury;

5. That defendant violated a duty that was prescribed by a contract;

6. Judicial notice; and,

7. Application of the doctrine of *res ipsa loquitur.*

STATEMENT OF FACTS (HYPOTHETICAL)

Jane Jones and her baby, passengers on the Silver Meteor from Washington, D.C., to Miami, Florida, were killed in a collision between the Silver Meteor and the Blue Special, both trains owned and operated by Southern Trains.

Jane Jones and her baby purchased first class tickets from Washington, D.C., on December 28, 1973. The trip was uneventful until the Silver Meteor reached the outskirts of the little town of Blainey, South Carolina, where the collision occurred. Several coaches were derailed, and as a result of the derailment, Jane Jones and her baby were crushed to death between the seats of the coach in which they were riding.

These are the facts you have obtained from the husband of the decedent. Your attorney now asks you to prepare a memorandum of law to establish negligence on the part of the defendant. You immediately know that it is a wrongful death action. Where do you start?

You might start with establishing step 5 in the list, "defendant violated a duty that was prescribed by a contract." Since we know the burden will be on your attorney to prove that the decedent had a legal right to be on the train, we must establish privity of contract. To do this you must have evidence of the purchase of first class tickets by Jane Jones and baby.

You therefore will do any of the following (or you may rely on the presumption discussed here):

1. Secure duplicate copies of the ticket, if they are available; or

2. Secure a copy of passenger list and have it authenticated by the appropriate officer or agency; or

3. Subpoena copies of this list for copying by way of deposition or by a notice and motion for production of documents (see Chapter 9, "Pretrial Discovery");

4. Or, if the tickets were purchased with a credit card or other means, secure copies of the invoice utilizing the procedures in step 3;

5. Or the husband could testify that he bought the tickets, gave them to his wife and put her and the baby on board the train.

Once you have established decedent's legal right to be on the train, your attorney can show that the defendant violated a duty of care in its negligent operation of an inherently dangerous instrument, that is a railroad train. See Steps 2, 3, and 7 in the foregoing list.

To aid you with this phase (if you cannot get the evidence that Jane Jones was lawfully on the train) you should have a "presumption of law" in her favor. "A presumption of law is a rule of law that courts and judges shall draw a particular inference from a particular fact, or from particular evidence, unless and until the truth of such inference is disproved . . . a rule which, in certain cases, either forbids or dispenses with any ulterior inquiry . . ." (*Black's Law Dictionary*, Revised Fourth Edition, West Publishing Co.). A presumption of law may be "absolute" or "rebuttable."

The presumption of law involved in our facts is the rebuttable presumption that Jane Jones was lawfully aboard the Silver Meteor. The presumption is that all passengers aboard a passenger train are presumed to be there lawfully. Presumption is the same as evidence that is presented to show that Jane Jones and her baby purchased a ticket and boarded the train at Union Station in Washington, D.C. Either the presumption or the evidence will shift the burden or proceeding to the party seeking to establish the contrary, that is to say, that Jane Jones and her baby did not purchase a ticket and board the train at Union Station in Washington, D.C., thereby not being lawfully upon the train at the time of the collision.

A legal passenger contract has now or will be established by your investigation here described or your attorney has decided or will decide to rely on the presumption of lawful passage as discussed.

The most important question for your consideration in establishing negligent conduct on the part of the defendant in this case is the application of the doctrine of *res ipsa loquitur*, "the thing speaks for itself." Even though you are not an attorney, you should basically understand this doctrine and how and when it is applicable.

If your attorney intends to rely on this doctrine, he does not have as great a burden of producing evidence to establish negligence on the part of the railroad.

However, the following facts should be investigated to determine:

1. *That the accident which occurred was the type of accident that would not have occurred had it not been for the negligence of the defendant.* An investigator might also have an on-site investigation to determine if the rails were defective; whether the brakes on the train were defective; whether they needed repairs; whether the trainman was drunk or had been drinking; whether he had poor eyesight; whether he wore glasses and if so, whether he had them on at the time of the collision, and so forth. If the doctrine of *res ipsa loquitur* applies, you do not have to prove the exact nature of a defect in the train or exactly what the employee did wrong.

2. *That the defendant (or agent, servant, employee) had exclusive control of the train.* To establish this, secure names, addresses, and capacity or title of the person driving or manning the train at the time of the collision and the immediate supervisor; get copies of payroll sheets and personnel files, and so forth. This information may be obtained by interrogatories directed to the railroad defendant.

3. *That the plaintiff in no way contributed to the accident, either voluntarily or otherwise.* You might establish this by seeking out survivors of the accident who may have witnessed the plaintiff and her baby; talked to her; aided her in some way; sat next to her on the train; and so forth. Contributory negligence is an affirmative defense that must be raised by the railroad company, but it doesn't hurt to be ready.

The facts of our case indicate a case for *res ipsa loquitur.* The reason: The trains were both wholly within the exclusive control of the defendant, and they are dangerous instruments. The attorney will decide what evidence he wants to present.

Now you must find some evidence of the fact that Jane Jones and her baby are dead as a result of the collision of the train in which they were lawful passengers *and* that the collision was the legal fault of the defendant railroad company.

You will not have to get evidence that a train is an inherently dangerous instrument. The attorney will ask the court to take judicial notice of that fact.

What is judicial notice? There are two types: facts which the court is bound to notice; and facts which the court may notice (discretionary with the court). See your state code of evidence to determine which applies to the fact you want the court to judicially notice.

You will check the law as to the duty of a railroad to its lawful passengers (as opposed to hobos hitching a ride, fellow employees, and so forth). Is it an insurer or must you prove negligence? If you must prove negligence, does the doctrine of *res ipsa loquitur* apply?

Generally, if a dangerous instrument is in the sole custody and control of the defendant, the doctrine of *res ipsa loquitur* does apply.

PROVING A PRIMA FACIE CASE

A. REPLEVIN CASE

Replevin means a redelivery to the owner of the pledge or thing taken in distress. At law it is any unauthorized act which deprives an owner of his property, either permanently or for an indefinite time. (See *Black's Law Dictionary,* West Publishing Co.)

A suit in replevin therefore would be a personal, possessory type action in which plaintiff must recover on the strength of his title in the property, not on the weakness of defendant's title. He must establish his right to possession of the property prior to the commencement of any action. For this reason, your initial interview with the client will be of great importance and should reflect the following:

1. Prima facie evidence of title; ownership and conversion by defendant—the unauthorized act.

2. And should go like this:

Plaintiff resides at 1510—104th Street, Los Angeles, California;

Plaintiff was the owner of a 1994 Ford Sedan, having purchased the same on October 1, 1994; that no one other than the plaintiff drove the vehicle or had keys to the same;

That plaintiff customarily parked his car in front of his house during and at the end of the day, not having a private garage adjacent to his place of residence;

That on December 31, 1994 plaintiff parked his car, as usual in front of his house at the end of the day. The next morning after watching the football game, plaintiff went out to get into his car and discovered that it was missing. He immediately called the police.

That during the subsequent investigative procedures, plaintiff saw his automobile parked in defendant's garage. That he advised defendant that the 1994 Ford Sedan parked in defendant's garage belonged to plaintiff.

That plaintiff had in his possession the papers indicating ownership and title and demanded that defendant return said vehicle to him. That defendant failed and refused to so comply.

Plaintiff now seeks the legal assistance of your employer.

Resolution: File a lawsuit for conversion and return of personal property; in the alternative, for a money judgment equivalent to the prevailing price of the automobile.

Step-by-Step Procedure

If thereafter the case goes to trial and a judgment is received, money or return of property, do the following:

1. Obtain an abstract of judgment, have the same certified and file it in the county where the property is located;

2. Secure a Writ of Execution from the Court;

3. Forward the Writ to the appropriate marshal or sheriff's office for execution on the judgment.

(Check your local state and Court rules to determine the time restrictions in connection with this procedure.)

B. SUIT BY A WIDOW ON A LIFE INSURANCE POLICY

To aid your attorney in successfully prosecuting this claim, you would have to establish prima facie evidence that the policy in dispute was issued upon the life of the decedent, and that he was the owner of said policy *before* his death.

Of course, possession of the policy with the name thereon of the insured and the deceased being the same, is the best evidence—but if for some reason the client could not locate the policy, what do you do? After discussion with your attorney, one of the following:

1. Send out a set of "special interrogatories" to the insurance agent issuing the policy with a request for attachments, i.e., a certified copy of policy and original application; or

2. Set up a deposition, Subpena Duces Tecum, requesting that he bring with him the policy and application or certified copies thereof for copying. Example of a set of special interrogatories would go something like this:

1. Do you know the decedent, John Jones?	Yes.
2. Did you write up the original application for the insurance policy in question?	Yes.
3. Did you see the insured sign said application?	Yes.
4. Where were you and the insured at the time of the signing of said insurance policy?	We were in his home in the kitchen, sitting at the kitchen table.
5. Would you be willing to make the same available for inspection and copying on a voluntary basis; or would it be necessary to secure a court order?	I would be willing to submit it for copying and inspection at any reasonable time during business hours.
6. Did you, subsequent to the above, deliver the policy to the insured and now deceased John Jones?	I did.

(At the time of trial, the widow of course, would corroborate the above by her testimony and identification of her husband's signature).

In connection with proof of death, if the same is denied as not having been received by the insurance company, a Notice to Produce should be served before the date of the trial, and if the defendant fails to produce such notice and proof of death, secondary evidence would have to be introduced. You, as the legal assistant, have the responsibility, therefore, of being sure that the client had notified the insurance company, complying with all the necessary and pre-requisite steps to secure payment of the insurance policy; and if you find that she had, then draft and file the Notice to Produce as indicated above.

Before going to trial, the Notice should be served on opposing counsel, describing in detail the written instrument which he is requested to produce at the trial, stating that in the event of his failure to do so, secondary evidence will be offered. This type of Notice should be sent out at least ten (10) days prior to the date of trial. Thereafter, if opposing counsel fails to produce, plaintiff's counsel can then offer in the Notice to Produce with Proof of Service as evidence.

C. UNLAWFUL DETAINER ACTION

The rule of law is that a tenant cannot, without the prior written consent of the landlord, create a new tenancy by holding over after the expiration of the lease.

Prima facie evidence to establish this right would be the following:

1. Legal capacity to sue—i.e., plaintiff in the action and owner of the property in question;

2. Possession of original lease agreement duly executed by plaintiff and defendant setting forth the rental agreement;

3. Evidence of acceptance of rental agreement and provisions thereof such as witnesses that defendant in fact moved in; mailbox identification; rent receipts for rent paid, etc.;

4. Evidence that defendant stayed in the premises for the period specified such as rent receipts for the past 12 months, etc.

Practical Step-By-Step Procedures for the Legal Assistant

The foregoing establishes the right and the evidence needed to convince the court. Now let us put it into a package.

1. As the first step to get the defendant out of the premises, you prepare and have personally served upon defendant a 30 Day Notice to Quit.

2. If after the 30 days your client advises that the defendant is still in the premises, then you file your Complaint for Unlawful Detainer. Bear in mind that each state may have a different time limitation so you should check your local state codes and rules of court to be sure you are filing these documents in a timely manner.

3. We have found it most helpful to prepare all of the documents at once, holding them in abeyance to be used as needed. This avoids the last-minute rush to get a document prepared and filed before the Statute runs. Your attorney would appreciate this extra effort on your part and it would save you a lot of wracked nerves.

4. In most states the defendant would have ten (10) days in which to answer a complaint for unlawful detainer, some states now make it thirty (30) days. In any event, the default procedure or preparation for trial thereafter is the same as with any other litigation.

D. ELEMENTS OF EVIDENCE AS TO WITNESSES

The major portion of any courtroom testimony is from the "mouths of" lay witnesses with a few "experts" thrown in. It is for this reason that the laws of evidence are extremely strict when accepting or not accepting what a witness states as to the facts of case. We will merely hit the highlights of the various facets of lay and expert witness testimony but will delve into detail how you produce these witnesses at a trial.

There are two major rules governing witness testimony—*competency* and *privilege*. These are further broken down into 10 or 12 subdivisions which we do not believe have significance to a legal assistant on a job situation.

A. *Competency:* As a general rule any and every person is qualified to be a witness and no one is disqualified to testify in any matter.

1. *Disqualification* of witness must be based on a statutory ground. *Example:* one who is incapable of understanding the duty of a witness to tell the truth; or one who is incapable of expressing himself concerning the subject matter as to be understood either through interpretation or otherwise. However, with a statutory provision, competency of witness to testify is a matter to be determined by the court and depends solely upon his (the witness') capacity to understand the oath and to perceive, remember and communicate that which he remembers.

2. *Personal knowledge of witness*—Even if a witness is competent, he or she can only testify to facts of his or her personal knowledge. And personal knowledge has been defined as "a present recollection of an impression derived from the exercise of the witnesses' own senses." [2 *Wigmore, Evidence,* Section 657 (1940)]. This being true, then any testimony by a witness that is outside of his personal knowledge would be inadmissible.

Therefore, the testimony of any witness must meet the following test:

a. He must be able to testify so as to be understood;

b. He must understand the nature and responsibility of the oath administered, and

c. He must have personal knowledge of the facts to which he is giving testimony (this statement is not true of an expert witness).

Let us skip to the next big category of restrictions:

B. *Privileges*

The reasons for invoking privileges as to witness testimony were for matters of public policy; stable social order and for religious reasons. That is why today anything said between an attorney and his client is considered "privileged information" or between the minister and his parishioner, priest and a penitent person; and why a wife (or husband) cannot be forced to testify against her husband (his wife). As you can see then, the mere fact that a witness is competent to testify does not mean that everything the witness has to say or knows can be inquired into.

When you get into the area of a witness "taking the Fifth" or refusing to testify because of some privilege, no presumption of guilt or innocence arises from the exercise of this privilege; and the fact that a witness has claimed the same cannot be used against him in any way.

The major and general provisions relating to privileges are as follows: (Your state may have other statutory privileges, you might check them if necessary.)

1. No privileges exist except those established by statute.

2. A privilege is waived unless raised at the earliest practical moment.

3. No one is permitted to comment on a person's invoking of a privilege.

4. Certain types of communications are presumed to be confidential and the party attacking the privilege has the burden of producing evidence of nonconfidentiality.

5. The trial court may require disclosure of the allegedly privileged matter in chambers.

To demonstrate some of the above, let us take an actual case situation and see how all this fits.

Statement of Facts

John Jones, was a visitor at the home of one Frank Williams, along with Harvey Evans and Earl Smith. While at the home of Frank Williams, they were served several drinks. During the course of the evening, several girls came in and there were more drinks served. Later in the evening, when everyone was in high spirits, John Jones, it is alleged, made some improper advances to Mrs. Williams. An argument ensued between Jones and Williams and there were some fisticuffs—however, Evans and Smith succeeded in separating the combatants, and Jones left the house.

Later Jones returned and was readmitted to the house. The prior tension between Williams and Jones still existed and made the other remaining guests uneasy. Shortly after his arrival Jones approached Williams and stated that he, Jones, did not like the way he was being treated and thereupon pulled a pistol from his pocket and shot Williams. Williams was rushed to the hospital and was pronounced "dead on arrival." Jones was arrested and charged with murder.

Let us say for discussion that you are now a legal assistant in a criminal law office and have received the above facts from the client. A cursory review of the facts indicated that the testimony of the witnesses to the alleged murder is going to be crucial. What do you look for? What documents do you prepare?

The character witness. In the case at hand, the defense may call character witnesses for the purpose of showing the general reputation of the accused, but the testimony of the character witness is confined to the reputation the party bears in his own community—where he lives and is personally known to the people at the time of the act.

So you look for evidence to support the fact that "John Jones, was a visitor"; and then "several girls came in" indicating that he was not personally known by them and he did not live in the community.

The reason—a person's reputation in some place distant from one's home is not admissible. The witnesses must have had an opportunity for observation of the habits and manner of life of the accused, which makes the character witness competent to form an opinion.

Character of the accused. As a general proposition of law, the character of a person cannot be shown for the purpose of proving his conduct. The exception to this rule allows the accused in a criminal case to prove such traits of character as tend to make it improbable that he would or could have committed the crime charged.

Therefore, search and find character witnesses who can testify to his good character in the community where he resides and works.

The expert witness. In the instant case, the testimony of the doctor who attended the deceased and pronounced his death would be necessary in the determination of the cause of death of the deceased. However, before expert evidence can be given, the one proposed to give the evidence must be qualified to testify as to his knowledge and his opinion in the case for the benefit and guidance of the jury. The expert witness must be qualified before he is permitted to testify. There is a distinction between "expert testimony" as to Fact and "expert testimony."

One embraces persons by reason of special opportunity for observation (like the doctor who pronounced John Jones DOA) who are therefore able to judge the nature and effect of certain matters better than persons who have not had opportunity for similar and like observation.

Further example: A person of ordinary intelligence, who is accustomed to seeing automobiles travel at various rates of speed, may testify as to the speed of an ordinary automobile. These witnesses are not really experts in the strict sense of the word, but are only *specially qualified witnesses.* This point is made to direct your attention to the possibility of the "doctor who pronounced John Doe DOA." Was he an intern? What is his professional background? What type of expert? This would be your evidence research to possibly negate his testimony.

The other class embraces those persons who by reason of a special course of training or education are qualified to give an opinion in certain matters of a peculiar nature and value—a value much greater than persons not specially trained on the subject, for example, speed of a 500 Indianapolis racing car as opposed to the speed of an ordinary automobile, i.e., Volkswagen.

How many cases of "dead on arrival" had the doctor handled? Was this his first case? What are his qualifications to make the judgment?

Deposition of a witness. In the statement of facts given, Earl Smith, a witness to the shooting is a student at the University of Buffalo at New York and by virtue of that fact will be physically unable to give oral testimony in the case. In situations of this kind where a witness is physically, mentally or for some other adverse reason incapable of attendance at a trial, the party for whom he is to testify is permitted to take his testimony by deposition; provided, however, that the person against whom the evidence is to be given has the opportunity to cross-examine the witness when the examination is taken.

In this connection, the deposition would be arranged either by way of a stipulation between the parties; or by way of Notice of the Taking of Deposition so that opposing counsel has an opportunity to arrange for said deposition or oppose the taking of same. For this reason, the Notice of Taking Deposition should be prepared and mailed to opposing counsel at least (and no less) than ten (10) days prior to the date of the taking of the deposition, i.e., if you plan to take the witness' deposition on May 18, 19—, then the Notice, with proof of service, should be mailed out by May 8, 19—. If the statute requires that it be a thirty-(30) day notice, then if the date is May 18, 19—, the Notice should be mailed out April 18, 19—.

CHAPTER 11

Trial Preparation and Procedure

This chapter discusses the practical duties of the paralegal before a trial begins. It covers the steps to be taken before the trial is opened. It includes gathering and assembling actual evidence and the preparation of the numerous procedural witness interviews.

It must be remembered that some trials are held without a jury. In such case, the judge hears the case and decides both the facts and the law.

In some states a party must demand a jury trial in a civil case if he wants one. If that is so, the jury trial may be demanded in writing at the end of a pleading or a separate demand for jury trial may be filed. Check your court rules.

In other states a jury trial, even in a civil case, is held unless it is waived (just as in a criminal case).

When a case is at issue (all necessary pleadings have been filed) and all pretrial motions have been disposed of and discovery has been completed, either party may have the case set for trial.

The legal secretary or paralegal usually prepares and files the necessary formal request to the court to set a trial date. Check your court rules for the exact procedure.

Your manual form file or your electronic form retrieval system will contain the standard form for setting either a jury trial or a nonjury trial.

Most courts set a pretrial conference date before the actual trial date.

When the pretrial court requires a pretrial conference memorandum, a knowledgeable legal assistant is invaluable to the attorney.

Such a memo usually requires a statement of the party's contended facts, lists of witnesses' names and addresses, lists of exhibits that will be offered as evidence, and any requests for preliminary rulings of law.

The legal assistant is familiar with both the facts and the law of the case by the time the case reaches the pretrial stage if she has been performing the practical duties described in this chapter up to that time.

GENERAL DUTIES OF A LEGAL ASSISTANT IN TRIAL PREPARATION

1. Acquisition and organization of trial materials (documentary and demonstrative evidence);
2. Interviewing client(s) and witnesses (make notes and relay attorney's instructions);
3. Setting up or arranging the files;
   a. Court document file (pleadings, motions, orders)
   b. Law memoranda file
   c. Evidence file (documentary evidence)
   d. Indexing of file contents
   e. Cross-referencing of file contents
   f. Making sure the file is up to date (this applies to the correspondence file as well as the aforementioned portions of the client file for this case)

STEP-BY-STEP PROCEDURE TO COMMENCE A TRIAL

1. Request the court for a trial date by filing the appropriate document with the court, with a copy to opposing counsel;
2. Upon receipt of the trial date from the clerk of the court, mark it on your desk calendar, on the pertinent case file folder, the office master calendar, and the trial attorney's calendar (2 a. If your court sets a pretrial date, do the same for that);
3. Advise the client of the trial date and set up an appointment for the client to come in for an office pretrial conference with the attorney

(3 a. If your court sets a pretrial date, it usually does not require or allow the client to be present in the pretrial conference but it usually requests that the client be immediately available to approve or refuse any settlement offer);

4. Advise any witnesses, including experts, of the date, and at the same time, mail to them the appropriate witness fees, if applicable;

5. If applicable, post your jury bond.

6. It is always nice, though not necessary, to also send out a notice of trial to the opposing counsel, if you are the plaintiff.

7. Depending on the nature of your case and your rules of court, the following are some of the documents you, as a legal assistant, might prepare in advance on the word processor for possible use by your attorney for trial:

   a. Written requests for jury instructions to be requested in the case (ask the attorney what special ones he wants). Use full captions of the case and title—Request for Jury Instructions.

   b. Defendant's first-time motion for nonsuit, motion, to dismiss, or for directed verdict if your court requires those motions to be in writing. (If required and prepared, use the full caption of the case and the appropriate motion title.)

   Note: There was a time when the preparation of the latter documents would have been a staggering undertaking, but with the advent of the word processor, you can now merely retrieve a case that has similar facts and circumstances, review it, and then customize it to fit your current needs. But be sure that you run an automatic citation check to obtain current case law, if you have access to a terminal.

8. Type questions to the jury (this just may be a list of questions on a plain sheet containing an abbreviated name of the case).

9. Coordinate activities relevant to the trial, such as: (1) appointment with witnesses prior to trial and (2) preparation of a profile of witnesses and their testimony;

10. Organize and index the evidence folder;

11. Prepare and locate exhibits;

12. Prepare the trial book;

13. Prepare and organize your investigation file;

14. Assist your attorney in preparing his opening and final arguments, if he desires such help, such as outlining both the plaintiff's and defendant's case from a daily transcript of the court record if it is available; if not, order it.

GATHERING AND ASSEMBLING EVIDENCE AND FILES FOR USE DURING TRIAL

EXHIBIT (EVIDENCE) FOLDER

It has been our experience that an "exhibit folder" (evidence folder) should be immediately made up for each client's file and original documents should be labeled and indexed and placed therein as they come in. This is true even if the case is a simple one, and it is mandatory in a very complex lawsuit. Your attorney must be able to find a document quickly and easily at any given point in the prosecution or defense of the action.

We have found the following procedure to be most helpful in preserving documentary evidence:

1. Maintain the original of any potential exhibit in the exhibit folder with a copy to the (1) evidence file and (2) chronological file folders.

2. Each document (or other type of exhibit) should be dated.

3. Note the source of exhibit either by stapling or clipping to the copy thereof. *Never* mark or clip the original.

4. Divide into categories, that is, purchase orders, contracts, tax returns, medical reports, and so forth. If it is a matter involving personal injury or malpractice, then you should of course set up a separate medical file with a further division into plaintiff and defendant medical reports, depositions, witnesses testimony, and the like.

5. Before the actual trial the exhibit folder (evidence folder) should be reorganized and placed in chronological order by subject matter and should be clearly marked (modern self-stick notes are a simple means of doing this). Whatever the method, *explain it to the attorney.* You may use an index or tab system.

Any clear system should save the attorney from an embarrassing search for documents during the trial.

PLEADING FOLDER

A separate folder for each case should contain the following:

1. Plaintiff's pleadings and motions and a separation division for defendant's pleadings and motions;
2. Summary of the allegations of the complaint;
3. Summary of the answer and affirmative defenses;
4. Summary of your plaintiff's reply, if any;
5. Summary of issues left to be tried;
6. Summary of facts to be proven at the time of trial.

TRIAL BRIEF OR TRIAL BOOK

A trial brief, if applicable (full-blown or issue) may be prepared. It could be placed in a separate folder with a list of any information about the jury panel and the list of *voir dire* questions.

In large law firms, the trial attorney may be given a "trial book" prepared according to specified firm instructions. It may be quite elaborate—color coded, indexed, and so forth.

A witness folder should contain:

1. Separate statements about each individual witness;
2. Any notes taken at an interview of a witness;
3. Any investigation reports;
4. Summary of any deposition; or
5. Statements made by a witness, and so forth.

The witness information would usually be included in the trial book. This has been covered previously.

A legal research folder for use during trial should contain:

1. Case or statute citations in support of your attorney's position on evidentiary or other trial matters;
2. Case or statute citations opposing any evidentiary matter your opponent may raise.

ALTERNATIVE METHODS OF RESOLVING A LITIGATION DISPUTE

The most common non-adversarial methods of resolving Court litigation are: (1) negotiation; (2) conciliation; (3) mediation; (4) mini-trials; (5) private judges; and (6) arbitration.

This section will deal with a step-by-step procedure for initiating and conducting arbitration.

Elements prerequisite to filing for arbitration:

1. Whether the arbitration award could exceed $25,000;

2. Time elapsed since complaint was filed; if close to five years, arbitration is advisable;

3. Investigation and discovery is complete and has been completed 15 days prior to the requested hearing date;

4. Documentary evidence available to support monetary award; and

5. Time required for arbitration hearing.

After the attorney has made the determination that the case is a candidate for arbitration, either via "Election for Arbitration" or "Stipulation for Arbitration," the following steps should be implemented:

1. Prepare appropriate letter to the Arbitration Committee/Administrator;

2. File Election/Stipulation re Arbitration;

3. Prepare *final* discovery (15 days prior to hearing) documents; then

4. Mail Notice of Intention to Introduce Documentary Evidence (25 days prior to hearing date);

5. Work with Arbitrator/Administrator re hearing date;

6. Prepare/mail Notice of Arbitration Hearing Date;

7. File Demand for List (Exchange) of Experts;

Determine from the Attorney

8. Length of time for hearing, if the liability of defendant is clear, and amount to settle. File Arbitration Trial Brief.

FOLLOW-UP PROCEDURES

1. By law, the Arbitrator is supposed to file the award within a ten-day period after the hearing. So, calendar this date.

2. Upon receipt of the Award, if it is not acceptable, file a Request for Trial within 20 days with the appropriate Court. THIS MAY NOT BE EXTENDED.

Or, in the alternative,

3. File an Application to Correct the Award, if needed, within ten days *after* receipt of the Award.

And/or—then,

4. A Motion to Vacate Judgment Entered is appropriate, and must be made within six months *after* Entry of Judgment under Rule 1615(d); *C.C.P.* 1286.2(a)(b)(c).

Note: The above and following are based on California procedure and should be checked and compared with your own state's trial procedure and court rules.

ATTORNEYS AT LAW
A PROFESSIONAL CORPORATION

Attorneys for Defendant

SUPERIOR COURT OF THE STATE OF CALIFORNIA
FOR THE COUNTY OF LOS ANGELES

_____ ,	]	CASE NO. C _____
Plaintiffs,	]	ARBITRATION BRIEF
	]	OF DEFENDANT
vs.	]	
	]	
_____ ,	]	DATE: October 17, 19___
	]	TIME: 4:00 p.m.
	]	LOCATION: Room 218
Defendants.	]	
_____	]	

STATEMENT OF THE FACTS

On October 23, 19___, plaintiff _____ injured the tip of his left middle finger at _____ by placing it in the doorjamb of the manager's office door. His parents, _____, voluntarily dismissed their claims for emotional distress caused by the witnessing of this incident.

On the date of the incident, plaintiffs had entered the store for the purposes of collecting what they believed to be their winnings in a Bingo Contest sponsored by the _____. They affixed their game pieces to a place card on a telephone booth ledge next to the manager's office. During this time, Mr. _____ entered and exited the subject door at least two times, the door thus closing at least four times in the presence of the plaintiff and his parents.

The door in question has an automatic closure mechanism. It cannot be manually slammed. When Mr. _____ entered the office door for a third time, plaintiff stuck his finger in the hinge side of the doorjamb where it was crushed by the closing door.

The plaintiff was treated at Kaiser Permanente Hospital by Dr. _____. His medical bills total $310.00.

CONTENTION OF THE PARTIES

Plaintiffs contend that _____ was _____ negligent through its employee, _____, by allowing the subject door to shut upon the plaintiff's finger.

Defendant contends that it is not liable for the plaintiff's injuries as plaintiff knew the dangers inherent by a closing door and further, the plaintiff's parents failed to exercise the proper, reasonable and necessary parental guidance in supervising their son.

STATEMENT OF THE LAW

As a general rule, owners and possessors of commercial property must exercise reasonable care in maintaining their premises in a safe condition for all purposes invited onto those premises. *Restatement* 2d, Torts, Section 283. The duty of care is not violated, however, where the condition is so obvious that it serves as a warning in and of itself, unless the harm was foreseeable despite the obvious nature of the danger. 4 Witken, *Summary of California Law* 2863, Section 594. Defendants have found no cases which classify a door with a closing mechanism as a dangerous condition. To place such a burden upon commercial landowners would render the effective operation of any business impossible.

In his deposition at page 27, line 18 through page 28, line 3, plaintiff stated that he was aware of a family member who had caught her finger in a car door four years prior to this incident. Thus, it appears that plaintiff assumed the risk or was comparatively negligent for his injuries. California *Civil Code* Section 1719. Additionally, his parents should be negligent for their failure to properly supervise their son. *Smith* v. *American Motor Lodge* (1974) 39 Cal. App. 3d.

EVIDENCE

Pursuant to California *Rules of Court*, Rule 1613, defendant has given notice of its intention to introduce documentary evidence at the Arbitration hearing. A copy of that notice was served and filed concurrently with this Brief.

DATED: September 21, 19__

_____

A PROFESSIONAL CORPORATION

BY _____

_____
Attorney for Defendant,

_____

ATTORNEYS AT LAW
A PROFESSIONAL CORPORATION

Attorneys for Defendant

SUPERIOR COURT OF THE STATE OF CALIFORNIA
FOR THE COUNTY OF LOS ANGELES

_____ ,	]	CASE NO. C _____
Plaintiffs,	]	NOTICE OF INTENTION TO
	]	INTRODUCE DOCUMENTARY EVIDENCE
vs.	]	AT ARBITRATION HEARING
	]	
_____ ,		DATE: October 17, 19__
		TIME: 4:00 p.m.
Defendants.	]	LOCATION: Room 218
_____]		

TO PLAINTIFF, _____ AND TO HIS ATTORNEY OF RECORD:
PLEASE TAKE NOTICE that, pursuant to California Rules of Court, Rule 1613, that defendant, _____, intends to introduce the following documents into evidence at the Arbitration hearing set on October 17, 19__, at 4:00 p.m. in Room 218 of this Court, located at 111 North Hill Street in Los Angeles:

1. The Declaration of No Records from Kaiser Permanente Hospital;
2. Plaintiff's Medical Records from Kaiser Permanente Medical Group;
3. Plaintiff's Medical Records from _____, M.D.;
4. Deposition transcripts and Interrogatory responses of _____, _____ and _____ as necessary for impeachment purposes.

DATED: _____, 19__

                            _____
                            A PROFESSIONAL CORPORATION

                            BY _____

                            _____
                            Attorney for Defendant,

                            _____

SUPERIOR COURT OF THE STATE OF CALIFORNIA
FOR THE COUNTY OF LOS ANGELES

_____,	]	CASE NO. _____
	]	
Plaintiff,	]	ORDER RE FINAL
	]	STATUS CONFERENCE
vs.	]	
	]	RULE 1106.5
_____,	]	
Defendant.	]	
_____	]	

All counsel must be present and comply with the following prior to trial and *at the Final Status Conference.*

1. MOTIONS IN LIMINE

All motions in limine must be in writing and served on opposing party and the Court fifteen (15) days prior to the Final Status Conference. Any opposition to the motions in limine must be in writing and submitted to opposing counsel and Court five (5) days prior to the Final Status Conference.

2. JURY INSTRUCTIONS

All requested jury instructions must be submitted to the Court at the Final Status Conference. Standard printed BAJI instructions should not be retyped. All blanks should be filled in appropriately and all inapplicable material deleted.

3. STATEMENT OF THE CASE AND CAUSES OF ACTION

a. All counsel must file a short statement of the case (no more than three paragraphs) to be read to the jury indicating the nature of the litigation and a statement of the facts. This is to be presented at the final status conference.

b. A separate statement shall be filed with the Court at the final status conference indicating by name and number the precise causes of action on which the plaintiff and cross-complainants actually intend to proceed to trial. This statement shall include the names and numbers of abandoned causes of action.

c. Defendants and cross-defendants shall specify by name and number the affirmative defenses on which they will actually proceed to trial and the affirmative defenses which are being abandoned.

4. TRIAL BRIEFS

All trial briefs shall be limited to fifteen (15) pages and shall be filed at the final status conference.

5. VOIR DIRE

Counsel shall submit to the Court, in writing, a list of voir dire questions counsel requests the Court to ask and questions counsel plans to use.

6. STIPULATED FACTS

Counsel shall meet prior to the Final Status Conference and prepare a list of facts which are not in dispute for the trial.

7. WITNESS LISTS

Each side shall prepare a list of the names of all witnesses, the order in which they will be called, the nature of their testimony and the anticipated length of their testimony.

8. EVIDENTIARY ISSUES

Specify in writing any major evidentiary issues anticipated, along with any points and authorities intended to be submitted on any of these issues.

9. EXHIBITS

a. Provide a complete list of exhibits on the Court's form listing each document and item of physical evidence pre-numbered.

b. During trial, each exhibit shall be pre-marked in the morning before the jury arrives.

c. During trial, all exhibits shall be offered at the close of one's case unless a foundational argument is anticipated.

10. DEPOSITIONS

All original depositions shall be lodged at the Final Status Conference.

DATED:

_____

_____

JUDGE OF THE SUPERIOR COURT

"FAST TRACK LITIGATION" (CALIFORNIA)

In California, the Courts have adopted what is called Trial Court Delay Reduction, commonly called "Fast Track Litigation."

The purpose of the initiation of the Fast Track Litigation procedure is determined by and is based upon the need to motivate trial Courts to implement rules to remove the backlog in the hearing of civil trial litigation.

The rules and regulations governing this Fast Track Litigation are the *Government Code* and the California *Code of Civil Procedure.*

Some of the key definitions utilized in this procedure are the "I/C Judge," whose duties are the handling of cases on an individual calendar and/or on an all-purpose calendar.

"M/C Judge" are those judges who would continue handling cases on direct assignment from Department 1.

The complaints filed in a Fast Track Litigation procedure are served within 60 days of filing, and a proof of service should be filed within 65 days of said filing.

Cross-complaints, without a leave of Court first being obtained, may not be filed by any party after the at-issue memorandum has been filed; or after the expiration of the deadline as set forth in the Rules.

The At-Issue Memorandum should be filed not later than 140 days of the filing of the complaint.

As it relates to discovery, all discovery should be completed not later than 180 days after the filing of the at-issue memorandum.

With reference to pleadings and motions, all answers shall be filed and served within 30 days of service of the complaint and cross-complaint, unless a motion or demurrer to such pleading has been filed within the statutory period.

In the event that a motion or demurrer is filed, the Court will, upon hearing of the motion or demurrer, make appropriate orders regarding the filing of further pleadings.

Any extensions are granted by the Court upon a showing of good cause, but the parties may not obtain any extensions by a stipulation.

As to the Notice of Status Conference, it is substantially the same as with other existing cases and shall be sent to the plaintiff following the filing of the at-issue memorandum. This notice shall be sent out by the clerk not more than 15 days after the filing of said at-issue memorandum and shall schedule the status conference at a time chosen by the assigned I/C Judge, but in no event later than 45 days after the filing of the at-issue memorandum.

Thereafter, the Court may refer appropriate cases to judicial arbitration.

Please note that where the Court determines that there is a possibility that the plaintiff will not obtain a judgment in excess of $25,000, it may consider, with a counsel stipulation for an amendment to the complaint, transfer of the case to the Municipal Court.

The Court shall set a Mandatory Settlement Conference and shall determine whether it is appropriate for the I/C Judge to hear and determine the MSC.

As to the setting of trial dates, this is done by the Court as soon as it determines the appropriate time of completion of reasonable discovery and other pre-trial preparation and is set in accordance with the *California Rules of Court* and in accordance with priorities authorized and mandated by law.

100-DAYS BEFORE TRIAL CHECKLIST

Name of Case: _____

Case Number: _____

Court and County: _____

Trial Date: _____

Date of Trial Setting Conference: _____

Date of Settlement Conference: _____

Last date of Discovery: _____
(30-days before trial date; Motions until 15-days
 before trial date —CCP, Section 224 (a), CRC,
Rule 333.)   _____
Any further investigation needed:
Notification to client/referring attorney:
Date completed: _____

Conference with client: _____

(Date scheduled)

Prepare a schedule of witnesses/phone
   numbers: _____

Preparation of Subpoenas and Subpoenas
　　Duces Tecum:
　　　　　　　　　　　　　　　　　　　　　＿＿＿＿＿＿＿＿＿＿＿＿＿

Notification of witnesses/experts re trial date:　＿＿＿＿＿＿＿＿＿＿＿＿＿

(Referencing weeks)

Jury Trial?
　　　　　　　　　　　　　　　　　　　　　＿＿＿＿＿＿＿＿＿＿＿＿＿

Has it been requested?
　　　　　　　　　　　　　　　　　　　　　＿＿＿＿＿＿＿＿＿＿＿＿＿

Have fees been paid?
　　　　　　　　　　　　　　　　　　　　　＿＿＿＿＿＿＿＿＿＿＿＿＿

(14-days before trial)

Have copies of Depositions been ordered?　＿＿＿＿＿＿＿＿＿＿＿＿＿

Demand for Inspection of Documents:　　　＿＿＿＿＿＿＿＿＿＿＿＿＿
Compliance in Response to Demand
for Inspection of Documents:　　　　　　＿＿＿＿＿＿＿＿＿＿＿＿＿

(20-days after service of Demand)

Last day to serve Cross-Questions to
　　written Depositions:
　　　　　　　　　　　　　　　　　　　　　＿＿＿＿＿＿＿＿＿＿＿＿＿

(15-days after service)

Last day to serve redirect questions re
　　written Depositions:
　　　　　　　　　　　　　　　　　　　　　＿＿＿＿＿＿＿＿＿＿＿＿＿

(15-days after service)

Last day to serve and file objections to
　　form of any question:
　　　　　　　　　　　　　　　　　　　　　＿＿＿＿＿＿＿＿＿＿＿＿＿

(15-days after service)

Last day to furnish Interrogatories or
　　Response to any person not heretofore
　　served, who has made a written request
　　for same:
　　　　　　　　　　　　　　　　　　　　　＿＿＿＿＿＿＿＿＿＿＿＿＿
Demand for physical and/or mental
　　examination of a party:
　　　　　　　　　　　　　　　　　　　　　＿＿＿＿＿＿＿＿＿＿＿＿＿

(Schedule exam at least 30-
days after service of De-
mand)

Response to Demand for physical or
  mental examination: _____

                                           (20-days after service of De-
                                           mand)

Depositions: _____

Prepare Request for Admissions: _____
Prepare list for exchange of expert
  witness information: _____
Make Demand for exchange of information concerning trial witnesses: _____

                                           (90-days before trial date)

Election for Arbitration filed: _____

Statement of Damages received: _____

Prepare pre-trial statement, if applicable: _____

Prepare Exhibits and evidence: _____

Is legal research completed?   _____

Prepare draft of Trial Brief, if applicable: _____

Last date to disqualify judge: _____

Prepare and submit Jury Instructions: _____

Prepare outline for voir dire questions: _____

Prepare Case Summary: _____

Prepare any Motions in Limine: _____

OVERVIEW OF IN-COURT TRIAL PROCEDURES

Under our system of justice the parties, plaintiff and defendant, have a right to have a trial either by a judge with a jury or trial before the judge alone.

The following is the procedure of a court trial sitting with a jury:

1. The first thing occurring in a trial with a jury is that the jury is selected and sworn in. At some point in time, your attorney may ask you to prepare what is called Voir Dire questions utilized in selecting those persons who will be sitting on jury.

2. Then the opening statements of plaintiff and defense counsels. These are outlines of what the parties will show by the evidence which would be introduced at the time the trial begins.

3. Witnesses are examined by the question and answer method. After direct examination, the opposing counsel is given the opportunity to cross-examine the witness. During these two procedures, objections may be made to the questions or the answers by either party.

4. At the conclusion of the plaintiff's case (evidence and witnesses testimony), defendant may move for a NON-SUIT or for a DIRECTED VERDICT in his favor. This Motion may be made on the grounds of insufficient evidence. If the defendant is successful in his Motion, the trial terminates at this point.

If, however, the defendant does not make one of the above Motions, or either of them is overruled, the defendant will present his evidence in the same manner as did the plaintiff. And again, at the end of the defendant's presentation of his evidence, the plaintiff may move for a directed verdict. It should be noted that the defendant may again make a Motion for a non-suit or directed verdict; or make his first Motion at the end of his case.

If, in the discretion of the court, the court does not grant either party's Motion, the case will be submitted to the jury. At this point counsels for both parties have the opportunity to give their closing arguments prior to the court giving its instructions to the jury.

5. At this point counsels for both parties have an opportunity to request the court to "charge the jury" in a particular manner as it relates to interpretations of the law as applicable to a given set of facts and/or exhibits which have been entered into evidence.

After hearing the closing arguments of both counsels and receiving instructions from the court, the jury retires to consider its verdict.

6. Upon reaching its decision, the jury can give a verdict for the plaintiff or defendant and state the amount. This is known as **GENERAL VERDICT**. If, on the other hand, the jury reports the facts only and leaves to the trial court the application of the law, this is called a **SPECIAL VERDICT**.

7. At this point either party can file a Motion for a New Trial. The grounds can be either based on error of the court; or that the verdict is excessive or inadequate or contrary to the weight of the evidence.

Other Motions which can be heard at this time are entitled Motions for Judgment Notwithstanding a Verdict, normally made by a plaintiff; and Motion in Arrest of Judgment normally filed by a defendant. These Motions are really in the nature of postponed Demurrers.

If none of the above Motions is granted, the court will enter judgment in accord with the verdict.

8. Thereafter, a **WRIT OF EXECUTION** is prepared which commands the Sheriff to attach the property of the defeated party, sell it and satisfy the judgment out of the proceeds.

However, the losing party may desire to carry the case to the Appellate Court and hence would file a Notice of Appeal which would require the preparation of **BRIEFS** directed to the Appellate Court. In this connection be aware that there are basically only three Briefs which are filed in the Appellate Court System:

(a) The Appellant's Opening Brief.
(b) The Respondent's Reply Brief.
(c) Rebuttal Brief.

Note: The trial before a judge alone would follow the same general sequence.

PROGRESS OF A CASE THROUGH TRIAL AND APPEAL

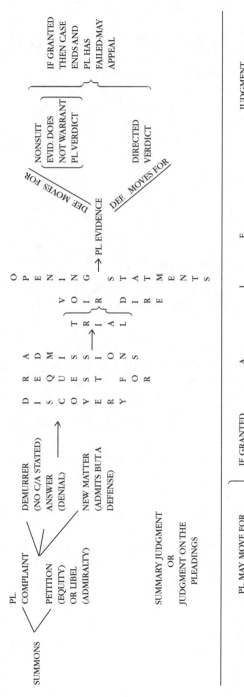

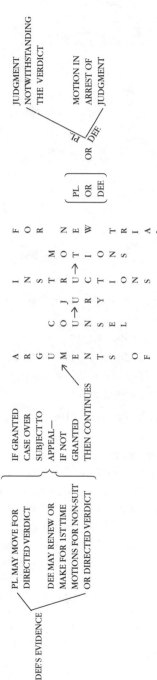

PL> – PLAINTIFF
DEF. – DEFENDANT

CHAPTER 12

Electronic Trial Preparation Procedures

COMPLEX LITIGATION

Basically, complex litigation consists of three important variables:

1. Multiple parties;
2. Multiple causes of action, as in a multiple party incident, wherein you have one or more plaintiffs and one or more defendants and cross-complaints and
3. A series of cases wherein issues of each are the same.

For example (but not limited thereto), a traffic accident involving multiple cars resulting in multiple injuries and/or multiple deaths; or an antitrust lawsuit wherein a small business is attempting to enjoin a large corporation from performing an act or acts that would prevent the small business from competing fairly in the marketplace; or to break up the monopoly of a large business in order that small businesses could compete successfully in the open market; or the "class action" suit like *David Darr* v. *Yellow Cab.*

PROBLEMS INHERENT IN COMPLEX LITIGATION

1. Administration of complex litigation can be a nightmare. The key to successful management and to insurance of an ultimate win of such litigation, is organization.

EXAMPLE

a. When you have an attorney attempting to handle, process and otherwise deal with 10,000 sheets (or more) of paper; and/or

b. Where you have different attorneys trying to handle the same 10,000 sheets (or more) of paper without communication and status report as to who is working on what.

2. A very real problem in complex litigation for the legal assistant develops where the plaintiff is a cross-complainant and is served with interrogatories and/or requests for admissions. How do you answer them? The conflict is obvious since, if you answer yes as the plaintiff, as the cross-defendant you would be saying no. *Caution, caution* is the name of the game, and consultation with your attorney is mandatory.

3. Another real problem in complex litigation for the legal assistant is documentation processing: how to

    a. Handle voluminous documents,

    b. Organize voluminous documents,

    c. Index voluminous documents,

    d. Authenticate voluminous documents,

    e. Code voluminous documents,

    f. Go about retrieving voluminous documents.

4. One of the most important aspects of complex litigation, which could present a real problem if not handled properly, is the awareness, location, and availability of witnesses, expert or otherwise.

VIP HINT

The legal assistant should make sure, far in advance of trial, that key witnesses are available. He should keep the witnesses apprised of the status of the case at all times, either through a status letter or other document, or simply by picking up the phone and talking to them about the case.

More important, the legal assistant should give all the witnesses, expert and otherwise, sufficient advance notice of the date of trial in order that they may plan their schedules to ensure their presence on the day of trial.

Furthermore, as to expert witnesses, the legal assistant should be sure that they have been paid according to their policy and that they have been paid far in advance of the date of trial, to assure their presence and appearance in court.

Note: You should never subpoena a "friendly witness." Have the subpoena, but don't serve it immediately. You inform the witness of the date and time of the trial and hold the subpoena to be served in case of a last-minute foul-up.

OVERALL DUTIES OF THE LEGAL ASSISTANT IN COMPLEX LITIGATION

Many of the principles discussed in this chapter in complex litigation are also applicable to the ordinary litigation. The use of electronic litigation support systems in all law offices, large and small, is increasing.

CHECKLIST OF OVERALL DUTIES OF THE LEGAL ASSISTANT WORKING WITH COMPLEX LITIGATION

1. Maintaining the file organization and preparing indexes and subindexes;
2. Coping with large amounts of accumulated evidentiary materials;
3. Researching and organizing data which will require quick retrieval of documents, and so forth;
4. Preparing and/or answering interrogatories and preparing for witness depositions taken by the other side;
5. Preparing for witness interviews and for taking depositions;
6. Controlling and organizing documents, which involves the preparation of summaries and subject matter, parties to the action, issues involved, and the like;
7. Controlling and organizing depositions, which may include the preparation of summaries, locating and indexing testimony for exhibits, preparation of exhibit list, and so forth.

ELECTRONIC LITIGATION SUPPORT SYSTEMS

The main purpose of the "litigation support system" (LSS), is to aid the attorney in the practice of his profession. This can be considered the primary reason why the use of computerized litigation support systems are a necessity in law offices that have an abundance of complex litigation lawsuits and why they are increasing rapidly in offices where litigation is on a simpler scale.

With the regular use of the litigation support system the attorney (and his legal assistant) is relieved of many time-consuming tasks. Furthermore, it frees the attorney to crystallize or slim-line the substantive issues. Additionally, it gives him time to plan the proper strategy to be used in trial preparation and presentation.

Moreover, attorneys have discovered that a computerized litigation support system is a means of (but not limited to) controlling exhibits during the trial of complex litigation, of locating and identifying exhibits or parts thereof, as well as the time and place of the appearance of the exhibit in the proceeding, and of locating relevant testimony, such as at what page and line in a transcript of an exhibit theretofore entered or in the testimony of a witness it can be found.

A law office may have its own litigation support system and/or subscribe to one of the commercial litigation support systems described later.

FUNCTION OF LSS

The primary function of a litigation support system is storage and retrieval. A computerized legal information retrieval system is, among other things, more than another research tool.

Note: It should be noted that litigation support systems do not replace judgment. The researcher (legal assistant) must evaluate and analyze the cases as to their relevancy and importance to the project.

Information readily available by use of a commercial litigation support system, such as those provided by Lexis and Westlaw, include the following:

1. Judicial searches;
2. Letter opinions;
3. Legislative searches;
4. Jury verdicts;
5. Judges and their record histories;
6. Citation of cases;
7. Dates of cases;
8. Judgments;
9. Documents by number;
10. Trial litigants, and so forth.

BENEFITS OF LSS

The prime benefits of any electronic litigations support system are as follows:

1. To ensure a complete, thorough review and search of documents available;
2. To expand the scope of the search to assure the complete efforts of the legal assistant;
3. To save the payroll costs of having a typist or legal assistant do the complex time-consuming legal research and analysis manually:
4. To reduce the time consumed by the legal assistant in performing preliminary legal research projects that seek appropriate legal data, for example, statutes, cases, opinion, and the like;
5. Furthermore, by way of example, litigation support systems make it possible for an attorney or his legal assistant to obtain answers to questions that they were heretofore unable to find in the traditional form of legal research. The Lexis commercial litigation support system, for example, provides the lawyer or his legal assistant, through its judicial segment, a means of determining a judge's previously written opinions relating to the issues involved in his case, prior to oral argument in front of the judge in question.

An in-office electronic litigation support system serves that same function for cases previously handled before local judges if it is programmed that way.

SCOPE OF COMMERCIAL LSS

The legal bibliographies recorded in the commercial litigation support systems include everything from state and federal statutory law, trial court and appellate court opinions, administrative regulations and decisions; to treaties, congressional hearings, municipal codes, restatement, and encyclopedias. Moreover, one can go from jurisdiction to jurisdiction, and from state to state, and if connected to the appropriate terminal or computer base, from country to country.

PRACTICAL USES OF ELECTRONIC LSS

If there is a specific area of legal assistant duties that has been extremely affected by computerized practice of law, it is in the area of trial preparation.

The gathering together of pertinent documents, the preparation of exhibits, the development of exhibits and exhibit books, trial and appellate briefs—all can now be accomplished much more quickly and efficiently through the use of word-processing equipment and other electronic information retrieval systems and equipment. The system may be one programmed for or used in your office, a commercial information retrieval system, or the efficient use and storage of your word processor machine disks, or any combination of those systems.

The use of a computer differs when engaged in a small-scale lawsuit as opposed to the very large litigation process. In small litigation cases, you normally use a computer to make a running tape as to the costs and to keep track of the costs involved in locating or searching for witnesses, expert or otherwise. You may use a manual office law retrieval system to find the law and a simple word processing disk collection to find the appropriate forms for the necessary court documents.

The office computer can best be used to keep track of the time spent by the attorney and the legal assistant in complex litigation. In complex litigation, you may be using the computer in the discovery process, such as indexing depositions of individuals, which can be taken as many as twenty times and that could conceivably be reworded on 2,000 pages.

In complex litigation, the Lexis, Westlaw, and Auto-Cite computers have changed the way legal assistants do legal research or verify citations contained in opposing briefs. Legal assistants may quickly gather information on judges' written opinions; names of lawyers who handled particular reported cases, as well as case law to be used in analyzing cases.

However, since facts are the major aspect of any case, the law pertinent to these facts must be correct and correctly analyzed. This being true, this correctness and analysis have an effect upon the outcome of a case in which your attorney is involved. For this reason the legal assistant still has to do manual editing. The human element of judgment is still needed. See discussion of Computerized Tools of Legal Research in Chapter 8.

The use of the LTMS, IBM 34, WANG, TRS-80, Datapoint, Vydec, and other information or word-processing machines has changed the way the legal assistant prepares lengthy documents; voluminous copies of documents; deducting and retrieving exhibits from these hundreds of documents; arranging, organizing, numbering, and analyzing documents for later use in trial preparation; and in setting up a management system to coordinate complex documents and discovery in complex litigation.

Moreover, with the LTMS system, for example, it is now possible for a legal assistant to sit down with a word processor person and set up a "conflict" and "adverse party" system. The names of all clients are listed in alphabetical order together with the names of other parties to the action, coded and given a number.

These systems may also be used to weed out clients who may already be accepted by the law firm. As a result, when a new client comes into the law firm, he is not accepted as a client until his name has been processed through these systems by way of a field search and visual scan of the office client lists and cross-referenced names.

EXAMPLE

Jane Doe has come into your office for a contract matter, and you want first to determine if there is a conflict of interest involved as to the client, such as whether or not there are any other cases being handled in the office for Jane Doe; or whether Jane Doe is a defendant in another case, and so forth. You can do this, prior to accepting her as a client, through the use of your computer conflict system to prevent any possible malpractice lawsuits or conflict-of-interest problem.

Another example of how many commercial LSS computers have affected the duties of legal assistants is their new capability, through the use of the computer, to determine prior to trial the attitudes expressed in written opinions of the judge before whom their attorney is to appear as they relate to cases like the one at bar. Or, if in your attorney's view the judge is questionable, you are now able to place the name of every judge into your computer system and receive every case that he has tried and his decisions or opinions on the subject matter involved. Such information about the judge's attitudes may make your attorney want to make an exception or cause the judge to be relieved or force him to disqualify himself from hearing and determining the present case.

If you are wondering how this is done, note that many of the commercial LSS are able to give you all the reported cases on which a particular judge has rendered a decision. The recorded dictation in a case lets your attorney know how the judge arrived at the decision, just as though you had found it by reading the case in your case report.

Another plus in the use of these computer systems is the access to the composition of law firms and the names of attorneys who have tried cases similar to the one at bar. In other words, you can now research the opposition.

Moreover, legal assistants are now able to program into this office computer the billing of their hours spent on cases as well as the time their attorney has worked on the case.

Furthermore, your computer can now advise you, particularly in a large law firm, what attorney is working on what case and what cases are related to other cases. This is particularly helpful when you are working on a complex litigation matter.

The preceding are just a few of the ways in which the computerized practice of law has affected the role of the paralegal.

CHOOSING THE APPROPRIATE ELECTRONIC LSS

A. What You Should Know About Word Processing and Data Processing

What is word processing? Simply put, word processing is recording, storing, and retrieving typed material. Word processing is to be distinguished from data processing, which records and manipulates information. Word processing is primarily a typing function.

Data processing is information processing accomplished by putting information into a computer for possible manipulation and later retrieval.

The material for use of a word processor is stored by means of specially treated magnetic computer strips of diskettes (some of which are fixed diskettes and some of which are removable diskettes. You are, however, almost always dealing with a disk of a removable nature, but still in a fixed area). Some computers understand mathematics, and some understand symbols. It depends on the vendor. The data-processing operator will be instructed how to place information into the computer in the language of the computer. A brief glossary of some data-processing terms appears at the end of this chapter before a bibliography on the subject of the use of computers in legal research and litigation.

In other words, operating a data processor is like learning another language. You take something someone says, and this is converted into the language of the computer. Then it is written in specific, logical terminology and changed into the format and language of the computer.

A data-processing system possessing a screen and operating solely as a computer generally has a central computer (data) bank from which various programs can be obtained and/or written. This vehicle has a printer attached to it that will print out such data as letters, documents, and so forth, on a continuous role of paper or on individual sheets of paper. Word-processing units, some of which possess screens similar to that of Lexis, Vydec, Lexitron, and the like but cannot perform computer functions, do not require such a bank because the memory unit is stored within the terminal itself.

B. Standard Word-Processing Machines

Many smaller law offices use standard word-processing machines with or without a computer system. These machines are supersophisticated typewriters. A data processor in itself saves time because it can type, correct, store, and print letters faster than a human being. For example, the average typist can put out possibly fifty to one hundred letters per day, whereas an electronic word processor can put out fifty to one hundred letters in a half hour, if necessary. Furthermore, the work is done more efficiently, can be stored in a space-saving manner, and cuts down on human error.

EXAMPLE

Take the individual who uses shorthand for dictation. This form of note taking could conceivably contain incorrect notes that were incorrectly written down because of lack of coherency, poor enunciation, or poor articulation in the speech of the speaker, and thus misunderstood. This would result in incorrect transposition in typing. On the other hand, with the use of an electronic word processor, one is able to see any errors immediately on the electronic screen and correct them immediately.

Finally, the word processor produces documents (written material) without the anxiety and frustration that normally accompanies meeting deadlines, such as in writing and correcting trial or appellate briefs, complaints, partnership agreements, contracts; or such documents as standard security agreements wherein you can make substitutions and change dates, and so forth, thus cutting down on administrative costs. This factor enhances office productivity, since the word-processing machine can operate by itself once given the command, leaving the legal assistant free to work on other projects requiring her physical presence.

Since most legal documents contain certain standard boilerplate paragraphs and segments, an office word-processing machine is a litigation support system in and of itself. All the legal assistant has to do is to customize the pertinent personal paragraphs in the documents that are on disk to meet the needs of the particular client and court document. She commands the electronic word processor to fill in the appropriate change in the standard paragraphs where needed.

C. On-Line Information Systems and Data Bases

The legal assistant should be aware of both the current in-office litigation support systems being used by law offices, courts, and agencies throughout the country, and also the commercial or outside information systems and data bases. See computerized legal research in Chapter 8.

The "on-line" systems in your office contain information that has been fed into your computer by way of a set of programs (numbers, symbols, phrases, or a combination thereof, and the like) for retrieval at a later date of the specific segments or other information required to complete your project.

Dialog (Lockheed). An example of this type of on-line information system (which can also be used as a litigation support system) is the Dialog (Lockheed). This on-line information system gives you bibliography information, directory, and statistical data bases. In addition, it provides scientific and technical information, as well as information in the social sciences, arts and humanities, business and finance, current affairs, and the television and newspaper media.

STEP-BY-STEP PROCEDURE FOR USING THE DIALOG SYSTEM

1. Select a subject, term, name of person, place or organization;
2. Combine two or more of these terms to narrow or broaden your search output:
3. Push the print-out button on your search while on-line;
4. Review through the subject terms as set forth. (Note: These subjects are alphabetically arranged.)
5. Check for related subjects in the on-line thesauri;
6. Search the full text of records for a specific term or phrase or those terms or phrases that reoccur or occur at the same time;

   (Note that in dealing with the Dialog system, you can return to previous search results even though you have changed data bases. The search logic in this computer's memory can be saved for future reference even weeks or months later.)

   Caution: Be sure that your selection of records or information is done in specific categories only, such as via subject headings, title, and so forth.
7. Then command the computer to give you off-line print-outs from the terminal.

D. Legal Time Management System Computer

The LTMS or Legal Time Management System Computer is another on-line data base operation. The primary functions of the LTMS are in the area of your office docket control: billing, accounting, file maintenance, and word processing.

EXAMPLE

Take the docket system. This system is basically a computerized operation that oversees the appointment calendar of your attorney, as well as any conference, court appearances, and so forth. This computerized system negates any forgotten appointments or court appearances or conflicts in appointments or court appearances, which allows the attorney to move more freely and the legal secretary and assistant to keep abreast of the attorney's free time or lack of it.

One of the more important aspects of the LTMS is its on-line capabilities to verify and check client names for possible conflicts of interest. This function is really a godsend when your office is handling a complex litigation matter involving multiple parties and causes of action. It negates the possibility of a malpractice suit based on a conflict of interest such as a partner in the office having ownership interest in one of the companies being sued or suing or another client of the office having an interest in one of the companies suing or being sued; or the partner may even be representing one of the clients in a multiple-party action in another case with similar facts.

On the other side of the coin, when you have multiple-party actions with multiple causes involved in a complaint, which results in a rather lengthy complaint, you can use a blank disk from your word-processing machine and put repetitive paragraphs onto the blank word-processing disk for later use.

Or, you can do a field search and check the system by name to remove the unneeded material and put it on a storage track that may be needed later in your trial preparation.

Or, you can do a status field search, which involves the items entered into evidence. Thereafter, you can prepare either a defendant trial-deposition exhibit and then use these exhibits to review what has been said by all parties in these exhibits or in their depositions.

Or, by using this same methodology, you can find out the connection between the defendant and the plaintiff, if any. This helps you to advise the attorney on what to do and helps you to prepare the various facts or trial books.

As you know, during trial preparation voluminous documents have to be numbered and arranged according to their pertinency to the case. For example, say you have alleged in the complaint allegations relating to the issue of monopoly. You would want to know where these documents were produced or what testimony given on the subject is pertinent, which would require the documents to be arranged and prepared as an exhibit; or you would want to know how they relate to depositions as taken by your office.

Furthermore, let us say that you had to prepare an exhibit involving a contract matter. This means that you would have to find out the nature of the contract, the people involved, and who agreed to or disagreed (or other) to the contract.

To determine this, a field search would have to be made. The results of a field search might reveal a document reflecting that a conference had in fact been held with members of the plaintiff's side and the defendant's side present, discussing and/or signing the contract. All these references and/or statements would then be part of, and prepared as, an exhibit.

CHECKLIST FOR DETERMINING WHEN TO USE AN LSS

An electronic litigation support system (LSS), obviously, will effect savings in time (and money) if used properly. The following are situations where its use would be advantageous:

1. Has your attorney taken on a case that involves 10,000 or more pages? If the answer is yes, logic tells us that it is bound to grow and become more voluminous as each party involved in the complex litigation case takes depositions and sends out interrogatories. This being true, consideration should be given to the use of the computer/word processor litigation support system.

2. If quick, definitive, accurate law answers and information are required, consider using a commercial outside data base research system (Westlaw, Lexis, and the like) as a litigation support system.

3. If the type of documentation to be used in your complex litigation is of a repetitive nature, then consider using a word processor litigation support system.

4. If time is of the essence in dealing with the retrieval of documents and information in your complex litigation, then consideration should be given to the use of the computer/word processor litigation support system.

5. If the volume of information needed is so formidable that it would save time and payroll for a legal assistant, legal secretary, or typist to gather the ma-

terials, then consider the use of a combination of the different types of litigation support systems available.

SUGGESTED SUBJECTS THAT CAN BE COMPUTERIZED

A. Computer/word processor documents and data that can be placed in a computer/word processor for subsequent retrieval are unlimited and growing in number. Whether you are in a small, medium, or large law firm, or you are a legal assistant working under the supervision of an in-house counsel in a corporation, bank, or other corporate entity, consider the following information to be placed in your litigation support system for a complex case:

1. Summary of facts;

2. The legal issues;

3. Cross indexing of facts;

4. Subject matter (main and spin-off);

5. Research, whether substantive law with supporting cases or something other.

6. The following discovery matters can be placed into the computer:

   a. Deposition digest consisting of:
      entire testimony of deposition;
      summary of deposition;
      transcript of deposition;
      or digest of a deposition according to subject matter.

   b. The above deposition methodology can also be utilized in connection with interrogatories.

7. Witness testimony (notes from first trial or pretrial hearing or conference, if applicable);

8. Former decisions of your local trial judges coded by subject matter of the cases that were heard before them.

9. Summaries and pages from trial transcripts;

10. Facts of similar cases wherein you might find a common denominator, such as a common supplier or distributor;

11. Key relevant documents obtained through daily production;

12. Client identifications for determining possible conflicts of interest as to representation of a client;

13. Payroll/accounting data, and the like.

B. Word processor: The following are examples of standard paragraphs that might be kept on word-processing-machine disks:

1. Failure to state a cause of action;
2. Failure to state a claim from which relief can be granted;
3. Failure of consideration;
4. Accord and satisfaction;
5. Estoppel;
6. Assumption of risk;
7. Comparative negligence;
8. Duress;
9. A counter-breach of plaintiff;
10. Wrong jurisdiction (court);
11. Wrong party;
12. Discharge of bankruptcy;
13. Statute of limitations;
14. Statute of frauds;
15. Imputed negligence;
16. Laches;
17. Lack of capacity to sue;
18. Exemption from prosecution;
19. Partial payment of obligation;
20. Another action pending;
21. Rescission;
22. Doctrine of *res judicata;*
23. Unclean hands;
24. Diplomatic immunity;
25. Other bases for motion to dismiss (demurrer);
26. Other affirmative defenses.

THE ROLE OF THE LEGAL ASSISTANT

In general, the main function of a legal assistant in dealing with electronic data is administrative, that is, making sure that everything is properly coded, delivered, and received by the word-processing or data-processing section, and that all files and cards are set up properly and in the same chronological or logical order as the file folders for the particular case.

Additionally, the legal assistant screens all documents received for relevancy and then sorts them into groups or bundles or separates individual documents. Thereafter, each group, bundled, or separate document is numbered, logged, and the degree to extent to which it is coded or screened out is accomplished at this stage. The documents with no apparent relevance are then indexed, boxed, and stored. Once all of this has been accomplished, each individual separate document and bundle of documents is again checked for processing, analysis, and distribution for electronic processing and/or photocopying.

Specifically, however, the major role of a legal assistant in the computerized practice of law is in the area of implementing and completing legal research projects, such as memorandum of points and authorities, motions to compel further examination, and so forth. Those memoranda and court documents are drafted by the legal assistant. The legal assistant may use the outside data base litigation support system to update points of law and authorities and may use the in-line system for some information. She may also call upon the word-processing system to type the memorandum or motion.

In line with the foregoing, consider the following specific examples of your role when using any of the litigation support systems.

STEP-BY-STEP PROCEDURE

While your attorney is involved in developing substantive issues, narrowing or focusing on the issues, and planning strategy for presenting his case, you will have the following problems with which to deal:

1. The preparation of a persuasive post-trial brief that should incorporate a brief summary of the pretrial brief and annotated exhibits received in the testimony. This should include pertinent summaries and the pages of the transcript where they were offered.

2. The preparation of a short summary which includes transcript page references (of testimony supporting the facts alleged and contained in the event statements which your attorney approved at the time of trial).

3. The preparation of appeal documents, if applicable, requiring you to select and pull from the computer both parts of a transcript and exhibits you

feel will be used or could be used on the appeal to support your attorney's motion to appeal and which would be incorporated in the appellate record and later used in preparing your appellate brief.

A practical hint: Since the legal assistant and LSS can play the greatest and most important role in complex litigation, it is hoped that you will have put into the computer all the necessary, pertinent documentation and analysis so that when they are needed they can be retrieved quickly.

Step-By-Step Procedures When Preparing Individually-Numbered Events in a Pretrial Brief

In your introduction be sure to include: the complete names and relationships of the parties concerned; the appearance date and title of the document (spelled out separately and distinctly) that makes a party–litigant a part of the action; the cause or causes a party–litigant is not involved in; and as to each party–litigant, the cause or causes of action pertinent. After this is done, you take the following steps:

First: Determine and spell out in detail what you intend to brief, that is, a one-issue trial brief, such as issue of liability only or measure of damages, and so forth.

Second: Determine and annotate the documents and exhibits your employer will be using, such as contracts, receipts, and so forth.

Third: Determine the witness testimony and depositions your attorney plans to offer in support of each event statement, such as third-party involvement; defendant's testimony, and so forth.

It has been stated that paralegals have difficulty in understanding and accepting the structure base and logic of computers and how to phrase a command or request to get the proper response.

Hence, a paralegal must know and be aware of the following:

1. Legal terminology, phrases, and general legal language. This is a necessity if you are to be competent in the use of a computer to the benefit of your attorney;

2. The library and the nature of the documents in the computer;

3. The language of the computer in order to phrase the response to solicit an answer to your request from the computer;

4. How to get "locked" into the proper library of the computer with only a case title for example.

EXAMPLE

Say you have an Illinois case and you are looking in a California library, or vice versa; or you are looking for a federal case in Illinois and you have a California state library. The end result, of course, is that the computer would be unable to find the case and would so respond.

Therefore, if the paralegal does not know what she is looking for or how to lock into the proper library and has locked into the wrong library, she will be unable to come up with the correct answer. (See discussion on Lexis.)

5. Of the utmost importance, the paralegal should check with the attorney or librarian to be sure that the firm has picked the right vendor; if not, the paralegal would be working with the wrong "lock-in."

Note: The information placed in these computers is governed by the vendor or the government, and this is done by way of pleadings already on film that were merely typed into the computer.

6. *Absolutely essential,* a legal assistant must know the difference between a word processor and a computer to understand how they interface and complement each other.

A STEP-BY-STEP PROCEDURE FOR COMPUTER INPUT

First, determine the problem. The items to be included when describing and defining the problem should be:

1. The status of the problem as of the day of your discussion and preparation of your computer input;
2. What your ultimate goal is in resolving the problem;
3. Whether or not it is open to alternative resolutions or approaches; and, of course,
4. Any restrictions, if applicable.

Second, determine what data will be needed to fulfill the requirements of the problem. In this connection, determine the availability of data resources and the capabilities (of the computer) needed; then compare the resources and capabilities to see if the computer can produce the desired results and/or give the desired material. At this point you could look for any alternative approach or resolution.

Third, design the approach and codes that will best ensure your receiving the material, when needed, in an expeditious manner. This is where you describe how the project will be accomplished by setting forth the processing steps and resources required.

Fourth, implement. By implement, we mean assemble your resources—personnel needed, and material required such as notes, transcripts, testimony, and so forth. (See Figure 12.1 for format.)

THE RETRIEVAL PROCESS

There are basically two methods (systems) for retrieving information. (See Figures 12.2 and 12.3 for examples.)

One system uses manual indexes, and the extracting is primarily limited to headnotes from cases, which, in effect, means you are only searching a file of indexes.

EXAMPLE

A master index, which is normally maintained by the assistant and her support staff, shows location of documents and how they are indexed and categorized. In some offices some indexing of documents lists is prepared. Furthermore, even in this simple organization of documents, you can utilize a code numbering or lettering system to be designed to various documents, parties, witnesses, legal issues, and so forth.

Figure 12.1 Project Summary Format

PROJECT SUMMARY

DEPARTMENT   PROJECT NUMBER

PROJECT NAME   DATE

PROJECT DEFINITION

Brief Description of Project: Describe in summary what the project is to do, its purpose, and the overall objectives.

Approach to Project: Describe overall approach. List any unusual features that must be considered in the development of the project.

Anticipated Problems: List any problems that are entitled to be encountered in the development of the project.

Project Completion: Precisely define the requirements that must be met for this project to be considered complete by both you and your attorney.

The other system is where the full text is being searched, requiring much more data or documentation preparation and computer input for storage.

In this instance, you would be searching through a complete deposition volume or a complete set of answers to interrogatories or a complete transcript of testimony, and so forth, looking for inconsistencies in statements made by witnesses or conflicting testimony about a particular issue, location, circumstance, or other.

These are documents that you would heretofore have placed into your computer storage bank.

Figure 12.2 Retrieval Example: Related Cases

REQUEST: Please transmit the name (only one) of the file you want to search.

NAME	FILE	NAME	FILE
SUP	Sup.Ct. 1/45 (25 C.2d) to 02/82*	CASES	Combined SUP & APP Files *Complete through Official Reports Advance Sheets No. 7 dated 3/11/82
APP	Cts. App. 1/55 (150 C.A.2d)** to 02/82* **Officially reported cases of the Courts of Appeal and Appellate Departments of the Superior Court of California	OTHERS	All Courts from All Other States in LEXIS

For further explanation, press the H key (for HELP) and then the TRANSMIT key.

LEVEL 1–11 CASES

1. THE PEOPLE, plaintiff and respondent, v. MICHAEL MEREDITH, et al., Defendants and Appellant, Supreme Court of California, 29 C.3d 682, July 20, 1981; Mofd. od opn. Aug. 19, 1981.

2. In re RICHARD PRICE, et al., on habeas corpus., Supreme Court of California, 25 C.3d 448, Oct. 15, 1979.

3. LEONARD D. JACOBY, et al., petitioners, v. THE STATE BAR OF CALIFORNIA, respondent, Supreme Court of California, 19 C.3d 359, MAY 3, 1977.

4. FRANKLIN BELL GASSMAN, petitioner, v. THE STATE BAR OF CALIFORNIA, respondent, Supreme Court of California, 18 C.3d 125, Sept. 24, 1976.

5. In re FRANK WILLIAM DEDMAN, JR., on suspension, Supreme Court of California, 17 C.3d 229, June 22, 1976.

6. DAVID R. CADWELL, petitioner, v. THE STATE BAR OF CALIFORNIA, respondent. In re DAVID CADWELL on suspension, Supreme Court of California in Bank, 15 C.3d 762 Dec. 22, 1975.

7. In re RAYMOND DORMIO on habeas corpus, First Dist., Div. One, 127 C.A. 3d 788, Dec. 30, 1981.

RESULT: These print-outs could be voluminous or minimal, depending on the nature of the case. It has been our experience that these print-outs should be kept confidential, and this, of course, is at the discretion of your attorney.

Figure 12.3 Retrieval Example: One Case

LEVEL 1–1 of 1 CASE

Estate of SINAH W. KELLY, Deceased. MARILYN WALROD EATON, et al., Appellants, v. FARMERS AND MERCHANTS TRUST COMPANY OF LONG BEACH et al., Respondents.

Fourth District
178 C.A. 2d 24
Feb. 15, 1960

OPINION:

. . . revoked, canceled, defaced, and obliterated the will here produced for probate. The answer denies this allegation. The affidavits in support of summary judgment are positive on the personal knowledge of affiants. That which refers to the first court of contest is by James H. Kindel and clearly shows that the testatrix did not herself cancel, deface, or obliterate any part of the will, and also that the penciled notations on the margin of the will were not done by the direction of the testatrix and that none of the writing of the will itself was, in fact. . . .

GLOSSARY OF DATA-PROCESSING TERMS

Application Program	A program written by or for a computer user for the purpose of solving a problem or set of problems that the user wants solved.
Coding	The act of, and the product of, writing the instructions constituting a computer program. Coding occurs after the program has been designed.
Computer	A data-processing machine that can perform arithmetic and logical operations under the control of a computer program, without need for human intervention once the computer program has been read into the computer and its operation has commenced.
Computer Program	A detailed and explicit series of instructions, in a form acceptable to the computer, prepared in order to achieve a certain result. Also referred to simply as a "program."
Data	The representation of information in some form recognizable by a computer.
Data Base	A collection of useful information, represented in a computer-readable form, all elements of which have a common format, and which is usually organized or organizable on the basis of one or more elements of that common format.
Design	A step-by-step functional and structural representation of what a computer program does, independent of the actual instructions used in the program.
Documentation	The collection of documents that describe and explain software in terms of its use, design, and coding.
Indexing	Ordering, according to some predetermined scheme, a group of items so that any given item or subset of items may be retrieved from the ordered group.
Listing	A printed list of the instructions comprising a program in the order in which they stand in the program.
Object Tape	A magnetic tape on which data is represented in a language that the computer can understand directly, without need for translation.

Programming Language	The set of rigidly defined representation, rules, and conventions used in the creation of a computer program; there are numerous programming languages in use, each with its own set of representations, rules, and conventions, which must be strictly adhered to.
Program Package	A computer program, along with information necessary or helpful for its use, created for marketing to any interested users.
Software	A generic term referring to programs, lists in machine-readable form, and documentation.
Source Language	The programming language in which a computer program is actually coded by the programmer, as opposed to any language into which that program may subsequently be translated by the computer in order that the computer may use it directly.

Note: The above terms and others used in electronic data processing may be put on word-processor disks for use in preparing pleadings, motions, interrogatories, requests for admissions, or other documents in a case where the definition of such terms are relevant and material to understanding the document to be typed.

COMPUTER BIBLIOGRAPHY

WordPerfect (with Direct Connect) IBM

Sylvan Log Dictionary

Jurisoft

Jurisoft Log Toolbox (criminal forms and briefs)

Jurisoft Cite-Rite

Jurisoft Full Authority Citations

Law Desk—Thomson Legal Publishing

Case Base—Thomson Legal Publishing

Lexis (Online service)—Mead Data Central

Westlaw (Online service)—West Publishing

PART THREE

THE LEGAL ASSISTANT'S ROLE IN THE SPECIALTY LAW PRACTICE

CHAPTER 13

How to Handle a Federal Bankruptcy Case

NATURE OF BANKRUPTCY

The purpose of the Federal Bankruptcy Act is to provide an honest debtor with a fresh start; as well as to protect creditors from their debtors; to protect creditors from each other, and to convert the debtor's assets in the case to be equally distributed among the creditors. (These assets could include certain state-exempt property belonging to the debtor, leaving the debtor with a complete loss of property and assets. This fact should be considered when determining whether or not to advise a client to file a federal Petition in Bankruptcy.)

JURISDICTION

A federal bankruptcy court has jurisdiction over all civil proceedings arising in or related to a bankruptcy proceeding that is held in its court. However, a federal bankruptcy judge can decline jurisdiction. In such case, the debtor would have to rely on state bankruptcy or receivable laws, and a state court would hear the matter and apply the state's bankruptcy laws or its state equivalent.

VENUE (FEDERAL)

Individuals: In the district where the debtor has resided for the longest portion of 180 days prior to the filing of a petition; location of his assets or place of business.

Corporations: In the state where it is incorporated; or where the corporation was licensed to do business and/or where they are actively doing business.

DOCUMENTS TO BE FILED

Generally, the following are documents to be filed in a federal bankruptcy proceeding and the new procedures.

PETITION

To commence a bankruptcy case, the first document to be prepared and filed is the "petition." This petition must be prepared and filed with the federal district of bankruptcy court clerk as follows: an original and three copies (see Procedure, page 294), and the caption on the petition must contain all the names theretofore used by the debtor within the previous six years.

The list of creditors contained within the petition should include the names and addresses of all creditors, as well as the account number, if applicable, and the estimated balance due on the accounts.

The schedules of assets and liabilities should be prepared according to 11 U.S.C. §521(1). However, the bankruptcy rules allow the filing of schedules separately, within ten days after the petition, if the list of names and addresses of creditors have not been filed with the original petition. Discuss this procedure with your attorney before you file or do not file the schedules concurrently with the filing of the petition.

Practical Hints

1. When preparing your list of secured creditors, footnote them as follows:

If it is a house, then say, "per broker's appraisal of _____ of _____," and attach a copy of the appraisal, or if it is an automobile, then say, "per Kelly's Blue-Book, dated _____ of _____, $_____ retail, $_____, wholesale."

2. Always include zip codes in addresses and complete description of goods claimed, for example, Zenith III TV set, 24", Westinghouse refrigerator; Whirlpool, and so forth (with serial number, if possible).

3. As to real property, make the client bring in the deed so that you can personally check it as to plot plan and tract number when recorded, and so forth. Use the legal description in the petition.

4. Before you list the personal property, check out the exemptions allowed under state law; or take the federal exemptions as provided for under 11 U.S.C. §105. *You cannot take both.* Make the determination of which is most beneficial to the client before you list the personal property. You must discuss this matter with your attorney and let her make the decision. (It might be the better part of valor if you develop a bible of exemptions and checklists in this regard. See Creditors Claims and Interest, page 271.)

Practical Step-By-Step Procedures Before Filing Bankruptcy Petition

1. After the initial interview between your attorney and the client, your consultation should be exhaustive.

2. In gathering the data needed for the petition, be sure to obtain the following data: name, address, telephone number, and Social Security number of the client; marital status; if a woman, her maiden name, together with the date of marriage (or marriages); if divorced, the date of the legal separation and/or entry of final divorce decree. This information could have an effect on what debts are dischargeable or not dischargeable in bankruptcy.

3. Prepare a *complete* list (and a complete list is what is meant) of any and all debts outstanding, current or in arrears, long past due or delinquent, however old, even out-of-state debts still pending.

4. Discreetly check to see if the balances given to you are on face correct by calling the creditors. The client may be too embarrassed to call and may have inadvertently given you an old invoice or statement.

5. Consult with the client's accountant, since the accountant would have a better understanding of liabilities of the client and have possession of any books and records, financial statements, and/or inventories of the client.

6. Check the judgment section of the court to determine if there are any outstanding judgments or lawsuits pending that the client may feel might not have any bearing on the petition in bankruptcy.

7. Another caution is the "family creditor," who the client says will not cause a problem. Verify the debt owed; obtain documentation if you feel the same is warranted. This might be one of the debts the client wants to protect from a preference suit, as indicated in item 3.

8. If property is involved, be sure that the legal description is correct: in whose name it is owned, and how (joint tenancy or other); when bought, and for how much, and so forth. This data will enable you to complete the filing of a declaration of homestead, if that has not already been done.

9. When all the above has been accomplished, *recheck* the debts with the client, for we often find that after the petition has been prepared and is ready to be filed, the client will call in to add still another outstanding debt. This can be (and is) frustrating to you and your attorney.

10. A suggested office procedure for verifying information with the client is to make a copy of the completed petition and mail it to the client to study and return. A five-to-seven day follow-up is recommended in these situations.

11. After receipt of a notice of the first meeting of creditors, check to see if any of them have been returned for lack of proper address, and if so, determine the correct address and remail the letter by registered return receipt requested in a timely manner in order that the creditor may file his proof of claim.

12. It would also be wise to list any assignees of claims as creditors and all property, regardless of the value. This is because failure to list them on the schedules may constitute a false oath by your client.

13. Finally, check and recheck; and check again to determine if the client has signed each and every page required and that those pages requiring notarization have been notarized. Too many times, petitions are returned by the court merely for lack of a signature. This can be crucial, if time is of the essence.

STATEMENT OF AFFAIRS

In addition to the above-described petition, the petitioner is required to file an original and three copies of a document entitled Statement of Affairs. This is a set of questions that require answers delving into the debtor's financial history and previous business transactions. If there is no answer, then you should write in the word "none," but all questions should and must be answered or explained.

AMENDMENTS AND SUPPLEMENTAL SCHEDULES

The additional schedules are governed by the Federal Bankruptcy Rules, *not* the Federal Bankruptcy Code. These bankruptcy rules permit amendments or supplemental schedules to be filed as a matter of course at any time before the case is closed.

FILING FEES

The fees for filing a petition in bankruptcy are as follows:

Chapter 7:	$120.00	Chapter 11	
Chapter 9:	$300.00	(Railroad)	$300.00

Chapter 11:   Chapter 13: $120.00
(Individual) $200.00

Since fees change frequently, you should check with the courts for any changes before filing. Please note that these fees can be paid in installments upon application to the court, and this application should be prepared and filed in duplicate. It should set forth the terms of payment of the installment payments, but may not exceed four payments.

Note: It is now possible for you to amend schedules of assets and liabilities at any time, but be sure to send the newest creditor listed all of the schedules heretofore filed.

CREDITORS' CLAIMS AND INTEREST

Any right to payment, whether or not it is reduced to judgment, is a claim that may enable the creditor to seek payment in the bankruptcy case. Furthermore, the claim is allowed so long as a foreseeable breach, if applicable, gives rise to a right to payment.

PROVABILITY OF CLAIMS

Provability of claims is eliminated under the new Act. Provability now depends on whether it is allowed, and nothing more.

However, personal injury cases with claims for damages are provable only if the claimant commenced a negligence action that was pending when the bankruptcy petition was filed. If not, the injured party would not have a claim in the bankruptcy case. This is also true of intentional tort claims that were not reduced to judgment.

FILING PROOF OF CLAIM

This filing of a "proof of claim" by a creditor is governed by the Federal Bankruptcy Rules of Procedure and Suggested Interim Bankruptcy Rules. It must be in writing and executed by the creditor or his authorized agent, unless filed by the trustee, debtor, or co-debtor. If it is a secured claim, the original or a copy of the writing or other evidence of the security must accompany the proof of claim.

Satisfactory evidence of a secured interest would be the copy of a financial statement showing that it was perfected. This perfection would have been done by way of a filing with the secretary of state of the state where the security interest was perfected under that state's commercial code and should be done within six months after the date set for the first meeting of creditors. In reorganization cases the time is prior to the approval of the disclosure statement.

Note: In Chapter 13 debt adjustment cases, the time is six months *after* the first date of the first meeting of creditors, unless it is a secured claim; then it should be filed before the conclusion of the first meeting of creditors.

If your attorney is working for a creditor, you should get a power of attorney to represent the creditor in all matters and to receive all notices and activity and documents flowing in the case. This should be filed along with the proof of claim. The creditor should send all invoices, bills, and bills of ladings and a statement of account in dispute as listed on the bankruptcy petition. Furthermore, if the creditor received the claim by way of an assignment, this assignment should be attached to the proof of claim.

THE SECURED CLAIM

Chapter 11 filings are affected by a state's version of the Uniform Commercial Code, Article 9, entitled Secured Transactions; Sales of Accounts, Contracts, Rights and Chattel Papers. These secured transactions would include secured personal property but not secured real property. State laws where real property is located determine whether a real property claim is secured.

EXAMPLE

Say you have got a house for $100,000 and then you make a down payment of $20,000. The balance due of $80,000 is to be secured by a promissory note and deed of trust. This is recorded where the property is located. Under state law this is a secured obligation. In case of a default, the trustee could ordinarily institute a foreclosure of the debt to satisfy the $80,000. See Scope of Automatic Stay later in this chapter.

EXAMPLE

Let's say that a business needs machinery and fixtures in a factory, and the individual goes to the bank to borrow money to pay for these items. The debtor signs a note for the money, a security agreement, and prepares and files a financial statement under the provisions of the state's version of Article 9 of the Uniform Commercial Code.

The bank *must* perfect this security interest by filing the financial statement with the secretary of state, which is in essence putting the public on notice; or perfecting this claim by possession of the security in the business. This is protecting itself and/or as it relates to trade fixtures should be recorded in the county in which the property or machinery is located. This is the state law that determines that the bank's claim is a secured claim for personal property in this example.

Then there are lien rights that create security rights such as:

1. A judicial lien plus some type of action by a court: attachment and execution for example.

2. A judgment lien obtained before the ninety-day period before the filing and where there was a levy on the property. This achieves the status of a secured claim as well.

3. Statutory liens such as tax liens (outside the ninety-day statutory period) and mechanics liens must be recorded in a timely statutory manner. These are deemed filed unless they are listed as undisputed or contingent. In Chapter 11 proceedings, these need not be filed in order to share in the distribution of assets. But in Chapters 7 and 13 they must be filed to be considered secured claims.

In no-asset claims, the question becomes moot, since the court and its auditors have determined that the case is a no-asset case, and hence you do not have to file a claim.

THE UNSECURED CLAIM

Basically, there are two ways to satisfy an unsecured claim under a Chapter 11 filing, which requires a fair and equitable distribution to this class of creditors.

1. Have the plan provide for full and complete payment of the unsecured debt, either through the payment of money or the retention of property of the debtor, equal to the value of the debt;

or

2. Under the Chapter 11 plan, do not give property or payment to any class of creditors that may be subordinate to the dissenting creditor.

EXAMPLE

If a dissenting creditor under the plan received payment or property worth only one half of its allowed claim, then the plan may still be considered fair and equitable if all junior or subordinate claims, including partners or stockholders, receive nothing and if no senior class is to receive more than 100 percent of its allowed claims.

CHECKLIST OF ALLOWABLE UNSECURED CLAIMS

1. A landlord's claim for loss of future rent resulting from the termination of a lease, which may be for an amount not to exceed the greater of one year or 50 percent of the remaining term of the lease, which does not exceed three years.
2. Allowance of employees' salary claim.
3. Contingent or unliquidated claims.
4. Transfer of voidable transfers of property belonging to the estate, that is, debtor.

CHECKLIST OF DISALLOWED UNSECURED CLAIMS

1. Unenforceability against the debtor.
2. Claim is for the unmatured interest.
3. Claim is subject to offset.
4. Excess property tax.
5. Claim is for services of an insider or an attorney.
6. Claim is for a post-petition decree for alimony, maintenance, and support.
7. Employment tax claim against employer.

INTEREST HOLDERS

"Interest holders" under the federal bankruptcy law fall into the following classes:

1. Common and preferred stockholders or
2. Limited and general partners.

To satisfy this class of creditors, the Federal Bankruptcy Code considers a fair and equitable treatment of their claims under the plan of reorganization if it is provided therein that these interest holders receive property equal to the fixed amount of the indebtedness or redemption price or present market value of the interest, whichever is the greater.

Alternatively, the plan, to be fair and equitable to the interest holder, could provide that no compensation be paid to subordinate interest holders, such as common stockholders and general partners. See 11 U.S.C. §1129(b)(2)(c)(ii).

ALLOWABLE POST-PETITION CLAIMS

1. Gap claims in involuntary cases.
2. Claims arising from the rejection of executory contracts or unexpired leases.
3. Claims arising from the recovery of property.
4. Priority tax claim.
5. Allowable post-petition claims under and pursuant to Chapter 13 petitions:
   a. Government proof of claim for taxes that became payable after the case was commenced and still pending.
   b. Consumer debts that constitute liabilities for property or services necessary for the debtor's performance under the Chapter 13 plan.
   c. Medical bills that occurred prior to the filing of the petition that relate to an injury of a debtor that has left the debtor incapacitated.

THE ROLE OF THE LEGAL ASSISTANT IN INTERVIEWING A CLIENT

In General

1. Attend the initial conference between the client and attorney.
2. Compile and assimilate data.

3. Aid client in completing the initial bankruptcy forms to obtain all pertinent information regarding the client's assets, liabilities, and so forth.

4. If time permits, merely give the forms to the client to complete the information within the privacy of the client's home.

5. If the foregoing is utilized, arrange for a later office appointment to review with the client the information on the sheet prior to discussing it with the attorney for final determination.

Specifics

Because of the new bankruptcy rules, regulations, and changes in the laws, the initial interview with the client is vitally important, since an individual debtor now can file either a Chapter 7 or Chapter 13 bankruptcy petition to ease the pain of being overly in debt.

These new options allow the debtor to take different approaches to obtain this relief from indebtedness, and as such, the requirements and form(s) necessary to be completed are different. For example, under Chapter 13 the schedules of assets and liabilities are merged into one document under Chapter 13 filing. This is one of the major reasons why a legal assistant should be present at the initial interview, because you, as a legal assistant, are the one whom the client will be contacting and be working with to complete the forms heretofore referred to, and later you will be verifying the answers with the client's creditors as to the client's outstanding debts, which may be contingent and/or unliquidated claims, and so forth.

Caution: In this regard, as it relates to the secured and unsecured claims, you should be careful to verify the nature and extent of the secured interests and what assets were pledged to secure those interests, and, of course, verification of any due and owing state, federal, or other type governmental taxes. In addition, be sure that you verify and tag any property that is exempt under the new bankruptcy laws.

Clients do not always tell the truth. Some do not understand the truth as to whether or not a security interest has been perfected.

THE CREDITORS MEETING

After the petition is filed, the bankruptcy judge appoints an interim trustee, and a regular trustee is elected or designated with full authority to do all those things necessary to protect the assets of the debtor until a determination has been made.

Thereafter, the debtor is required to appear at a public meeting of the creditors in Bankruptcy Court. This meeting is normally held between twenty and forty days after the petition is filed. The clerk of the Bankruptcy Court normally presides over this meeting unless the creditors vote to designate someone else. They may also elect a regular trustee and/or creditors committee at this point in the proceeding.

The purpose of this meeting is to give the creditors and the trustees a chance to question the debtor as to the reason for filing the petition, the assets involved, and any other matters pertinent to the petition and the debtor's right to be discharged in bankruptcy.

As the legal assistant, you should prepare the client for this hearing by causing him to reread the schedules in the petition statement of affairs, go over his account books and bank statements, tax returns, canceled checks, and so forth. *Remember, the attorney will not be with him at this meeting.*

Note, moreover, that security holders, that is limited partners, shareholders, or others, may wish to have their own meeting. This is allowed under the Interim Bankruptcy Rules.

PETITIONS THAT CAN BE FILED

Bankruptcy petitions are divided into two basic types: voluntary and involuntary. The Federal Bankruptcy Code and the Federal Bankruptcy Court Rules govern who may file and the procedure to be used in filing both types of petition.

VOLUNTARY PETITIONS

A voluntary petition may be filed by the following persons in the following manner:

A. Individuals

An individual can file a voluntary petition whether or not he is insolvent or eligible to be relieved of the liability for his debts through a discharge in bankruptcy. Specifically, under the old act, if you were discharged in bankruptcy, you could not refile until six years had passed; however, under the new bankruptcy code, you may file a petition in bankruptcy and proceed as a debtor under Chapter 7 to liquidate your assets.

B. Minors

The foregoing procedure includes minors who have incurred debts for the purchase of the necessities of life and incompetents through their guardians *ad litem.* The only requirement is that the person either reside in the United States and/or have a domicile or place or business or property in the United States. This means that even aliens can file for discharge of their debts as long as they fulfill the foregoing prerequisites.

C. Private Family Trust or Estate

Private family trusts and mismanaged estates cannot file a Chapter 7 bankruptcy petition seeking liquidation.

D. General Partners

Voluntary petitions may also be filed by all the general partners on behalf of the partnership; or a partner may file a voluntary petition either with or without one or more of the other partners. Note, however, that the mere filing of an individual petition by a partner does not discharge the other partners from their personal liabilities to creditors of the partnership.

E. Corporations

Corporations may file a voluntary petition in bankruptcy for the purpose of liquidation and distribution of assets to creditors. This is because the bankruptcy code defines "person" to include a corporation, and as such, a person is eligible to file a liquidation petition. See 11 U.S.C., §101(30), et. seq.

F. Joint Petitions

The only joint petitions allowed (more than one debtor) are in the case of a husband and wife. The effect of a petition on the property rights of the other spouse is determined by the Bankruptcy Court and *not* by state law.

If only the husband files, remember that the state community property laws are subservient to the Bankruptcy Court regulations. See Section 302(a) of the Bankruptcy Code.

G. Joint Administration

This procedure occurs when the court orders cases involving two or more related debtors in a partnership or corporation, or the like, to be administered jointly.

Should this occur, joint administration would include the use of a single docket for the administration matters and a joint listing of claims and a combined list and notification of creditors. However, it is possible to file two separate and distinct petitions.

EXAMPLE

Suppose there is a California corporation that owns 100 percent of the stock in a New York corporation, but it has its principal place of business in California and the subsidiary in New York has its principal place of business in California. In this instance, separate petitions must be filed.

H. Consolidation

Consolidation, on the other hand, merges the assets and liabilities of each debtor involved. This procedure is used where there is such a commingling and/or intermingling of assets and liabilities that the court cannot separate them.

INVOLUNTARY PETITIONS (LIQUIDATION)

Under the Code there are only two instances where involuntary petitions may be filed: liquidation under Chapter 7, and reorganization under Chapter 13. This section discusses involuntary petitions for liquidation.

The purpose of filing a petition for liquidation is to assure equal distribution of the debtor's assets among his creditors, without showing preferential treatment. Additionally, this type of petition increases the assets of the debtor to the benefit of a creditor and the voiding of certain liens and encumbrances.

A. Who May File

Before taking such a course of action, that is, forcing the debtor to file an involuntary petition, there are certain courses that should be exhausted first.

1. Have you taken any legal action to collect the debt? If so, does the prospect of recovery outweigh the inconvenience and expense of a collection effort?

2. Does the debtor have enough money to pay at least a percentage or partial payment of the total indebtedness? If this is true, you may want to collect by taking the matter to court and seeking redress under the remedies offered under state law.

3. Is your client/creditor aware of the locations of the debtor's assets, and if so, remember that state law provides for post-judgment discovery for this purpose? For example, under state law you have such remedies as garnishment, attachments, receiverships, and other such procedures for protection of your client/creditor.

4. Can the debtor be rehabilitated? In this instance, we are talking about an insolvent debtor who may be able to pay a small fraction of the debts if all his assets are liquidated and who just may have the ability to improve his economic condition and in the future make periodic payments in larger amounts. If this is the case, the court leans toward giving the debtor the opportunity to do so.

Who may file an involuntary petition? Any employee of a debtor who is also a creditor; any insider of the debtor who is a creditor; and any creditor who received a preference, fraudulent conveyance, statutory lien, post-petition transfer, or any other lien or interest in the debtor's property that is voidable by a trustee in bankruptcy. As to these creditors, see 11 U.S.C. Section 303(b); 11 U.S.C. Sections 101(2) and 101(25).

It only takes one petitioning creditor to start an involuntary bankruptcy proceeding of a debtor, if the debtor has fewer than twelve creditors or indentured trustees, which is the required number. But note that these listed creditors may be excluded by the court in determining whether or not there are the required twelve creditors needed to file an involuntary petition against the debtor.

Reason: These creditors may not be counted by the court because of their special privity with the debtor, such as an employee who might lose his job if the debtor is liquidated in bankruptcy or the insider who might be so closely connected to the debtor (for example, his father or uncle) as to be biased toward the debtor, and so forth. It is for this reason that it is easier for a single outside creditor to commence on involuntary petition against a debtor.

As a matter of practice and procedure, if there are twelve or more creditors, the petition must be executed by at least three of the petitioning creditors in order for the petition to be filed and accepted by the court. Moreover, the claims as between these creditors must be in an aggregate amount of $5,000. We are, of course, referring to claims that are unsecured collectively to the extent of $5,000.

Secured creditors cannot commence an involuntary bankruptcy case against a debtor, but a partially secured creditor may act as a petitioning creditor to the extent of any deficiencies over and above the value of its secured claim.

B. Against Whom Can an Involuntary Petition Be Filed?

Any person, including a corporation, who may file a voluntary petition for liquidation may be the subject of an involuntary bankruptcy case except for farmers and not-for-profit corporations. See 11 U.S.C. §303(a).

C. Filing an Involuntary Petition Relating to Liquidation

1. At the time of filing the involuntary petition, it should be executed by the petitioners in the office of the clerk of the Bankruptcy Court, at which time a filing fee of $60 is paid.

2. An original petition and three copies thereof must be filed unless the court rules provide otherwise. See Suggested Interim Bankruptcy Rules 1002(b) (1) and 1003 (a).

3. This filing commences a legal action. It should contain allegations made in the form of a pleading. Hence, the petitioners must identify the debtor in the caption, together with any names that he may also have been known by within the previous six years.

4. Furthermore, this involuntary petition should contain the names and addresses of all the petitioners and an allegation asserting the claims each petitioner has against the debtor that would amount to the aggregate sum of $5,000 or more.

5. Note that the nature and amounts of petitioners' claims should be described briefly, but clearly.

6. The petitioners should allege in this petition the jurisdiction and the venue of the court; and

7. The petition must allege that at least one of the grounds for an order for relief is satisfied.

D. Step-By-Step Procedure After Filing an Involuntary Petition

1. The clerk of the Bankruptcy Court issues a summons to be served on the debtor, together with a copy of the petition. (It should be noted that it is the petitioner's choice of serving the summons and petition either by personal service or by mail.) Service, however, must be made within ten days from the issuance of the summons. Failure to serve the summons and petition within this time will result in the petitioner's having to obtain a new summons from the court.

2. The service of summons and petition must be made by first-class mail. (As in all other cases, it is suggested that this service by mail be made by certified mail, return receipt requested.)

3. If there is an attempt to make personal service, this personal service may be made by anyone who is an adult and not a party to the bankruptcy proceeding.

4. If you are filing the involuntary petition against a partnership, you should comply with the Suggested Interim Bankruptcy Rules, Rule 1004(b), which requires that service be made in five days after the filing by the petitioning creditors or partners and that it be mailed by first-class, return receipt requested to the last known address of each general partner who has not joined in the petition, or not heretofore served. (It is legal, however, to deliver a copy of the petition to a general partner.) See Suggested Interim Bankruptcy Rules, 1004(b).

E. Step-By-Step Procedure in Preparing an Answer to an Involuntary Petition for Liquidation

1. The debtor in question, whether an individual, corporation, partnership, or general partner, may file and serve an answer.
2. Creditors may not file an answer to contest the petition.
3. The answer may be in the same form and contain the same type of defenses as in civil actions filed in the federal courts.
4. The answer may include a statement of claim against the petitioning creditor to defeat the purpose of the petition only. This is because an affirmative judgment cannot be sought by way of a counter-claim in a bankruptcy case.
5. The answer must be served and filed within twenty days after the issuance of the summons, unless the time is extended or limited by order of the court for service to be made by publication.
6. *Note that no other pleadings are permitted after an answer is filed and served.* The exception to this rule is when the court orders the petitioners to reply to the answer.
7. As to the debtor, per se, he may make a motion to dismiss the petition for lack of jurisdiction, or for failure to state a claim upon which relief can be granted.
8. The debtor may also file a motion for a more definite statement.
9. The debtor may also make any other motions that are permitted under Rule 12 of the Federal Rules of Civil Procedure.

Note: Under Chapter 11, U.S.C. §302(a), permission is given for joint petitions to be filed only against husbands and wives, though in some cases involuntary petitions can be filed against a corporation or other debtors who are closely connected, to be followed by either a joint administration of assets or a complete consolidation of bankruptcy cases.

THE AUTOMATIC STAY

A. Scope of the Automatic Stay

The "automatic stay" affects the following:

1. The commencement or continuation of any legal proceeding against the debtor that was or could have been commenced before the filing of a bankruptcy petition is automatically stayed (stopped) when a federal bankruptcy petition is filed. This includes any judicial, administrative, and arbitration proceeding, whether or not it is before a governmental tribunal. It also applies to every step of a proceeding, including the issuance of a process such as levy, garnishment, and/or other supplemental proceedings.

2. The enforcement of a judgment obtained before the petition was filed, either against the debtor personally or against property of a bankruptcy. In this instance, creditors may not proceed with levy or execution to satisfy any prebankruptcy judgment.

3. Efforts to obtain possession of property of the estate, or property from the estate. Property of the estate includes the debtor's property as of the date of the petition. The stay covers these acts so as to give the trustee ample time to discover and evaluate the respective rights in the property before the creditors start grabbing.

4. Any attempt to collect or recover on a claim against a debtor that arose before the bankruptcy petition was filed.

5. The settling of any debt that a creditor owes to a debtor against the debtor's liability to the creditor.

6. The commencement or continuation of a proceeding before the U.S. Tax Court concerning the debtor.

    Note: The statutory period of time affecting the collection efforts is 180 days. That is to say, collection efforts can be made by the claimant ninety days before the filing of a bankruptcy petition. However, any claim filed or collection efforts made after ninety days or on the ninety-first day is voided by the filing of the bankruptcy petition.

7. See Federal Bankruptcy Code and Federal Bankruptcy Rules for adversary proceedings in the bankruptcy court.

B. Exemptions from the Automatic Stay

Exemption from the automatic stay are as follows:

1. Criminal actions against the debtor may proceed despite the bankruptcy petition.

2. The collection of alimony, maintenance, and support is not affected by the automatic stay to the extent that it is from property that is not part of the bankruptcy estate.

3. Perfection of a lien or property interest to make it effective against the trustee in bankruptcy under Section 546(b) of the Bankruptcy Code is permitted.

4. Governments may proceed to enforce their police and regulatory powers, such as by prosecuting actions to prevent violations of health, consumer protection, environmental, or other similar laws.

5. Governments also may take steps to enforce injunctions or judgments, other than money judgments, obtained prior to bankruptcy in the exercise of their police or regulatory powers.

6. The automatic stay does not cover certain setoffs or mutual debts and claims relating to commodity claims actions.

7. Despite the automatic stay, the Secretary of Housing and Urban Development may commence an action to foreclose on a mortgage insured under the National Housing Act.

8. The automatic stay does not apply to the issuance of a notice of tax deficiency issued by a governmental agency.

DISCHARGE IN BANKRUPTCY

There are certain categories of indebtedness that free the debtor from forever paying his debts, leaving creditors unable to file any type of civil litigation for repayment of the debts discharged in bankruptcy in the future. Those are dischargeable debts.

There may be grounds to object as to a discharge as to all debts or just to certain debts. The categories of debts from which there can be no discharge are:

1. Taxes;

2. Debts incurred by fraud;

3. Unscheduled debts;

4. Embezzlement, larceny, and fiduciary's fraud;

5. Alimony, maintenance, and support;

6. Willful and malicious injury;

7. Fines and penalties;

8. Student loans; and

9. Multiple bankruptcies, such as debts from a previous bankruptcy in which discharge was denied.

A. Step-By-Step Procedure for Objecting to Discharge of Bankruptcy

1. The person wishing to object to the discharge must commence an adversary proceeding by filing a complaint before the deadline set by the court.

2. Thereafter, a summons is issued by the clerk of the Bankruptcy Court, together with a notice of trial or pretrial conference.

3. The complaint should state a ground for objection.

4. At his option the debtor may contest the complaint by filing an answer. If he docs, a trial will be held.

5. The debtor can make motions to dismiss or request a bill of particulars or more definite statements of the objections.

6. The parties may engage in discovery, in accordance with federal court rules in conjunction with the bankruptcy rules governing adversary proceedings.

CHECKLIST OF CROUNDS FOR DENIAL OF DISCHARGE

1. The discharge is for individuals only.

2. Fraudulent transfers or concealment of property.

3. Failure on the part of the bankrupt to keep books and records.

4. Commission of a bankruptcy crime on the part of the bankrupt, such as:
   a. Knowingly and fraudulently making a false oath or account;
   b. Knowingly and fraudulently presenting or using a false claim;

  c. Knowingly or fraudulently getting or receiving a bribe:

  d. Knowingly and fraudulently withholding records.

5. Failure to explain loss of assets.

6. Refusal to obey a bankruptcy court order or to answer questions (which may be in the form of a subpoena).

7. Commission of prohibited acts in connection with an insider's bankruptcy.

8. Prior discharge within six years.

9. Prior Chapter 13 discharge.

10. Waiver.

B. Revoking a Discharge

There are three reasons for revoking a discharge:

1. Fraud on the part of the debtor.

2. Concealing the acquisition of the property of the estate on the part of the debtor, before the case is closed, or one year after the case is closed.

3. Refusal to obey orders to answer questions. It should be noted that those persons attempting to revoke a discharge may make their request within one year after the granting of a discharge if it is based on fraud or concealment. Other than for fraud or concealment the request must be made before the bankruptcy case is closed.

C. How to Reaffirm a Debt

A bankruptcy debtor may choose to reaffirm an otherwise dischargeable debt under certain circumstances without violating the federal bankruptcy law.

Restrictions and limitations on reaffirmations are:

1. The reaffirmed debt may be enforced only to the extent that it is enforceable under applicable nonbankruptcy law.

2. The reaffirmation agreement must have been made before the granting of a discharge to be enforceable.

3. The debtor has the right to rescind the reaffirmation agreement within thirty days after it becomes enforceable.

4. Whenever the case involves an individual and a discharge is either granted or denied, the court is required to hold a hearing at which the debtor either must be informed that the discharge has been granted or given the reason why a discharge has not been granted. If the debtor wishes to reaffirm a discharged debt, the judge is obliged under the code to inform the debtor at a hearing that (1) such reaffirmation is not required under any law, or agreement, and (2) the legal effect of such reaffirmation and consequences of default.

5. In the case of reaffirming an individual consumer debt, except for obligations secured by a real estate mortgage, the reaffirmation agreement is not enforceable unless the court determines that it does not impose undue hardship on the debtor or his dependents and that it is in the best interest of the debtor to reaffirm.

HIGHLIGHTS OF THE NEW BANKRUPTCY CHAPTERS

CHAPTER 7 LIQUIDATION OF ASSETS

Chapter 7 of the new Federal Bankruptcy Code deals with voluntary petitions, commonly called "straight bankruptcy" petitions and also known as The Adjustment of Debts of an Individual's Regular Income. It states that any individual, including a partnership or a corporation, may file a voluntary Chapter 7 bankruptcy petition; and that furthermore, any person qualifying to file a voluntary petition may be the subject of an involuntary petition filed by creditors.

Moreover, during this proceeding, a bankrupt is no longer responsible or liable for debts for which he has been discharged, while he is attempting to equitably distribute his assets among his creditors.

It should be noted here that only an individual can be discharged and liquidate his assets under this proceeding and only after a determination has been made as to whether or not there are any grounds for objection by creditors of the debtor.

EXAMPLE

A fraudulent transfer of property within the past year prior to filing a bankruptcy petition or the debtor as having been discharged in a trial bankruptcy proceeding within the next previous six months.

1. Certain taxes that accrue prior to the filing of the petition; and

2. Alimony and child support payments.

Corporations and partnerships cannot be discharged from their indebtedness in bankruptcy in which liquidation and equal distribution of assets become a primary purpose for filing the petition. This is because this process could reduce the claims asserted by creditors. The same is true of banking institutions and insurance corporations. The reason: They have received money from the public.

CHAPTER 11 BUSINESS REORGANIZATION OF DEBTS AND ASSETS

One of the most revolutionary modifications in bankruptcy law resulting from the Bankruptcy Reform Act of 1978 was the consolidation of Chapters 9, 11, and 12. As it stands, all business reorganization of debts can now be handled under Chapter 11 of the new bankruptcy code. This chapter is divided into subchapters as follows:

Subchapter (1) Officers and Administration

Subchapter (2) The Plan

Subchapter (3) Post-Confirmation Matters

Subchapter (4) Railroad Reorganization

Because of the complexity involved in these subchapters, we will give only an overview of Chapter 11, since it will be the attorney's job to apply the subchapters and their provisions to the client's needs and desires in his reorganization plan.

A. Who May File for Reorganization Under Chapter 11

Whereas Chapter 7 and 13 give the individual person a fresh start, Chapter 11 gives the business debtor relief from financial distress.

As with other reorganization petitions, Chapter 11 petitions can be instituted by way of either a voluntary petition by the debtor or by way of an involuntary petition filed by the creditors of the debtor.

The Federal Bankruptcy Code states that any business entity that can file a voluntary petition for liquidation is eligible to file a petition for reorganization. Moreover, though farmers and nonprofit organizations are eligible to file voluntary petitions for reorganization, they cannot be compelled to reorganize.

The specifics of the nature and scope of the Plan for Reorganization as to who may file a plan, the contents of the plan, impairment of claims and interests, post-petition disclosures and solicitational acceptance of the plan, modification of the plan, and confirmation of the plan are governed by Title 11, Bankruptcy Code, Subchapter 2, Sections 1121 to 1129. The post-confirmation matter can be found in Chapter 3 of the code, Sections 1141 through 1146.

B. Conversion and Dismissal

Specifically discussing conversion or dismissal, the following is submitted for your review. The details can be found in Title 11, United States Bankruptcy Code, Subchapter 1, Section 1112.

Should your attorney decide that it would be in the best interests of the business debtor to convert a Chapter 11 to a Chapter 12, the following should be checked by you to determine eligibility:

1. If the client/debtor, at the time of the application for petition to reorganize, is a *debtor in possession;*
2. If it is an involuntary petition that was originated under this chapter; or
3. If it was not petitioned to be converted under Chapter 11 at the request of another, that is, creditor, equity holder, and so forth.

Note: The Court may convert a Chapter 11 reorganization case to a case under the provisions of Chapter 13 if the debtor makes such a request or, if the debtor has been discharged, under Section 1141(d) of Title 11.

The court may also convert a case under Chapter 11 to a case under Chapter 7 if the debtor is a farmer or a corporation that is not a monied business or commercial corporation, unless the debtor requests such conversion.*

C. Prerequisites for Conversion of a Chapter 11 to a Chapter 12 Filing

In order for the business debtor to qualify for a conversion, you must be sure that the following elements exist:

1. That the business debtor has suffered a continuing loss of property and that there is an apparent absence of likelihood for rehabilitation;

---

* See Title 11 U.S. Code Bankruptcy, Subchapter 1, Chapter 11, page 241.

2. That the business debtor is unable to effectuate a plan;

3. That there has been an unreasonable delay on the part of the business debtor that is prejudicial to his creditors;

4. That the business debtor has been unable to produce a plan within the time set by the court;

5. That there has been a denial of confirmation of a proposed plan a denial of a petition for additional time to file another plan or modification of any previous plan;

6. That there has been a revocation by the court of an order of confirmation of the plan and/or a denial of confirmation of another plan or modification thereof;

7. That there has been, on the part of a business debtor, demonstrated inability to effectuate consummation of a confirmed plan;

8. That there has been on the part of the business debtor a material default with respect to any confirmed plan; and

9. That there has been a termination, by the court, of a confirmed plan, resulting from an occurrence of nonoccurrence of a condition specified in the plan.

CHAPTER 13 WAGE-EARNER PETITION

Chapter 13 of the Federal Bankruptcy Code governs a bankruptcy petition. The wage-earner petition gives the debtor the opportunity to arrange installment payments with his creditors rather than liquidate his assets. But more important, it is aimed to aid the debtor avoid the stigma of being adjudged a bankrupt under the old act. Under the old act, the wage-earner petition was limited and available only to wage earners and not to self-employed persons; furthermore, under this petition secured creditors had the right to veto any plan that adversely affected them, and it did not prevent creditors from going after the spouses and/or relatives of a petitioning bankrupt. The new act solves those problems.

Note that the following chapters of the new Federal Bankruptcy Code affect Chapter 13 as those chapters relate to practice and procedure to be followed.

For example, Chapter 1 of the code contains the applicable and general conditions and definitions; Chapter 3 of the code contains the procedure for commencing the case, including the powers of the trustees, the automatic stay provisions, the meeting of creditors, and so forth, all of which are applicable to Chapter 13. Chapter 5 of the new Federal Bankruptcy Code contains matters such as claims, priorities, exemptions, property of the bankrupt, and other such related matters, which apply to Chapter 13 unless in conflict with provisions of Chapter 13.

Chapter 13 applies only to petitions to adjust debts of and for individuals.

A. Who May File Under Chapter 13

Under the new Federal Bankruptcy Code, any person who can establish the stability and regularity of income to ensure that payments can be made to creditors under Chapter 13 may file a Chapter 13 petition. The exceptions to this rule are stockholders or commodity brokers, but included are self-employed individuals such as pharmacists, grocery store owners, plumbers, farmers, and the like. Interesting also is the fact that individuals living on pensions or receiving Social Security benefits and the like are eligible to file under Chapter 13.

But there is a catch to this, and it is as follows:

At the time of the filing of a Chapter 13 petition, the individual with regular income must owe less than $100,000 in unsecured, noncontingent or liquidated debts and/or noncontingent, liquidated, or secured debts of less than $360,000.

Furthermore, if it is a joint petition, that is, husband and wife, the aggregate amount owed may not exceed $100,000 in unsecured debts and/or $350,000 in secured debts.

A Chapter 13 proceeding can be commenced only by the filing of a voluntary petition by the individual debtor or, if it is a joint case, by the husband and wife. The procedure for filing a Chapter 13 petition is the same as that used when filing a Chapter 7 petition; that is, the rules governing venue, jurisdiction, transfer, and so forth, apply to the wage earner petition under Chapter 13. As with Chapter 7 petitions, the Chapter 13 petitioner must list all creditors and submit schedules and the statement of affairs.

B. Limited Automatic Stay

The protection against debt collection and the enforcement of liens as provided for in liquidation and the reorganization cases applies to Chapter 13 filings as well. However, that protection is limited in order to protect the lender against loss of substantial rights as against a co-debtor's liability. It should be made clear to the client–debtor that this automatic stay is only a procedural delay, which does not affect the right of a creditor to full satisfaction from either the debtor or the co-debtor.

The automatic stay under a Chapter 13 wage-earner petition merely means that the lender must wait for payment of a debt under the Chapter 13 plan. Furthermore, the automatic stay in this instance arises only when consumer debts are involved and they are debts of an individual debtor and not upon any debts that arose as the result of the conduct of business and furthermore that the stay is automatically lifted when the Chapter 13 proceeding is either closed, dismissed, or converted.

Note: If there is a danger that the statute of limitations will prevent a creditor from collecting his just debts from the debtor, the code provides that "the period in which the creditor may sue the co-debtor does not expire until either the end of the original statute of limitations, or thirty (30) days after notice of determination of the stay, whichever is later." See S. Rpt. No. 95-989, 96 Cong. 2nd Sess. 139 (1978).

C. Post-Petition Claims

The general provisions of the Federal Bankruptcy Code governing the filing of proofs of claims, allowance of claims, secured and priority claims, and the like, in liquidation cases are applicable to Chapter 13 filings. However, there are special provisions made for the filing of post-petition claims.

There are just two types of post-petition claims which are allowed under this Chapter filing (though it is not mandatory that they be filed):

1. A claim for taxes which becomes payable while the case is still pending; and
2. Claims based upon a consumer debt.

When these types of claims are filed, they will either be allowed or disallowed under the same provisions which determine the allowability of post-petition claims in other chapters. Furthermore, to provide this allowance, these claims are handled as if they had arisen before the date of the filing of the petition.

D. Conversions/Dismissal

Initially, it is noteworthy that the code specifically provides that a Chapter 12 liquidation may not be converted into a Chapter 13 case, unless specifically requested by the debtor.

Involved in and pertinent to conversion or dismissal of a Chapter 13 filing are the following:

1. The debtor's right to convert or dismiss;
2. Dismissal or conversion for cause:
   a. Unreasonable delay by the debtor, which is adjudged prejudicial to the creditors;

b. Nonpayment of court fees and administrative costs;

c. Failure of a debtor to file a plan in a timely manner as required by Chapter 13;

d. Denial of confirmation of a plan and a denial of additional time to file another or modified plan;

e. A material default of a debtor in connection with term or terms of the confirmed plan;

f. Revocation of the order of confirmation and denial of confirmation of a modified plan, and

g. The termination of a confirmed plan.

3. Conversion to Chapter 11 for a more complex reorganization of the debtor's debts.

E. Specific Effects of Chapter 13

1. *Additional Rights.* A Chapter 13 debtor has all the rights of a Chapter 7 debtor, as well as the additional rights as follows.

2. *Retention of property.* One particular advantage in a Chapter 13 proceeding is that the debtor may retain her property (home, automobile, and so forth) while making payments to creditors. The Chapter 13 trustee does not take possession or ownership of the property of the debtor as in Chapter 7.

3. *Reinstatement of defaults.* A Chapter 13 debtor may cure defaults on mortgage or deed of trust payments, including defaults that could no longer be cured under nonbankruptcy law.

4. *Co-debtor stay.* Chapter 13 debtors who have had personal loans cosigned by friends or relatives obtain an automatic stay of actions by those persons upon the filing of Chapter 13. If the Chapter 13 debtor does not pay the creditor in full, the creditor may obtain permission from the Bankruptcy Court to proceed against the co-signer. The creditor must file an adversary proceeding for relief from co-debtor stay.

5. *Rejection of executory contracts.* The Chapter 13 debtor can get out of agreements to purchase or rent property and other contractual obligations that are not to her benefit.

6. *Confirmation of plan.* If the Bankruptcy Court is satisfied that creditors will receive more under a Chapter 13 plan than they would on Chapter 7 Liquidation, the plan meets the "best interests" test. If the court is also satisfied that the debtor is making "meaningful payments" in good faith, the debtor may be able to obtain "confirmation" of the Chapter 13 Plan.

7. *Secured creditor cram-down.* If secured creditors (other than those holding the deed of trust or mortgage on the debtor's residence) do not agree to repayment terms offered by the Chapter 13 debtor, the court can force the creditors to accept reduced payments so long as the "value" of the security is given to the creditor.

8. *Super discharge.* A Chapter 13 debtor who obtains confirmation of a Chapter 13 plan is entitled to a discharge of all debts except taxes and alimony, even those that cannot be discharged in Chapter 7.

SPECIFIC CHANGES IN FILING PROCEDURE AND DISTRIBUTION UNDER THE NEW FEDERAL BANKRUPTCY ACT

CHAPTERS 7 AND 13

Chapter 7 (Liquidation) and Chapter 13 (Debt Adjustment of Individuals with Regular Income) cases require the following in filing.

Procedure: One original and three copies of the petition under Chapter 7 or 13 should be filed with the clerk, who files a copy of the petition regarding release under subchapter 3 of Chapter 7 to the Securities Investor Protection Corporation, and one copy of the petition under subchapter 4 of Chapter 7 to the Commodities Futures Trading Commission. (See Rule 1002.)

CHAPTERS 9 AND 11

Chapter 9 (Adjustment of Debts of a Municipality) and Chapter 11 (Reorganization of Debts) cases must be filed in the following manner.

Procedure: One original and six copies of the Petition under Chapter 9 or 11 should be filed with the clerk. The clerk thereafter transmits two copies to the Securities Exchange Commission, two copies to the District Director of the Internal Revenue Service in which the case is filed, one copy to the secretary of state of the state in which the debtor is located, and one copy of a Chapter 11 petition is filed with the secretary of Commerce.

If the petition for relief is filed under sub-chapter 4 of Chapter 11, the clerk of the Bankruptcy Court will file a copy with the Interstate Commerce

Commission and one copy with the secretary of the Department of Transportation. (See Rule 1002.)

PARTNERSHIP PETITIONS

A voluntary petition may be filed by all the general partners on behalf of a partnership.

Where there is an involuntary petition (by creditor or less than all of the partners), when filed within five days thereafter, the petitioning partners or petitioning creditors should send a copy of the involuntary petition by first class mail, postage prepaid, to the last known address, or hand deliver a copy to each general partner who did not join in the petition, or who has not been served.

CHAPTER APPENDIX OF BANKRUPTCY FORMS

The following sample forms for use in federal bankruptcy courts illustrate the use of the required debtor and creditor information that has been discussed in this chapter.

Printed forms are available (for a price) from the bankruptcy court clerk's office, or they may be reprinted. The advantage of the packaged forms is that there are the required number of copies of each form. Check with the Bankruptcy Court clerk as to the availability of the packaged forms for use in that court.

In addition to court forms, two specimen bankruptcy problems are included, together with an office form for obtaining necessary information from the client. (See Figures 13.1 through 13.10.)

Figure 13.1   Bankruptcy Information Form

Although we are asking questions about all of your property, it does not mean that you will lose it by filing for bankruptcy.

Complete all questions fully and completely based on all information available to you. If you do not have the information available, make your best effort to obtain the information from all sources.

1. NAME AND RESIDENCE INFORMATION:

    A. Full name: _____

    B. Marital status (if married and separated from your spouse, please state "Separated" or if divorced state "Divorced"): _____

        Your spouse's name: _____

Figure 13.1   (Continued)

C. Social Security number: _____

Your spouse's Social Security number: _____

D. List any other names used by you or your spouse (including maiden name) in the last six years: _____

_____

_____

E. Current address: _____

                      Street   City   County   Zip

F. Telephone number: _____

                              Home   Work

(1) List spouse's current address and telephone number, if different than above:

        _____

        _____

G. List all addresses you have had in the last six years. If husband and wife are both filing bankruptcy, list addresses for each for the last six years: (Include street, town and zip code)

_____

_____

_____

_____

_____

2. OCCUPATION AND INCOME:

A. Usual type of work you do: _____

B. Name and address of *current* employer: _____

_____

C. Spouse's usual type of work: _____

_____

D. Name and address of spouse's CURRENT employer: _____

_____

E. How long were each of you at your current job: _____

_____

Figure 13.1 (Continued)

If not employed by present employer for at least one year, state the names of the prior employers of either of you and nature of your job.

_____

_____

F. When do you receive payment of your salary (weekly, twice monthly, monthly, etc.)?

_____

G. Have you or your spouse been in business by yourself or with others during the last six years? Yes ____ No ____ If yes, give the name of the business, its address, and the names of others in business with you or your spouse.

_____

_____

_____

H. Amount of wages that you and your spouse received for last year:

Your wages: _____

Your spouse's wages: _____

Amount of wages that you and your spouse received for the year before last:

Your wages: _____

Your spouse's wages: _____

Amount and type of payroll deductions:

_____

_____

Amount of any other income received by you and your spouse last year (specify source such as welfare, child support, unemployment compensation, etc.):

_____

Amount of any other income received by you and your spouse for the year before last (specify source): _____

_____

Amount of income which you and your spouse believe you will receive during the next twelve months:

_____

_____

Figure 13.1 (Continued)

Is your employment or your spouse's employment subject to seasonal change or variation?

_____

3. TAX RETURNS AND REFUNDS: (Bring a copy of your income tax returns with you to our office.)

   A. Did you file a federal income tax return during the last three years?
      Which year or years? _____
      Did you file a state income tax return during the last three years?

      _____

      Which year or years? _____

   B. Where did you send tax returns for the last two years? Give city and state to which each form was mailed.
      State: _____
      Federal: _____
      State: _____
      Federal: _____

   C. Have you received any income tax refunds this year? Yes ___ No ___
      Amount: State $ _____ Federal $ _____

   D. What income tax refunds do you expect to receive this year? _____
      Amount: State $ _____ Federal $ _____

4. BANK ACCOUNTS AND SAFE DEPOSIT BOXES:

   A. Name and address of each bank in which you have had any account (checking, savings, etc.) during the past two years. Include every name on the account and the name of *every* person authorized to make withdrawals.

      _____

      _____

   B. Name and address of each bank you had any safe deposit box in during the past two years. Include name and address of all persons with a right to open the box, describe the contents of the box, and if given up, when:

      _____

      _____

Figure 13.1 (Continued)

C. Are you a member of a credit union? Yes ___ No ___ If yes, give its name
and address and how much you have saved there:

_____ $ _____
    Name   Address   Amount

5. **BOOKS AND RECORDS**

A. Have you kept books of accounts or records of any nature or type whether
formal or informal which relate to your finances during the last 2 years?

Yes ___ No ___ If yes, where are these books or records now
(Give names and addresses and include information about checkbooks,
bank statements, invoices, statements of accounts, etc.)?

_____

_____

_____

B. If any of the records of your financial affairs have been lost or destroyed
during the past two years, tell when and how:

_____

_____

_____

6. **PROPERTY HELD FOR ANOTHER PERSON:** Do you have in your possession
any property, furniture, etc. that belongs to another person? Yes ___ No ___ If
yes, what is the property, who owns it and what is it worth? Include name and
address of the owners:

Type of Property	Value	Owned by	Address	Relative Yes or No

7. **PRIOR BANKRUPTCY:** Were you ever involved in any prior bankruptcy action? Yes ___ No ___ If yes, bring *all* papers relating to the action to our office.

8. **RECEIVERS AND ASSIGNEES:**

A. Is a receiver or trustee holding any of your property? (Generally, a receiver is
a person appointed by a court to receive and preserve the property or funds
involved in a legal proceeding. A trustee is generally a person appointed by
the court who is required by law to care for property and administer its dis-

Figure 13.1 (Continued)

position) Yes_____ No _____ If yes, bring in all papers relating to the property and the person's appointment.

_____

Trustee's Name   Address

B. Did you give, transfer, deliver, pledge or assign for any reason whatsoever any of the property (including wages) to a creditor within the past year? Yes ___ No ___ If yes, describe the property, its worth and give the name and address of the person you gave it to:

Type of Property   Value   Name and Address of Person Who Has It

_____

_____

_____

_____

_____

_____

9. PROPERTY HELD BY ANOTHER PERSON: Does anyone have anything of value that belongs to you? For example, have you loaned any of your property to another person or does a person other than a creditor hold any of your property for any reason? Yes ___ No ___ If yes, who has the article, what is that person's address and what is the article worth:

Article   Who Has the Article/Address   Value

_____

_____

_____

_____

10. LAWSUITS AND ATTACHMENTS:

A. Have you been a party to a lawsuit of any kind during the past 12 months? Yes ___ No ___ If yes, bring in all papers pertaining to any lawsuits in which you have ever been involved.

B. Are you suing anyone, or do you have any possible reason for suing someone, for injuries to yourself or other members of your family? Yes ___ No ___ If yes, who are you suing, for how much are you asking and why are you suing?

_____

_____

Figure 13.1 (Continued)

C. To your knowledge, does anyone have any reason for suing you (*e.g.*, car accident)? _____

_____

D. Have you had any property sold in a sheriff's sale or seized by a creditor or creditor's representative during the last 4 months? Yes ___ No ___ If yes, bring any papers concerning those actions. Below, give a description of the property and the names and addresses of any creditors involved, as well as the dates involved.

_____

_____

E. Has your bank account or paycheck been garnished in the last 4 months?

Yes ___ No ___ If yes, give the following:

Who Received the Money	Amount Taken	Dates:	From	To

_____

_____

_____

11. LOANS REPAID:

A. If you have made any payments within the last 12 months to creditors from whom you have a loan of any type whether secured or unsecured (not medical bills, charge accounts or other open accounts), give the name of the creditor, the dates of the payments and the amount of the payments:

Creditor	Payment Dates	Amount of Payment

_____

_____

_____

_____

_____

B. Have you paid off any loans in full in the last 12 months? Yes ___ No ___ If yes, give the following:

Creditor	Address	Date Paid	Amount Paid	Relative Yes or No

_____

_____

_____

_____

Figure 13.1 (Continued)

12. PROPERTY TRANSFERS:

   A. Describe any gifts other than ordinary and usual presents to family members and charities during the past one year. Include the date of transfer and name and address of who received the gift:

   _____

   _____

   B. Describe any sales or other transfers of any of your property during the past one year. Include the date of the transfer and the names and addresses of the people who received the property:

Property	Amount Received For It	Date	Person It Was Sold to/Address

   C. State the amount of money you actually received for the sale or transfer of any of the property you listed in A and B above:

   _____

   _____

   _____

13. REPOSSESSIONS AND RETURNS: If any property was repossessed (taken by a creditor) or returned during the past one year, give the following:

Description of Property	Date of Return or Repossession	Creditor	Address	Value

14. LOSSES:

   A. If any property was lost in the past one year due to fire, theft or gambling, describe the property and its value, give the date of the loss and identify all persons involved.

   _____

   _____

Figure 13.1 (Continued)

B. Did insurance pay for any part of the loss? Yes ____ No ____ If yes, give date of payment _____ and amount paid _____

15. PAYMENTS OR TRANSFERS TO ATTORNEYS:

A. Give the date, name and address of any attorney you consulted during the past one year:

_____

_____

B. Give the reason for which you consulted an attorney during the past year:

_____

_____

C. Give the date and amount you have paid an attorney or any property you have transferred to any attorney:

_____

_____

D. If you have promised to pay an attorney within the past year, give the amount and terms of the agreement:

_____

_____

16. BUSINESS: If you are in business, list the names of all the partners in your business, or if your business is a corporation, the names of all of the officers, directors and stockholders of the corporation:

_____

_____

_____

_____

_____

17. DEPENDENTS:

Does either spouse pay or receive alimony, maintenance or child support?

Husband: _____ How much? _____

Wife: _____ How much? _____

If support received, for whose benefit is it received? _____

_____

Figure 13.1 (Continued)

List all dependents other than present spouse for whose support either spouse is responsible. Also state their relation to you. _____

_____

_____

18. BUDGET:

    A. Please estimate what you believe will be you and your spouse's average future monthly income for the next 12 months:

       Others (describe) _____ Amount _____

                          _____ Amount _____

    B. If there is a co-signer or guarantor for any of your debts, give co-signer's or guarantor's name and which debt he or she co-signed for or guaranteed:

_____

_____

_____

_____

    C. Have you ever been a co-signer or guarantor for someone else's debts? Yes ___ No ___ If yes, give the following:

Creditor	Address	Amount Owed	Date You Co-signed	Person You Co-signed For

ASSET LIVING

1. REAL PROPERTY:

    Do you own real estate? Yes ____ No ____ Describe and give the location of all real property (lot, house, burial plot, etc.) in which you hold an interest: (if you have the deed or mortgage bring them with you to our offices)

_____

_____

_____

    Outstanding mortgage balance: _____

Figure 13.1 (Continued)

Name of mortgage company: _____

Purchase price: _____ Year purchased: _____

Address: _____

Present value of your house: _____

Is there a second mortgage? Yes ____ No ____ If yes, give the name and address of the company: _____

2. PERSONAL PROPERTY:

   A. Cash on hand: _____

   B. Do you have any deposits of money in banks, savings and loan associations, credit unions, utility companies, or with landlords or others? If yes, list the name and address of the company and the amount of deposit:

      _____

      _____

      _____

      Husband: _____ (take home pay)

      Wife: _____ (take home pay)

   C. Please set out the estimated average amount of the following monthly expenses you believe will be incurred over the next 12 months

      (1) Rent or mortgage: _____

      (2) Utilities: _____

      _____

      _____

      _____

      (3) Food: _____

      (4) Clothing: _____

      (5) Laundry and cleaning: _____

      (6) Newspapers, periodicals, etc. _____

      (7) Medical and drug expenses: _____

      (8) Insurance (not deducted from wages): _____

      (9) Transportation: car loans: _____

                           other: _____

      (10) Entertainment and recreation: _____

      (11) Dues (if not deducted from wages): _____

Figure 13.1 (Continued)

(12) Taxes not deducted from wages and not included in mortgage payment: _____

(13) Alimony, maintenance or support: _____

(14) Other support of dependents not at home: _____

(15) Other (specify): _____

_____

_____

_____

CREDITORS

1. SPECIAL CREDITORS:

   A. Do you owe wages to anybody? Yes ____ No ____

      To whom? _____

      Address: _____

      How much: _____

   B. Do you owe taxes to anybody? Yes ____ No ____ If so, to whom and how much:

      U.S.A. _____ Amount _____ State _____ Amount _____

      County _____ Amount _____

   C. List your major personal property items such as furniture, tools, appliances, stove, refrigerator, TV, sewing machine, etc., giving approximate age and value (what you think you could get for it if you sold it). Itemize as completely as possible:

Item	Approximate Age	Value (what you could get for it if you sold it)

Figure 13.1 (Continued)

If any of the above items are being financed through a company, list the item and the name and address of the company below and bring the financing papers to our offices:

_____

_____

_____

Give an estimate of the value (what you could get for it if you sold it) of the following:

All your furniture: _____ All your clothing: _____

All minor appliances: _____ All your jewelry: _____

All your other household goods (such as dishes, utensils, food, etc.):

_____

D. CARS, MOBILE HOMES, TRAILERS AND BOATS:

  1. Do you have any cars? Yes ___ No ___ If so, give the year, make, model, value and who is financing it: (Also give the amount owed and to what company or bank it is owed)

     _____

     _____

     _____

  2. Do you have any mobile homes, trailers, and/or boats? Yes ___ No ___ If so, give brand, year, value and who is financing it: (Also give amount owed)

     _____

     _____

     _____

E. ACCESSORIES:

  1. Do you own any life insurance policies? Yes ___ No ___

    Company/Address: _____

    How long have you had the policy? _____

    Cash surrender value: _____

  2. Do you own any stocks? Yes ___ No ___ Value of stocks: _____

  3. Do you own any bonds? Yes ___ No ___ Value of bonds: _____

Figure 13.1 (Continued)

4. Do you have any interest in or own any machinery, tools or fixtures used in your business or work? Yes _____ No _____ If yes, describe and state what you could sell it for:

_____

_____

5. Do you have any books, prints or pictures of substantial value? Yes ___ No ___ If so, estimate the value of them:

_____

_____

_____

_____

6. Do you have any stocks, bonds, certificates of deposit or the like? Yes ___ No ___ If so, estimate the value of them:

_____

7. Do you own or claim any other property not mentioned above? (Include livestock or animals other than family pets). Yes _____ No _____ If so, what: _____

   Value: _____

   Have you had any previous marriages? Yes _____ No _____
   If so, what is the name of your former spouse? _____

8. Does anybody owe you any money, alimony or child support? Yes ___ No ___ Who: _____

   How much: _____

9. Do you owe any alimony or child support? Yes _____ No _____
   If so, how much and to whom: _____

   _____

10. Have you been involved in any automobile accidents in the past two years? Yes _____ No _____

11. Do you expect to inherit any money within the next six months? Yes ___ No _____

12. Do you expect to receive any settlements from any insurance companies?

   Yes _____ No _____ Amount: _____

Figure 13.1 (Continued)

F. BUSINESS:

1. If you own or operate a business, does the business have any equipment or furniture of any type used in the business? Yes _____ No _____ If so, list all items and their estimated value:

   _____

   _____

2. Does the business have any outstanding and unpaid accounts receivable? Yes _____ No _____ If so, list the name and address of each person owing money to the company and the amount owed:

   _____

   _____

3. Does the company have any inventory of finished or unfinished goods or merchandise for sale? Yes _____ No _____ If so, list and give your best estimate of value:

   _____

   _____

4. Do you or does your business own or have an interest in any type of property about which we have not asked? Yes _____ No _____
   Please describe the property and the value you would give it:

   _____

   _____

   _____

I certify that the information contained in this application is true and correct to the best of my knowledge.

Dated: _____   _____

                                      _____

                                      Applicant(s)

Figure 13.2 Specimen Problem 1

Using a Chapter 13 (wage-earner petition) to restrain your creditors:

Harold M. has been sued by a finance company. They are demanding that he pay them $800. Harold had borrowed from them and gave them a "chattel mortgage" on his furniture. Harold could not pay the $800, so he went instead to downtown Los Angeles and filed a Chapter 13. Here is what Chapter 13 is doing for Harold.

It took about two hours for Harold to file his Chapter 13. As soon as he did so, the lawsuit brought against him by the finance company was "frozen." The finance company could not go ahead with the lawsuit.

Harold did not have to give up his furniture. He kept it. Through the Chapter 13, the chattel mortgage on the furniture was "avoided" or done away with. The finance company cannot ever get it.

The Chapter 13 operates as a restraining order on *all* creditors. The finance company had to stop telephoning him and demanding payment. The collection agencies had to stop harassing him—no more telephone calls to his employer, or to his home. Chapter 13 stops all such.

Harold had an old judgment outstanding against him, and that creditor sent the marshal to Harold's place of work to run an "attachment" against his earnings. Harold and his boss told the marshal that a Chapter 13 had been filed and gave him the number. The marshal then left, as he had been restrained from running the attachment.

Harold added up his debts, and they came to a total of $4,200. He added up his living expenses—rent, food, gasoline, and so forth—and figured out that the most he could pay his old creditors was $50 a month. He then arranged through the Chapter 13 plan that he would pay $50 a month for a period of thirty-six months, and that is what the creditors got. The creditors, including the finance company that had sued him, received less than half of what they wanted, but under the Chapter 13, they were entitled only to what Harold could afford. Harold did not have to pay the balance of the money he owed.

As shown by the foregoing, the new Chapter 13 plan was designed with the purpose of permitting a debtor to get full relief from his debts by paying what he can afford, and not the whole amount. This way he is able to avoid bankruptcy, and he does not have to borrow money.

Figure 13.3 Specimen Problem 2

THE NEW CONSOLIDATION PLAN

If you use the new Consolidation Plan, you do not have to borrow money, and you do not have to file bankruptcy. It is a new way to handle your creditors.

As soon as you must file your application for a Consolidation Plan, the creditors *must* leave you alone. They cannot sue you, cannot telephone you any more, cannot telephone your employer to put pressure on you, cannot tie up your paychecks, cannot pick up your automobile, and cannot even write a letter to you.

How would you like to pay your creditors only what you can afford (not what they want), and as long as you are doing this, the creditors *must* leave you strictly alone? This can be done through the new Consolidation Plan. Here is how it works:

First, you write down on a sheet of paper how much money you bring home each month. Next, add up your ordinary monthly living expenses—rent, food, medical, utilities, transportation, and so forth. Subtract the monthly living expenses from the amount you bring home. What is left is what you can afford to pay on the old bills. That is all you have to pay. This is divided up among the creditors.

What you do is to pay into the Consolidation Plan, once a month the amount that you can afford to pay. You make these payments for a limited period, usually twenty-four months. By then, the creditors may have been paid very little, but that is all they get, and they cannot come at you to make you pay the rest of it.

If you are buying things on time, like a car, a TV, stereo, or the like, you can either tell them to come and get it or work out a deal to pay the reasonable value of the property in reduced monthly payments.

Foreclosure on your home: The new Consolidation Plan stops the foreclosure immediately, and you have a period of time within which to get on your feet, so you will not lose your equity in the real property.

Figure 13.4 Voluntary Case: Debtor's Petition

UNITED STATES BANKRUPTCY COURT
FOR THE _____ DISTRICT
OF _____

In Re	)	Case No.:
	)	
	)	VOLUNTARY CASE: DEBTOR'S
	)	PETITION
	)	
Debtor(s)	)	
(Any other names used by	)	
Debtor within the last	)	
six years should also be	)	
placed here.)	)	
	)	
_____)		

1. Petitioner's Post Office address is _____

_____

2. Petitioner has resided (or has his domicile, or his principle place of business; or his principal assets) within this district and has had the same for the proceeding 100 days (or for a longer portion of the proceeding 100 days, than in any other district.)

3. Petitioner is qualified to file this petition and is entitled to the benefits of Title 11, United States Code of a voluntary debtor.

(Optional/if appropriate)

4. A copy of petitioner's proposed plan, dated _____, is attached. (Or petitioner intends to file a plan pursuant to Chapter 11 or Chapter 13 of Title 11, United States Code.)

WHEREFORE, petitioner prays for relief in accordance with Chapter 7, (Chapter 11 or Chapter 13) of Title 11, United States Code.

_____
Petitioner

_____
Address

I _____ the petitioner named in the foregoing petition hereby certify under penalty of perjury that the foregoing is true and correct.

Executed on _____

_____
Petitioner

Figure 13.5 Voluntary Case: Debtor's Joint Petition

UNITED STATES BANKRUPTCY COURT
FOR THE _____ DISTRICT
OF _____

In Re   )   Case No.:
)
)   VOLUNTARY CASE: DEBTOR'S
)   JOINT PETITION
)
      Debtor(s)   )
(Any other names used by   )
Debtor   within the last six years)
should also be placed here.   )
_____   )

    1. Petitioner's Post Office address is _____

_____

    2. Petitioner has resided (or has his domicile, or his principle place of business; or his principal assets) within this district and has had the same for the proceeding 100 days (or for a longer portion of the proceeding 100 days, than in any other district.)

    3. Petitioner is qualified to file this petition and is entitled to the benefits of Title 11, United States Code of a voluntary debtor.
(Optional—if appropriate)

    4. A copy of petitioner's proposed plan, dated _____, is attached. (Or petitioner intends to file a plan pursuant to Chapter 11 or Chapter 13 of Title 11, United States Code.)

    WHEREFORE, petitioner prays for relief in accordance with Chapter 7, (Chapter 11 or Chapter 13) of Title 11, United States Code.

_____
Petitioner

_____
Address

I_____ the petitioner named in the foregoing petition hereby certify under penalty of perjury that the foregoing is true and correct.
    Executed on _____

_____
Petitioner

Figure 13.6 Involuntary Case: Creditors' Petition

1. Petitioners, _____ , , of _____ , and _____ _____ , of _____ , and _____ , _____ , of _____ , are creditors of _____ of _____ , holding claims against him, not contingent as _____ to liability, amounting to the aggregate, in excess of the value of any lien held by them on the debtor's property securing such claims, to $5,000 or over. The nature and amount of petitioner's claims are as follows:

2. The debtor has had his principal place of business (or his domicile or his principal assets or has resided) within this district for the 180 days preceding the filing of this petition (or for a longer portion of the 180 days preceding the filing of this petition than in any other district.)

3. The debtor is a person against whom an order for relief may be entered until Title 11, United States Code.

4. The debtor is generally not paying his debts as they become due as indicated by the following:

_____

_____

or (within 120 days preceding the filing of this petition, a custodian was appointed for or has taken possession of substantially all of the property of the debtor as follows: _____

_____)

WHEREFORE, petitioners pray that an order of relief be entered against _____ under Chapter 7 (or 11) of Title 11, United States Code.

Signed: _____

_____

Attorney for Petitioner
Address: _____

_____

_____

(Petitioners Sign if Not
Represented by Attorney)

_____

_____

_____

Petitioners

Figure 13.6 (Continued)

I, _____ , one of the petitioners named in the following petitioner, certify under penalty of perjury that the foregoing is true and correct according to the best of my knowledge, information and belief. Executed on this _____ day of _____ , 19_____.

_____
Petitioner

Note: This form may be adapted for use where a petition is filed against a partnership by fewer than all of the general partners.

The requisites for an Involuntary Petition are specified in 11 U.S.C. 803.

Figure 13.7. Proof of Claim

UNITED STATES BANKRUPTCY COURT
FOR THE _____ DISTRICT
OF _____

In Re   )   Case No.:
)
)   PROOF OF CLAIM
)
            Debtor(s)   )
(Any other names used by   )
Debtor within the last   )
six years should also be   )
placed here.)   )
_____)

1. The undersigned, who is a claimant herein resides at (put down person's current address)

_____

(If, however, the claimant is a partnership claiming to be a member he should not only give his address but state that he is a member of a partnership and the composition of that partnership and the location of their business and make a statement to the fact that they are authorized to make proof of the claim on behalf of the partnership.)

Figure 13.7 (Continued)

(If the claimant is a corporation claiming through an authorized officer then he should state where he resides and that he is president, vice-president or whatever of a corporation, and the corporation is organized under the laws of the state or other; and that the corporation does business at a local address and that he is the officer authorized to make proof of the claim on behalf of the corporation.)

2. The debtor was at the time of the filing of the petition initiating this case, and still is indebted to the claimant in the sum of $ _____ .

3. The consideration for this debt (or grounds for liability) is as follows: (*Here you should state whether or not the same was an unsecured debt or a secured debt or any other basis upon which the claim is filed.*)

4. (If the claim was based upon a written instrument) The writing on which this claim is founded is attached hereto (or cannot be attached for the reasons set forth in the statement attached hereto).

5. (If applicable) This claim is founded on an open account, which became or will become due on _____ , as shown by the itemized statement attached hereto. (Unless it is attached hereto or its absence is explained in an attached statement, no note or other negotiable instrument has been received on account or any part of it.)

6. No judgment has been rendered on the claim except (*Here you should state if any payments were made or any other means of diminishing the debt.*)

7. The amount of all payments on this claim had been credited and deducted for the purpose of making this proof of claim.

8. This claim is not subject to any set-off or counter-claim except for the following: (*Here set forth any action made on the part of creditor to offset this claim.*)

9. No security interest is held for this claim except (*If security interest in the property of a debtor is claimed then this question should be answered.*)

(The undersigned claims the security interest under the writing as set forth in paragraph 4 above, is attached hereto; or under a separate writing which cannot be attached hereto for the reasons set forth in the attached statement. Evidence of perfection of social security interest is also attached hereto.)

10. This claim is a general unsecured claim, except to the extent that security interests, if any, described in paragraph 9 is sufficient to satisfy the claim.

DATED:

_____

(Signature)

Figure 13.8 Complaint for Relief from Automatic Stay

ADVERSARY PROCEEDINGS FORMAT

The following is the initial pleading filed to obtain relief from an automatic stay.

In Re	)	ADV. No.: 81-(JM)
	)	
MARIE PROTEIN	)	Bk. No.: 81-(JM)
	)	
vs.	)	COMPLAINT FOR RELIEF
	)	FROM AUTOMATIC STAY
NATIONAL BISCUIT	)	
COMPANY	)	
	)	
_____	)	

In this proceeding the summons is issued and the court (trial or a preliminary hearing) sets the date, all of which is done within two distinct 30 day periods (see Rule 710).

Figure 13.9 Order for Relief

UNITED STATES BANKRUPTCY COURT

FOR THE _____ DISTRICT

OF _____

In Re	)	Case No.:
	)	
	)	ORDER FOR RELIEF
	)	
	)	
Debtor(s)	)	
	)	
(Any other names used by	)	
Debtor within the last	)	
six years should also be	)	
placed here.)	)	
	)	

On consideration of a petition filed on _____ against the above-named debtor, an order for relief under Chapter 7 (or 11) of Title 11 of the United States Code is GRANTED.

DATED:

_____
Bankruptcy Judge

Figure 13.10 Discharge of Debtor

DISCHARGE OF DEBTOR*

It appearing that the person named above has filed a petition commencing a case under Title 11, United States Code, on _____ , and an order for relief was entered under Chapter 7 and that no complaint objecting to the discharge of the debtor was filed within the time fixed by the court [or that a complaint objecting to discharge of the debtor was filed and, after due notice and hearing, was not sustained]; it is ordered that

1. The above-named debtor is released from all dischargeable debts.
2. Any judgment heretofore or hereafter obtained in any court other than this court is null and void as a determination of the personal liability of the debtor with respect to any of the following:
    (a) debts dischargeable under 11 U.S.C. §523;
    (b) unless heretofore determined by order of this court to be nondischargeable, debts alleged to be executed from discharge under clauses (2), (4) and (6) of 11 U.S.C. §523(a);
    (c) debts determined by this court to be discharged under 11 U.S.C. §523(d).
3. All creditors whose debts are discharged by this order and all creditors whose judgments are declared null and void by paragraph 2 above are enjoined from instituting or continuing any action or employing any processes to collect such debts as personal liabilities of the above-named bankrupt.

DATED: _____

          BY THE COURT

          _____

          Bankruptcy Judge

---

* This form is a revision of Official Form No. 24. It takes into account the feature of 11 U.S.C. §523 which, in turn, were derived from the 1970 amendments to the Bankruptcy Act.

~ CHAPTER 14 ~

Setting Up a Corporate Entity

This chapter deals primarily with, and gives an overview discussion of, the pitfalls, questions which may arise, and steps to be considered when setting up any type of business venture. It will therefore outline certain step-by-step procedures regarding the accumulation of the proper documents, such as articles of incorporation, which can now be found in printed form. We state this simply because it will be your duty as the attorney's paralegal to gather these documents and do the legal research pertinent thereto.

First and foremost, what is a corporation? The law books tell us that a corporation is considered to be an entity, a legal person separate and apart from persons interested in controlling it.

There are several classes of corporations which we will discuss. Please note in your research that these different classes of corporations are organized under different statutes and may not be the same in your state.

1. The *public corporation,* which includes such entities as the cities, towns, tax districts, irrigation districts, departments of water and power, etc., and may also include the Federal Deposit Insurance Corporation and the Federal Savings and Loan Insurance Company.

2. The *corporations not for profit,* which are organized for purposes other than monetary gain. These types of corporations are normally for religious, social, educational or charitable purposes. And the designation as a nonprofit corporation bestows a preferred tax exempt status under the *Internal Revenue Code.*

319

3. The *corporations for profit,* which are organizations that issue stock and sell the same for profit. These corporations can be classified as publicly owned corporations, closed corporations and professional corporations.

The closely held corporation normally concerns itself with a small group of stockholders and oftentimes they are all members of the same family. You might research this in your state to see if special corporate laws are applicable. (See Exhibit A.)

4. The *professional corporation,* commonly known as the "professional association," which we see all the time with lawyers and doctors, etc.

In addition to the above classifications of corporations, you also have what is called the *de jure corporation* and the *de facto corporation.*

The *de jure corporation* is one which has been formed in compliance with all of the applicable state laws and may have the right to sue and be sued.

Exhibit A

Publicly Held Corporations

ADVANTAGES	DISADVANTAGES
1. Easier to raise capital.	1. Difficulty in borrowing money since no one in the corporation will be personally responsible; and the corporation does not have adequate assets.
2. Keeps the officers more honest because of the requirement to file report with the SEC and annual report to the stockholders.	
3. Easier to purchase or merge with other businesses or corporations.	2. Profit must be distributed upon demand even if the officers wanted to retain it in the business.
4. Easier to expand business:	3. Extensive paperwork, bookkeeping, financial reports, etc.
i) sale of stock	
ii) issuance of debt securities, bonds, etc.	4. Decisions of directors subject to attack by stockholders.
iii) issuance of additional class of stocks.	

Privately Held Corporations

ADVANTAGES	DISADVANTAGES
1. Higher profit for individual owner.	1. Higher risk for individual owner - bankruptcy.
2. Decisions can be made quickly and without too much resistance.	2. Easier to dissolve the corporation.
3. If necessary, profit can be retained in the business for reinvestment and expansion.	3. Since there will be more difficulty in raising money, it will be harder to expand the business.
4. Easier to borrow money, if the officers are willing to co-sign a note.	4. Much harder to sell stock to private investors for expansion of the business.

Opposed to the *de jure corporation* is the *de facto corporation* which merely exercises corporate powers and franchises under the color of law, absent compliance to applicable state laws. Here again, you are cautioned to research your state corporate laws to see if there are any peculiar laws pertinent to these two corporations in your state.

After you have decided which type of corporation you will recommend to your employer for his client, then you have to determine under which tax laws it should be governed.

You may want to recommend that the newly formed corporation be treated as a "C" corporation or as a subchapter "S" corporation for purposes of federal income tax. As you know, a "C" corporation is automatically taxed unless its shareholders elect to be treated as an "S" corporation.

The "C" corporation is considered separate and apart from its shareholders as opposed to the "S" corporation, which treats its shareholders as partners. In this connection, you should review and research the Internal Revenue Code, election by a small business corporation.

KEY FACTORS TO BE RESEARCHED

1. **Determine how much capital or credit** will be required and if the client will be supplying all of it.
2. **What will be the liability?** Unlimited personal liability is a characteristic of a sole proprietorship and a general partner. You do not have this disadvantage under a corporate structure.

3. **Transferability of interest.** The corporation offers easy transferability of ownership interest, which makes it easy for one to liquidate his investment.

4. **Legal status.** It is important to know whether or not the proposed corporation (1) holds property; (2) can transfer ownership and (3) whether it can sue or be sued. All of these rights are available to a corporation.

5. **Longevity.** A partnership or sole proprietorship has a severe disadvantage in this area: **Reason:** death or withdrawal by a partner. A corporation goes on forever.

6. **The abilities and background of the promoters.** If a promoter can provide capital but does not have experience or management abilities, the sole proprietorship and the general partnership are unequitable business forms. And,

7. **Tax ramifications.** In this instance, you are talking about the issuance of stock; if at all.

The result of the issuance of several classes of stock, who owns them and how much, will affect the control of the operation.

STOCK ISSUANCE

The two principal classes of stock issued by a corporation under the laws of its state and the provisions of its articles of incorporation are:

(a) Common stock;

(b) Preferred stock.

Common stock is the most common type of stock issued by a corporation. It is the responsibility of the common stockholder to elect the board of directors, which has the responsibility of hiring persons to manage and operate the corporation. A common stockholder has no voice in the running of the corporation beyond the annual vote for the board of directors. And further, common stockholders are only entitled to share the assets of a corporation upon its dissolution.

Preferred stock owners' preference is a grey area in that it could pertain to the division of dividends or to the division of assets upon dissolution; or both.

VALUE OF THE STOCK

Stock can either be par-value stock or no-par-value stock. Stock, which has on its face the value thereof, is considered to be par-value stock. Stock upon which there is no value assigned is considered to be no-par-value stock. Preferred stock, as a general rule, has a par value, while common stock, on the other hand, can either be par-value or no-par-value.

Other types of stock can be *treasury stock,* which is stock previously sold by the corporation and later reacquired by the corporation. Then there is *watered stock,* which is stock when issued as fully paid up, but the purchase price therefor was paid with property of inflated value.

In discussing this with your attorney, either in a memorandum or a face-to-face conversation, be sure to bring up the Securities Act of 1933, which regulates the sale of securities in interstate commerce, as well as the Securities Exchange Act of 1934, which regulates initial offerings and the over-the-counter markets. This latter Act requires the registration of stock exchanges traded in interstate commerce and SEC-regulated, publicly held corporations.

To underscore what I have said, let us now deal with a hypothetical case scenario to bring the point home.

Your office has been consulted by A, B and C to give an analysis with regard to the operation of Special Metals, Inc. They have need for capitalization. They seek advice as to the methods for distributing the stock to the public to raise capital.

The background of the company is as follows:

A. The Company

Special Metals, Inc. was incorporated under the laws of the State of Ames, which follows the Uniform Securities Act and the Model Business Act in regulating corporations. Its principal asset consists of a "new process" for handling special metals. It has its executive offices and plant in the City of Langdell. Special Metals, Inc. has been organized to serve as a supplier of special metals and plastics, primarily for the electronics industry; and to act as a specialist consultant in the use and handling of special metals for electrical components.

The company will be working in research and development of new processes in the handling of special metals geared to the special needs of consumer problems.

The company is a new business, has no history of earnings or operations, and has no established competitive position. Investors, therefore, will have to assume the usual risks associated with any new business venture. Although the company has conducted various market surveys which indicate a broad potential market for its special process, no assurance can be given that Special Metals, Inc. will be successful in selling its product or realize any profits.

B. Incorporators

A, B and C, individually, have very little money or equity in personal or real property to sustain a corporation. Together they can raise $60,000, which is inadequate to establish a "space age" type of corporation, let alone buy the necessary equipment, plant site, raw materials, etc., needed to get a corporation of this nature off the ground.

A, B and C, for the majority of their adult life, have been employees, never employers with the accompanying knowledge of business management and operation.

A, B and C's prime assets lie in the area of their expertise in scientific procedures and metal processing, as well as creation of ideas; the "know-how" in experimentation; and their complete dedication to and conviction about their process. The creation of ideas was their job while in the employ of "X" Corporation.

It would appear, therefore, that the role to be played by A, B and C in Special Metals, Inc. would be in the nature of control and decision-making in the area of research and development; training of personnel and survey of markets for the sale and use of the process.

For this reason, it is conceivable that A, B and C would be of great help in selling not only the product of the company to the public but the stock of the corporation as well.

C. Stock

The price of the stock to be sold hereunder has been based upon the funds estimated by the company to be reasonably required to begin operations and not on book value, earnings, asset value or any other recognized criteria.

The threefold purpose of going public with stock is to raise money; de-termine interest in the company for the sale of the product of the company, and for profit.

One of the problems of Special Metals, Inc. is that the cash reserve is quite thin, i.e., $60,000, reduced to $59,700 since $300 was used as a deposit on a 90-day option to buy or lease a plant in Langdell. Furthermore, the only real as-set of the company is the "new process" for handling special metals. Addition-ally, the lack of a business tract record of A, B and C will cloud the matter and make it difficult to get financing. With this in mind, let us proceed to analyze the offers of financing proposed to date, in light of the federal and state re-strictions in the sale and purchase of securities.

D. Available Sources

I. L and P, a young lawyer and accountant, friends of A, B and C, offered their services in exchange for stock in the company. This would net them between $2,000 and $5,000 and might place some restrictions on the stock as to any tax exemptions.

The law is grey as to whether you can exchange stock for services, but it is clear that L and P can buy stock in the company for cash. As to the ac-countant: The Tax Commission looks down on the transfer of stock in ex-change for services. Reason: the Registration Statement required to be filed with the Securities Exchange Commission must be certified by "an indepen-dent public accountant" before it is filed as a step in going public with its stock; or to distribute its stock under the Securities Act of 1933. This Act pro-hibits issuance of stock to an accountant for his services in connection with the organization of a company, "if these services include preparation of the Registration Statement."

This provision is intended to protect the public investor and secure for the benefit of the public "detached objectivity" as to the financial status of the company. It is felt that an accountant with a financial interest in the company might lose his objectivity in preparing the Registration Statement.

As to the lawyer, the law is quite clear, and leaves the decision pretty much up to the business ethics of the lawyer as to whether or not he will accept stock in the company in exchange for his services. It is the position of the Commission that "though he owes a responsibility to the public, his first duty is to his client; and the protection of the interest and rights of said client." Therefore, it probably might not be a good idea for the lawyer to accept stock in Special Metals, Inc. because of the friendly relationship and the potential legal malpractice liability. On the other hand, should he choose to do so, he should fully disclose the nature and extent of his interest in Special Metals, Inc.

Perhaps L and his clients would be willing to furnish money and/or property needed, in exchange for securities of the corporation, which could be one or more types of stock and/or bonds.

II. L then put A, B and C in touch with a small investment firm which offered a "best effort underwriting," assuming all risks and guaranteeing approximately $400,000 but it wanted a 15–20 percent commission. A, B and C should reject this offer as the commissions alone would leave approximately $200,000 for the new company and their projection figure is $500,000 minimum. They must still allow for costs of legal fees, accountant charges, printing, sales promotion, etc.

III. A, B and C then contacted a large public underwriting company who offered a $500,000 guaranteed capitalization which would have included the cost of equipment, but who wanted a controlling interest in the company in exchange. This procedure should be rejected, as it would wipe out any tax exemption available under the Securities Act. This Act provides for continued control of the company to qualify it for said exemption; i.e., 80 percent of the shares of stock immediately upon the transfer of outstanding stock in the company. Under the terms of the foregoing proposition, this would not be the case.

IV. Sometimes a potentially large supplier or bank may provide money on notes of the company to be co-signed by the promoters. Such was the case when A, B and C visited an industrial commission and a small business investment company. The problem here was the feasibility of securing a bank loan which would insist on some type of security for the loan. Furthermore it would have required A, B and C to co-sign a loan, making them personally liable, instead of the corporation. This procedure, too, should be rejected, inasmuch as the company is too new and the market too speculative at this point. Plus, it would entail a great deal of time and expense to work out the financing arrangements. A loan from a finance company would not be in the best interest of Special Metals, Inc. at this time.

V. D, a stockbroker friend of A, B and C, suggested that they return to their original idea of private solicitation as a means of financing their company and its operations. There are a few wealthy individuals willing to pay five times more for the stock than the asking price. This measure would have the effect of setting up a small-knit corporation. This might be the way to go, provided, however, that Special Metals, Inc. could qualify as a small business corporation.

E. Litigation

None pending, but possible.

Reason: As indicated earlier, A, B and C were employees of "X" Corporation. While so employed, A, B and C developed a "new process" for handling special metals used in the component parts of "X" Corporation. This process is the prime and principal asset of Special Metals, Inc. All of the experimentation was done on company time, in the company plant, using company materials. A, B and C received salaries all during these procedures.

Admittedly, A, B and C advised the officers of "X" Corporation of the results of said experimentation, but they did not disclose the precise nature of the production processes which they had developed. While "X" Corporation was not interested in utilizing the new process in connection with its component parts (though aware of the "bright prospects" and future of the process), it is conceivable that it may change its mind when Special Metals, Inc. displays the success of the new process.

The question therefore arises as to whether or not A, B and C had a right to use the new process developed at the expense of "X" Corporation for their own use and benefit, and to the possible detriment of "X" Corporation.

The scope of unfair competition is not limited to any particular type of deception. The legal concept of unfair competition has evolved as a broad and flexible doctrine with the capacity for further growth to meet changing conditions. There is no complete list of activities that constitute unfair competition. In this example A, B and C developed a process at the request of their employer for its business activity. It was to be used by said employer. The slightest use, therefore, or invasion of information subsequently developed, would be advantageous to any competitor to the detriment, however remote, of "X" Corporation. A, B and C's misappropriation and/or conversion thereof, could be considered an act of unfair competition in setting up Special Metals, Inc., using this "new process."

F. Summary of Analysis

Special Metals, Inc., is a small business. It has no business track record and its incorporators have always been employees. They have no "business" track record or business management experience.

It will be difficult to raise money for this type of small business and the investors will have to assume all the normal risks (and perhaps more) associated with any new business venture.

The capital investment of Special Metals, Inc. is very thin.

The authorized shares of stock to be issued are only 122,000, the sale of which would net approximately $500,000 with no other shares of stock outstanding or in issue. This status of affairs would result in the necessity of issuing either additional shares of stock or securing debt bonds to raise more money, if and when needed. The stock structure should be revamped to allow for this contingency.

A possible lawsuit to enjoin the use of the "process" should be given careful consideration as a future substantial problem which could affect the sale of stock and the success in growth of the business.

WHAT WOULD BE YOUR RECOMMENDATION TO YOUR EMPLOYER?

INCORPORATION

STEP-BY-STEP PROCEDURES

(Be sure to check your local state statutes and corporations code before implementing these procedures)

In bringing a corporation into existence, there are certain steps which are necessary and prerequisite to be followed by your attorney; the role that you play is as follows:

1. Determine from the client the name of the corporation. (In our hypothetical case, the name was "Special Metals.") If not already accomplished, this name should be reserved with your local state department applicable. In California, it is the Secretary of State Division of Corporations.

    In most states, there is a "reservation" fee. This can be accomplished by calling the branch of the corporation division of the Secretary of State, if applicable in your state.

2. Then you prepare the necessary incorporating papers, such as the Articles of Incorporation. (See sample at the end of this chapter.)

3. It is also at this juncture that you prepare a Certification of Authority to issue stock. This is secured from the State Securities Department. Simultaneously, you should prepare the corporation's bylaws. In most states today, these are printed forms.

4. The next step is to have these documents, above described, executed by the pertinent partners and/or directors.

5. Thereafter, documents should be filed with the appropriate state department of your state. Here again, you should check your local state statutes regarding this procedure.

6. Prepare the notice and/or letter advising the incorporators of their first meeting. The date and time of this meeting should have been discussed with the incorporators.

7. Then prepare the necessary letter or notice regarding the first meeting of the directors. This would have been done at the meeting of the incorporators, (who may also be the original stockholders), when normally the board of directors would have been elected.

8. Then the stock certificates for the outstanding issue of stock should be prepared. The delivery of the stock certificates would have been determined at the board of directors meeting.

NOTE: IN SOME STATES, THE ARTICLES OF INCORPORATION MUST BE CREATED FROM SCRATCH. This being true, please be sure that you include, in your incorporation papers or articles, the purpose of the business. In some states this is called a "purpose clause." However, this might also be a form in your state; please be sure to check this.

If in your state, these articles are to be prepared from scratch, be sure to include the following: (a) name and address of the original incorporator; (b) names and addresses of the directors; (c) the number of shares of stock issued and delivered, if any; (d) designation of a resident agent; (e) the principal office of the corporation; (f) the fiscal year of the incorporation; (g) date for the annual stockholders' meeting; (h) initial capital of the corporation; (i) the authorized capital stock, including a breakdown of a number of shares of common and preferred stock; and (j) the number of shares which are either par-value or non-par-value.

Articles of Incorporation

I

The name of this corporation is:_____.

II

The purpose of this corporation is to engage in any lawful act or activity for which a corporation may be organized under the general corporation law of the State of _____, other than the banking business, the trust company business or the practice of a profession permitted to be incorporated by the _____ Corporation Code.

III

The name and address in the State of _____ of this corporation's initial agent for service of process is _____.

IV

This corporation is authorized to issue only one class of stock; and the total number of shares which this corporation is authorized to issue is _____.

DATED: _____, 19__

_____

I hereby declare that I am the person who executed the foregoing Articles of Incorporation, which execution is my act and deed.

_____

The above is an example of an alternative set of articles of incorporation. Of course, there are others which can be created which are in more detail and which may include the name and address of the incorporators as well as the names and addresses of the initial directors, and the duration of the corporation. A sample of a set of articles of incorporation for a nonprofit organization is also attached.

[Nonprofit Public Benefit Corporation]

ARTICLES OF INCORPORATION

OF

(CORPORATION NAME)

I

The name of this corporation is _____.

II

A. This corporation is a nonprofit public benefit corporation and is not organized for the private gain of any person. It is organized under the Nonprofit Public Benefit Corporation Law for charitable purposes.

B. The specific purpose of this corporation is to _____
_____.

III

The name and address in the State of California of this corporation's initial agent for service of process is:

_____.

IV

A. This corporation is organized and operated exclusively for charitable purposes within the meaning of Section 501(c)(3) of the Internal Revenue Code.

B. No substantial part of the activities of this corporation shall consist of carrying on propaganda, or otherwise attempting to influence legislation, and the corporation shall not participate or intervene in any political campaign (including the publishing or distribution of statements) on behalf of any candidate for public office.

V

The property of this corporation is irrevocably dedicated to charitable purposes and no part of the net income or assets of this corporation shall ever inure to the benefit of any director, officer or member thereof or to the benefit of any private person. Upon the dissolution or winding up of the corporation, its assets remaining after payment, or provision for payment, of all debts and liabilities of this corporation shall be distributed to a nonprofit fund, foundation or corporation which is organized and operated exclusively for charitable purposes and which has established its tax exempt status under Section 501(c)(3) of the Internal Revenue Code.

DATED: _____

_____
(Signature of Incorporator)

CHAPTER 15

How to Assist in a Criminal Law Practice

A legal assistant should be familiar, not only with the classification and types of crimes, but also with all aspects of criminal procedure, including pretrial and post-trial motions. The legal assistant should be able to conduct initial interviews with the client, when appropriate, and know what information is necessary to determine what Court documents are needed in preparation for the defense of the case. More importantly, the legal assistant should be fully aware of the fiduciary relationship between the client and the attorney.

Additionally, the legal assistant must have a working knowledge of specialized areas of criminal law and procedures that arise most often in criminal cases, such as: legality of arrests; searches and seizures (both with and without warrants); the admissibility of confessions or other statements of the defendant; the hearsay rule and its exceptions; the names of the various crimes as stated in the applicable criminal statute. The legal assistant should also know the elements of the crime, that is, that combination of intent and act which make up the crime and which must specifically be proved in order to secure a conviction.

The following discussion is based upon criminal law and practice in the State of California, the Federal Rules of Criminal Procedure, Evidence and Appellate Practice.

GENERAL DISCUSSION

Criminal law deals with: what is and what is not a crime.

The burden is on the state to prove "beyond a reasonable doubt." All the defendant has to do is sit there.

He technically does not even have to put on a defense, if he determines or feels from the State's witnesses that the State has not proven its case.

ELEMENTS: FOR EXAMPLE . . .

Burglary: This is a "breaking and entering into the dwelling place of another—in the nighttime—with *an intent* to commit a felony or serious crime therein."

NOW

Every crime is made up of certain elements and each of these elements MUST BE PRESENT. If not, there may not have been a crime committed.

So, let's examine the definition of Burglary:

1. *First* element: *entry into* the dwelling place of another (could be a driveway or backyard, etc.).
2. *Second* element: *breaking*—this could be opening a window or screen door, or just walking through an open door.
3. *Third* element: it has to have been *"at nighttime."*
4. *Fourth* element: there has to be "mens rea," the "intent" to commit a *serious crime therein.* This is *vitally* important: THE INTENT TO DO THE ACT.

ACTUS REUS

A criminal intent unaccompanied by a criminal act is not punishable in law.

There *must be* some affirmative action. Just thinking and planning is not a crime.

Problems with Actus Reus:

1. *Status or condition of person:*
   a. Vagrant;
   b. Unemployed;
   c. Meandering without purpose;
   d. No apparent means of subsistence.
2. *Responsibility for any conduct he (she)*
   a. Originates;
   b. Sets in motion;
   c. Solicits;
   d. Supports; or
   e. Incites.

AND

Relationship of the parties

Who actually commits the Actus Reus:

> a. Principals;
>
> b. Accessories;
>
> c. Aiders;
>
> d. Abettors;
>
> e. Agents.

3. *Does this conduct or act really cause the injury or harm?*

   The State must prove that a causal relationship exists:

   a. Between the act done; and

   b. The harm resulting therefrom.

   In other words:

   a. That the defendant acted;

   b. That the defendant caused the result.

Defenses:

> a. Defendant not responsible because of an *"intervening cause."*
>
> b. Defendant not responsible because of *"concurrent causes";*
>
> c. Defendant not responsible because of an *"independent intervening cause";*
>
> d. Defendant not responsible because of a *"superseding cause".*

Example: "A" beats up "B" and throws "B" into the street. "B" is subsequently run over by a car, and dies.

Question: Is "A" liable for murder?

> Was there a break in the chain of responsibility?
>
> Is "B"'s death caused totally by independent causes?
>
> When do third parties become partially responsible?

4. *When is an attempted act a legally complete Actus Reus?*

   a. Finding the accused guilty DOES NOT require successful completion of a crime.

   b. An "attempt" is an unfinished crime.

AND

5. *Is it impossible to commit the "Actus Reus"?*

   a. *Physically impossible:*

      (1) Pickpocket who attempts to steal from a person who has no wallet; or

      (2) Drug buyer wanting to purchase drugs from a dealer, who has none.

   b. *Factually impossible:*

      (1) Assault on a store "mannequin";

      (2) Abortion on a non-pregnant woman; or

      (3) Shooting a pillow thought to be a human body.

All had the intent—and punishable—not same degree.

   c. *Legally impossible:*

      (1) Perjury committed outside a legal proceeding;

      (2) Juvenile committing an "adult" crime; or

      (3) Can a party be convicted of rape when a person consented?

Conclusion:

If the *act* is impossible to *commit,* the Actus Reus may not be properly proven for the purposes of establishing criminal liability. IT MUST BE ACCOMPANIED BY A MENTAL STATE—MENS REA—AN INTENT TO COMMIT.

A. CLASSIFICATION OF CRIMES

1. *Felony:* very serious and punishable by imprisonment in state penitentiary.

2. *Misdemeanor:* less serious and generally punishable by a fine or commitment to a county jail.

B. PLEAS

1. Guilty. This can be either to the offense charged or to a less serious offense pursuant to an agreement with the prosecuting attorney.

2. Nolo Contendere. This is available in some jurisdictions and has the same effect as a plea of guilty, except that it cannot be used against the defendant in civil actions arising out of the same incident that gave rise to the criminal charges.

3. Not Guilty. (Self-explanatory)

4. Not Guilty by Reason of Insanity. This is sometimes pled in conjunction with the not guilty plea.

5. Double Jeopardy. Double jeopardy (or once in jeopardy). This is pled when a defendant has already been tried for the offense, unless the defendant successfully secured a new trial after an appeal; or after a motion for new trial was granted by the trial Court.

Rather than entering one of the above pleas, a defendant, in some jurisdictions, can enter a demurrer which in effect states that the complaint or information does not state a cause of action against him. After a hearing on the demurrer, the Court can either "sustain" the demurrer (and thus either dismiss the complaint or allow the prosecution to amend it), or can "overrule" the demurrer, at which point the defendant must enter a plea.

C. CRIMES FALL INTO THREE BASIC CATEGORIES

1. Crimes against the person;

2. Crimes against property; and

3. Crimes against the habitation.

D. TYPES OF CRIMES

1. First or Second Degree: murder;

2. *Voluntary or Involuntary:* manslaughter;

3. *Grand or Petty:* burglary, robbery, rape or theft;

4. *Arson;*

5. *Mayhem;*

6. *Kidnapping.*

CRIMES AGAINST THE PERSON:

A. *Homicide:*

1. *Murder: purposely or knowingly* done, or is committed recklessly, manifesting *extreme* indifference to human life.

2. *Manslaughter: An act of passion.* An act of extreme mental or emotional disturbance which has a reasonable explanation.

3. *Felony Murder Rule:* addresses itself to any and all members of a *"conspiracy to* commit a *major criminal felony* . . . where murder is a foreseeable result."

B. *Assault:* An intentional, unlawful offer of corporal injury to another by force to create well-founded fear of imminent peril, with apparent present ability to execute, if not prevented.

1. *Simple Assault:* One committed with no intention to do any other injury falls short of actual battery.

2. *Aggravated Assault:* One committed with the intention of committing some additional crime; or one attended with circumstances of peculiar outrage or *atrocity.*

3. *Reckless Endangerment:* Reckless taking of *chance* without intent that accident or injury would occur.

C. *Kidnapping:* Forcible removal of any person from his or her own country <u>now</u>, and/or <u>home</u> and/or confinement.

And today may include: "for the purposes of:"

1. Ransom, reward, shield or hostage;

2. Facilitating commission of a felony;

3. Inflicting bodily injury or terrorizing victim; and/or

4. Interfering in the performance of any governmental function.

D. *Sexual Offenses:*

Now includes men, women, boys and girls.

And, an "earnest-resistance requirement"; and "penetration, which includes *anus* or *mouth.*"

1. *Rape/Aggravated Sexual Assault*
   Elements:

   a. Sexual intercourse (penetration);

   b. Lack of consent (implying force or threat of harm); and

   c. Any "person"—rape has become "*neutral.*"

2. *Sexual Conduct:* lewd and lascivious behavior and public exposure of "naked body."

Note: As it is apparent that crime throughout the country is ever increasing, some of the indispensable elements which make up violent crimes against persons may not be needed for the Courts to interpret that there has been a violent crime committed.

For example, you might want to check your local state codes to determine the applicability of the need for "penetration" in rape. It may be that now, in some states, molestation may have superseded the actual act. This means that any improper touching of a person such as a child under age, or a woman who did not agree to the act of sex, like with husband or "date," could be considered molestation or rape.

Then there are the new federal laws regarding what constitutes sexual harassment. These are brought to your attention since they were deliberately not discussed in this criminal law section. In other words, check your local state codes with reference to what elements are necessary and/or mandatory to a felony conviction as to violent crimes against persons.

CRIMES AGAINST PROPERTY

A. *Larceny/Theft:* "the taking of property of value—no lawful right to possession—and movement—transfer of the property."

   Elements of Larceny/Theft:

   a. Taking of property of value;

   b. No lawful right to possession; and

   c. Movement, transfer or "asportation" of the property.

B. *Theft by Deception and Fraud:*

   1. Must relate to material issues of fact. Scams; cancer cures; door-to-door rip-offs; consumer protection: purposely creating an impression in the mind of the owner to induce consent when the impression is false.

C. *Theft of Services/Public Utilities:*

1. Restaurant: check or tab not paid and the restaurant is left with no means of collection.

2. Non-payment of utility bills, etc.

D. *Theft of Lost or Abandoned Property:*

Anyone who comes into control of property, "knowing" it to be *mislaid, lost or delivered by mistake,* commits a theft, if he or she DOES NOT TAKE REASONABLE MEASURES to return the property to the person.

EXAMPLE

Say you found a brown bag in an alley containing $50,000 in unmarked bills and no identifying markings. You turn the bag and its contents over to the police to process. They have to hold it for six months (this time may vary in your state) while they check for the owner. Thereafter you have to wait an additional thirty days before you can legally claim the money as yours.

E. *Theft by Extortion* (found under Larceny/Theft Statutes)—when a person obtains a threat, often used by organized crime

1. Inflict bodily injury or other offense;

2. Falsely accuse anyone of an offense;

3. Expose secrets;

4. Take or withhold official action;

5. Cause a strike or boycott;

6. Withhold legal testimony;

7. Threaten any harm.

F. *Receiving Stolen Property:* One who pays a bargain price for goods, *knowing* that it was a "low" price for the value can be viewed as knowing the goods were stolen. Example: $35 for an Apple One computer. Actual knowledge can be inferred from the facts.

G. *Robbery:* primary difference between *Robbery* and *Larceny* is *the amount of force exerted.*

Robbery inflicts serious bodily injury; or threatens another with, or purposely puts him in fear of IMMEDIATE, serious bodily injury.

Robbery, therefore, is an offense of the person as well as property.

More physical than Larceny.

Court's dilemma: shove, grab, push—are these violent enough?

CRIMES AGAINST THE HABITATION

A. *Burglary:*

   1. Entry;

   2. Purpose to commit a crime (any crime);

   3. No license or privilege.

   Gone is the "nighttime" requirement (except New York).

B. *Arson:* "does not" require a successful destruction—mere charring is sufficient—*intent* to burn, destroy and set fire to property and *done with knowledge* that this conduct involves substantial risks.

CRIMES CLASSIFIED AS "INCHOATE"

(Primary public defenders and District Attorneys)

A. *Conspiracy:*

   1. Two or more people have conspired;

   2. To engage in conduct constituting a crime;

   3. Have agreed to aid in the planning or commission of the crime; and

   4. Have committed an overt act in furtherance thereof.

B. *Solicitation* (hiring a hit man)

   Individuals who: promote, facilitate, command, incite or encourage others to commit criminal offenses. Both are equally liable.

   Defenses:

      a. Notify the person solicited that you renounce the crime; and

      b. Give timely warning to appropriate law enforcement; or

      c. Try to stop the criminal behavior.

JUSTIFIABLE DEFENSES

A. *Public Authority:* when the State authority has its agents commit an act which would be a criminal act if committed by an ordinary individual.

B. *Domestic Authority:* parents and schoolteachers inflicting non-deadly force upon children.

C. *Self-Defense:* becomes by permitting you to use any *known* deadly force which reasonably feels necessary to terminate a physical attack on your person.

D. *Defense of Others:* In most jurisdictions, the general law is that you may only defend others if you stand in some kind of *public* or *family* or *personal relationship* with them.

E. *Defense of Property:* force for force. You do not have the right to "shoot" aggressors.

F. *Crime Prevention:* reasonably necessary to protect a "breach of peace." It must be a felony. NO DEADLY FORCE—changed recently.

EXCUSES:

1. You did it;

2. It is not justifiable beyond a reasonable doubt;

3. It is forgiven because of the circumstance beyond your control

    a. *Infancy*—No Mens Rea

        (1) Below age seven;

        (2) 7–14 it is rebuttal.

    b. *Insanity*

    c. *Involuntary intoxication*

    d. *Mistake of fact*

    e. *Mistake of law:* ignorance of law is no excuse as a matter of practicality.

    f. *Duress:* (coercion) when you can show you have acted under the threat of another in fear of your life or serious bodily harm.

    g. *Necessity:* out in a storm, needing some place to stay, you break into a vacant house. No alternative *but to open and use it.*

    h. *Coverture:* "My husband made me do it." Committing a crime at the direction of another.

    i. *Conduct of the victim:*

        (1) *Consent:*

            (a) *Affective* consent will be a defense to the commission of the crime

        (2) *Inaffective consent:*

            (a) Fraud, misrepresentation

        (3) *The guilt of the victim:* an individual who deals with a "fence" or, if someone left himself or herself wide open to a criminal act.

j. *Condoning an Act After It Has Been Committed:* It is totally irrelevant. It is a crime against our society, not just the individual victim.

k. *Entrapment:* When law enforcement participates in the setting up of a crime, which would not have happened, without the intervention of the agency.

THE CLIENT INTERVIEW

More than in any other phase of law practice, your attitude toward and treatment of a client should be professional; not only because of the nature of the case, but because of the nature of the beast. There will be times when you are appalled at the alleged crime, or not in sympathy with the alleged act of violence, or by the indulgence in a sex act, or by participation in the use of narcotics or other drugs, but you are not there to sit in judgment—you are there to help the client.

The initial interview of a client charged with a criminal offense is one of the most crucial steps in a criminal proceeding, since you are dealing with a person's life and freedom of movement as opposed to loss of, or damage to, property.

Time is of the essence, since the period between arrest and trial is very short as compared to a civil action, which may not come to trial within eighteen months or two years from the date of filing the complaint. For this reason, the time in which discovery can be initiated and conducted is compressed. In this connection you should be doubly careful; first, obtain from the client the minute details of the arrest to determine if his rights were violated in any way and if there were any illegal acts committed by the arresting officers. Second, if the client is a member of any minority by race, creed, color, or sex or is poor and indigent, you may be faced with the additional problem of communication. Hence, you should be well versed and knowledgeable about the concerns and customs of various cultures and ethnic groups with whom you may have to deal. The following are some of the factors you should bear in mind when interviewing a client in a criminal matter.

THE CULTURAL GAP

1. Client's interests
2. Client's capabilities
3. Client's motivation

4. Behavioral patterns: what are normally accepted in his world are controlling to him.

5. Language barrier: this could be just the slang he uses or a foreign language necessitating his translating English (in his head) to his own language. Often the words do not mean the same in his language, or the word might have two meanings in our language.

FAMILY STRUCTURE

1. Who is the head of the household, if any?

2. What is the client's responsibility in the home?

3. What is the earning power of the husband? The wife?

4. Who and how many people are depending on him?

These facts help shape the client's attitude about himself and will aid you in preparing the client for both trial and the rehabilitation process. It will give you insight into his behavior and what, if anything, your attorney can do to help. Also, depending where he is in the family structure, you might get an insight as to why he really committed the crime, if he did. Sometimes too much pressure or responsibility or an unfaithful spouse is the real culprit. Your attorney, in any event, should be aware of these and any other possible motivating factors that you may become aware of during the interview.

Attitude Toward the Establishment

If you are interviewing a member of a minority, how he feels about crime and punishment is vitally important. His cooperation in implementing the trial strategy to be planned by your attorney is a must. You should be aware that punishment by the establishment is not as important to him as is the punishment of his peers. Committing a crime could be a way of obtaining "approval" or to "be a man" in the eyes of someone close or would not be considered a crime by him, period. Hence, going to jail could be a reward or a means of making his point.

Finally, be aware of your client's shrewdness and possibly comprehensive knowledge of the law and the sentences accompanying his particular crime. If he is not a first offender, he is probably much more educated than you are in this area. Even first offenders seem to know the "ropes." On the other side of the coin, the client may be too willing to talk or cooperate. There is the other feeling of being prepared or willing to say whatever is expected, rather than what he really wants to say.

This short course in practical psychology will aid in determining what the truth really is, as told by the client, or will perhaps help you draw the truth from him and win his confidence. This will make your attorney's job much easier.

Some Basic Questions to Ask

1. Obtain a detailed statement of the facts surrounding the alleged crime, that is, the alleged murder in our hypothetical set of facts. (a) How it really happened? (b) What the client actually did? (c) Who really started the fight? What he really intended to do when he went home and returned? And so forth.

2. Ask questions about the client including: (a) personal history, including marital status, finances, education, work experience, occupation, hobbies: (b) Any prior record of violence; (c) Any prior felony convictions; (d) Whom to call to aid in obtaining money for a bond'? (e) Did he commit the crime for which he was charged? (And believe him when he answers no.)

PRETRIAL PROCEDURE

In many jurisdictions, when the client is charged with having committed a misdemeanor, a complaint is filed against him. The defendant appears in court for the "arraignment" (usually within a specific statutory period after the filing of the complaint), to enter the "plea." He may plead guilty and have the matter set for sentencing, or he may plead not guilty and have the matter set for trial. (Of course, the other alternatives set forth earlier are also available.) Depending on the verdict reached after the trial, either the case will be dismissed or the defendant will be ordered to return for sentencing.

When a felony is charged against the client, the subsequent procedure may become somewhat more complicated, since the offense charged is more serious.

For instance: After the arrest, the defendant must be arraigned within a specific time period, and assuming a guilty plea is not entered, the court may set the matter for preliminary hearing (again within a set time period). If, after the preliminary hearing, the court decides that sufficient cause exists to hold the defendant for trial, the client may then be rearraigned in another court, and the matter may be set for trial.

Time limitations are almost always set by law, and if the prosecution deviates from them without the defendant's consent, you can proceed to prepare a motion to dismiss.

A. Pretrial Motions

1. Motion to reduce bail. If an excessive bail has been set, the following is a sample motion to reduce the bail:

(Name)
(Address)
(Telephone No.)

Attorney for Defendant, John Doe

SUPERIOR COURT OF THE STATE OF CALIFORNIA
FOR THE COUNTY OF _____

PEOPLE OF THE STATE	)	No._____
OF _____	)	MOTION TO REDUCE
	)	EXCESSIVE BAIL
Plaintiff,	)	
vs.	)	
	)	
JOHN DOE,	)	
	)	
Defendant	)	
_____	)	

Defendant John Doe, through his counsel (name of counsel), hereby moves the Court for an Order reducing defendant's bail from the previously set sum of $100,000, which is unconstitutionally excessive, to the sum of $25,000, an amount that should guarantee defendant's appearance at all stages of the proceedings.

This motion is based upon the transcript of the preliminary examination, which the Court has read and considered, the declaration of John Doe, attached hereto as Exhibit A, the declaration of _____, attached hereto as Exhibit B, the point and authorities annexed hereto, and such . . .

This sample motion illustrates a format for all pretrial motions in criminal case.

2. Motion to quash or set aside complaint or indictment. If there was no "probable cause" to arrest the defendant or, in matters heard by a grand jury if the evidence was not properly presented to the grand jury, a motion to quash may be used in some jurisdictions—ref. Federal Rules of Criminal Procedure 12(b)(1). See also Motion to Dismiss following.

3. Motion to dismiss. This may be made based on formal defects in the information or indictment. The attorney must decide whether it is wise to make such a motion as it may educate the prosecutor unnecessarily—ref. F.R.Cr.P. 6(b)(2) and 12(b).

The following is a sample motion to dismiss stating several possible grounds (use only the grounds applicable to your particular case).

In the United States District Court for the

_____ District of _____

_____Division

UNITED STATES OF AMERICA

vs.   No. . . . . . .

John Doe

MOTION TO DISMISS INDICTMENT

The defendant moves that the indictment be dismissed on the following grounds:

1. The court is without jurisdiction because the offense, if any, is cognizable only in the _____ Division of the _____ District of _____.

2. The indictment does not state facts sufficient to constitute an offense against the United States.

3. The defendant has been acquitted (convicted, in jeopardy of conviction) of the offense charged therein in the case United States vs. _____ in the District Court for the _____ District of _____, Case No. _____ terminated on _____.

4. The offense charged is the same offense for which the defendant was pardoned by the President of the United States on _____ day of _____, 19__.

5. The indictment was not found within three years next after the alleged offense was committed.

Signed:_____

_____

Address

Dated: _____, 19_____

4. Motion for change of venue. This order can be done on the court's own motion, but you can file the same if your attorney feels her client will not get "a fair and impartial trial" within the county where the alleged crime was committed.

5. Motion for discovery under court rules of criminal procedure. Your attorney has the right to be aware and informed of the district attorney's case and possible witnesses. That was not so in the "good ole days."

6. Motion to suppress evidence. You would use this motion where evidence has been obtained through illegal search and seizure. It applies to physical evidence, statements made by the defendant when not advised by counsel or through wiretapping, prior convictions, and so forth—ref. F.R.C.P. 12(b)(3) and Federal Evidence Code.

This motion is normally presented days prior to the date of trial or at the preliminary hearing, but most criminal court rules allow it to be filed at any time before trial.

A sample of a motion to suppress evidence and for the return of the seized property follows.

In the United States District Court for the
_____ District of _____,
_____ Division

United States of America

Plaintiff,

vs.   No._____

John Doe

Defendant.

_____

MOTION TO SUPPRESS

John Doe hereby moves this Court to direct that certain property of which he is the owner, a schedule of which is annexed hereto, and which on the night of _____, 19 _____ , at the premises known as _____ Street, in the city of the District of _____, was unlawfully seized and taken from him by two deputies of the United States Marshal for this District, whose true names are unknown to the petitioner, be returned to him and that it be suppressed as evidence against him in any criminal proceeding.

The petitioner further states that the property was seized against his will and without a search warrant.

_____
Attorney for Petitioner
Address

Dated: _____, 19_____

7. Motion to sever. This motion is used when there are two defendants charged with the same crime or who acted jointly in the commission of a crime and either attorney feels it would be in his client's best interest it they had separate trials. In federal cases and in some states the prosecutor can also request relief from prejudicial joinder on motion and order of court—ref. F.R.C.P. 14 and 12(b)(5).

8. Motion for appointment of an expert. This motion is used if the attorney feels that an expert witness, that is, psychiatrist, pathologist, and so forth, would be necessary for the defense and if the client does not have sufficient funds to hire an expert. You are referred to your local court rules to determine how an expert can be appointed at court expense for an indigent defendant. Psychiatric examination on motion of the federal prosecuting attorney is governed by F.R.C.P. 12.2(c).

A state court sample order for an examination at the request of the defendant follows:

(Name)
(Address)
(Telephone No.)

Attorney for Defendant.

SUPERIOR COURT OF THE STATE OF _____
FOR THE COUNTY OF _____

PEOPLE OF THE STATE OF CALIFORNIA,	)	CASE NO._____
	)	
Plaintiff,	)	MOTION FOR ORDER
vs.	)	APPOINTING PSYCHIATRIST
	)	(_____Evid. Code,
JOHN DOE,	)	Sections _____, _____, _____,)
	)	
Defendant.	)	
_____	)	

(Name), counsel for defendant herein, moves the court for an order appointing _____ M.D. as psychiatrist for defendant herein, to examine said defendant and to report her findings to defendant's counsel only.

    A confidential psychiatric examination is necessary and material, and is authorized by Sections 370, 952, and 1017 of the Evidence Code, so that counsel can be fully advised and can advise defendant whether to present a defense based on insanity or on defendant's mental or emotional condition.

Dated: _____, 19_____

_____
Attorney for Defendant

B. Pretrial Discovery in a Criminal Case

In a criminal case, pretrial discovery may be made by deposition. Some criminal court rules and the Federal Rules of Criminal Procedure 15 require a court order to take a necessary deposition. Some state courts have more liberal pretrial deposition rules. Check your criminal court rules.

Even though deposition may be taken only on order of court and even though interrogatories, as such, are not available under criminal court rules of procedure, pretrial discovery is possible under other rules that require disclosure of evidence and other information by the prosecutor to the defense lawyer. Some of these rules are mandatory and some are permissive.

The Federal Rules of Criminal Procedure 16 provides for reciprocal disclosure by the prosecutor and the defendant. The reciprocal rules require disclosure of names and addresses of witnesses, statements (written or recorded), as well as documents and tangible objects that are in the custody and control of the government and that are either material to the preparation of the defense or intended for use as evidence.

Certain information is not subject to disclosure.

Some state criminal procedure rules have a "notice of alibi" rule similar to that of the Federal Rule of Criminal Procedure 12.1. The prosecutor must make the first move (a written demand) to invoke this rule under the federal and many state rules.

Your attorney may not want to take advantage of the reciprocal rules of disclosure, and the prosecutor may not want to take advantage of the notice of alibi rule for practical strategic reasons, but the legal assistant should be aware of these rules in case either one does want to use those rules.

EXAMPLE

1. Motion for deposition alleging reasons—ref. F. R.C.P. 15.

2. Notice of defense based on mental condition—ref. F. R.C.P. 12.2.

3. Written demand by prosecutor stating time, date, and place at which the alleged offense was committed. It is in response to that written demand that a notice of alibi, listing names and addresses of alibi witnesses, must be served on the prosecution by the defense attorney (usually 10 days)—ref. F. R.C.P 12.1.

4. Request by defendant for disclosure—ref. F. R.C.P 16(a) and (b).

Check your local criminal court rules or rules of criminal procedure for other strategies available by pretrial written motion or written request.

JURY SELECTION

Unless the attorney wishes to challenge the entire grand or petit jury panel (for example, on the grounds of racial or sexual discrimination, which may, of course, give rise to overall investigatory problems), the legal assistant's main concern as the trial approaches is in assisting in the preparation of the *voir dire* examination by the attorney on the day of trial.

This may involve the preparation of specific questions to be directed to the various members of the jury by your attorney, questions that are designed to elicit information showing pretrial bias on the part of any and all members of the panel.

Very often, however, your attorney will prepare his own *voir dire* questions just prior to the court's calling the jury, since questioning may vary with the nature of the offense charged and the special peculiarities inherent in certain classes of offenses, or the attorney may have a standard list of *voir dire* questions upon which she may elaborate prior to each trial.

Useful data on potential jurors may be compiled as follows by:

1. Obtaining the areas of their residence from the local Department of Voter Registration, tax assessor's office, and so forth;
2. Checking their political affiliations;
3. Checking what petitions they may have signed;
4. Checking their cars to determine what stickers, if any, they have pasted thereon; and,
5. Determining if they have any children, animals, and the like—anything you feel might give the attorney insight as to their personality.

TRIAL PREPARATION PROCEDURE

Preparing the case for trial involves:

1. Coordinating the activities pertinent to the trial;
2. Interviewing witnesses;
3. Setting up depositions of witnesses;

4. Preparing witnesses for examination and cross-examination;

5. Preparing exhibits;

6. Preparing list of names and addresses of witnesses to be subpoenaed, if any; and

7. Preparing the trial book (similar to the exhibit book in a civil action), which contains:

   a. A police report;

   b. Profile of the witnesses and their testimony;

   c. Investigation file; and,

   d. Research memoranda.

If there are physical items of evidence to be offered by the defense, such as photographs, and the like, be sure the attorney has them in his possession on the day the trial begins. In this connection, it has been our experience that a brief memo explaining the various items of evidence and when they are to be first identified and marked during the trial is quite helpful to your attorney.

At the trial itself, you should be familiar with the standard of "proof beyond a reasonable doubt" applicable in a criminal proceeding, as opposed to "proof by a mere preponderance of the evidence" or the "clear and convincing proof" standards applicable to a civil matter.

An initial thoroughgoing effort at discovery before the trial, as described earlier in this chapter, will enable your attorney to evaluate the nature and strength of the evidence to be presented by the prosecution, so that he may plan how best to present the defense.

At times the prosecution's case will be so weak as to be unable to withstand a defense motion to dismiss at the close of the prosecution's case. But do not expect this blessing too often, if at all, since many weak cases are weeded out either before they are formally filed or at the preliminary examination.

All defense witnesses should be thoroughly interviewed by you and your attorney, since, unlike in civil proceedings, depositions in criminal proceedings are somewhat rare. Make notes of statements made by witnesses as you interview them or record the questions and answers, if the interviewed witness agrees, on tape.

WITNESSES

Witnesses can be of several types: (1) direct witnesses, (2) alibi witnesses, (3) character witnesses, (4) expert witnesses, and so forth. If any of your witnesses testified under oath previously concerning the offense charged, it is important that you secure a transcript of that testimony to ensure that there is no variance in later testimony.

If there is a variance due to a memory lapse, then the witness will want to refresh his recollection before testifying, and this is done by review of the transcript. Here you can be of great assistance to your attorney, for if you suspect that the witness's variance is attributable to intentional misrepresentation, or perjury, you can advise your attorney so that he may avoid the pitfalls that will result from calling that particular witness to the stand.

The foregoing procedure, that is, reviewing the transcript with a potential witness, aids your attorney in achieving the best results and cuts down the possibility of cmbarrassment or of being caught by surprise in the middle of a trial.

1. Direct witness. A person who saw the actions of the accused at the scene of the crime or saw actions of others that are relevant to the case.

2. Alibi witness. A witness who can testify to facts which place the defendant somewhere other than at the scene of the crime (See Notice of Alibi criminal court rule and annotations of cases interpreting that rule.)

3. Character witness. A witness who may know nothing about the facts of the alleged crime but who knows the reputation of the community of the defendant for the character quality involved in the offense such as:

    a. Larceny—honesty

    b. Assault—peace loving

    c. Sex crime—morality and chastity

4. Expert witness. A person qualified in a scientific or other relevant field to answer a relevant hypothetical question by stating an opinion or by giving relevant demonstrative or opinion evidence.

Prior to subpoenaing character witnesses, it is important to find out, through pretrial evidence disclosure as discussed earlier, whether or not the defendant has a prior criminal record. If so, get the details of the charge and the disposition of the prior case.

If the defendant has a criminal record, it may not be wise to raise the issue of his reputation by calling character witnesses.

Note: In some states, the issues of credibility of the defendant as a witness may be raised as soon as he takes the witness stand in his own behalf and the prior criminal record can be introduced, whether or not character witnesses are called.

Know, by studying the appropriate provisions of your evidence statutes (and by consulting with the attorney on case law), how much of the "rap sheet" the prosecution will be able to get before the jury, if you put on character witnesses or she calls the defendant to testify.

PREPARING JURY INSTRUCTIONS

Proper preparation of jury instructions is critical. Many jurisdictions have standard, preprinted jury instructions that can be ordered or duplicated. There are, however, instances in which your attorney will want special jury instructions typed "to order." You should know when these jury instructions must be presented to the court. In California, jury instructions ordinarily must be handed in to the judge prior to commencement of the argument of counsel.

DOCUMENTING OPENING AND FINAL ARGUMENTS

Your attorney may want you to assist in preparation of his opening and final arguments. As a guide, you should briefly outline the facts of both the prosecution and defense case, and note the items of evidence that are to be or have been introduced and which of these, if any, would be most helpful to your attorney's argument. Your attorney will advise you what other items or arguments he may wish to include. Then develop a legal memorandum accordingly.

After the verdict has been rendered, if it is adverse to the client, your attorney may want you to interview, or assist him in interviewing, the jury, to determine what led them to the verdict and if there were any irregularities during the deliberations that might give rise to a motion for new trial. This is not allowed in some states or may be counterproductive.

POST-TRIAL PROCEDURE IN A CRIMINAL CASE

If the jury returns a not guilty verdict, the proceedings are usually at an end then and there, unless the client is held to answer on other charges.

If a guilty verdict is returned, various post-trial motions may be in order. Very often, a motion for new trial may be made. In addition, the defendant may apply to the court for probation. If the client has the funds, the attorney may, if an appeal is to be filed, move that the court admit the defendant to bail pending appeal.

PRACTICAL STEP-BY-STEP POST-TRIAL PROCEDURE AFTER VERDICT

1. After the verdict has been rendered, file a motion for new trial (if applicable), or a motion for release from custody on bail pending sentence.

2. Interview the jurors after the trial to determine how they reached the verdict.

3. Assuming that your motion for a new trial is denied and the client is sent to jail or released on bail pending sentencing, he can be given:

   a. Time in jail or prison;

   b. Straight probation; or,

   c. Probation conditioned upon certain community service, medical treatment, or other condition.

After conviction, a great deal can be done by the legal assistant in preparing the defendant for the inquisition of the probation department. The report of the assigned probation officer is analogous to a civil service personnel file in that it follows the defendant not only to the jail, but becomes a matter of public record and can affect the defendant's status in the community for the rest of his life.

The legal assistant, therefore, not only interviews the defendant after conviction as to prior offenses, employment history, and so forth, but delves into areas which could mitigate the punishment and/or reduce the sentence, such as a feeling of remorse and penitence or a desire for possible psychiatric examination or treatment and, of course, job rehabilitation.

If an application for probation is made, every effort should be made to present the probation officer the strongest justification for admitting the defendant to probation. Very often, letters of recommendation can be presented to the probation officer from friends, family, employers, clergymen, and so forth, and these letters can be reviewed by the court at the time of sentencing without running afoul of the hearsay rule.

If delegated the responsibility, you should instruct the client to be perfectly candid and remorseful (that is, if the client is in fact guilty) when talking with the probation officer. As a practical matter, the attorney often deals directly with the probation officer, not only to secure the best possible recommendation for sentencing, but also to determine if the probation officer arrived at the recommendation fairly and properly.

If the client's criminal record is extensive, the probation officer will often recommend that the client spend a period of time in the county jail or state prison. (Mandatory death penalty statutes involve special problems of "finality" and of constitutionality which will not be discussed here.) And for this reason, sometimes the client will be psychologically prepared to "do time." In this connection, sometimes your attorney, or you (if delegated this task), must assume the duties of a parent-confessor-psychologist in preparing the client for incarceration.

In any event, the preparation for the sentencing hearing by your attorney, or you, can often be more important than the trial itself. This can especially be seen in cases where the client pleads guilty and waives the constitutional rights attached to a trial by jury. To this end, you should review all the various classes of post-trial motions authorized by statute in your jurisdiction so that you may be best prepared to utilize many or all of them for your attorney and his client.

APPEAL IN A CRIMINAL CASE

If a motion for new trial is denied, the defendant may want to appeal. Although procedures on appeal may vary from jurisdiction to jurisdiction, you will very often find that a prepared "notice of appeal" must be filed within a specified time period after judgment is rendered.

Your duties, once the notice of appeal is filed, may include a formal request for the preparation, by the clerk of the Record on Appeal, which consists of, for example, the Clerk's Transcript (Record during Trial), the Reporter's Transcript, copies of all motions filed, jury instructions, and so forth. In short, the appellate court must have before it a complete picture of these proceedings.

You must be aware of the strict time limits within which requests must be made, briefs filed, and motions made to the appellate court. See the Appellate Rules of Procedure for the appellate court to which the appeal is being taken.

Oral arguments made by the attorneys are often as important as the written brief, and you may be called upon to assist in the research needed to prepare the written brief and assist in the preparation of oral arguments, or both.

Even after an appellate decision is rendered, various jurisdictions permit the defendant to file a "petition for rehearing" (if the decision is adverse), and you may be called upon to draft the petition for rehearing. Appellate court rules usually require that the reasons for need for rehearing be set forth in the petition.

If that petition for rehearing is denied, file a petition for hearing in, or review by, the state's highest court (*certiorari*). Or, if a constitutional question has been raised in the state courts, there may be grounds for an eventual appeal to the Supreme Court of the United States. See 1980 Revised Rules of the United States Supreme Court on the rules volumes of the United States Code Annotated.

SUMMARY
GENERAL PROCEDURE OF THE CRIMINAL PROCESS

A. *Arraignment:* when the accusatory instrument has been filed—*information* or *indictment*—and the defendant is informed of the charge against him/her and informed of his/her rights, especially the assistance of an attorney. *Attorney needed* at this "critical" stage.

   1. *Custodial Interrogation:* "*Custody*" much broader than arrest. A person is in custody when the circumstances would lead a reasonable person to believe he/she was not free to go.

   2. *"Interrogation":* statements made in the presence of the suspect although not specifically directed to him/her, which invite an incriminating response have been held to be "interrogation."

B. *Bail or ROR:* factors considered in these are:

   1. Nature of offense;

2. Penalty that may be imposed;

3. Probability of voluntary appearance of the defendant or flight to avoid punishment;

4. The pecuniary and social status of the defendant;

5. The general reputation and character of the defendant;

6. The nature and strength of the proof as bearing on the probability of his/her conviction.

ROR = Release on person's own recognizance.

C. *Disposition Without Plea of Guilty*

1. Upon or after arraignment in a local criminal Court upon an information or misdemeanor complaint and

a. Before entry of a guilty plea; or

b. The commencement of trial, the Court may, on its own motion, or that of the prosecutor or defendant and with the *consent* of *both parties,* order that the action be *"adjourned in contemplation of dismissal."* Reasons: no witnesses; state's case is so trivial that it will not endanger the community.

D. *Specialized Hearings or Dispositions*

1. To adjudicate:

a. First-time/or small-time drug offenders;

b. Youthful offenders and violent juveniles;

c. First-time offenders;

d. Candidate whose crimes are so small that their disposition should be accelerated.

E. *Preliminary Hearings*

1. Arraignment of a felony complaint, which is indictable by a grand jury and which cannot be disposed of in the local criminal Court.

Purpose:

a. To determine whether there is sufficient evidence to bring the matter before the grand jury;

b. To test the sufficiency of the evidence and, if it does not establish "prima facie evidence." If not, then the case can be dismissed. Sufficient evidence will cause the defendant to be held over for grand jury action.

F. *Grand Jury:* 10–23 citizens hear testimony presented by the prosecution. Does *not* determine *guilt* or *innocence,* just sufficiency of evidence to prosecute. There is NO judge. Returns an "indictment for felonies" *and* indictable misdemeanors, recommends to prosecutor to file an *"information"* in the criminal Court, *or* dismisses the charge by returning a "no true bill."

G. *Plea Bargaining*

Purpose:

1. Dispose of heavy *criminal* loads;
2. Witnesses not available or reluctant to testify;
3. Prosecutor's evidence is lacking or questionable;
4. Enables prosecution to dispose of an indictment on a reasonable basis, and in the interest of the public;
5. For the defendant, it eliminates a long trial or conviction of a higher degree of crime.

H. *Omnibus Motions Filable:*

1. Motion for severance;
2. Motion for suppression of evidence;
3. Motion for psychiatric examination;
4. Motion to quash the indictment or information;
5. Motion for change of venue;
6. Motion to excuse the trial judge;
7. Motion to dismiss—speedy trial; sufficiency of evidence;
8. Motion to continue;
9. Motion to suppress identification testimony.

I. *Trial Process*

1. *Jury selection:* (voir dire);
2. *Opening statements:* recitation of strategy and tactics; interpretation of law as applied to the facts;
3. *Direct examination*—witnesses;
4. *Cross-examination*—witnesses;
5. *Redirect or rebuttal*
6. *Summation or closing:* counsel summarize their position;

7. *Jury instructions:* judge instructs jury in the law as it relates to the facts;

8. *Verdict:* jury deliberates, returns verdict.

J. *Post-Verdict Motions*

   1. *Petition for Writ of Habeas Corpus:* filed within ten days after finding of guilt. N.O.V. Discharge on the basis of insufficient evidence.

   2. *Motion for New Trial* and *In Arrest of Judgment:*

     a. Verdict contrary to law and evidence;

     b. Verdict against weight of evidence;

     c. Court erred in not suppressing testimony;

     d. Court erred in not admitting confession;

     e. Court erred in its instructions to jury.

   3. *Application for Modification of Sentence*

DUE PROCESS

CONSTITUTIONAL RIGHTS OF THE ACCUSED

1. Right to confront the accuser;

2. Right to a speedy trial;

3. No secrets;

4. Proper search and seizures;

5. Exclusionary Rule;

6. Right not to testify against yourself;

7. Right not to be charged twice for the same crime on the same charge.

CONSTITUTIONAL CONSIDERATIONS

First: privacy, freedom of speech, religion, association.
Fourth: search and seizure, warrants, probable cause.
Fifth: federal due process, self-incrimination, double jeopardy.

Sixth: confrontation, presence, jury trial, speedy trial, counsel.
Eighth: cruel and unusual punishment, excessive bail and fines.
Fourteenth: state due process, equal protection of the law.

HYPOTHETICAL CASE

Johnny, a 22-year-old male, who is mentally the age of seven, is walking down the street at dusk one warm summer eve.

Mary, a 25-year-old woman, is preparing for bed. She has, in error, left up the window shade on her ground floor bedroom window, and the window is open.

Johnny sees Mary. After Mary gets into bed and turns out the lights, Johnny walks over to the window. He places his hands on the window sill. Mary, thinking it is her lover, calls out, "Is that you, darling? Come in."

Johnny climbs through the window and into Mary's bed. Mary realizes her mistake and screams. Johnny is frightened and leaps from the bed. Mary turns on the light, screams a second time, and reaches for a gun she keeps in the side table by the bed.

Johnny picks up a bookend and throws it at Mary, knocking her unconscious.

Johnny heads toward the front door. Halfway there, he sees an expensive camera. Picking it up, he calls out, "Can I have this?" Getting no response, he takes it and leaves.

Define the crimes and defenses of Johnny and Mary.

Your attorney has given you the above facts and has asked you to do a preliminary analysis of said facts and come up with a recommendation as to what crime or crimes have been committed, if any; and what defenses to said crimes are available to the client. Consider the following: the defendant, Johnny, is mentally retarded and has the thinking capacity of a seven-year-old. Would he therefore be capable of attempted rape? Would he be guilty of trespass? And what about breaking and entering? And lastly, would he be guilty of assault and battery? Or guilty of a house robbery?

If any of the above are true, would his defense be that he was mentally retarded and did not know what he was doing, or was not capable of understanding what he was doing? This being true, all things being equal, is he guilty of any crime at all?

As to Mary, what was her culpability in this scenario? Is she guilty of contributory negligence or negligence in preparing for bed, leaving the shade to her window up and the window open? Was this an open invitation to anyone walking by her window, seeing her prepare for bed? Was she negligent in assuming that it was her lover and inviting in the person without a confirmation?

This hypothetical case sets forth some of the questions that you would have to determine and for which you would have to do some legal research.

✑✑ CHAPTER 16 ✑✑

How to Handle a Contract Action

Since the basic substantive law of contracts is an extremely broad and vast field of law, no attempt to delve into every aspect of it is intended here. This chapter contains a brief overview of the basic elements you should understand to draft a contract.

WHAT IS A CONTRACT?

A contract is a legally enforceable agreement between two or more parties. It may be oral or written. It is a promise by one party or set of promises between two or more parties. It may be oral or written. In any event, the law recognizes a duty to perform these promises and allow recovery of damages for the lack or failure of performance of said agreements or promises. The law requires some promises to be in writing to be legally enforceable.

Generally, contracts are divided into formal and informal types. A simple or informal contract may be just a letter. The formal contracts are normally those which are written in formal legal language and may be under seal.

These contracts are further described as being unilateral and/or bilateral and should contain an offer, an acceptance, and above all, some type of consideration.

To aid in analyzing contractual problems, consider the following:

Unilateral contract. In this type of contract you have an offer, a promise by one to do something in return for the act of another. Whenever you have a unilateral contract, you always have one side which is executory (the offeror) and one side which is executed (offeree). The act which is done to create the contract is the consideration. In this unilateral contract, the acceptance and performance are done at the same time so that there is no further duty on one party, but he does have the right to demand performance from the original promissor.

EXAMPLE

A promises B that he will pay B $100 if B enrolls in and completes a Stop-Smoking Program. B enrolls in the program and completes the course. A owes B $100 upon completion of the program.

Bilateral contract. In this contract both parties make promises. It is an unconditional promise on both sides, with each side bearing and assuming a risk related to producing the expressed or implied results.

EXAMPLE

A promises B that A will sell B a certain farm in return for B's promise to A that B will pay A a certain amount of money and execute a note and mortgage for the balance of the purchase price on the closing date specified in the deed.

If a contract is not valid (enforceable by law) the agreement of the parties may be void or voidable.

Void contract. This is an agreement which was unenforceable from its inception. There was no contract. Examples of such a contract would be an illegal contract (such as gambling or price fixing in violation of federal law). A contract can be void as a matter of public policy. It is possible for it to meet every other requirement of a valid contract, such as an offer, acceptance, consideration, and so forth, but as a matter of public policy, or because it is illegal, be void.

A moral contract may meet all these qualifications but be void because a statute required that it be enforceable at law (such as an agreement to sell real estate to lease for more than one year or to guarantee the debt of another person).

Voidable contract. Such a contract may bind only one of the parties to the contract and give an option to the other party to withdraw if he so chooses. This type of contract normally arises when one of the parties has been induced by fraudulent misrepresentation to make his promise, and he later discovers the misrepresentation. He can hold the other party to the performance of his duties under the contract and perform his part or he may rescind the contract and not perform his part.

Quasi-contract. This contract is implied by law even though it could not be implied in fact, and even though the parties did not enter into an expressed agreement. A contract is implied in law where one person actually performed with the knowledge and consent of the other, and the person thereby accepted the benefit of the performance and would be unjustly enriched if the law would not imply a contract.

ELEMENTS NECESSARY TO CREATE A CONTRACT

Following is a list of elements necessary to create a contract:

1. Offer (oral or written if not required by law to be written);
2. Acceptance (oral or written, if not required by law to be written);
3. Consideration (money or promise);
4. Capacity of the parties to Contract (not a minor or incompetent or drunk or drugged);
5. Intent of the parties to contract (objective meeting of the minds);
6. Object of the contract (it must be lawful *and* not be against public policy).

OFFER

An offer is a definite expression or overt action which starts a contract. It is what is offered to another for the return of another's promise to act. It cannot be ambiguous. It must be spelled out in terms that are specific and certain, such as the identity and nature of the object which is being offered and under what conditions and/or terms it is offered. If the offer is accepted, by the offeree, the offer can be enforced as a contract.

Negotiations. Negotiations of a contract between prospective parties to a contract are not offers in the true sense of the word. The individuals involved are merely discussing the possibility of offering something.

Advertisements. These generally do not contain a specific promise to sell. They are usually statements that certain items are available for an offer to purchase at the advertised price by the unknown members of the public who may read the ad.
Note: There are many consumer protection laws which prohibit deceptive advertising.
Rewards. A reward offer is a unilateral contract. If the act to be rewarded

is performed with the intent of accepting the offer, the unilateral contract may be enforced by the person who performed.

Commercial sales offers. An offer between merchants as defined in your state commercial code must be communicated. It should be noted, however, that under the Uniform Commercial Code, which has been adopted by all states, an offer of a contract of sale does not fail for lack of an in-depth statement of terms, even though one or more terms are left open, if the parties have intended to make a contract and there is a reasonably certain basis for giving an appropriate remedy.

ACCEPTANCE

As a general proposition of law, the acceptance of the offer made by one party by the other party creates the contract. This acceptance, as a general rule, cannot be withdrawn; nor can it vary the terms of the offer, or alter it, or modify it. To do so makes the acceptance a counter-offer. Though this proposition may vary from state to state, the general rule is that there are no conditional acceptances by law. In fact, by making a conditional acceptance, the offeree is rejecting the offer. However, the offeror, at his choosing, by act or word which would show acceptance of the counter-offer, can be bound by the conditions tendered by the offeree.

Here again, the Uniform Commercial Code, as it has been adopted in your state, governs acceptance by a merchant (including manufacturer sellers of commercial goods to wholesale buyers of commercial goods) of an offer made by a merchant. The rules differ somewhat between a merchant and a consumer and between nonbusiness people.

CONSIDERATION

Consideration for a contract may be money or may be another right, interest, or benefit, or it may be a detriment, loss, or responsibility given up to another. Consideration is a necessary element of a contract.

Caution: The consideration must be expressly agreed upon by both parties to the contract or be implied in fact by the express terms of the contract. A possible or accidental benefit or detriment alone is not a valid consideration. The consideration must be explicit and sufficient to support the promise to do or not to do, whichever is applicable. However, it need not be of any particular monetary value.

It should be noted that mutual promises are adequate and valid consideration as to each party, as long as they are binding. This general rule goes to conditional promises as well.

To take it a step further, the general rule is that a promise to perform an act which you are already legally bound to do is not a sufficient consideration for a contract. The application of this general rule may differ from jurisdiction to jurisdiction, as the courts tend to sustain agreements involving liquidated or undisputed debts where there has been a partial payment of a pre-existing obligation.

Furthermore, it has been held that an express promise to pay or perform made to the party entitled to such performance under a contract will be enforced. It is suggested, because of these variances in holdings, that you consult case law in your case for ordinary contracts and your state commercial code for sales of goods between merchants.

CAPACITY OF THE PARTIES

It is a general presumption of law that people have a capacity to enter into a contract. A person who is trying to avoid a contract would have to plead his lack of capacity to contract against the party who is trying to enforce the contract; that is, he was a minor adjudged incompetent or drunk or drugged, and so forth.

When filing a suit to enforce a contractual promise, you allege an offer, acceptance, and consideration, as well as a failure to perform with resulting damages. You do not plead lack of capacity unless you are trying to avoid the contract.

The trend in the courts today is toward upholding the validity of a promise made by a minor to pay a debt incurred while he was still an infant, where the contract was for necessaries.

> EXAMPLE
>
> Where a minor, eighteen years of age, enters into a contract to buy school clothes on the installment plan, and upon reaching the age of majority he still owes on the debt, he can be forced to pay the balance due. This is also true in some jurisdictions as it relates to a minor woman under the age of majority entering into a contract and upon marriage being forced to pay the debt incurred prior to her emancipation. This rule would not apply to a mink coat or a fancy sports car.

The general rule, therefore, is that infants cannot avoid the responsibilities for the necessities of life. They can disaffirm a contract at any time before they reach their age of majority, and within a reasonable time after they become of age.

As to an incompetent's capacity to contract, being eccentric or a bit balmy does not make the defense available *per se.* An adjudged incompetent lacks the capacity to contract for himself. The contract must be made with his court-appointed guardian to be enforceable.

INTENT OF THE PARTIES

It is a basic prerequisite to the formation of any contract (oral or written) that there must be a mutual assent or a meeting of the minds of the parties on all essential elements and terms of the proposed contract. There can be no contract unless all the parties involved intended to enter into one. This intent is determined by the outward words or actions of the parties, not their secret intentions. That is why mere negotiations to arrive at a mutual assent to a contract are not considered offer and acceptance even though the parties agree on some of the terms being negotiated. That is also why fraud or certain mistakes may make a contract voidable.

EXAMPLE

1. A mistake resulting from ambiguity refers to the ambiguity of the language contained in the contract where the meaning placed thereon by each party could reasonably vary, though it is an honest interpretation. Under these circumstances, the court will generally determine that there is no mutual agreement—hence no contract.

2. A mistake as to a material fact is, as a general rule, a mistake of the mind, where one party reasonably thought something was present or expected, when in fact it was not. Courts will grant relief in this instance, if there is not resulting injury to innocent third parties.

3. A unilateral mistake will not necessarily void a contract unless there are other elements present such as misrepresentation, ambiguous language, or the other party to the contract had knowledge of the mistake and took advantage of it.

4. A mistake in the drafting or typing of the contract may be remedied through reformation, if the parties really did agree and intend to contract. In this instance, your attorney would have to prove it was clearly a typographical error made in the typing of the instrument or that the words were transposed, rearranged, and the like, by mistake, as opposed to a lack of understanding by the parties of the language used. This is important to you, since as the legal assistant you will be drafting the contract. The basic action or pleading for reformation would be one in equity.

OBJECT OF THE CONTRACT

A contract is not enforceable if its object is illegal or against public policy.

In many jurisdictions contracts predicated upon horse races, dog races, lotteries, and other forms of gambling are illegal contracts. Yet in some states these types of contracts are valid.

Federal and some state laws make contracts in restraint of trade, price-fixing, and monopolies illegal. Therefore, a contract which violates those statutes would be illegal and unenforceable.

In some states a noncompetitive clause in an employment contract is against the public policy of free enterprise or against a statute making unlimited noncompetitive contracts illegal. For that reason, an overbroad noncompetitive clause in a contract should be avoided by the employee. Most states require that such a clause be limited in both time and geographical area.

Contracts in derogation of traditional concepts of marriage are against public policy in some states. In drafting a contract (such as marital and nonmarital contracts), the legal assistant must be aware of that public policy.

If the legality of part of a contract may be in doubt, the contract should contain a severance clause.

EXAMPLE

Should any portion of this agreement be judicially determined to be illegal, the remainder of the agreement shall not be affected by such determination and shall remain in full force and effect.

Any contract governed by the Uniform Commercial Code as adopted in your state is subject to the unconscionable provision of Section 2–302 of the U.C.C.

In pleading to avoid a commercial contract, facts should be alleged which would show that the contract or a provision thereof is unconscionable.

PURPOSE AND EFFECT

To render contracts which are not in writing—voidable and unenforceable because of fraudulent misconduct.

AREAS OF APPLICATION OF THIS DOCTRINE

1. Sale of real property;
2. Interest in land beyond a one-year period;
3. When the terms of the contract cannot be performed within a year;
4. Promises to answer for the obligation of another; and
5. When the contract is for the sale of goods, in excess of $500, for a will; bonds; stocks, etc.

NATURE OF WRITING

It can be a mere scrap of paper, or a telegram accepting an offer with a confirming letter, a formal contract or a written agreement. Without any such writing you either have a void contract, which is no contract at all, or an unenforceable contract which has no remedy in a Court of law.

COLLATERAL PROMISES

There must be three (3) parties to a collateral promise to make it valid. It must be in writing against the promise to be performed, in the event the original promise is not performed.

EXAMPLE
Surety or undertaking bond.

EXAMPLE

"A promises to pay B $100." (This is the original promise.)

"C promises to pay B the $100 if A does not pay B." (This is the collateral to the obligation A has to B.)

CONDITIONS TO CONTRACT

CONDITIONS PRECEDENT, SUBSEQUENT, AND CONCURRENT

Condition precedent. This is where one party must do something before performance by the other party is required.

For example, a buyer's ability to get a certain amount or proportion of financing may be a condition precedent for a contract to sell land, or in an insurance contract, if there is a condition that a claim must be made within a certain period after an accident, that is a condition precedent to the insurance company's obligation to pay the claim.

Conditions subsequent. This is where a valid contract is terminated or a required performance is changed if a specified thing happens after performance of the contract has begun.

EXAMPLE

The payment of required premium is a condition subsequent to an insurance contract. If the premium is not paid on time or within any prescribed grace period, the condition subsequent is broken or condition requiring for future performance under a contract is a condition subsequent. Breach of that condition is a breach of contract unless the breach is waived or consented to by the other party.

Conditions concurrent. If there is something to be done on both sides and no time for performance is set, these conditions are concurrent.

EXAMPLE

I will give you my car for $100."

The performance is assumed to be meant to happen at the same time. Performance on each side is dependent on performance of the other side at the same time.

THIRD-PARTY BENEFICIARY CONTRACTS

A contract made between two or more people may be made for the benefit of a person who is not a party to the contract. That type of contract is called a third-party beneficiary contract.

The general rule in most states relating to third-party beneficiaries is that these persons have the right, in their own name, to enforce contracts made for their benefit, despite the fact that they are not a party to the contract.

Under present law the courts, in enforcing the rights of third-party beneficiaries under this circumstance, look to the intent of the contracting parties to determine if they, in fact, intended that the third party benefit from the contract.

You should be aware at this juncture, however, that although this third-party doctrine is applicable to various types of contracts, for it to be applied there must be more than an incidental, indirect, or consequential benefit inuring to the benefit of the third-party beneficiary by reason of the contract.

Example—creditor beneficiary

A owes B money. A makes a contract with C, who promises to pay A's debt to B. A and C are the initial contractual parties, but the nature of the contract is purely for the benefit of B, who is in fact the creditor of A. As a creditor beneficiary under the contract between A and C, B can exercise some rights.

Furthermore, under present law, a third-party-donee beneficiary also has the right to enforce a contract made for his benefit, since most courts no longer require privity of obligation between the donee-beneficiary and the promisee.

Finally, you should know that the third-party beneficiary rights, as set forth there, vest immediately upon the making of the contract between the promisor and the promisee, even if the actual benefits will not take place until a later date.

Example - donee beneficiary

Father has a son he wishes to be well cared for. Father contracts with the bank to draw a trust on behalf of his son. Then later, the father says that the bank is not doing a satisfactory job for the benefit of the needs of his son.

The son is a donee beneficiary of the contract between the father and the bank, and as a result can enforce his rights under that contract.

ASSIGNMENT OF CONTRACT

In most states, the rights under a contract are assignable, unless the contract provides otherwise or unless the contract requires the performance of some unique service (as a particular actor or opera singer or a particular hand craftsman).

Most landlords and many others prefer that the contract state that it is *not* assignable "without the written consent of the owner (or seller or mortgage or other appropriate party)."

A right to assign may be conditioned on some other action or event, or the right to assign may be denied.

EXAMPLE

This contract (or mortgage) is not assignable by the buyer (or mortgagor or other appropriate party).

Assignment can also occur where one person to a contract conveys his "beneficial rights" to another person. *Note that only "the right" is assignable. It does not extinguish the duty.* Though the rights are assignable, the duty to perform can *only* be *delegated*, but the person to whom the right is assigned must accept the duty to perform.

Note further that *you cannot* assign claims for wages; Workers' Compensation; personal services; insurance; credit; future rights or any assignment or delegation which may be in violation of public policy.

TYPES OF ASSIGNMENTS

1. Gratuitous or outright as a gift. (*These are revocable.*)
2. Assignments for value, as in a contract between assignor and assignee (collection agencies). (*These are irrevocable.*)

BREACH OF CONTRACT

DEFINITIONS OF A BREACH

What is a breach of contract? When one of the parties fails and refuses to perform under the terms of the contract without a valid or legal reason or excuse.

Should this occur, the *injured party* to the contract can either:

1. Rescind the contract, *period;*
2. Sue to recover any monies expended;
3. Sue for the value of services rendered to date; or
4. Maintain the contract and sue for damages because of the breach.

DEFENSES

Where there are legal reasons for one's failure to perform the terms of a contract, the Court permits the following as defenses:

1. *Prevention:* exists when one party acts in a manner as to prevent the other party from carrying out its contractual obligation.

EXAMPLE

I contract with you to clean my house. You arrive and find that the house is surrounded by a ten-foot wall with guard dogs. Clearly, you would not attempt to scale that wall and come in to my house for fear of the dogs attacking you.

Note: The fact that you may lose money on the contract is not a defense of prevention. You cannot be forced to carry out a nonprofitable contract which may send you into bankruptcy. This is not prevention, just bad faith and/or bad business.

2. *Anticipatory Breach:* this occurs when a party to the contract acts or says things in a manner which indicate that he/she will not perform the contractual obligations.

EXAMPLE

Say you claim a delivery of widgets and that I am going to pay you after the first delivery of said widgets. After the first order is made, I tell you I will not pay for them or that I will not pay for any more.

The "words" convince you that the other party is not going to pay you. Therefore, validity is excused from the contract. In other words, the contract speaks.

3. *Prospective Inability to Perform:* exists when the actions or circumstances surrounding the contract indicate that the party will not perform according to his/her words.

EXAMPLE

"Going Out Of Business Sale" posted on the door.

EXCEPTION:

Having title in an escrow. Here, we find that you did not own the property in question. But title to the property may be there when escrow closes. The key is whether or not you have title at the time of the closing of the escrow.

You are forgiven for performing, if the other party fails to perform, when one side breaches a contract, or does not perform their part of the contract. This constitutes a breach, but the breach has to be a "material" breach.

EXAMPLE

The tenant and the landlord each has, among other things, an obligation to deliver three gallons of bottled water every three weeks. No water is delivered for five weeks. This failure is not a "material breach." On the other hand, if you are a chemist and you use water for your experiments, the water becomes a material breach, since water is used in the main line of your work.

4. *Waiver of Duty to Perform:* running with the example of the bottled water, let us assume that you did not need as many bottles of water; or that you do not need any more water, period. This is a waiver of a duty to perform by the landlord to you.

Here, for your own protection and that of your employer, you should get any and all modifications in writing and additionally, the description of a job. This, because the job may be one which is impossible to perform.

EXAMPLE

The car you are going to paint has been destroyed. Hence, you cannot paint the car.

5. *Personal Service Contracts:* A defense to these types of contracts is death or illness of the person for whom you are to perform the service. These types of services are special and unique.

EXAMPLE

Asking Van Gogh to paint a house instead of painting a portrait.

6. *Frustration of Property:* This exists when performance is possible, but the value of the service no longer exists. To explain: renting a room, or buying a house near the ocean, where a highway is placed near the room or the ocean, or even a toxic dump.

7. *Mutual Discharge and Cancellation:* this occurs when both parties agree that the terms have been carried out; or want to withdraw from the contract.

Note that in most states, the superficial procedure distinctions between law and equity have been abolished, but the complaint to be filed must contain statements of fact which will state a proper cause of action in either law or equity. Alternative counts may be pleaded in most states.

Other Defenses

Some affirmative defenses (legal excuses) that can be raised in a law action for damages for breach of a contract are:

1. Disclaimer written or agreed to in the contract;
2. Unconscionability (sale of goods, contract security agreement, or other contract subject to the U.C.C.);
3. Waiver;
4. Accord and satisfaction;
5. Payment or completed performance;
6. Excuse for nonperformance;
7. Novation;
8. Estoppel;
9. Failure of consideration on the part of the plaintiff;
10. Statute of frauds;
11. Statute of limitations;
12. Illegality;
13. Others.

Some affirmative defenses which can be raised in an action for specific performance of a contract are:

1. Subject matter of the contract is not unique, so damages would suffice to make plaintiff whole;
2. Estoppel;
3. Laches;
4. Fraud;
5. Duress;
6. Mistake;
7. Illegality;
8. Others.

Facts to state a cause of action for rescission would include facts to show:

1. Breach;
2. Anticipatory breach;
3. Damages;
4. Fraud;
5. Duress;
6. Mistake.

DRAFTING THE PLEADINGS

A breach of contract was defined in the foregoing section. Excuses for nonperformance were also discussed in that section. A cause of action is based upon that failure to perform. The cause of action is stated in the complaint. The excuses for nonperformance are stated as affirmative defenses in the answer.

COMPLAINT

In preparing a complaint for a breach of contract, be direct and to the point, and use as many theories as you can. The reason—if you fail in one, your attorney may be able to win in another. This procedure is used to ensure that the client will come out whole, or as if the contract had in fact been performed, the latter being the overall purpose of a breach of contract action. Use separate counts for each alleged course of action.

EXAMPLE

In an action for specific performance, which can force a seller to sell to a buyer, when the seller, for whatever reason, decides that he does not want to sell, you should draft your complaint to include facts and prayer not only for specific performance of the contract, but also for the return of the deposit and damages for the breach as it relates to, for example, the buyer, who had to put his furniture in storage until the house was out of escrow, and so forth. If the house was being built to specifications, then any monies expended in this effort, that is, purchase of special rugs, linoleum, fixtures, and so forth, and any other allegations which would support money damages would be recoverable.

The following counts are for law actions involving contracts.

1. *Indebtatus assumpsit*—money had and received;
2. *Quantum meruit*—work and labor (reasonable value for services);
3. *Quantum valebant*—goods, sold and delivered (implied contract);
4. Open book account (account stated);
5. Action for the contract price paid and consequential damages.

In your complaint, there must be allegations of fact to show violation of the contract rights of the plaintiff by the defendant and a statement to the effect that demand for performance, payment, and so forth, was made and that the defendant "failed and refused" and "continues to fail and refuse" to perform in accordance with the contract or to pay for performance rendered by the plaintiff.

In these counts you must allege an express promise to pay an amount agreed upon between the parties, together with the reasonable amount of the services and damages sustained as a result of the breach. Note that it is possible that the plaintiff may recover less than the complaint pays for, but it cannot recover more than he paid for.

Caution should be taken in spelling out the demands of the complaint, since if it leaves the defendant in doubt, or if it is ambiguous, not only will it be subjected to a demurrer (if applicable in your state), but the defendant may make demand for a Bill of Particulars. This Bill of Particulars would require the plaintiff to set forth a more detailed statement of the acts violated or contract breached.

A defense, most commonly used to a common count, is that of pleading a "set off" such as a counterclaim (which is no longer used in California) or cross-complaint, which is filed concurrently with the answer to the complaint, or by way of affirmative defenses included in the answer to the complaint.

The following are some examples of notice of pleading of some of the more usual contract counts:

GOODS SOLD AND DELIVERED

1. Within two years last past, and on or about _____, 19___, at (CITY), (STATE), plaintiff sold and delivered to defendant goods, wares, and merchandise of the reasonable value of $_____, for which said defendant agreed to pay plaintiff.

2. No part of said sum has been paid (except the sum of $_____, and there is now due, owing, and unpaid the sum of $_____. (Or in number I here substitute, "agreed amount" in place of "reasonable value").

ACCOUNT STATED

1. Within four years last past, and on or about _____, 19___, at (CITY), (STATE), plaintiff was furnished to defendant at his special instance and request, upon an open book account, goods, wares, and merchandise of the aggregate-agreed (reasonable) value of $_____.

2. No part of said sum has been paid (except for the sum of $_____), and there is now due, owing and unpaid from defendant to plaintiff, the sum of $_____.

WORK AND LABOR

1. Between _____, 19___, and _____, 19___ at (CITY, (STATE), plaintiff rendered services to defendant as a _____. Such services were rendered and performed at the special instance and request of defendant, and defendant then and there promised to pay plaintiff the reasonable (or agreed amount) value thereof.

2. The reasonable value (or agreed amount) of such services at the time they were rendered and at the time defendant promised to pay, was the sum of $_____.

3. No part of said sum has been paid (except for $_____).

MONEY HAD AND RECEIVED

1. On _____, 19___ at (CITY), (STATE), defendant became indebted to plaintiff in the sum of $_____ for money had and received by defendant for the use and benefit of plaintiff.

2. On or about _____, 19___, and before the commencement of this action, plaintiff demanded payment thereof from defendant.

3. No part of said sum has been paid (except for the sum of $_____).

Note: Where an action is based on a written contract, whether the action is in law or equity, most court rules of civil procedure require that a copy of the executed contract be attached to the complaint or counterclaim alleging it.

The first step a legal assistant should take before preparing a breach-of-contract complaint is to read the contract carefully.

A practical hint is to make a photocopy of the contract so that you can "mark it up" as you read it when you locate provisions relevant to the client's problem.

ANSWER

The answer may just consist of a general denial. Or it may contain affirmative defenses and possibly a counterclaim.

For various affirmative defenses available in a law action for breach of contract, see page 373 of this chapter, and for various affirmative defenses in an equitable action on a contract, see page 376 of this chapter.

If a contract involves the sale of goods between merchants, see the implied warranty sections in your state's version of the Uniform Commercial Code 2–312 (title and against infringement); 2–313 (express warranty of description); 2–314 (implied warranty based on dealing or usage of trade); 2–315 (goods fit for particular use); 2–316 (goods are merchantable for ordinary use); 2–317 (goods will conform to sample); 2–318 (to third parties as to consumer goods). Also see exclusion and modification of warranties and sections in your commercial code for performance by seller and performance by buyer.

If either the cause of action or affirmative defense to a contract action is fraud, the facts constituting the alleged fraud must be spelled out with particularity.

EXAMPLE

A. Do not allege "The contract was procured by fraud of the seller" and then stop. Do allege:

   1. The contract was procured by fraud of the seller against the buyer as follows:

      a. The seller–distributor did not have a full output contract with the manufacturer, as he specifically stated to the buyer that he had to induce the buyer to place his Christmas order with him and pay $5,000 in advance to the seller.

      b. The seller knew or should have known that he could not deliver to buyer in time for the Christmas season because of his lack of the above contract with the manufacturer.

    c. The seller intended to use the advance payment demanded of the buyer for . . .

    d. The seller agreed with X Company, a direct competitor of buyer, that he would do these alleged actions for the purpose of harming buyer's Christmas business.

2. And further allege that the buyer had a right to rely on the seller's statement and did rely on it.

    a. The buyer had a right to rely and did rely on the representation of the seller when he placed the order that seller did have a full output contract with the manufacturer.

    b. And so forth.

DAMAGES

Damages is the sum of money which the judge (in a nonjury case) or the jury by its verdict awards the contract claimant as compensation, recompense, or satisfaction for the wrong sustained by reason of the breach of contract.

There must be not only a breach of the contract (a wrong or injury done). There must also be damage resulting from the wrong. Only nominal damages can be awarded if no evidence of damage is given by the person who alleges breach of contract.

Exemplary or punitive damages are not ordinarily recoverable in breach-of-contract actions. In some states, there are exceptions, where the actions in breach of contract were so wanton and reckless that they constituted an independent tort.

The damages ordinarily recovered in an action for breach of contract are compensatory damages.

Compensatory damages may be either general or special.

1. General damages are those which are the natural or necessary result of the breach, such as the difference between the value of the actual performance and the contract price.
2. Consequential damages are special damages, such as the loss of profits as a consequence of nonperformance by the other party.

Liquidated damages may be stated in a contract and are agreed to within the contract. The courts tend to construe them as penalties. Normally, they are held invalid unless they are reasonable in amount in relation to the value of the contract and the difficulty in determining consequential damages.

RECAPITULATION—SUMMARY OF DAMAGES

COMPENSATORY DAMAGES

You can sue to be compensated for any actual dollar injury that is clearly identified in the contract.

EXAMPLE

You can sue for the cost differential to mitigate your damages. That is, get another person to finish a job someone else started. In this instance, you can sue for the difference between the amount you paid that person and what it actually cost you.

CONSEQUENTIAL DAMAGES

These are damages of lost profits or expectations which occur as the result of someone breaching a contract.

SPECULATIVE DAMAGES

What you would have gotten, had someone performed the contract based on your pro forma work without a tried and proven track record.

PUNITIVE DAMAGES

These are normally awarded only in circumstances where the behavior of a party is offensive, so offensive that the Court wants to discourage any repetition. In other words, to punish the defendant. These types of awards are normally given in medical malpractice cases; and cases involving insurance companies or automobile companies.

OTHER DAMAGES

1. Specific Performance: here, you are merely suing for that which the contract calls for.

EXAMPLE

I do not want your money, I want the house. It is unique and different.

This occurs when, for example, you want to buy my house because it looks like a Spanish castle; I change my mind and decide not to sell the house. I want to give you the money back and you say, no, I want the house because it looks like a Spanish castle.

2. *Rescission/Restitution:* in this instance, you are asking the Court to cancel the contract and give you back whatever you put in it. You are saying, I do not want damages, I just want my money back.

DISCHARGE FROM PERFORMANCE

1. Death of one of the parties;
2. Illness, to the point of incapacity;
3. Illegality of the contract on grounds of fraud, misrepresentation, against public policy.

DAMAGES RECOVERABLE AT LAW

1. *Compensatory:* costs between difference of performance and what the contract called for;

2. *Damages proximately caused by breach:* or loss incurred as a direct result of bad faith bargaining.

3. *Injunctive relief:* this is an implied covenant (promise) to restrict someone from doing something to another person's detriment. This is "extraordinary relief"—for an extraordinary wrong.

4. *Liquidated damages:* agreed-upon damages, normally set forth in a contract. It must be stated in the contract to be enforceable in a Court of law. *Construed as penalties by the Court.*

5. *Reliance damages:* money actually spent in reliance of the contract.

GLOSSARY

Aleatory Contract	A gambling contract.
Ambiguous	Having two or more meanings. Not clear; vague.
Antenuptial	A contract entered into before marriage to determine control over disposition of the individual assets of each party.
Arbitration	The submitting of a matter in dispute to the judgment of disinterested persons, or person, called arbitrators, whose decision is binding upon the parties.
Assignment	A transfer of a contractual right.
Bilateral Contract	Where it is contemplated by the offeror that the offeree shall make a return *promise* to give certain performance.
Chose in Action	A right to demand by action a debit or sum of money.
Condition Concurrent	A type of condition precedent which exists when the parties to a contract are bound to render performance at the same time.
Condition Precedent	A condition which delays the establishment of a right until a specified event has happened.
Condition Subsequent	A condition which has the effect of terminating liability for a breach which has already occurred.
Consideration	That which is bargained for and given in exchange for a promise.
Constructive Condition	Conditions which do not arise out of the agreement of the parties but are imposed by the Courts as a matter of fairness and justice.
Counter Offer	A manifestation by the offeree of a present willingness to deal on different terms.
Credit Beneficiary	A third party qualifies as a creditor beneficiary where no purpose to make a gift appears and performance by the promisor will satisfy an obligation owing by the promisee to the beneficiary.

Disputed Claim	An unsettled assertion of a right.
Divisible Contract	A contract wherein the performance of the parties is divided into two or more separate units, and performance of each part by one party is the agreed exchange for a corresponding performance by the other party.
Donee Beneficiary	A third party qualifies as a donee beneficiary where it appears that the intent of the promisee in obtaining the promisor's promise of performance is to make a gift to the beneficiary.
Equivocal	Having two or more meanings; purposely ambiguous.
Estoppel	An admission or declaration by which a person is prevented from bringing evidence to controvert it, or prove the contrary.
Gratuitous Assignment	An assignment for which no consideration is given.
Gratuitous Promise	A promise for which the promisor does not bargain for anything in exchange for his promise.
Illusory Promise	One which by its terms imposes no obligation upon the person making it.
Incidental Beneficiary	A third person who will benefit from performance of a contract, but who does not qualify as a donee or creditor beneficiary.
Insolvency	The state of one who has no property sufficient for the full payment of his debts, or who is unable to pay his debits as they fall due in the usual course of business.
Irrevocable	Incapable of being revoked.
Legal Detriment	Unilateral contracts: promisee is doing something which he was not previously obligated to do, or is giving up a legal right. Bilateral contracts: each promisee is promising to do something which he was not previously obligated to do, or is promising to give up a legal right.
Liquidated Debt	Fixed; ascertained. The exact amount that must be paid.

Mortgage, -ee, -or	A conveyance of property, real or personal, to a person called the mortgagee, to secure the performance of some act, such as the payment of money, by the mortgagor.
Novation	A new contract which works on immediate discharge of a preexisting contractual duty and creates a new duty in its stead.
Option Contract	A power or right to choose which has been "paid for."
Quasi Contract	Recovery based upon the theory that the defendant has been unjustly enriched at the plaintiff's expense and that, as a matter of fairness, the defendant should reimburse the plaintiff for the benefit conferred.
Reformation	The correction of an instrument so as to make it express the true intentions of the parties.
Rejection	A manifestation by the offeree that he does not intend to accept the offer or to give it further consideration.
Repudiation	An apparent inability to perform.
Rescission	Rescinding or putting an end to a contract by the parties, or one of them.
Restitution	A restoring of whatever benefits have been conferred under a contract.
Revocation	A manifestation by the offeror that he no longer intends to enter into the proposed contract.
Unilateral Contract	Where it is contemplated by the offeror that he shall not be bound by his offer until he has received *performance* by the offeree.
Unliquidated Debt	The amount that must be paid is not ascertained.
Usury	Originally, interest charged for the use of money. Now, illegal interest only.
Vendee	One to whom anything is sold.
Vendor	One who sells anything.
Voidable Promise	Of imperfect obligation, so that it may be legally annulled or, on the other hand, cured or confirmed at the option of one of the parties.
Waiver	A surrendering of a right to decline to take advantage of.

CHAPTER 17

How to Assist in Estate Planning and Administration

GENERAL DUTIES

The general duties of a legal assistant in estate planning and administration involve the gathering and recording of financial information for use by the attorney in his advisory function in estate planning and his guidance in the administration of a decedent's estate.

1. *Planning*—interviewing the client for information after the client's initial interview with the attorney; gathering facts; and assembling assets in preparation for drafting a will.
   Administration—similar duties in preparation for the probate of a will or intestate (without a will) administration of a deceased client's estate.
2. *Planning*—drafting the initial inventory of assets and appraisal documents.
   Administration—gathering assets and preparing court inventory.
3. Researching the federal tax laws and their ramifications for possible application in the estate-planning process or their application to the estate of a deceased client.
4. *Administration*—developing financial data required for the completion of the appropriate state and federal tax forms.
5. *Planning*—preparing memoranda regarding the estate planning for the attorney.

6. *Planning*—drafting of initial trust agreements.

7. *Administration*—initiating administration of an estate; preparing court documents; and preparing filing and notice procedures necessary for obtaining an appointment to administer a decedent's estate.

8. *Administration*—accumulating marketing, acquiring, listing, and inventorying the assets of the estate.

9. *Administration*—preparing interim and final accounting documents; preparing petitions for sale or distribution; preparing court petitions; and following discharge of executor or administrator or trustee in case of a trust.

10. *Planning*—reviewing and updating wills to keep abreast of the changes in the law and of the status of the client.

This chapter will deal with the theory and concept of preparing wills and trusts, as opposed to the completion of routine estate administration forms.

As a legal assistant you will be primarily responsible for the drafting portion of your attorney's estate practice on behalf of his client.

Word-processing machines have made that task much easier, but understanding the meaning of the clauses stored on your disks will make your drafting more efficient and more interesting.

TYPES OF WILLS

There are three basic types of wills:

1. The formal, witnessed will, which category includes the self-proved will provided for in Section 2–504 of the Uniform Probate Code, which has been adopted in some states.

2. The holographic will, which must be totally in the handwriting of the tester to be valid, including the signature and date signed. Note that this form of will is only valid as to personal property and in some jurisdictions it is not recognized at all. You should consult your local statutes for this procedure. For example, in Alabama the holographic will is not recognized.

3. The nuncupative will, which is an oral statement subsequently reduced to writing (within a statutory time limit) by the person who heard the testator make the statement. This latter type of will could be a deathbed statement of intent or a battlefield expression, and the like, and is only applicable

to nominal or minimal assets of personal property. Here again you should consult your state statutes, since the treatment of nuncupative wills varies from state to state.

The foregoing wills can be further broken down into mutual and joint wills, though the latter is not very often used, and is discussed only for your information and comparison. The propriety of their use would, of course, be in accordance with state statutes.

The joint will is one document containing the desire and intent of two testators as to the disposition of their property. It is a testamentary gift document signed by two or more testators. It is administerable on the death of one of the testators. If the will is revoked as to one, it is still in force as to the non-revoking testator.

Mutual wills, which are considered to be wills with contracts incorporated within the document wherein each testator agrees not to revoke the terms thereof. In some states, there are accepted rules under the law of contracts where a party may contractually agree to do or not to do something in his will, in consideration of another's promise or other consideration. Because of this variance in recognition and procedure, you should check your local statutes relating to mutual wills and their contents and independent contracts to make a will.

ELEMENTS OF A WILL

As a general rule, the basic elements required to be present for a valid will to exist, with caution taken, however, to incorporate them in accordance with local state laws, are as follows:

1. It must have been executed with testamentary intent.
2. Testator must have had testamentary capacity. That is, he must have had the ability, at the time the will was drawn and executed, to do that which he intended.
3. The execution, assuming capacity, must be done of testator's own free will, that is, without undue influence, duress, or the like.
4. It must have been duly executed and be in compliance with statutory requirements.

A will cannot be accepted for probate if it is not "duly executed."

A will, even though accepted for probate, may be cancelled or set aside by a "will contest" if it was executed as a result of fraud, undue influence, or duress or the testator lacked testamentary intent or capacity.

Your local probate court rules will contain the procedure to raise the question (as by contest or petition to set aside the will).

THE CODICIL

A codicil is a subsequently drawn document, which can be a part of the original will or a separate document in place of the original will and may revoke a portion of or amend a previously drawn will, or it may just name an executor. In any and all such events, a codicil must have all the testamentary elements of a will, unless otherwise provided by law.

Other aspects of a codicil are that it can republish a will, it can and may invalidate a prior will, or it may make valid that which had become a revoked prior will.

This being true, a will speaks of the date of the latest codicil to that will. The date of the codicil becomes the date of the entire will and for all purposes of intent, you would use the date of the codicil for interpretation of the will.

Watch out for ambiguities in your codicils. A patent ambiguity appears obvious on the face of the document. A latent ambiguity does not. To avoid latent ambiguity be specific in describing property to be bequeathed or devised.

EXAMPLE

In changing the house devised to B, when the testator has in fact sold the house referred to in his will and has since purchased another house, you should spell out the house with specificity, giving the legal description and the common street address.

REVOKING A WILL OR CODICIL

There are primarily four ways in which a will or codicil can be revoked:

- By the execution (dating and signing) of a new formal will;
- By drawing a codicil which is inconsistent with the original will;
- By burning or destroying the will or codicil; and

- By a change in the circumstances of the testator, that is, marriage, divorce, and so forth.

Any revocation must be done by a person who has the testamentary intent to revoke and the testamentary capacity to revoke. There must be an overt, undeniable expression to revoke. You should check your probate codes to determine the overt acts which can be done to destroy a will, for only those physical acts set forth in the applicable code or statute will be effective as to the destruction of a will. If there is no such statute authorizing this type of revocation, the testator cannot destroy or effectively revoke his will in this manner. Almost all states have this type of statute.

Some of the overt, physical acts to destroy and thereby revoke a will are as follows:

- The testator can burn the entire will;
- The testator can just severely burn or scorch an existing will or codicil; or,
- The testator can tear up the will or codicil or just tear it enough to show the intent to revoke.

IMPLIED REVOCATION

Implied revocation may arise by word or deed of the testator.

Generally, an implied revocation can exist if there are inconsistencies in the will or codicils to that will. Partial inconsistencies in a will can be integrated by reasonable interpretation and made into a valid will, but total inconsistencies render both the will and the codicil to that will invalid and of no force and effect.

An example of an implied revocation by an act of the testator rather than by an ambiguity in the will itself could be the following:

> "A Testator executed Will No. 1, then later on executed Will No. 2, which expressly or impliedly revoked Will No. 1; later on, testator (though not creating another will) performed some physical act (such as tearing or burning it), which in effect revoked Will No. 2.

In the last example, the key factor in determining which will was in force and effect is the intent of the testator—what was really meant by the physical act performed by the testator.

INDEPENDENT RELATIVE REVOCATION

This doctrine merely means that the alleged revocation was dependent upon, and relative to, certain facts being mistaken by the testator. That is, if the testator knew the truth (true facts) or was mistaken about the truth (or true facts), he would not have done what he did in his will. This would render any revocation ineffective. It is a presumption in the law, and the language of the will supports this presumption unless it is express revocation.

To invoke this theory of Independent Relative Revocation there must be a revocation to begin with; the intent to revoke must have been predicated upon a mistake of fact or law; and the truth must not be within the knowledge of the testator making the revocation. Had the truth been known by the testator, the revocation would not have taken place, and the revocation would not have been consistent with the intent of the testator.

By way of example, let us say that through trickery or some other devious device, you prevent your boyfriend from changing his will after he left everything to you; then he dies. If the legal heirs can show that the testator would have revoked his will except for your trickery or deceit, the will would be totally ineffective. As a matter of course, the law will not allow a person to profit by his unlawful act. He would merely be the trustee in a constructive trust for the benefit of the true heirs.

The doctrine here described is comparable to the fraud doctrine available to set aside a will that was duly executed.

THE LEGAL CHECK-UP

Alice and Boyd marry and make wills, leaving property to each other. At the time of the dissolution of the marriage, generally speaking, if the dissolution is the result of a legal proceeding, gifts from one spouse to another as contained in a will will be invalidated unless there is some language in the will making it clear that the testator intends to give the gift regardless of whether he is divorced. However, in some states the entire will is revoked by a divorce.

The attorney should be aware of the client's change of status or circumstances and should explain to the client who is in a divorce proceeding as plaintiff or respondent what effect divorce may have in the client's present will. The client may want to rewrite his or her will, or at least add a codicil to the will, changing the beneficiary and/or leaving only the spousal rights required under the laws of Intestate Succession and such other rights as provided by law. It saves a lot of headaches later on.

However, this change or possibility is sometimes covered in a property settlement agreement, wherein it is stated that each spouse, among other things, shall have no interest in the other's estate, or take any inheritance. It repudiates and/or surrenders any right to a gift in the testator's will. It is not, however, applicable to the children of the parties, unless the testator specifically writes them out of his will.

In this instance, it may be possible for you to use your word-processing system to simplify and/or substitute appropriate paragraphs. However, bear in mind that simple wills are not conducive to word processing except for the boilerplate paragraphs, such as Paragraphs 5, 6, or 7 in the sample will following, which deal with the appointment of an executor, the powers of an executor, and other such repetitive phrases. If the will contains a testamentary trust agreement, however, it is possible to utilize the word-processing system for those paragraphs that are repeated over and over again and are considered to be standard paragraphs as used in most trust agreements of that nature.

USING THE WORD PROCESSOR IN UPDATING WILLS AND TRUST AGREEMENTS

Giving a client's will or estate-planning documents a legal check-up in today's modern law office can be accomplished much faster and more simply with the advent and use of legal support and word-processing systems.

EXAMPLE

When reviewing and/or auditing your probate files, if you determine that some of the clients have been divorced, or a spouse or child has died, or a child has reached the age of majority, or a child has been adopted, or some other pertinent condition or clause in the will or trust agreement has been invalidated for whatever reason, you can now, by viewing the document on the screen of your support system, make the necessary changes using the word-processing system, such as change of name, change of clause or condition, and so forth, by typing in the new information or the new change or address or by making any type of correction in language simply by pushing a button.

Moreover, it has been established that by using a computer and word-processing system in developing wills and trusts agreements, there will be no errors or misspelled words. In some offices there has been attached to the computer machine a dictionary disk of programmed pertinent words, phrases, and definitions commonly used in wills and trust agreements.

It is a good idea to develop a program or programs or libraries of pertinent business, probate, estate planning, and probate tax liability forms and the like which have been written and developed in your office. This is because they can be stored in a data base of information for later retrieval. It is clear that these disks are most useful when, for example, a client is leaving on a vacation and wants to have his will drawn up or a codicil added before he leaves. If this is the case, you can merely push the appropriate code and bring up his will; push another code and bring up a similar will from which you can get the new changes, phraseology, and so forth, printed out. Thereafter, you can review the client's will together with the will on the screen and merely by switching paragraphs around or making word changes, print out the addition or clause or phrase that your client wants. This can be done in a matter of twenty to thirty minutes, where previously it might have taken an hour or more.

Figure 17.1 is a sample form of a self-proving attestation clause.

Even though a will was not self-proved at the time of its execution, the Uniform Probate Code 2-504(b) (and the states which have adopted it) allows an attested formal will to be made self-proving at a later date by the same witnesses and the testator executing the appropriate form and attaching it to the original attested will. (See Figure 17.2.)

Figure 17.1   Self-proving Attestation Clause

I, _____, the testator, sign my name to this instrument this _____ day of _____, 19_____, and being first duly sworn, do hereby declare to the undersigned authority that I sign and execute this instrument as my last will and that I sign it willingly (or willingly direct another to sign for me), that I execute it as my free and voluntary act for the purpose therein expressed, and that I am eighteen years of age or older, of sound mind, and under no constraint or undue influence.

_____
(Testator)

We, _____ and _____ , the witnesses, sign our names to this instrument, being first duly sworn, and do hereby declare to the undersigned authority that the testator signs and executes this instrument as his last will and that he signs it willingly (or willingly directs another to sign for him), and that each of us in the presence and hearing of the testator, hereby signs this will as witness to the testator's signing, and that to the best of our knowledge the testator is eighteen years of age or older, of sound mind, and under no constraint or undue influence.

_____   _____
(Witness)   (residence of witness)

_____   _____
(Witness)   (residence of witness)

State of _____

County of _____

    Subscribed, sworn to and acknowledged before me by
_____, the testator and subscribed and sworn to before
me by _____ and _____ wit-
nesses, this _____ day of _____, 19_____.

_____
(Notary Public)

My commission expires:

Figure 17.2   Self-proving Attachment to Attested Will

State of_____

County of_____

We, _____, _____, and _____, the testator and wit-
nesses respectively, whose names are signed to the attached or foregoing instrument, being first duly sworn, do hereby declare to the undersigned authority that
the testator signed and executed the instrument as his last will and that he had
signed willingly (or willingly directed another to sign for him), and that he executed
it as his free and voluntary act for the purposes therein expressed, and that each
of the witnesses, in the presence and hearing of the testator, signed the will as witness and that to the best of his knowledge the testator was at that time eighteen
years of age or older, of sound mind and under no constraint or undue influence.

_____
(Testator)

_____ of _____
(Witness) (residence of witness)

_____ of_____
(Witness) (residence of witness)

Subscribed, sworn to and acknowledged before me by
_____, the testator, and subscribed and sworn to before
me by _____ _____, and
_____, witnesses, this _____ day of
_____, 19_____.

_____
(Notary Public)

My commission expires:

DRAFTING A WILL

We will include here a checklist for drafting a will, a sample of a basic simple will, and practical hints for using electronic word and data processing in preparing a will or drafting a codicil.

CHECKLIST FOR DRAFTING A WILL

1. *Introductory clause* introduces the testator and gives instructions for payments of last debts.

2. *Declaratory clauses* spell out the desires of the testator for disposition of his personal and real property, that is, "bequests" of personal property and "devises" of real property. Such bequests or devise may be specific or general.

EXAMPLES

For a specific bequest, specifically identify the object being given. You should describe the property. "I give 'A' my ten (10) shares of General Motors stock." Not "I give my stock to A." Anything that tends to identify the nature or specificity of a gift is a specific gift.

A gift of personal property is usually called a bequest.

A gift of real property is usually called a devise.

In some states, the person who drafts the will must be very precise in using the appropriate gift transfer word.

3. *Appointment clause* sets forth the name of the executor (and trustee, if applicable), and the powers of said individuals.

4. *Residuary clause* disposes of any and all property not otherwise disposed of in the will.

5. *Signature clause, which is self-explanatory.*

Note: When drafting a will, you are cautioned to *always* (and I cannot emphasize this too greatly) keep the line for the testator's signature on the same page with at least two lines of the attestation clause at the bottom. This is vitally important. If the attestation clause with the signatures becomes detached and lost, the will will be considered invalid.

6. *Attestation clause* is also self-explanatory. Note, however, that in some states only two witnesses are required, and in some states it may be

three. You are cautioned to check with your local probate code for the required number.

In states where the self-proving will is allowed as provided in the Uniform Probate Code, the specific statutory language must be used. Two witnesses are required plus a notary public.

SAMPLE FORM OF SIMPLE WILL

LAST WILL AND TESTAMENT OF MARY ANN JONES

1. Opening paragraph: (not numbered)

I, MARY JONES, of Los Angeles, California, being of sound mind and disposing mind and memory, do hereby make, publish, and declare this instrument to be my Last Will and Testament, hereby revoking any and all previous wills or codicils that may have been executed by me.

2. *The body of the will:* The paragraphs in this section usually bear numbers and these numbers are normally spelled out in capital letters, such as FIRST and SECOND and underlined.

For example:

FIRST: I direct that my executor, hereinafter named, pay all my legal obligations and just debts as soon after my demise as may be possible.

SECOND: I give, devise and bequeath unto my brother, John Doe, etc. (specific bequest)

(Use separate, numbered paragraph for each specific bequest if there is more than one.)

THIRD: I give, devise, and bequeath all the rest, residue, and remainder of my real, personal, or mixed property wherever situate to my husband, John Jones, his heirs and assigns forever.

(It is important to have a "residuary clause" in any will. If there is no residuary clause, most states treat the residuary estate as intestate and it would be distributed as provided in the state intestate succession laws, not to the other person or persons named as specific beneficiary in the will.)

FOURTH: I hereby make, constitute, and appoint my husband, John Jones, as Executor (or personal representative in some states) of this my Last Will and Testament.

(The last paragraph before the signature is not numbered. It is called the witness clause.)

(For example:)

IN WITNESS WHEREFORE, I, MARY ANN JONES, have hereunto set my hand and seal this _____ day of_____, 19___.

MARY ANN JONES,
Testatrix

The foregoing instrument, consisting of four (4) pages, including this page was at the date hereof, by MARY ANN JONES, signed as and declared to be her will, in the presence of us, who at her request and in her presence, and in the presence of each other, have subscribed our names as witnesses thereto. Each of us observed the signing of the will by MARY ANN JONES and by each other subscribing witness and knows that each signature is the true signature of the person whose name is signed.

Each of us is now more than twenty-one (21) years of age, and a competent witness and resides at the address set forth after his name.

We are acquainted with MARY ANN JONES, and aver that she has the legal capacity to make this will, is of the age of majority (or in accordance with local statute), and to the best of our knowledge is of sound mind and is not acting under duress, menace, fraud, misrepresentation, or undue influence.

We declare, under penalty of perjury (or such other provision as required by local statute), that the foregoing is true and correct.

Executed on this _____ day of _____, 19__, at _____,
(COUNTY)   (STATE)   (CITY)

_____ , _____

_____ residing at _____

_____

_____ residing at _____

_____

Instead of the above "attestation clause," you may use the one that complies with your particular state statute.

Be sure that the testatrix initials each and every page of the will and thereafter give her a copy and put the original in the attorney's safe deposit box at the bank or wherever he keeps original wills. It often happens that the client will want to keep the original. In either such event, govern yourself according to the policy of your employer, the wishes of the client, and the state in which you work.

INFORMATION CHECKLIST FOR ESTATE PLANNING

This may be prepared by the legal assistant and submitted to the attorney for planning.

FAMILY AND PERSONAL INFORMATION

Name and address of client:_____

Occupation of client:_____

Name and address of employer:_____

Client's date of birth; place of birth:_____

Wife (or husband's) name; date of birth; place of birth:_____

Children's names and dates of birth:_____

_____

Other relatives to be mentioned in will: name, addresses, and relationships:

Persons who would take if there is no will (state's intestate succession law):

Previous marriages (names and dates):

Other pertinent facts about family relationships: names of grandchildren; personal resources of beneficiaries (e.g., earnings in profession or occupation, legal and equitable interests, powers of appointment); disability of beneficiaries.

GENERAL OUTLINE OF ESTATE PLAN

Primary beneficiaries:
Name   Relationship   Property or shares of estate—how given (outright or otherwise)

Other beneficiaries:
Name   Relationship   Property or share of estate—how given (outright or otherwise)

INVENTORY OF ASSETS

BUSINESS INTERESTS

Is business conducted as a sole proprietorship, partnership, or close corporation?_____

Name and address of the business:_____

_____

Names of the client's business associates. How many shares of stock (or what percentages of the business) are owned by each associate and by client?

What office is held by each associate and by client?

Who are the directors, if a corporation?

What functions in the business are carried on by the client and by each associate?

Are there any key employees? What are their names, addresses, and titles?

Where are the corporation's legal and bookkeeping records kept? Name of accountant?

Have the stockholders or partners entered into a business continuation agreement with the client? Is there a partnership agreement in writing? A stockholder's agreement? A buy and sell agreement? Stock redemption agreement with corporation?

What is the estimated value of the client's interest in the business?

BANK ACCOUNTS

Names and addresses of all banks in which accounts are held; *number of each account;* names on each account (i.e., joint, tentative trust, etc.); nature of account (i.e., checking, savings and loan, building and loan, etc.); amounts at present in each account.

Where are bank books, checkbooks, and bank statements kept?

SAFE DEPOSIT BOXES

Name of safe deposit company, address, box number, names and addresses of other persons having access. Who has keys? Where are the keys kept?

FINANCIAL INVESTMENTS; STOCKS AND BONDS

Names of brokerage houses where accounts are maintained; addresses; names of persons who handle client's accounts.

Where are statements and other records kept?

Are stocks owned individually in client's names, or jointly with others? Does he own any stock as custodian for a minor?

Where are the stock certificates kept?

What is estimated value of stock owned?

What is estimated value of bonds owned?

What other property interests does client have in this area, such as stock options, etc.? What is estimated value of such interests?

Does client own any U.S. Savings Bonds? Are they in individual, co-owner, or beneficiary form? What are names of co-owners and beneficiaries? What is the face amount of bonds owned? What is their present value?

REAL ESTATE; HOMES

Does client own home, condominium, or cooperative apartment? Is it owned in his individual name, as joint tenant with right of survivorship, as tenant in common, as tenant by the entirety, etc.? What is name of other owner and relationship to client? Where is the property located?

What is approximate description of property? What is value of property? What is the amount of the mortgage, or mortgages, and other liens of the property? What is value of client's equity interest? What is total equity in property?

What other property does client own for his own use, i.e., summer homes, winter homes, or hunting lodges, etc.?

Fire, title, and other insurance on above property; name and address of insurance company, kind of insurance and coverage; policy number; amount; expiration dates; name and address of broker familiar with client's property and liability insurance?

REAL ESTATE; INVESTMENTS

Location, description, ownership, valuation, and equity in real property owned as an investment. Names and addresses of associates, amounts of mortgages and other liens on property, and by whom held. Addresses of mortgagees and lienors. Fire, title, and other insurance on above property. All pertinent information with regard to this realty.

MORTGAGES OWNED

Amount and nature of each mortgage owned; property on which mortgage owned-location, description, ownership, valuation; other liens on said property; names and addresses of associates in ownership of mortgage. Value of client's interest in mortgage.

PENSION, PROFIT-SHARING, OR STOCK BONUS PLAN; KEOGH PLANS AND IRA ACCOUNTS

Name of plan; name and address of plan trustee; name of insurance company if group annuity or other insured retirement plan; number of group annuity certificate; is plan contributory or noncontributory; how much has client contributed; option already elected; options still available, amount of annuity or other distribution on retirement; amount of death benefit?

Where are copies of plans, certificates of participation and client's account books kept?

BENEFIT PLANS OF CLIENT'S EMPLOYER

Group life insurance plan; split dollar life insurance; other death benefit plan; stock option plan; disability income, accident, sickness, medical, or hospitalization plan; name of insurance company or service organization; number of policy or certificate of participation; amount; names, addresses, and relationships of beneficiaries; options still available under policy; option already elected?

Where are copies of plans, policies and certificates of participation kept?

DEFERRED COMPENSATION AGREEMENT WITH EMPLOYER

Date of execution; provisions for retirement and death benefits; funded by insurance policy purchased by employer; name of insurance company issuing policy; number of policy; amount; options still available; option already elected; other funding arrangement?

Where is agreement kept?

LIFE INSURANCE AND ANNUITY POLICIES

Name of insurance company issuing each policy; number of policy; amount; names, addresses and relationships of beneficiaries; any loans under policy; any assignment; options still available under policy; option already elected; settlement agreement; any dividends at interest or applied to purchase of additional insurance; life insurance trust; participation in life insurance (group or individual) program of employer; National Service Life Insurance?

Other types of personal insurance policies owned by client (disability income, accident, sickness, hospitalization, etc.); name of insurance company; number of policy; participation in program of employer?

Policies owned by client on lives of others; name of insurance company; number of policy; amount; names, addresses, and relationships of beneficiaries; cash values; who pays premiums?

Where are policies and certificates of participation in employer's insurance plans kept?

Family or other noncommercial annuities?

SOCIAL SECURITY AND VETERANS ADMINISTRATION BENEFITS

Social Security Account No.; veteran or not; serial number, branch of service, dates of service?

OTHER PROPERTY

Money owed client personally as distinct from business credits; all facts in connection with said credits.

Rights of client under living trusts set up by himself or others; all facts in connection therewith.

Rights of client under testamentary trusts; all facts, etc.

Interest of client in unadministered estates of relatives or others; client's expected inheritance from parents or others; all facts, etc.

General or special powers of appointment held by client; all facts, etc.

All facts in connection with jewelry, furs, silverware, art works, books, stamp collections, coin collections, and similar property owned by client.

Value of household furniture owned by client.

Automobiles; boats.

All other property or interests in property not covered previously.

All facts relating to insurance on any of above property.

Cemetery plot; location, custody of deed, owned in what names; perpetual care or not?

DOCUMENTS REQUESTED OF CLIENT

Previous will or wills

Spouse's will

Antenuptial or other property agreement with spouse

Other instruments as indicated by answers to questions on foregoing pages

Examples: Partnership or stockholders' agreement; life insurance and annuity policies; pension, profit-sharing and other benefit plans; deferred compensation agreement; deeds of house and business property; leases; tax receipts; maps; surveys; fire and other insurance policies; mortgages and notes owned; copies of trust agreements and wills under which client has power of appointment or other rights; copies of income and gift tax returns; bills of sale and other evidences of ownership.

TAX OUTLINE

PROPERTY UNDER WILL

Real estate valued at	$ . . . .
Securities valued at	$ . . . .
Business interests valued at	$ . . . .
Other property valued at	$ . . . .

A. $ . . . .

Life Insurance

Includible in gross estate

B. $ . . . .

PROPERTY OWNED WITH OTHERS (at value includible in gross estate)

Joint bank accounts	$ . . . .
Jointly owned real estate	$ . . . .
Jointly owned securities	$ . . . .
Jointly owned other property	$ . . . .
Property owned by the entireties	$ . . . .
Community property	$ . . . .

(Note: Exclude property listed above under "Property under Will")

C. $ . . . .

OTHER PROPERTY NOT UNDER WILL (to extend includible in gross estate)

Living trusts	$ . . . .

Powers of appointment $ . . . .

Gift taxes paid on taxable gifts
within 3 years of death $ . . . .

Other $ . . . .

                                                                    D. $ . . . .

COMPUTATION OF TAX

(1) Gross estate [Total of A, B, C, & D] $ . . . .

(2) Estimated administration and funeral expenses,
     and debts of decedent $ . . . .

(3) Marital deduction $ . . . .

(4) Other deductions (e.g., charitable transfers) $ . . . .

(5) Taxable estate [(1) − [(2) + (3) + (4)] $ . . . .

(6) Taxable gifts made after 1976 $ . . . .

(7) Tentative tax base [(5) + (6)] $ . . . .

(8) Tentative tax [from table] $ . . . .

(9) Gift taxes paid on gifts made after 1976 $ . . . .

(10) Tax before unified credit [(8) − (9)] $ . . . .

(11) Allowable unified credit [from table] $ . . . .

(12) Approximate federal estate tax payable [(10) − (11)] $ . . . .

UNIFIED ESTATE & GIFT TAX RATES

Column A	Column B	Column C	Column D
Taxable amount over	Taxable amount not over	Tax on amount in Column A	Rate of tax on excess over amount in Column A (Percent)
0	$10,000	0	18
$10,000	20,000	$1,800	20
20,000	40,000	3,800	22
40,000	60,000	8,200	24
60,000	80,000	13,000	26

Column A	Column B	Column C	Column D
80,000	100,000	18,200	28
100,000	150,000	23,800	30
150,000	250,000	38,800	32
250,000	500,000	70,800	34
500,000	750,000	155,800	37
750,000	1,000,000	248,300	39
1,000,000	1,250,000	345,800	41
1,250,000	1,500,000	448,300	43
1,500,000	2,000,000	555,800	45
2,000,000	2,500,000	780,800	49
2,500,000	3,000,000	1,025,800	53
3,000,000	3,500,000	1,290,800	57
3,500,000	4,000,000	1,575,800	61
4,000,000	—	1,880,800	65

The tax computed by use of the foregoing table is without allowance for any credit for state or foreign death taxes paid or credit for tax on prior transfers.

MAXIMUM UNIFIED CREDIT AGAINST ESTATE TAX

For decedents dying—	The credit is—
in 1982	$62,800
in 1983	79,300
in 1984	96,300
in 1985	121,800
in 1986	155,800
after 1986	192,800

The allowable unified credit is the maximum unified credit reduced by 20% of the aggregate amount that was allowed as a specific exemption for gifts made after September 8, 1976.

DRAFTING A TRUST AGREEMENT

For drafting a trust agreement see sections on word processing and data processing (use of computer) in this section.

A. Definition and Nature of a Trust

A trust is a legal entity. A trust agreement creates a fiduciary relationship between two or more persons wherein one is entrusted with the property, real or personal, of another and holds legal title thereto, for the use and benefit of the other(s). The "beneficiaries" have an "equitable title" or interest in the property so held in trust. The trustee has the legal title.

The trustee has complete control of the trust property subject to the terms of the trust agreement and state law regulating trusts. The consequences of this power of the trustee are far reaching. For this reason, but not necessarily limited thereto, a will containing trust agreements should be meticulously and carefully drawn and reviewed by your attorney. It can be one of the most important documents you will ever draft in a probate matter because of the long-range effect on the property of the testator and the heir-recipients thereof.

Hence, it is vitally important that during the initial interview with the client, he states with specificity his intent as to the trust agreement and the powers of the trustee and reviews the tax ramifications applicable to the gifts therein set out.

Trusts are normally established to ensure the future support of the surviving spouse, the future support and education of the children of the testator, and to preserve the capital or body of the estate. The trust agreement usually provides for particular payment income to specified beneficiaries. Accumlating income from the trust property is limited by tax law.

Trust agreements may be "testamentary" or *inter vivos.*

B. Parties to a Trust

1. *The trustor, or settlor,* who is the party who creates the trust.

2. *The trustee,* who is the party of the second part with fiduciary responsibility as to the property being entrusted to him. He holds the legal title to the property so entrusted.

3. *The beneficiary,* who is the party for whom the property is being held by the trustee.

In an *inter vivos* trust, the trustor or settlor may also be a beneficiary during his lifetime.

C. Elements of a Trust

1. *Intent.* There must be an intent to create a trust. You do not have to use the word trust, just prove that there was an intent to create a fiduciary relationship and a fiduciary duty. You may use words which express hope or de-

sire without their being a demand or command. But be sure to make it effective immediately.

2. *Property or trust res.* The property must be identifiable. You must describe the trust *res* with great particularity. (Note that a debt owed by the trustor is not a specific property; it is merely a general obligation of the estate.)

3. *Parties.* The parties to the trust (who may be a class of persons) must be designated. Any incompleteness as to the designation of a trustee or beneficiary would make the trust ineffective. There must be an appointment and designation of people *now.* The parties must have the capacity of a settlor or trustor as with any other document, that is, capacity, and so forth. The actual name of the trustee is not too important or necessary, but the provision for a trustee should be spelled out in the document. The court can always name a trustee, but it cannot name the other parties.

4. *It must be for a legal purpose.* That is, it must be a trust which is not against public policy.

D. Types of Trusts

All trusts, regardless of what they are called, fall into two basic categories: active or passive, depending on the duties of the trustee:

1. In an active trust the trustee has to do a lot.

2. In a passive trust the trustee has little to do in managing the trust.

TYPES OF TRUSTS

1. A "private trust" is an express trust for a particular individual or named individuals or designated class of individuals.

2. A "charitable trust" is an express trust for undesignated persons of a definite class for a charitable purpose.

3. An "express trust" is one which is expressly and definitely created by the trustor (settlor) by his conduct, words, writing, or all together. There is specific intent on the part of the trustor to create the trust.

4. A "resulting trust" is one inferred by operation of law. This is declared when a court finds that a person *intended* a trust but did not effectively create a trust by a written or oral statement.

5. A "constructive trust" is one resulting by operation of law. It is normally used to prevent fraud or unjust enrichment. It is a sort of remedial device and is a trust merely because the law says so. Such a trust could be one decreed by

a court to avoid fraud against creditors or to avoid fraud against heirs of a decedent's estate where the testator had made an absolute deed to a person before his death but intended that person to hold the property in trust for the heirs of others. This type of trust could be declared by the court on petition of the creditors or heirs. The trustee under this circumstance would be the record title owner holding the property for the benefit of the creditors.

6. The "spendthrift clause" protects the beneficiary against his own folly. If a spendthrift clause or clauses is included in a trust agreement, the beneficiary's creditors cannot attach the property; and the beneficiary cannot encumber the same.

7. An "inter vivos trust" is a trust created by the settlor (trustor) while he is living. The settlor may also be the beneficiary during his lifetime of an *inter vivos* trust created by him. The *inter vivos* trust may be "revocable" or "irrevocable."

8. If it is revocable, it is one in which the trustor has power comparable to total ownership. This is a totally flexible instrument. In California, if the trust does not say anything about it, it is presumed to be a revocable trust. Therefore, if you want to make it an irrevocable trust, you must spell it out in detail; otherwise, the court will presume that the trust is revocable.

This revocable trust can be set up during life and can be funded or unfunded. The funded *inter vivos* trust is payable immediately upon death, without benefit of probate, directly to the beneficiaries named in the trust. The unfunded *inter vivos* trust is payable upon death to the trustee rather than to the members of the family directly. This vehicle is sometimes called the "pour-over trust," and its advantage is that the assets of the estate cannot be attacked by creditors, it also has certain tax advantages.

9. A pour-over trust is an existing trust recognized under the terms and provisions of a will. The trustee performs the provisions of the trust, or the will. The will in this instance merely provides funds for the trust.

10. A totten trust is created by the deposit of one person of his own money in a bank in his own name, as a trustee for another. It is a tentative trust, revocable at will until the depositor dies or completes the gift in his lifetime. It becomes an absolute trust at his death, if it was not disposed of entirely during the life of the trustor.

EXAMPLE

B. Jones goes to the bank and opens a bank account in the name of "B. Jones, in trust for my wife C. Jones."

This type of trust does not go through probate.

CHECKLIST OF CLAUSES WHICH CAN BE INCLUDED IN TESTAMENTARY TRUST AGREEMENTS

It is in this area of your duties that the word-processing system can be most helpful and timesaving, as generally most trust agreements are long and complicated with many paragraphs and subparagraphs. Furthermore, most of these paragraphs and subparagraphs are boilerplate and repetitive, as they are used in most types of trust agreement. In this connection, therefore, consider the following clauses, among others, that can be described as boilerplate clauses:

1. Trust for spouse and family not qualifying for the marital deduction-beneficial interest.

2. Trust for spouse to qualify under the Economic Recovery Tax Act of 1981 (ERTA). Note suggestion to put specific reference to the act in the clause concerning unlimited marital exemption—ref. Section 403 of ERTA

3. Trust for several individuals

4. Trust for one individual

5. Trust for a class of persons

6. Spendthrift trust clauses

7. Annuity trust clauses

8. Income accumulation trust clauses

9. Cemetery trust clause

10. Exculpatory clauses

11. Power to terminate trust clauses

12. Invasion of principal clauses.

STATE LAWS AFFECTING ESTATE PLANNING

Some state common laws or statutes that may affect estate planning and the drafting of a will are as follows:

1. *Integration rule.* This is the rule in some states that requires every page of a will to be present and connected at the time of the signing of the will by the testator. This is the basis for requiring each and every page of a will to be initialed by the testator and for the inclusion in the attesting paragraph of the will the number of pages of the will.

2. *Law of the situs.* The courts will look to the laws of the state in which the will was drawn when probating an estate to determine if it is a valid will even if it is being probated in a different state.

Note: A will is offered for probate in the state where the deceased resided at the time of his death.

EXAMPLE

The testator lives in California and owns property in Missouri. His personal property will be disposed of according to the laws of California, but the real property will be disposed of according to the laws of Missouri. An ancillary administration may have to be instituted in Missouri.

It should be noted that most states try to uphold the provisions of a will made in another state if possible and will change the practical effect of provisions therein contained only if they conflict to a great extent with the laws of their state.

3. *The cy-pres doctrine.* The rule of "cy-pres" is a common-law rule for the construction of instruments in equity by which the intention of the party is carried out as near as can be, when it would be impossible or illegal to give it literal effect. Thus, where a testator attempts to create a gift to a charity that is no longer in existence, the court may endeavor, instead of making the devise entirely void, to explain the will in such a way as to carry out the testator's general intentions and allow the gift to a similar charity. Some states do not apply the cy-pres doctrine or apply it only in very limited situations.

4. *The rule against perpetuities.* This rule was originally an English common-law rule. Some states have adopted statutes to get a similar result.

In California, the Rule Against Perpetuities applies to trusts which are geared to the accumulation of money over a period of fifty years or more. The common rule stated that property of any type must vest, if at all, not later than twenty-one years, plus a life (or lives) in being, but a charitable beneficiary with a "now" vesting interest may accumulate property.

Note: A baby within the womb has been considered to be a life in being within the definition and terms of the Rule Against Perpetuities.

In some courts, where an interest violates the rule against perpetuities, only that interest is void; the balance of the interest is not affected. This is because the courts will do anything within their power to avoid forfeitures and losses. This is a good point to remember when preparing and working with trusts or wills and the interests conveyed to others therein.

FEDERAL TAX LAW AFFECTING ESTATE PLANNING

As you know, the federal estate tax, as provided for in the Internal Revenue Code, is a tax imposed on all of the property owned by the decedent jointly or severally at the time of the death, be it real or personal, tangible or intangible, and wherever located. It includes not only the value of property owned outright, but also the value of any interest he may have had in the property as of the time of his death (jointly owned).

The value of the taxable estate is determined by deducting from the value of the gross estate (as described here) the exemptions, credits, and deductions allowed in the estate-tax section of the Internal Revenue Code.

The Economic Recovery Tax Act of 1981 (ERTA) made major and revolutionary changes in the exemptions, credits, and other tax benefits allowable in estate planning. It should be made clear, however, that the basic statute, the Internal Revenue Code of 1954, remains in effect. The Economic Recovery Tax Act of 1954 (hereinafter referred to as ERTA) made changes by amendment to the Internal Revenue Code of 1954.

These new provisions are of such a highly sophisticated and complicated nature that any attempt here to set forth a fully detailed discussion would be an exercise in futility. Furthermore, because of the major surgery performed by the amendments made to the Internal Revenue Code of 1954 resulting from the enactment of ERTA, you, the legal assistant, should immediately check the estate-planning files, wills, and trust documents of your attorney's clients so that he can determine the need for changes or additions to these documents by reason of ERTA.

PRACTICAL USE OF COMPUTERS IN DRAFTING WILLS AND TRUSTS

COMPUTERIZED TOOLS OF LEGAL RESEARCH

If, in drawing up a trust agreement for the client, you want to make sure that the desire of your client and the language used in the trust agreement have not been invalidated by law resulting from a recent court decision, you could go to Lexis or Auto-Cite or Westlaw to see if any cases have come down dealing with the new subject matter. Then, if so, follow the procedures outlined in Chapter 8 regarding the use of electronic legal research as it relates to the follow-up or next steps in processing a case to determine its current status.

And/or you could go to Nexis to determine if there have been any articles or cases that may have been used regarding the probate of an estate in which a similar trust agreement was the subject of controversy but was settled out of court.

WORD-PROCESSING TOOLS

In addition to the preceding, the word processor becomes a most valuable drafting tool, as you can retrieve from it heretofore programmed and coded boilerplate paragraphs and even unusual or rarely used terms and conditions which have been recorded because they were used in trust agreements which are similar in factual situations, terms, and conditions.

The foregoing samples and information can merely be customized for your current client.

Moreover, these current or customized paragraphs and trust agreements can be reviewed for accuracy and change prior to the final print-out and/or filing for future reference.

EXAMPLE

Let us say that you have already programmed your software and it is displayed on the screen for review. It is at this point that you can correct any mistakes, such as a misspelled name which appears throughout the document. You can tell your computer to correct the spelling wherever the name is used in the document. Or, at this point, you can rearrange paragraphs either by removing them entirely or by changing their position in the document.

If you have merely retrieved a document similar to the one you are doing, it is at this point that you can change the names and other personal information to customize it for your current needs.

THE ADMINISTRATION OF AND PROBATING OF ESTATES

The following step-by-step procedures are geared to California practice and set forth by way of example what you should look for and be guided by. It is suggested that you look to your local court rules and statutes for the procedures used in your jurisdiction.

INITIAL STEPS (GENERALLY)

Generally, as to both intestate and testate probate proceedings you should:

a) Search for burial instructions and/or will to dispose of the body;

b) If applicable, open safe deposit box for burial instructions, and/or will;

c) Determine if a special administrator is needed;

d) Have copies made of will for later use in administration procedures;

e) Locate witnesses to prove the will; or if it is a holographic will, someone who can prove the handwriting of the decedent;

f) Prepare petition for issuance of letters testamentary; letters of administration with the will annexed; or letter of administration, whichever is applicable;

g) Determine who is to be the petitioner, and,

h) Ascertain names, addresses, ages of heirs at law and/or named beneficiaries.

PROBATING THE ESTATE

A. Intestate

Step-by-step Procedure

1. File petition for Letters of Administration.

2. Notice of hearing. (Be sure any and all heirs or suspected heirs are notified of the hearing date via registered mail at least 10 days prior to the date of said hearing; or whatever time limit is the policy of your state.)

3. File any contest to petitioner, petitioning for Letters of Administration.

4. *Preparation for hearing:*

   a) testimony establishing death;

   b) residency requirements;

   c) known heirs and unknown heirs; etc.

5. *Order appointing administrator.* This should be prepared in original and three copies and placed in your attorney's file so that he may have same at the hearing.

6. *Letters of Administration.* These should be prepared before the hearing and placed in the attorney's file so that he may have them on the date of the hearing. Make an original and three copies, others may be secured when and as needed.

7. *Administration of the Estate:*

   a) Publication of Notice to Creditors. All claims should be filed within four months from the date of publication.

   b) Request appointment of an appraiser.*}

   c) Prepare an original and three copies of the Inventory and Appraisement. An original and one for the court, one for the appraiser and one copy for your file.

   Note: in each of the above documents, be sure that the petitioner has signed in all spaces provided for the signature.

   d) Powers and duties of administrator:

      1. Liquidate assets;

      2. Raise funds by selling property and/or collecting outstanding debts due the estate;

      3. Pay all outstanding debts as soon as possible, including state and federal taxes due and inheritance taxes, if any;

      4. Pay expenses of administration and attorney's fees, if any.

8. Distribution and Settlement of Estate:

   a) Preliminary distribution (if warranted);

   b) Final distribution;

      1) A period of six months from date of first publication of Notice to Creditors must have lapsed before there can be a distribution (time element may be peculiar to your state);

      2) Current and final accounting should be prepared before there can be a final distribution to heirs, etc.;

      3) If first and final accounting is approved by the court, then the attorney can distribute the funds in the estate;

      4) File application to the court for final discharge;

      5) File application for termination of proceedings when the estate is exhausted.

---

* In some states this is now automatically done by the court.

B. Testate

1. File petition to probate will and for Letters Testamentary (or for Letters of Administration with Will Annexed if appropriate).

2. Send out notice of hearing to all named heirs, beneficiaries, etc. and unknown.

3. Prepare the necessary documents for issuance of your Letters before the hearing date so that the attorney may have them in the file.

   a) Order for Letters Testamentary;

   b) Letters Testamentary;

   c) Subscribing witness affidavit and proof of will (in some states this procedure has been changed and a printed document is now used and in some states a certified copy of the original will must be submitted to the witness for verification as to signature);

   d) Prepare the order admitting will to probate;

   e) Secure bond, if required.

4. *Administration of Estate:*

   Use the same procedure as set forth under the General Outline for probating an estate wherein there was no will, and the paragraphs a through d of subparagraph 7 and 8 regarding distribution and settlement of the estate.

C. Estates Involving Minors and Guardians

The provision for the appointment of guardians on behalf of minors or incompetents is in many state statutes, or is governed by committees for the insane with the appointments being made by the court.

The duties and trust of the guardian are administered under the control of the court, and the power to remove a guardian for cause is generally vested in the court making or approving the appointment.

These guardianships can be generally classified as follows:

1. A constructive guardianship;

2. A natural guardianship;

3. A testamentary guardianship;

4. A general guardianship; or

5. A guardian ad litem.

Since the basis for their determination may vary from state to state, it is conceivable that the procedure for their administration and control will also vary from jurisdiction to jurisdiction. Hence, you are referred to your local probate rules for the controlling procedures. The following procedures are set forth as examples only, and emphasize the duties which can be performed by legal assistants in this area of an attorney's practice, and are guided by California practice and policy.

The powers and duties of a guardian are basically the same as those for any "estate" except that you must be sure to keep accurate and complete records of any and all expenditures for the support and care of the minor and/or incompetent; you also must make semi-annual or annual accountings to the court (whichever time limit has been established by the court); and any and all expenditures, regardless of how small, must be approved by the court *before* they are expended.

Although all sales or transfer of any asset in any "estate" must receive the approval of the court, it is most important in that of a minor and/or incompetent, in order that the minor may have an income or money when he has attained the age of majority; and/or for the incompetent's protection.

Termination of these types of guardianships occurs when:

1) the minor has reached the age of majority and you make a full and complete accounting to him and the court;

2) and when the incompetent has been restored to capacity in the eyes of the court or has died. Then his estate becomes a true "estate" matter and should be handled accordingly.

You should also secure final discharge papers and termination of proceedings documents when the duty of the guardians has been discharged completely and to the satisfaction of the court.

STEP-BY-STEP PROCEDURE

Minors:

1. File petition for Letters of Guardianship.
2. Send out notice of hearing to interested parties.
3. Prepare the following for hearing:
   a) Order appointing guardian;

      b) Letters of Guardianship;

      c) Secure bond, if required.

Incompetents:

1. File petition for Letters of Guardianship.
2. Send out notice of hearing to all interested parties, including relatives, creditors, etc.
3. Prepare the following for hearing:

      a) Order appointing guardian;

      b) Letters of Guardianship;

      c) Bond, if required.

CHRONOLOGICAL STEP-BY-STEP PROCEDURE IN HANDLING AN ESTATE MATTER*

1	Collect and compile personal data needed to handle estate.
2	Evaluate data needed to write legal and correct will(s).
3	Write will(s).
4	Collect and compile information for trust agreement.
5	Write legal and correct trust agreement.
6	Transfer assets to a Trust.
7	Write specific Power of Attorney Document.
0	Probating Decedent's Estate.
1	Compile personal data of decedent.
2	Determine whether probate is necessary from personal data.
3	Evaluate data to develop a petition for probate.
4	Document legal petition for probate.
5	Write affidavit of minutes to the will.
6	Document bond for estate executor.
7	Write text of court order to admit will to probate.
8	Compile information for heirs.
9	Write a Note to Interested Persons.
10	Arrange required publishing of death notice with newspaper.
11	Locate and inform heirs of the death and arrange required actions.

---

* Source: Oregon Department of Education, Curriculum Development Unit, Vocational and Career Education

12   Locate and establish control of estate assets.

13   Appraise value of estate assets.

14   Document assets and their value.

15   Pay off liens and/or court judgments against the estate.

16   Determine necessity of ancillary probate.

17   Write documents required for ancillary probate.

18   Pay or reject claims against the estate.

19   Compile needed data and write out income tax return.

20   Write out fiduciary tax returns.

21   Prepare Federal estate tax return.

22   Request final audit in writing.

23   Apply for release of assets.

24   Administer checking account.

25   Estimate total cash needed to close the estate.

26   Advise heirs and devisees of the status of the estate.

27   Accomplish a final accounting for the estate.

28   Write a Notice of Final Accounting.

29   Write court order approving the Final Accounting.

30   Arrange transfer of assets to heirs.

31   Prepare receipts.

32   Assemble information for Supplementary Final Accounting.

33   Prepare Supplementary Final Accounting.

34   Compile and write court order to close estate.

35   File Claim against estate.

36   File objection to final accounting.

CHRONOLOGICAL STEP-BY-STEP PROCEDURE IN HANDLING A CONSERVATORSHIP

1   Collect and organize data needed to set up conservatorship.

2   Compile petition for appointment of conservator.

3   Prepare Order for citation.

4   Prepare citation.

5   Prepare Acceptance of Service of Citation and Waiver.

6   Write document needed to place Conservator under.

7   Write court order appointing Conservator.

8   Document Inventory of assets under Conservatorship.

9   Administer conservator checking account.

10   Provide annual accounting for conservatorship.
11   Compile tax returns affected by conservatorship.
12   Write court order approving annual accounting.
13   Compile conservatorship final accounting.
14   Write court order approving conservatorship final accounting and direct distribution.
15   Fill out conservatorship direct distribution receipt.
16   Write court order closing conservatorship.
17   Prepare conservator's petition for sale of real property.
18   Prepare and serve citation for Sale.
19   Write court order to sell real property under conservatorship.
20   Write conservator's petition for sale of personal property.
21   Write court order to sell personal property under conservatorship.

GLOSSARY

Administrator	An individual appointed by the court to manage the estate of a decedent who has died without leaving a will (feminine is an administratrix).
Administrator with Will Annexed	An individual appointed by the court when a decedent has left a will in which there has been no executor or executrix appointed or the named executor fails to act.
Codicil	An addition to or change in a will that has already been executed by the testator or testatrix.
Devise	A gift of real property under a will.
Devisee	An individual to whom real property is given under a will.
Executor (Executrix)	An individual (or entity such as a bank) appointed by a decedent in his will to carry out the terms and provisions of his will.
Holographic Will	A will entirely written by hand, dated and signed by the testatrix and/or testator.
Intestate	The state of an individual not having prepared and left a valid will for probate.

Legatee	An individual to whom personal property is bequeathed under the terms of a will.
Letters of Administration	The formal instruction of authority and appointment given to an administrator by the proper court, empowering him to enter upon the discharge of his office as administrator (administratrix).
Letters Testamentary	The formal instruction of authority and appointment given to an executor by the proper court, empowering him to enter upon the discharge of his office as executor (executrix).
Nuncupative Will	An oral will declared, or dictated by a testator, *before* witnesses and *afterwards* reduced to writing.
Public Administrator	A public official who has prior right to administer an estate, when no other qualified person seeks appointment as administrator.
Residuary Legatee	One who receives the residue of an estate after payment of the testator's (testratrix's) debts, devises and legacies.
Special Administrator	An individual who is appointed, by the court, under certain conditions when the circumstances of the estate require an immediate appointment of a personal representative.
Testate	The state of having died leaving a valid will for probate.
Will	An instrument in which a qualified person legally and intentionally directs the disposition of his or her property to become effective after his or her death.

CHAPTER 18

How to Handle a Family Law File

One of the prime functions of a legal assistant in a law office with a family law practice is that of interviewing the client and obtaining the necessary facts relating to the marriage, the children, if any, and the property of the parties. Thereafter, she will be able to analyze and determine what marital state was created, whether there is a child custody problem, and what is the separate, personal property of the parties as opposed to the community property or joint property (depending on the state where the parties reside).

The most common mistake made is that of assuming all property automatically upon marriage becomes community or jointly owned (depending on the state where the parties reside) property. It is for this reason that a legal assistant should know the difference between the two and how they interact and can change their character.

One of the causes of emotional distress and bitterness at the time of a dissolution of a marriage is the improper division of the property of the parties.

Inasmuch as the format and procedures used in pursuing a family law matter vary from state to state, an in-depth, step-by-step procedure would be impractical.

Hence, this section on family law will be an overview discussion of the theory and concept of the marital state and a capsule breakdown of property before, during, and after a marriage.

What Is the State Called Marriage?

Marriage is a civil contract, the parties to which are (1) a man, (2) a woman, and (3) the state. It is not a commercial contract in that it cannot be contracted away. It can be dissolved only by the state law, in conformity with "public policy."

Throughout all discussions with clients regarding a marital problem, bear in mind these two words—public policy—since they are the underlying determining factor of all laws relating to marriage and the dissolutions of marital bliss.

ELEMENTS OF STATUTORY MARRIAGE

A so-called legal marriage is a marriage authorized by state statute. The statute usually requires a license to marry plus a marriage ceremony by a person authorized to perform marriage such as a minister, priest, notary public, captain of a ship, judge, and the like.

Absent a license to marry issued by the state, it is a void marriage in spite of a marriage ceremony regardless of its formality, except in a state that recognizes common law marriage.

Furthermore, "mandatory statutes," directed to the parties, state that the parties shall not be validly married if there is a preexisting marriage not dissolved by law.

And, "directory statutes" advise county clerks that they shall not issue a marriage license unless there is evidence that a blood test has been taken. But it is a valid marriage even though the clerk may not have had the blood certificate physically present at the time of issuing the certificate.

The general rule as to statutory marriage or another state's recognition of a common law marriage is that a marriage valid where celebrated is valid everywhere except where it is against public policy.

ELEMENTS OF A COMMON LAW MARRIAGE*

There is a sharp disagreement and conflict as to the validity of such a marriage, but in a state or court jurisdiction where it is accepted this type of marital arrangement carries with it all rights of inheritance, descent, and distribution, as well as other property rights. Hence, the prerequisites should be clear-cut and defined as follows:

1. There must be a mutual consent and agreement between the parties;
2. There must be cohabitation between the parties; and,

---

* California does not recognize common law marriages. The Family Law Act states that you must be legally married.

3. There must be full and complete representation and a holding out to the community at large that the parties are living as husband and wife for a specified (statutory provision) period of time. If there is no statutory provision, it is deemed to be a "common law" marriage as each of the above elements are present.

Another method sometimes used to establish a marriage is the proxy marriage. Where recognized, it is considered a valid marriage. It is allowable without cohabitation if an authorized representative of each party is present at the proxy ceremony. Absent such statutory regulation, such a marriage is void and of no force and effect. Though this doctrine of the proxy marriage is not recognized in every state, most states have such a statute on the books.

OTHER RELATIONSHIPS DISTINGUISHED

1. Putative relationship: A "putative relationship" exists when one or both of the parties enter into an invalid marriage but do so in good faith, believing that neither one has any impediment affecting the validity of the marriage. In jurisdictions where this type of relationship is recognized, as in New York and Texas, a mistake of fact or law may be present and still not negate the lawfulness of a putative relationship, in this instance, only the innocent spouse of the putative spouse. The one who knows that the marriage is invalid is the "meretricious spouse."

2. Meretricious relationship: A meretricious relationship exists where both parties have knowledge of the invalidity of the marriage performed or where they are just living together. It is not a sufficient community and does not constitute any legally recognized relationship.

3. Rights of the parties in meretricious and putative relationships: One of the major problems arising in these types of relationships is the status of any property accumulated and the disposition thereof when the relationship is terminated. The laws relating to the disposition of property vary in the states recognizing these relationships, but most tend to favor the putative spouse.

EXAMPLE

In the case of the wife as the putative spouse, should she find that her husband has a living wife somewhere and thereafter obtains an annulment of the marriage, her rights as the innocent spouse in the putative relationship are fully protected, and she is entitled to the same share that she would have been entitled to had it been a valid marriage.

In the case of a "legal wife" who survives a meretricious husband, cases treat the husband as having had two surviving spouses. As a result of this treatment, one half of the property of the husband goes to the putative wife and one half goes to the legally recognized community, or the legal wife. The reasoning is that since the putative innocent spouse contributed to the putative community, she is entitled to what she contributed; and of course, the legal wife is entitled to one half of the legal community.

The recent trend to couples living together without benefit of matrimony or statutory or common law has changed some of the former legal rules about the rights of parties to a meretricious relationship.

The Common Law Methodology of marriage appears to have taken on a new legal status, and the state of flux in the law relating to alimony, maintenance, and support appears to have stabilized as the result of the recent judicial decision in the California case of *Marvin v. Marvin.** Since the Marvin case, some other jurisdictions have recognized and applied some of its principles where there was no marriage intended.

As you will recall, in that case the parties were living together without the benefit of a traditional marriage ceremony or other *prima facie* evidence of a legal marriage or intent to marry, and the court made its decision based on the relationship as between the parties over the many years of their living together as "husband and wife."

More recently, the relationship between homosexuals living together and their legal rights have been brought to the attention of the judicial system when one of the parties sued for palimony. At the moment, the law in this area of palimony and property rights, is in a state of flux.

The effect of the decision in the *Marvin v. Marvin* case on family law practice and the legal precedents set established the following:

1. An unmarried person can recover from a person with whom he or she had lived, in accordance with an agreement; or,

2. By way of the conduct between the parties it could be *implied* that there was a contract; or,

3. The court can consider equitable remedies based upon the value of the relationship or on the basis of a "constructive trust"—*quantum meruit.*

---

* *Marvin* v. *Marvin*, 18 Cal 3rd 660, (1976); 122 Cal App 3rd 871 (8-11-1981).

These principles may be applied to a contract between homosexuals if such a contract would not be considered illegal because it is against public policy or statutes in a state *quantum meruit.*

In dealing with the large divorce case, such as the Marvin case, perhaps you should consider "bifurcating" the property settlement agreement and/or division of property from the actual divorce proceeding because of the possible tax ramifications. It is suggested that you check with your attorney about this.

MARITAL AGREEMENTS

An "antenuptial agreement" between a husband and a wife before marriage, but in contemplation of marriage, regarding separate personal property must contain a complete disclosure of all separate property of the properties, and, as well, a representation of each party by an attorney of his or her own choosing.

If the wife is not represented by counsel, the agreement may be invalidated by the court. Therefore, in drafting your agreement, be sure to include a statement to the effect that there was a full disclosure of all separate property of the parties; and that each party was represented by counsel.

Since there is a duty, established by law, that a husband should support his wife, he cannot contract away that duty. He can sometimes contract away "spousal support," but in your agreement you must show that the wife has fair and reasonable means to support herself.

A "post-marital agreement" may be made by the parties and enforced by the court where divorce is contemplated or where the parties intend to continue the marriage relationship if there is full disclosure and separate representation by attorneys.

Some homosexuals living together have called upon attorneys to draft a "nonmarital agreement" for them since the Marvin case.

The section of family law of the American Bar Association has published an excellent and informative paperback book with sample forms for all the above contracts. Its title is *Marital and Non-Marital Contracts* by Joan Krauskopf. It can be purchased from the ABA Press, 1155 East 60th Street, Chicago, Illinois 60637.

DIVORCE (DISSOLUTION OF MARRIAGE)

In all states a statutory marriage must be dissolved by order of court. In states where a common law marriage is recognized, divorce or dissolution of marriage proceedings would be the only definitive way to end such a marriage (children, property rights, and so forth).

Many states still require specific grounds for divorce to be stated in the petition or complaint. Others have adopted the "no-fault divorce" concept. In the latter, it is sufficient to allege that the marriage is irretrievably broken without stating the specific reasons for the breakup. Check your state divorce code or statutes for the grounds you must allege. State case law interprets those statutes.

State court rules of civil procedure and local court rules govern what court documents must be filed and the times for filing.

DISSOLUTION OF MARRIAGE (NO-FAULT DIVORCE)

About sixteen of the fifty states still require a complaint in divorce to state grounds for divorce other than the mere ultimate fact that the marriage is "irretrievably broken." The grounds to be stated may not be the real reasons the plaintiff (petitioner) wants a divorce, but at least one of the grounds must be alleged in the complaint (petition) to state a cause of action in divorce.

State statutes provide the basis for getting a divorce. They state the grounds: irretrievable breakdown of the marriage (no-fault), adultery, desertion, mental or extreme cruelty, physical cruelty, impotence (not infertility), nonsupport or willful neglect, insanity, alcoholism, drug addiction, or conviction of a felony, among others.

In all states, the "substantive grounds" for divorce must be stated in the complaint to state the cause of action. In no-fault divorce states, it is sufficient to state that the marriage is irretrievably broken, without stating grounds or facts showing why. In other states, the particular ground for obtaining the divorce must be stated in the complaint, and the defendant may demand a bill of particulars or motion for more definite statement to get the facts if the divorce is being contested.

In all states the "jurisdictional grounds" for divorce must also be stated in the complaint (petition). Jurisdiction is based on the place and length of residence of the parties. Residence requirements (immediately preceding the filing of the action) vary from none in Alaska and six weeks in Idaho and Nevada to one year in Iowa, Rhode Island, South Carolina, and West Virginia. Some of the states with longer residence requirements have exceptions where the plaintiff was married in the state, if the cause of action for divorce arose in the state, or if both parties reside in the state.

Important: Check your state court rules for divorce procedure. Check your state statute(s) for the grounds for divorce in your state.

In most no-fault divorce states, the plaintiff (petitioner) must include allegations in the complaint (petition) that will entitle him or her to other relief if he or she wants it: division of property, custody of children, attorney's fees, partition of jointly held property, and so on.

The court will apply equitable principles of law in deciding those questions.

Note: If grounds or jurisdictional facts are not stated in the complaint for divorce, it is subject to a motion for dismissal (demurrer). If facts that show the petitioner is entitled to any or all of the other relief mentioned here are not stated in the complaint and prayer, the court may not even consider those questions.

A. Jurisdiction

Jurisdiction is the authority and capacity of the court and its judicial officers to take cognizance of and decide the case before it. It must have jurisdiction over both the subject matter and the parties. The question of "domicile" goes to the subject matter in a divorce case.

Jurisdiction over the parties is obtained by "service of process." See Chapter 4 on court systems and procedures.

Service. Service in a divorce court (with certain limitations) can be:

1. Personal service, which is the physical service of process on the person of the defendant. This must be accomplished to have *in personam* in jurisdiction; and

2. Constructive service, where the individual has been served by publication, which is merely a notice of pending in *rem* proceeding; and

3. Marital status is considered a thing (*rem*), so constructive service may be made in a divorce or dissolution case to determine the right to divorce or dissolution (of the marital status), but other matters cannot be disposed of unless there is personal service.

Domicile. Domicile can be of the following types:

1. Marital domicile, which is the place where the husband and wife established a home in which they live as husband and wife and where

the marriage contract is being performed. Since in some states this element of domiciliary may be relevant as it relates to the question of jurisdiction at the time of a separation between the parties, you should consult your state statutes for resolution.

2. Domicile of origin is where the person was born or lived with his parents; and,

3. It can be where the person chose to live.

Domicile itself has two necessary elements: (1) to establish domicile of the plaintiff sufficient to give a court jurisdiction of a divorce where the defendant resides in another state, the plaintiff must be physically present in the state and must (2) have the subjective intent to remain in said state for an indefinite period of time.

Additionally, all states have a further domiciliary requirement for the plaintiff, that is three months, six months, six weeks, one year, and so forth, immediately prior to the filing of the complaint or petition.

Where a husband and wife are domiciled in one state and the respondent is personally served, a divorce granted by that state is given full force and effect everywhere.

Divisible Divorce. The doctrine of divisible divorce allows a valid *ex parte* divorce to be granted in one state and property rights to be settled by a court in another state.

EXAMPLE

A wife secured a divorce in Nevada and remains there. There is no property owned jointly by the parties in Nevada.

The husband lives in Arizona, where there is property. Wife cannot sue for support and alimony or for the division of the property in Arizona. Nevada can grant the divorce, but the State of Arizona would have to order support and alimony payments and divide the property, since these require *in personam* jurisdiction. This is called a divisible divorce.

B. Procedure

Documents fileable—noncontested divorce. In most states a divorce proceeding is started by a petition for dissolution of marriage or complaint in divorce. If a response document is not filed by the respondent within the statutory period, for example, thirty days in California, the divorce decree is automatic, after the filing of the Interlocutory Decree and normal confidential and financial declaration papers. (Of course, these procedures vary from state to state.)

In California, for example, there is now the summary judgment type of proceeding, which requires the following qualifications, but serves as a noncontested divorce proceeding:

1. Jurisdictional requirement;
2. Irreconcilable differences;
3. No children of the marriage;
4. The marriage is not more than five years' duration at the time of filing;
5. No real property;
6. No unpaid obligations in excess of $3,000;
7. The fair market value of community assets is less than $10,000;
8. Mutual waiver of rights to spousal support;
9. Appeal and mutual desire of the courts to end the marriage.

In other jurisdictions, the case can be set for hearing immediately after the time for filing an answer has passed.

Documents fileable—contested divorce. The following preparation must be made when filing for a contested divorce:

1. Prepare summons (marriage), the reverse side of which (in some states) tells you what other documents should be prepared to accompany it for filing with the court. These additional documents may vary from state to state so check your state divorce statute or code. The summons must be personally served on the defendant if he can be located. The plaintiff must have resided in the state where the divorce is filed for the length of time prescribed by state statutes.

2. Then prepare the petition for divorce or complaint in divorce. If you use a printed form, be sure you choose the appropriate one.

3. Look to the state statutes and local court rules to determine the grounds for divorce and if you need to attach to the petition for divorce any exhibits, such as a property settlement agreement, inventory of household goods and furnishings, financial statements, and so forth.

4. If there is a danger of physical harm to your client by the spouse, the attorney may want you to prepare a temporary restraining order to be signed by the court.

5. A confidential conciliation statement may not be applicable in your state.

The same caution should be used in completing this document as is outlined in number 3 above.

6. The financial declaration is called the financial statement in some states. It is also a vital document, as it advises the court of the financial condition of both parties, thereby aiding the court in making a ruling as to who pays what, and when. Be sure it is as complete and correct and as current as possible.

Note: Your attorney and the client must sign this document. In some states the financial statement must be made under oath but need not be signed by the attorney.

7. In preparing notices and orders to show cause and other various notices—motions and orders to show cause regarding contempt, modification, joinder of parties, and so forth—you should work closely with your attorney and check your local rules applicable regarding service, and so on.

These documents should be meticulously and carefully prepared, since they deal with the needs of the petitioner relating to child support, alimony and the ability of the respondent to pay same, as well as the disposition or hypothecating of real and personal property of the community property in California and other community-property states.

8. To prepare the request or declaration regarding default (marriage), do the following:

a. Check to determine if a current financial declaration is of record; if not, attach a carbon copy to your request for default.

b. A copy of this request for declaration must be mailed to the last known address of the respondent. You *cannot show* "unknown" as it relates to the address of the respondent.

c. In some states you cannot get a default judgment for the petitioner, but the case can be set for trial and tried *ex parte.*

9. Your checklist preparing your attorney for trial ends in preparing your attorney for the hearing (or trial) in a dissolution proceeding; therefore, be sure to include the following:

a. The required number of copies of the interlocutory judgment of dissolution (regarding marriage), which you had prepared beforehand; and

b. Copies of any property settlement agreement, as well as the original for filing with the court, if necessary; and

c. Notice of entry of judgment regarding marriage.

Note: Naturally, if it is a full-blown trial, then all documents normally prepared and included for a trial would be applicable here.

ALIMONY AND CHILD SUPPORT

Alimony and child support are usually decided in a divorce (dissolution of marriage) case.

The following are basic issues in a divorce case:

1. Jurisdiction of court (based on the residence of plaintiff);
2. Required grounds for divorce;
3. Custody of minor children, if any;
4. Division of property by agreement of the parties or by order of court.

Note: In dealing with a large divorce settlement perhaps you might want to consider "bifurcating" the property settlement and/or division of property from the actual divorce proceeding because of the possible tax ramifications. It is suggested that you discuss this possibility with your attorney–employer.

5. Child support if there are minor or disabled children;
6. Spousal support. (If this is determined to be income to the wife and therefore taxable to the wife, husband can deduct this spousal support. Check the Internal Revenue Code and the Code of the Federal Regulations on the subject).

Further note: In some states, a trial court has in its jurisdiction whether to terminate jurisdiction over spousal support, unless the record clearly shows that the wife cannot take care of herself once the spousal support is terminated.

To determine whether or not the wife can take care of herself and appraise the assets of the husband, if he is the respondent, the legal assistant should gather the kind of evidence to be submitted to the court that would indicate that the wife can or cannot take care of herself at the time of the termination of the spousal support.

This should include a financial declaration as to both parties, supporting schedules, earning capacity of each party, separate property of each party, historical background as to education and work experience of the wife, and so forth.

In connection with this, your attorney may consider discovery at this point, such as depositions, interrogatories, and so forth, to determine the separate assets and earning capacity of each party. This is to support the plaintiff's ability to obtain employment, once the divorce is final.

7. Attorneys' fees and costs.

8. In some states, jointly owned property that is held as "tenants by the entireties" by husband and wife during the marriage remains jointly owned but the divorced partners are tenants in common instead of tenants by the entireties from the moment the divorce or dissolution decree is entered.

Note: In some of those states, a spouse may prove a "special equity" in the jointly owned property by proving that she paid for the property from funds unconnected with the marriage (as by inheritance or part of a former divorce settlement). That spouse must also prove that no gift to the other spouse was intended when the property was put in both names.

9. In some states the jointly owned property may be ordered partitioned by the court if grounds for partition were alleged in the petition or complaint for divorce and that relief was asked for in the prayer contained in the petition or complaint.

The general rule in most states is that a husband is liable for the support of the wife. This duty is based upon and is an integral part of the marriage contract.

The husband's liability as to support is based upon the wife being his agent with express or implied authority to pay, as a matter of law, for the necessities of life, that is, food, clothing, education, support and maintenance for the children of the parties, medical expenses, and the like. To this end, the wife has the power to pledge the husband's credit to produce these necessities—as long as they are still married, whether physically together or not.

Once a divorce or separate maintenance decree is made by a court, obtaining money ordered by the court for the support and maintenance of the children and for alimony is another matter. There is a definite procedure for exercising these rights and fulfilling the decree of the court; these step-by-step procedures can be found under the domestic relations or family law section of your state civil code or code of procedure.

For example, in California once there has been a hearing on a petition for dissolution of a marriage, the court issues its orders to the respondent (if by default, he does not have to be present; but the petitioner is required to forward him a copy of all pleadings and minute orders of the court), requiring him to do or not to do certain things, including but not limited to (1) paying a specified sum of money to the petitioner for the support and maintenance of the children of the parties, if any; (2) alimony (if not waived); (3) attorney's fees; (4) provision for visitation rights; (5) provision for the disposition of any property: and (6) any restraining order pertinent thereto.

Hence, you have the following orders that may be issued by the court:

1. Order for support and maintenance;
2. Order for child custody;
3. Order regarding visitation rights of the parties;
4. Order for attorney's fees and costs; and
5. Injunctive or restraining orders.

ENFORCING SUPPORT ORDERS*

There are basically two methods that may be used to proceed to enforce these orders of the court: (1) civil and (2) criminal.

STEP-BY-STEP PROCEDURE

A. Civil Method

1. This could be a contempt order or modification order in which a declaration is made as to the amount of the arrearage, the amount ordered to be paid and when, and the balance due. If it is a modification, then a statement should be included setting forth a change in circumstances, requiring a reduction in payments.
2. This document is filed with the court and a failure of compliance on the part of the respondent (or defendant) results in a money judgment being entered upon which is obtained a writ of execution.
3. This writ is delivered to the marshal to levy on the property of the respondent (or defendant), that is, bank account, automobile, salary, and the like.
4. The proceeds are physically taken from the bank or the marshal will take the car, and so forth, in satisfaction of the money judgment for back support payments.

---

* California procedure set forth by way of example only.

This payment may be followed for attorney's fees, alimony payments, and child support.

B. Criminal Method

This procedure is used when the party is in contempt of a court order for which he can be imprisoned. But there must be a hearing to determine his violation and disobedience of a lawful court order. Since it is a quasicriminal proceeding, he has to be personally served and physically present at the hearing, though he need not take the stand to testify. He can remain silent, but the initiating party must prove beyond a reasonable doubt that:

1. He had knowledge of the order, either by being in court on the day it was decreed, or had been personally served with a true copy thereof;
2. He has the ability to comply with the order; and
3. He willfully disobeyed the court's order at the time he had the ability to pay.

DIVISION OF MARITAL PROPERTY

IN COMMUNITY PROPERTY STATES

As indicated earlier, one of the greatest problems to be resolved in a family law matter is the division of the property accumulated during the marriage of the parties. The courts and legislators had the presence of mind to develop a means by which this could be accomplished on a more equitable basis with the least amount of trauma; hence the classification of property into personal and community in community-property states.

1. Personal property: This kind of property is normally that which consists of things temporary and movable, such as animals, furniture, jewelry, books, and cars; or stocks, bonds, patents, and copyrights. It can include cash on hand and separate checking and savings accounts, all of which were acquired, in this instance, prior to a marriage between the parties.

2. Community property: Under this classification, husband and wife form a kind of partnership and the property acquired by either during the marriage belongs to both. It is therefore necessary, when dealing with a dissolution where there is community property, to consider the date of the acquisition of the property in order to fully determine the rights of the parties therein.

This community-property plan regulates property rights as between a husband and a wife in the United States and is based upon express legislation, and it is controlling in the following states: Arizona, California, Idaho, Louisiana, Nevada, New Mexico, Texas, and Washington. Oklahoma has an optional community property plan.

In California, all property that is owned by married persons can be one of only three things:

1. Husband's separate property;
2. Wife's separate property; and
3. Community property.

Under this plan, the property acquired during the marriage as the result of the efforts of both husband and wife belongs to the community. This type of property may include any and all property, other than gifts, devises, or inheritance.

One of the problems in dividing the property in a dissolution of marriage proceeding is to be able to place the property into the proper category. This is done by tracing the source of the property.

A. Sources of Community Property

What does community property include? Earnings and real property acquired during the marriage are the community property of both, while gifts received from third parties are the personal property of either the husband or wife.

Earnings include whatever benefits are appended to employment such as pensions, profit sharing plans, bonuses, stock options, and the like. If these other sources flow from the employment, they are community property.

1. Pension plans. Whatever the plan stipulates as to the rights of the husband thereunder is applicable to the interest of the wife in said plan.

EXAMPLE

Husband was to be in the plan for fifteen years to be eligible. The lump sum is $10,000 at maturity, or $200.00 per month. Wife's interest in the plan, as determined at the date of divorce, would be one half of $10,000 or one half of $200.

If one spouse has a completely perfected right prior to marriage, then that property would be separate property of that spouse.

EXAMPLES

Husband buys an automobile prior to marriage. He makes the down payment out of his separate property. He then gets married and thereafter makes the monthly payments out of his earnings. These payments would be community property. He would then own one half of the automobile and the wife would own one half. The amount of the down payment, being separate property, would be apportioned at the time of the divorce between the parties.

An author is writing a book and it takes him six months to do so. He gets married upon completion of the manuscript. Thereafter, the book is published and he receives $10,000. His right to this money was a perfected right since no income was involved. This money would not be apportioned at a divorce hearing.

By way of explanation, simply put:

A perfected right says, "I do not have to do anything else to get the money. It is due me."

The nonperfected right says, "I have to do something before I get the money." This right would be subjected to apportionment out of community property.

2. Apportionment of insurance proceeds. You have to prove the source of the money used to purchase the insurance policy. If paid by community funds, the proceeds from the policy will be in the same ratio as the proceeds used from community funds. So it would be apportioned.

EXAMPLE

Husband buys a $10,000 policy (before marriage) and (after marriage) pay $500 in premiums before he dies. This would be apportioned as to the amount of premiums paid. Look to the ratio of the premiums to determine the community interest.

If the husband uses separate property in community property to purchase this life insurance and names the wife as the beneficiary, then this is a gift to the wife and she is entitled to the whole thing. The children would not have an interest in the policy and would not be successful in attacking the policy.

If the marriage is terminated by divorce, a problem arises as to the insurance policy, which has a value only at the time of death. A mathematical formula as to the cash value is the determining factor, and it is then apportioned as to what is separate and what amount is community property.

3. Gifts, bequests, devises, and inheritances. All are separate property of the recipient, unless there is some agreement to the contrary between the parties. To prove a gift there must be a showing of actual or constructive delivery of the gift of property.

"Constructive delivery" means the gift was never actually placed in the hands of the person, but rather was placed in a bank, or in trust in the donee's name (compare and distinguish a totten trust). This shows the intent to make a gift. It can be inferred.

"Actual delivery" is where the gift is physically handed to the person. The intent at the time of the delivery of the gift is determinative of whether or not it was a gift of separate property, either to the wife or husband. If it is not community property, it is the separate property of each. If no intent was shown as to distribution when given, they each have a one-half individual interest in the gift.

4. Damages (money) from personal injury. The general rule is that the cause of action is community property, but the funds received therefrom would be separate property. The present state of the law in California has lumped them together, so that the entire personal-injury recovery is community property. It is suggested, therefore, that you check your local statutes in this regard.

Exceptions to the foregoing are that any personal injury recovery will be separate property in the following ways:

1. If at the time of the receipt of the money there is a final judgment of dissolution;

2. If the parties are living separate and apart pursuant to a decree of legal separation or interlocutory judgment of dissolution. If either of the foregoing exists, the proceeds are then the separate property of the recipient except that if the wife is the injured spouse, then you need only physical separation for her funds to be separate property. The community is entitled to reimbursement for any money paid out for expenses arising out of this accident. Even if the personal injury funds are community property, the wife would have management and control over her own personal injury property.

Formerly, the cause of action was common property and since the husband had management and control of the community property, he could select the attorney and authorize the settlement. The wife could have management and control only after receipt of the funds.

That used to be the case. Today, the wife has management and control from the time of the accident.

5. Credit acquisitions. The general rule is that credit is property. The status of property acquired on credit is determined by the status of the credit involved. If the property is acquired on the basis of either spouse's separate credit, then that property is separate property.

If community funds were used to make the payments, even though the intent of the creditor was to look to the separate property of the husband, there is a "presumption in the law" that it is a community asset, though it may be considered a separate liability of the husband because of his management and control. If it is a worthwhile asset, they will divide it between the parties; but if it is worthless or nil in value, the husband may have to pay.

6. Rents, issues, and profits. Coming from common property, these remain common property; and the rents, issues, and profits from separate property remain separate property, unless there has been some service rendered by the spouse during the marriage on a particular piece of separate property which may increase its value.

EXAMPLE

Husband owns a house before marriage. From the income he pays taxes, and so forth. He takes over the management of the house (say, an apartment house), wherein he renders maintenance and painting services, and the like, thereby increasing the value of the separate property. If this occurs, you may have a community interest.

B. Change of Character Property

The character change of property is governed by the transmutation doctrine, which defines transmutation as any act taken by the parties that changes the character of property. This character change is not to be confused with change in form. (Check your local code to determine the applicability of this doctrine in your state.)

EXAMPLE

Say you have $100,000 in the bank. You take it out of the bank and buy an apartment building. This is merely an exchange of cash for real property. It is still considered separate property. In other words, money change in form does not change the character of the property.

Examples of changes in character of property would be: (1) conversion of community property to separate property; and (2) separate property to community property by agreement.

These can be accomplished by way of an oral agreement. (Joint-tenancy property may be transferred only by means of a written agreement.) The oral agreement, however, will operate only as a change of status of property, not as a conveyance of the property. To create a joint tenancy, it *must be* in writing to fulfill the requirements of the four unities of (1) interest, (2) time, (3) title, and (4) possession.

Neither spouse can make a gift of community property to himself in an attempt to change the character of the community property to personal property.

C. How Do You Change the Character of Property?

Transmutation can be accomplished in three ways: (1) Ratification, (2) waiver; and (3) estoppel.

EXAMPLE NUMBER 1

Husband attempts to change the character of the property by making a third party the beneficiary of an insurance policy, using community property to pay the premiums. This is invalid, but the wife can ratify the act and make it legal by doing some overt, affirmative act or by orally agreeing to it.

EXAMPLE NUMBER 2

The waiver approach is merely negative-type conduct or is passive ratification. Using the foregoing insurance-policy situation, the wife does nothing about it. She neither agrees to the payment of the premiums nor does anything overt or affirmative to approve it. In other words, she has knowledge of what the husband did, but does nothing, thereby waiving her right to object to the change in character of the community property.

EXAMPLE NUMBER 3

Estoppel is the detrimental reliance of one party on the acts of the spouse. Husband says to the wife, "I am thinking of purchasing a life insurance policy and naming a third person as the beneficiary." Wife says it is a good idea. Husband, then relying upon her agreement, buys the policy naming his mother as the beneficiary. The wife is estopped from taking any adverse action, since the husband based his action on her accord.

IN OTHER STATES

The division of marital property in states which do not have "community property" laws usually allows one of the divorced parties to keep the property according to its record title unless the other party proves some special equity in the jointly owned property.

Since a *tenancy by the entireties* in a special common law tenancy applies only to husband and wife, most state statutes provide that these tenants by the entireties become *tenants-in-common* of the jointly owned property after the decree in divorce or no-fault dissolution of marriage. There are presumptions of gift to a spouse to be reckoned with. There are special contributions of funds unconnected with the marriage to be considered.

The legal assistant must be familiar with the case law in the state which has interpreted the no-fault dissolution of the marriage statute or the divorce code to determine what information should be obtained from the client before preparing a petition for dissolution or divorce.

Note: Don't take the client's word for anything. Have the client bring in car titles, deeds, mortgages, stock certificates, or get them by request for documents under the discovery rules of most states.

COMMON-SENSE ADVICE

The following is a list of some common-sense advice that is worth passing along to your client during your interview, or in a form letter if a divorce or dissolution action is being contested:

1. Take a vacation from each other to let irrational anger cool off before negotiations begin.

2. Understand the benefits of a careful balance between alimony, child support, and unallocated maintenance payments, and satisfy yourself that your lawyer has calculated them to the optimum advantage of both parties.

3. Consider whether there are good reasons to reverse the usual practice of automatically granting custody of the children to the mother. Agree on a visitation schedule and stick to it.

4. Make a list of joint assets built up since the marriage. Be realistic, especially concerning the wife's intangible contribution. Remember that the house, the furniture, and the car traditionally go to the spouse who will be maintaining a home for the children.

5. Discuss assets each partner owned before the marriage, and leave them out of the settlement.

6. Investigate the tax ramifications of who gets the house. If you have joint ownership and the wife gets the house, the husband will in effect be selling his half and may have to pay a capital gains tax on half of the difference between the acquisition price and the current market value.

7. Remember a divorced wife has no rights to her ex-husband's estate. A life insurance policy is often used to provide her with financial security in the event of his death. Determine whether it is more advantageous, from a tax standpoint, to make her the owner of the policy—in which case the premiums, in the form of alimony would be deductible. If the wife remains the beneficiary, she will have to check to see that payments are kept up and that the policy is not canceled.

8. Take into account the fact that the husband usually pays the fees of both lawyers, although it may be possible to pay the wife's fees in the form of deductible alimony. Remember that the husband normally provides health insurance coverage for the wife. The children are usually covered by his business health plan; check to see if the company plan provides a rider for the ex-spouse.

9. A divorced spouse can obtain benefits under a former husband's Social Security record if the marriage lasted at least ten years and the divorced spouse is 62 years of age, or older, and unmarried. Prerequisite: the husband must be 62 years of age. The parties may have been divorced for two years and get those benefits even if the worker is not retired.

10. Try to get divorce in your own state. Quickie divorces are still available in Haiti and the Dominican Republic, but they might be declared invalid if contested. A trip to a divorce-mill state or territory like Idaho, Nevada, or the Virgin Islands creates extra costs—transportation, hotel bills, and duplicate legal fees—all of which further deplete the post-divorce assets available to either partner.

UNIFORM CHILD CUSTODY JURISDICTION ACT

This act is not a reciprocal law. It can be put into full operation by each individual state regardless of its enactment in other states.

The full benefit of the act will be felt, however, when all or the majority of the states adopt it. Many states have adopted it. Check your state statutes or code and *read the act* if it has been adopted by your state. In such case, you must follow it and plead the necessary allegations in all child custody cases and in divorce petitions which pray for determination of child custody.

If you are interested and your state has not adopted the official uniform act or its equivalent, you may get a copy of the act and other uniform acts by writing to: National Conference of Commission on Uniform State Laws, 645 North Michigan Avenue, Chicago, Illinois 60611, (312) 321-9710. The price for the copies is nominal.

CHAPTER 19

How to Assist in a Real Estate Practice

As a legal assistant working in a law office with a heavy real estate practice, your duties may vary, from accumulating data and information needed to complete the various instruments of conveyance, such as deeds or mortgages, to monitoring mortgage foreclosures, real estate closings, examining title reports, and in some law offices, to preparing and plotting legal descriptions of land.

In some jurisdictions, you will also be preparing all types of leases, land sale contracts, and secured transactions agreements, as well as drafting complaints, answers, and other documentation dealing with unlawful detainer proceedings such as attachments and undertakings, quiet title, and partition actions.

Because of this continuing contact with the operation and effect of the laws relating to the changes in the character, purchase and sale, and transfer of real property from one person to another, you should know the rules affecting ownership and transferability of real estate.

EXAMINING THE NATURE OF REAL PROPERTY LAW

Real estate as it is commonly called (property) almost always deals with a portion(s) of the original land and objects which are permanently affixed to it.

In actuality, it is the study of the globe on which we all live and our rights to the use of a portion of the globe, and things permanently affixed to that globe. For example, a building can be bulldozed, yet it is considered to be real property because of the difficulty in removing it from the "globe." Lighting fixtures are in the same category. Crops of wheat and the like are covered by the same law, for until they are physically removed, they are considered permanent fixtures of the land. At that point, they become a part of personal property.

What are some of the rights which run with the ownership of property? Most of us look at buying property like buying a television set. When you buy the television, what you acquire is absolute and free title and total unencumbrance. There is no body of law which can restrict your use of your television. But buying a piece of real property is analogous to buying an automobile. To explain . . .

First of all, you will never have "free title." Why? If you do not pay cash, you share the car with the lender. If you want to sell it, you have to go to the lender and get permission, who will then give you the "pink slip."

Even if you own the car outright, you still do not own it. You have to pay traffic tickets, for example. The Department of Motor Vehicles can prevent you from selling it or even driving it. There are smog device regulations that have to be complied with before you can sell it or even drive it. The law requires that you drive 25 to 35 miles per hour, or 55 to 65 miles an hour. At no time can you use your car as you see fit, because of the rights and obligations you have to other people. This is unlike a television set, which you can turn off and on as you will, throw it out the window if you like, beat it up, destroy it or give it away, if that is your desire.

The bundle of rights which run with the ownership of property has an interlocutory relationship with other people who own property, and hence, limits and restricts your use of your property. It will never be free and clear of these series of encumbrances.

GENERAL DUTIES OF THE LEGAL ASSISTANT

The general duties of the legal assistant in a real estate practice are as follows:

- Accumulating data and information needed to complete various instruments of conveyance;
- Preparing contracts for purchase and sale of land;
- Preparing and plotting legal descriptions of land;
- Preparing deeds;
- Preparing mortgages;

- Preparing all types of leases;
- Examining title reports, abstracts, or preliminary title insurance binders;
- Preparing statements for real estate closing. Use your office closing statement form as a checklist for information and documents you will need at the closing.
- Drafting complaints, answers, and other legal pleadings (breach of contract to purchase or sell land, action for specific performance of contract to sell land, landlord-tenant actions, and the like);
- Monitoring mortgage foreclosures;
- Preparing secured transaction agreements where personal property is being sold with real property, as in the sale of a business or the selling of a residence with a mobile home or selling a business real property with movable equipment.

The following is a sample list of what a legal assistant might do in a case where two people want to form a partnership or execute a joint venture agreement to purchase a certain piece of real estate.

1. After your attorney has held the initial meeting with the client, use your form checklist of questions and basic information to review and complete any unanswered questions. If you do not have such a checklist develop one from the attorney notes in the file.

2. Do your research relating to the tax ramifications of the real estate transactions, as well as any other legal aspects.

3. Develop and then prepare a Time and Responsibility Schedule to aid you and your attorney to keep on top of certain things to be done, that is, documents placed in escrow, money due from lender, title search begun or received from title company, and the like.

4. Prepare the partnership agreement or joint venture agreement as directed by your attorney.

5. Prepare or review the real estate purchase and sale agreement.

6. Gather your exhibits to be attached to the purchase and sale agreement, that is, plot plans, schedules, assignments of leases, subleases, notes, deed of trust, and the like. Make sure all the exhibits have been dated and properly and completely executed.

7. After approval, have the agreements typed and have them mailed out for signatures with exhibits attached.

8. Prepare your escrow instructions. In some jurisdictions these may be a printed form.

9. After the foregoing has been accomplished, draft your consent to assignments and subleases and prepare estoppel certificates. In some jurisdictions this latter may also be a printed form.

10. Send out a request for a preliminary title report from the title company.

11. Once the entire package has been executed by all parties, including the sales agreement and partnership agreement and initialing the exhibits, have the certificate of partnership recorded in the county where the property is located. If a limited partnership is involved, check the state limited partnership statute.

Note: As with all voluminous documents, check and recheck to see that every page requiring a signature has been signed and that every page requiring notarization has been so notarized.

12. Then draft any and all remaining documents needed to be deposited into escrow.

13. Check all closing documents and prepare the closing statement, showing amounts to be paid at closing by the respective parties.

14. Deliver all closing documents and the closing statement to your attorney for his use at the closing.

WHAT IS REAL PROPERTY?

Real property is land and personal property which is affixed to it as part of the land. Trade fixtures and equipment may or may not be so attached to the land as to become real property. A mobile home may become so affixed to the land as to become real property. Whether personal property has become part of the land is a question of fact in most cases. A contract may specify whether personal property which is attached to the land becomes real property. This could create a question of both law and fact if a dispute arises.

Note: A "mortgagee" of land would be particularly interested in knowing what is included as part of the mortgaged land. If there is any doubt, the mortgagee should be giving a "security interest" in the personal property in plain language in the mortgage or in a separate security agreement. A "financing statement" should then be filed to perfect the security interest under the applicable state commercial code.

INTERESTS IN REAL PROPERTY

Some interests a person may have in real property are:

Fee simple. An estate in fee simple is an absolute interest in land.

Life estate. A life estate is an estate in land for the length of one's life or the life of another. The life tenant has the right to possession during his life or the life of that other person named in the deed.

Reversionary interest. A reversionary estate is a non-possessory interest in land, the residue of an estate remaining in the grantor after he has conveyed away some lesser estate. It will be possessory only on the termination of the lesser state transferred.

EXAMPLE:

A to B for life with the reversion to A on B's death.

Remainder interest. A remainder estate is also a non-possessory interest in land, which vests after a predecent estate ends. It is created by an act of the grantor in favor of some person other than the grantor. It remains out of possession of the grantor forever, rather than reverting back to the grantor.

EXAMPLE:

A gives to B for life, and at B's death, to B's son.

This is a typical remainder interest. The property remains out of the possession of the grantor and is non-possessory until it vests in the heirs of B.

Periodic estate (leasehold interest). This is a tenancy for a designated period of time. An example of this type of estate is month-to-month tenancy.

Tenancy at will. This is a tenancy created for an uncertain term by agreement between the Landlord and Tenant. Either party may terminate by giving notice at any time. It may be oral or in writing. A tenancy at will cannot be assigned.

Easement. Another possible interest or right in the use of land is the easement. Though the theory of, and laws relating to, easements may vary from state to state, as a general proposition, an easement is a right of interest in the land of another, existing apart from the ownership of land. It can be a positive or negative right and/or interest in land. It may be created by a conveyance giving limited or unlimited use or enjoyment.

An easement is to be distinguished from a mere "license" to use land for a specific purpose. A license is a personal revocable and unassignable privilege to do certain acts on land (such as place a billboard in a field). A license may be created orally, but it is wiser to have it in writing.

An easement may be an affirmative easement where the owner of the easement has the right to enter upon another's land, or it may be a negative easement under which the owner of the land cannot use a specified part of his own land.

An easement can be "appurtenant" or "in gross":

a. An easement appurtenant is established where there are at least two tracts of land, and the owner's use and enjoyment of one tract is benefited by the easement. The easement is appurtenant to the other tract of land. The land benefited is called the "dominant estate" and the tract burdened by the benefit is called the "servient estate." Example is the right to ingress and egress over another's land.

b An easement in gross, on the other hand, is generally a personal right benefiting the owner personally, *not* any land he owns. These rights are generally granted to install and maintain electric power or sewers.

An "easement by prescription" is obtained by adverse use for a continuous period prescribed by the statutes or common law of the state in which the land being used is located.

Simply put, it is virtually the same as gaining land by adverse possession. The elements required to establish an easement by prescription are as follows:

a. Hostile intent and possession;

b. Open and notorious use;

c. Continuous and uninterrupted use.

This use applies, generally, only to an easement, as opposed to getting the land by adverse possession, together with title to the land. (See pp. 454 and 455 for samples of easement forms.)

Condominium ownership. This is a type of ownership of real estate. The condominium purchaser gets a recordable deed to a unit or apartment in a condominium complex. It is subject to the terms of the Condominium Declaration which has been filed by the developer. The owner is required to pay the taxes and insurance for his unit or apartment. He may sell, lease, mortgage, or even include his condominium premises in his will. Additionally, he shares with other unit owners certain rights to use common areas and facilities such as halls, basements, lobby, elevators, and storage space located on the land upon which the condominium apartments are built. A condominium association is usually formed by the unit owners. The association then deals with the developer on behalf of the owners.

The condominium concept of real estate ownership is created and held together by the Master Deed (Condominium Declaration), which spells out and affirms separate ownership of the individual units and the sharing of the obligation for commonly used areas.

To ensure the aforementioned separateness of ownership and joint sharing of obligations, the residents may elect a Board of Managers to supervise all activities and enforce the rules and regulations of the master deed or condominium declaration.

Cooperative ownership. The cooperative form of ownership, on the other hand, though similar in some ways to the condominium ownership, provides individual buyers a stockholder position in the cooperative corporation which actually owns the multiple unit property. The cooperative corporation stockholders receive a *proprietary lease* from the corporation instead of a deed to their respective units.

And, unlike condominium ownership, renters of a cooperative own only a percentage of the corporation and are assessed sums of money periodically (monthly, quarterly, and so forth) to cover the payment of taxes, mortgages, repairs, and the like. A cooperative owner cannot sell or otherwise dispose of his co-op as he does not "own" his own apartment. The sale of his stock in the cooperative corporation is governed by the terms and conditions of the articles and by-laws of the cooperative corporation.

The obligations and rights of the tenant–stockholder will be spelled out in his proprietary lease from the corporation, which usually incorporates the by-laws of the corporation by reference.

House rules and by-laws which govern the activities of the tenant–owner will be incorporated in the proprietary lease by reference or be spelled out in the lease.

The board of directors of the corporation manage the cooperative complex, pay taxes, make repairs, enforce rules, and so on.

OWNERSHIP IN REAL PROPERTY

Sole and Individual Ownership

The grantee's title to property will be sole and individual if his name only appears on the deed (in some states a spouse has an inchoate dower interest).

Joint Ownership With Another

If there is more than one grantee named in a deed, or joint ownership of the real estate is created, a remainder interest or reversionary interest may result, depending on the language of the deed.

Joint tenancy. If the deed names two or more grantees and includes the words "with right of survivorship," a joint tenancy is created in the whole of the land, which cannot be disposed of without the consent of all until the last survivor is the sole owner. If the grantees are husband and wife, see the comment following.

When a joint tenancy exists between two or more people, each is theoretically considered to own the entire property until the death of the other joint tenant(s). In effect, then, a joint tenancy merely creates an estate which vests in the last surviving joint tenant. Only the last surviving tenant can dispose of the property by will.

Tenancy-in-common. If the deed names two grantees without words of survivorship (see exception in case of husband and wife in comment following), a tenancy-in-common is created in most states.

This type of tenancy exists between two or more persons who each own an individual interest in the property, but each can, during his or her lifetime, dispose of that undivided interest by deed and can, of course, bequeath it by will. A tenancy in common may be specifically created by such words as:

> I, AB, do hereby grant to JS and LY, as tenants in common, each as to an undivided one-half interest in the following described real property: (here you should insert the legal description).

In most states, the undivided interest owned by a tenant-in-common may be the subject of a partition action, whereas a joint tenancy or tenancy by the entireties may not be partitioned.

Tenancy by the entireties (between spouses). The deed language required to create this particular type of tenancy varies widely from state to state and can depend on whether the state in question is a community property state or not.

Some states that are not community property states require that a deed to husband and wife use the words "with right of survivorship" to create the joint tenancy, which is then called a "tenancy by the entireties." Some states hold that any deed naming both husband and wife as grantees and including the description "his wife" or "her husband," automatically creates a tenancy by the entireties even though there are no specific words of survivorship. Some states will allow a court to declare that a tenancy by the entireties was created if the two grantees are in fact husband and wife even though the relationship was not spelled out in the deed.

Obviously, the surest way to create a tenancy by the entireties would be to give the two names plus the relationship, plus the words "with right of survivorship."

EXAMPLE

John Doe and Mary Doe, his wife, with right of survivorship.

INSTRUMENTS OF TRANSFER OF INTERESTS IN REAL PROPERTY

As the title, effect, and description of instruments of transfer may vary from state to state, the following are submitted as guidelines so that you will at least know what to look for when gathering information and completing these documents.

DEEDS

A deed to real property is the legal instrument by which the grantor transfers title to his interest to the grantee.

A deed should contain the following:

1. Name of the grantor;
2. Words of conveyance, that is, I give; I hereby grant, sell, or transfer;
3. Name of the grantee;

4. Legal description (not just the address) of the property being conveyed;

5. Signature of the grantor;

6. Witnesses to the grantor's signature, if required by state law where the property is located;

7. Date on which the signature was affixed; and

8. A notary acknowledgment of said signature.

Practical hints: When conveying property, the grantor must use the same name as when he received the property, that is, "D. Bard Smith to Mary Smythe" and then "Mary Smythe to Jane Oslow," not "Mary Smith to Jane Oslow."

A deed must be acknowledged to be recorded; however, it is valid as between the grantee and grantor without acknowledgment.

There are various types of deeds:

1. Grant Deed (special warranty deed).

   a. That the grantor has not previously conveyed the property to another; and

   b. That the grantor has not made any liens or other encumbrances in or on the property.

2. General warranty deed is one which contains a covenant of warranty of title and an obligation to defend that title for the grantee against anyone.

3. A quitclaim deed is a deed of conveyance the purpose of which is to convey all the interest of the grantor, whatever it is. He does not warrant anything. Its use is intended to pass any title, interest, or claim which the grantor may have in the property.

It can be used in an easement situation or if there is a break in the chain of title. In giving a quitclaim deed, the grantor is not giving any implied warranty to the grantee as to title in the property. The grantor is merely giving whatever interest, if any, he possesses, in the property. It could be nothing, but he or the grantee thinks he may have an interest, and the quitclaim deed will clear the title of any claim the quitclaim grantor may have.

Simply put, a quitclaim deed is generally used where a person has an interest that cannot be defined, has no monetary value, or where the grantor wants to pass his title but is not willing to make any warranties.

4. Void deed is a deed that is void from inception and cannot be cured.

5. The voidable deed is one given to a minor who cannot acquire title, or because there are statutes to the contrary. This can be by virtue of fraud, mistake, or receipt from someone mentally or legally incapable of transferring property.

RECORDING NON-COURT DOCUMENTS: THE DEED: ONLY EVIDENCE OF TITLE (CALIFORNIA PROCEDURES)

I. They do not have to be recorded. They are just as *valid* unrecorded. Recording *only affects subsequent rights.*
   In the above instance, a *Complaint to Quiet Title* would be in order.
   Recordable Instruments:
   A. Any writing, signed and delivered from one person to another *giving an interest, right* or *duty;* and *in payment of a debt;*

   B. Those specifically provided for by statute. *Statutes Affecting the Recordation of Conveyance:*

      1. *Notice Recording Statute:*

      Ex.: A to B, then A to C, thereafter B records and C records later.
      Note: In a *Notice Recording Statute* state, in the above example, B is under a duty to give *notice of conveyance* to C. Failure to give such notice could cause him to lose against C in a quiet title action.

      2. *Race Statute: Ex.:* A to B; then A sells the same property to C.
         a. C immediately records, and thereafter B records.
         b. C would win the lawsuit under the theory of this statute, obtaining clear title to the property.
         c. B would have recourse against *A* for damages.
         d. It would not matter whether C knew about B or not. Under the Race Statute, it is *first in time, first in right.*

      3. *Race Notice Statute:* This is peculiar to the State of California, and applies to people who have no notice of a recorded document regarding property purchased, or to be purchased. As a result, "a buyer without notice is unprotected as against an unrecorded transfer."

      What Constitutes Notice = Two (2) types:

         1. *Constructive Notice:* which is actual recordation of the instrument of conveyance—notice to the world.

   2. *Actual Notice:* This is being aware of negotiations or agreements
for purchase and sale of property between others:

   Ex.: A actually knew about a transfer to B, because someone told him
about it.

EASEMENT

(CREATING A RIGHT OF WAY FOR INGRESS AND EGRESS
FOR LIMITED TIME, ALLOWING JOINT USE)

   1. This agreement made in the City and County of _____ on this
_____ day of _____, 19_____ , by JOHN DOE who lives at _____, hereinafter
called the party of the first part and JOHN SMITH, residing at _____, in the City,
County, and State of _____, hereinafter called the party of the second part.

WITNESSES AS FOLLOWS:

   2. That the party of the first part, his heirs and assigns, grants and conveys
unto the party of the second part to his heirs and assigns an easement in, to, upon,
and over all that paved portion of a certain roadway situated at:

   Note: Once again, give a full detailed legal description of the property to be
conveyed.

   3. It is understood that said easement is for the sole purpose of ingress and
egress, and it is agreed and understood that it is not to be construed as an easement given to the exclusion of the party of the first part or his heirs and assigns, or
to others later granted a similar right.
   4. That the party of the second part, and his heirs and assigns, covenants with
the party of the first part, and to his heirs and assigns, to at all times maintain and
repair, at his or their expense, said easement for its proper upkeep and maintenance.
   5. That the party of the second part is to hold the said right-of-way easement
for a period of _____ years. (Here put a time limitation, such as five years, twelve
years, and so forth.)
   6. IN WITNESS WHEREOF, the parties hereto have executed this agreement on
the date above first written.

                                    _____
                                    (Owner of servient land)

   Note: Be sure to add an acknowledgment for recording the easement in the
county where the servient land is located.

EASEMENT, BASIC FORM
(LIMITED USE EASEMENT FOR UNLIMITED TIME)

This agreement made in the City and County of _____ on this _____ day of _____, by JANE DOE, who lives at _____, in the City of _____, hereinafter called the party of the first part, and MARY SMITH, residing at _____, in the City, County, and State of _____, hereinafter called the party of the second part;

WITNESSES AS FOLLOWS:

That the party of the first part represents and warrants that she owns and has fee simple title to that parcel of real property located in the City of _____, County of _____, and State of _____, bounded and described as follows:

Note: Here you should set out the complete legal description of said property including the tract, block, and boundary lines.

That the party of the second part desires to use said property for:

Note: Here you should describe completely and with clarity the *exact* nature and type of easement desired, that is, walkway, to build a fence, and so forth.

It is mutually agreed as between the parties under the following conditions as follows:

The party of the first part does hereby grant, assign and set over to the party of the second part:

Note: Describe the nature and type of easement granted, with any and all *restrictions* that your client may deem necessary. Also include servient owner's right to share use, if that is desired.

Except as herein granted, the party of the first part shall continue to have the full use and enjoyment of the property.

The party of the second part shall bear full responsibility for the use and enjoyment of the property and shall hold the party of the first part harmless from any claim of damages to person or premises resulting from the use, occupancy, and possession of said property by the party of the second part.

Furthermore, to have and to hold said easement unto the party of the second part and to her successors and assigns forever.

IN WITNESS WHEREOF, the parties hereto have executed this agreement on the date above first written.

_____
(Owner of servient land)

MORTGAGES

Depending on the state, a mortgage is treated as creating a lien or title. Most states apply the "lien theory."

A mortgage may be created by an instrument called a mortgage (which may secure a note or a bond), a mortgage deed, a trust deed, or an agreement for deed.

1. Trust deed gives the trustee legal title to the real property until the debt is paid. The elements of a trust deed are:

    a. The trustor or debtor;

    b. The trustee who holds the legal title for security of the debt;

    c. The beneficiary or lender; and

    d. An obligation.

You should also include in the trust deed words of conveyance and a description of the property as heretofore mentioned.

EXAMPLE

A to B for $20,000. B pays $5,000 down, then borrows $15,000 from C, a banking institution, or other, and obtains promissory note for $15,000. B is the maker of the promissory note, and the bank is the holder of the note. The note is for $15,000 plus interest. The bank is also the lender beneficiary and obtains security for the note that is the trust deed; or it could obtain a lien on stock commensurate to the $15,000 borrowed by the trustor. This promissory note must contain the following:

    a. The name of the borrower–lender, and a description of the trust deed (or other collateral) with specificity;

    b. It must be signed by the borrower and dated and acknowledged by a notary public;

    c. It must have a complete description of the property herein.

When the note is paid in full, a reconveyance is signed and recorded in favor of the borrower.

2. Mortgage

    a. Mortgagor who is the debtor retains title;

    b. Mortgagee who is the lender acquires a lien on the property.

This document should contain the operative words of the mortgage, a description of the property, and of course, incorporation reference or attachment of the note or bond that is being secured by the mortgage.

3. Mortgage deed

a. Mortgagor who is the debtor gives conditional title to the mortgagee.

b. Mortgagee who acquires title to the land only if the mortgagor fails to pay the note or bond that is being secured by the mortgage deed.

4. Land sale contract (agreement for deed). This is another means of creating what amounts to a mortgage on real property and is done without giving title to the property. It is a written agreement for the purchase and sale of real property between a vendor and a vendee.

The vendee gets an equitable title to the property and possession thereof so long as he complies with the terms of the contract or agreement for deed.

The vendor has the legal title and no possession, as opposed to a grantor and a grantee relationship, where the grantor gives away all of his right, title, and interest in and to the real property.

Some of the restrictions or limitations to the vendor-vendee relationship are:

a. The contract or agreement can be rescinded or foreclosed (depending on the jurisdiction where the property is located) if the purchaser doesn't pay or comply with other terms of the contract of agreement.

b. The purchaser or vendee cannot change the property without the consent of the vendor.

LEASES

In some states a leasehold interest in real property is considered personal property. A lease is at least a possessory interest in real property even if it is not considered an estate in real property.

Drafting Guide for Leases

A lease must describe the demised premises with sufficient certainty to avoid ambiguity. Language similar to that required in the drafting of a deed may be used in describing leased premises but is not required in most cases.

The same general rules that apply to reservations and exceptions in deeds apply equally to reservations and exceptions in leases. If a reservation or exception set forth in a lease is repugnant to any estate previously granted, the lease is inferior to that prior interest in the land.

Checklist

Consider the following checklist of those elements to be considered when drafting a lease of residential property.

1. Date;

2. Names and status of the parties, and their interests in the property;

3. Demise or conveyance clause;

4. Description of, and reservations or exceptions affecting the property leased, including any garages or parking spaces or other common facilities (such as pool or tennis courts) that may be pertinent;

5. Duration of and limitation of terms of occupancy and date on which the occupancy commences;

6. Any restrictions relative to use of the demised premises;

7. Limitation on number of occupants, if applicable; and

8. Amount of and mode, place, and time for payment of rent.

Be aware of state statutes creating special landlord and tenant laws and court rules for summary procedure in landlord and tenant cases.

Note: Most states require a lease for a year or more to be written. If that is required, an oral lease for such a period is unenforceable. Check your state statute on fraud.

A basic lease form follows:

BASIC LEASE

A. (DATE)
This lease agreement, entered into on this _____ day of _____, 19_____.
B. (PARTIES)
By and between _____, hereinafter referred to as the lessor, and _____, hereinafter referred to as the lessee.
C. (PREMISES)

In consideration of the rental below-described and of the covenants stipulated herein, the lessor agrees to lease the following-described premises located at _____ Avenue, _____ City, _____ County, State of _____, and legally described as follows:

Note: Here should be set forth the full legal description of the commonly described rental unit, that is, Lot 1, Block 2, in Tract 40, City and County of Los Angeles, State of California, as per map recorded in the office of the County Recorder, in Book 100, at page 67.

D. (Term)
To have and to hold the premises unto the lessee, its successors and assigns, for the term of _____ (years or months) commencing on the _____ day of _____, 19____, and ending on the _____ day of _____, 19____.

E. (Rent)
That the rent for the term of this lease is _____ Dollars (\$_____), payable without demand or notice in monthly installments of _____, on the _____ day of each and every month of the term beginning on the _____ day of _____, 19____.

Note: Here again, you can incorporate at this juncture the acknowledgment of the first and last month's rent in advance, as well as a security deposit. In some instances, this is optional and/or negotiable, as between the parties.

F. (Use)
The use of the premises shall be for _____, and for no other purpose except with the written consent of lessor.

G. (Assignment)
The lessee may not assign this lease or sublease any part of said premises without the written consent of the lessor.

H. (Lessor's Maintenance Responsibilities)
The lessor hereby agrees to keep the entire exterior portion of the premises in good repair and maintenance.

Note: Here is an opportunity for you to insert any other responsibilities of the lessor that your client may wish to have spelled out for clarity to avoid confusion in the future.

I. (Lessee's Maintenance Responsibilities)
The lessee hereby agrees to maintain the interior portion of the premises in good repair at all times.

Note: Here is an opportunity for you to insert any other responsibilities of the lessee which your client may wish to have spelled out for clarity to avoid confusion in the future.

J. (DEFAULT REMEDIES)

Said lessee hereby covenants and agrees that if a default shall be made in the payment of rent or if the lessee shall violate any of the convenants of this lease, then the lessee shall become a tenant at sufferance, waiving all right of notice, and the lessor shall be entitled to re-enter and take possession of the demised premises.

Note: This is tantamount to your three-day or thirty-day notice that leads to an unlawful detainer action.

K. (TERMINATION)

The lessee agrees to quit and deliver up said premises at the end of the term of this lease in good condition, ordinary wear and tear accepted.

L. (OPTION)

The lessee has the option to renew the lease for a further term of _____ (years), beginning with the _____ day of _____, and ending with the _____ day of _____, for a total rent of _____, payable _____ Dollars ($) per month. All other terms and conditions of the lease agreement shall remain in full force and effect.

IN WITNESS WHEREOF, . . .

M. (SIGNATURES AND WITNESSES)

Note: Residential leases are not usually recorded so an acknowledgment is not necessary. If, for any reason, the lease is to be recorded, an acknowledgment should be added and executed.

PROPRIETARY LEASE (COOPERATIVE APARTMENT)

This Proprietary Lease, dated the _____ day of _____, 19_____ by and between _____ a (State of Incorporation of the cooperative corporation) having an office at _____ hereafter "Lessor"; and _____ hereinafter called "Lessee."

WHEREAS, the Lessor is the owner of the property and building in the City and County of _____, commonly known as _____ (number of street) _____ , hereafter called the "Building"; and

WHEREAS, the Lessee is the owner of _____ shares of the Lessor, to which this lease is appurtenant and which had been allocated to Unit Number _____ in the Building;

TERM

NOW, THEREFORE, in connection of the premises, the Lessor hereby leases to the Lessee, and the Lessee hires from the Lessor, subject to the terms and conditions hereof, Unit Number _____ in the Building (hereinafter referred to as the Apartment). (It is here that any other terms and conditions can be placed that bear on the lease to the apartment.)

1. Rent (basis upon which it is set)
2. Lessor's repairs
3. Services by Lessor
4. Damage to Apartment or Building
5. Inspection of books of account/annual report
6. Changes in terms and conditions of Proprietary Lease
7. Penthouses, terraces, and balconies
8. Assignment of Lessor's rights against occupant
9. Cancellation of prior agreements
10. Quiet enjoyment of premises
11. Indemnity/hold harmless
12. Payment of rent
13. House rules
14. Use of premises
15. Subletting
16. Assignment of lease or transfer of shares
    a. Consent: of debt of Lessee
    b. Consents generally as it relates to stockholders' and directors' obligations to consent
    c. Release of Lessee upon assignment of subletting, resale
17. Pledge of shares and proprietary lease
18. Repairs by Lessee
19. Lessor's right to remedy Lessee's default
20. Increases in rate of fire insurance
21. Alterations
22. Proprietary lease subordination to mortgage and ground lease
23. Mechanic's lien
24. Right of entry (the right of the Lessor to have a key to each unit apartment).
25. Waivers
26. Notices
27. Reimbursement of Lessor's expenses
28. Lessor's immunities
29. Termination of lease by Lessor
30. Lessor's right after Lessee's default
31. Waiver of right redemption
32. Surrender of possession
33. Lessee's option to cancel
34. Extension of option to cancel
35. Continuance of a cooperative management after all leases have been terminated
36. Unsold shares

37. Foreclosure procedures
38. Covenants
39. Waiver of trial by jury
40. Lessor's Additional Remedies (Lessee can be more than one person)
41. Effect of partial invalidity
42. Notice to Lessor of default
43. Unity of shares and lease
44. Charges of utilities
45. No discrimination as to race, creed, or religion, etc.
46. All changes to be in writing

Note: This form and checklist is just a skeleton, giving basic subjects that should be covered in a proprietary lease.

Be further guided by your state's general real estate and contract laws and any specific statute pertaining to cooperative apartments.

PURCHASE AND SALE OF A PIECE OF PROPERTY

1. Buyer and seller begin with a listing agreement, which is a contract between you as seller and your licensed real estate broker, granting the broker the right to become your agent and to represent you with potential buyers of that real property. Salespeople are agents of the broker.

2. This agreement must be in writing. It is a contract for the sale or lease of property and must be in writing. Failing this, it will be subject to the Statute of Frauds. The broker has an agent relationship with you.

3. Buyers do not have an agent as a matter of law. They are the seller's agent and have a fiduciary duty to the seller to make an offer, and this offer must be in writing. Note: a counter-offer constitutes a rejection. This offer must be signed without change for it to be binding on the seller.

This binding contract sets up the escrow and establishes your right as a property owner. Remember, other people's rights are involved when you buy a piece of property. Whether their rights are going to encumber and restrict your right to the use of the property is unimportant. Further note that the terms of the contract under which you can get out of the contract, and sue for liquidated damages, depend on which party failed to complete and follow through with their part of the contract.

In the above instance, the parties "agreed" upon the liquidated damages. This clause must be in all caps and initialled by all parties. So, when you as the paralegal are drafting a purchase and sale agreement, be sure to bring this to your boss's attention and see that it is done.

PREPARING A SET OF ESCROW INSTRUCTIONS

The role of an escrow company is one of a "neutral stakeholder." The escrow company holds the money and the deed to the property and other pertinent documents until the escrow is closed. A breach of escrow instructions by the escrow company is a basis for a lawsuit on the part of either party.

The escrow company will issue a preliminary title report which is documentation of any and all pieces of rights to your piece of real property. It is a search of all of the records of the County Recorder (in your state) dealing with liens against the real property, which have an impact as to the use of said real property.

The Deed of Trust is a three-party document consisting of the following parties:

1. Beneficiary (lender);

2. Trustee (holds the deed); and

3. Trustor (sends the money).

CHAPTER 20

How to Handle a Tort Action

SECTION 1: THEORY

As a working legal assistant, you will not be required to have an in-depth knowledge of the substantive law of torts, but you will need a working knowledge of the concept and theory of the laws affecting tort actions or casualty claims.

This chapter will give you much of the basic knowledge you will need to properly prepare a complaint in a personal injury, property damage, products, or strict liability lawsuit or a medical malpractice claim. To this end, emphasis is placed on the basic elements of tort law relating to negligence, duty owed, liabilities of the parties, and some of the defenses used in defending a claim based on negligence.

THEORY AND CONCEPT OF NEGLIGENCE

As a general proposition a tort is any wrongful act or omission against another. There must be the existence of a legal right and a violation of this right under a legal duty which would give rise to a cause of action in tort. Specifically, a tort has been defined as a private wrong or injury to person or property or other violation of a right not dependent upon contract.

A crime is also a tort, if the crime committed injures the person, property, or rights of another. The injured person may file a civil action against the "criminal" to recover the damages suffered. The crime itself is a public wrong, but the damage to the victim is a private wrong.

A crime must be proved beyond a reasonable doubt. A tort must be proved by the preponderance of the evidence.

Most crimes require intent. A tort may be the result of carelessness (negligence), regardless of the intent.

Generally, to establish a valid cause of action based on negligence, the following elements must be present:

1. A duty owed to the plaintiff by the defendant;

2. A breach of that duty by the defendant;

3. Breach of the duty must be the actual and proximate cause of the injury to the plaintiff,

4. Damages resulting from the breach of the duty.

THE DUTY OF CARE

Every negligence action is based on the "duty of care," which the defendant owes to the plaintiff. That duty may be a statutory duty or just a duty to exercise the reasonable care under the circumstances which would be expected of a reasonable, prudent man. It should be noted that the duty of care may vary depending on the factual situation and may or may not be governed by statutes.

These variances in types of duty owed between the parties may be based on the status, capacity, and age of the persons involved.

These variances may also be due to the special relationships between the parties, that is, employer-employee relationships; parent-child relationships; landlord-tenant relationships; master-servant relationships, expert-client relationships, and the like.

Where no statute has been violated by the defendant, case law is the precedent for determining whether his actions constitute breach of his duty of care to the plaintiff.

GENERAL LEGAL DOCTRINES AFFECTING LIABILITY

In every tort action, liability of the defendant must be established before he can recover damages for his injury. He cannot recover damages just because there was an "accident."

He must prove liability (breach of the duty of care, and the breach was the cause of the injury complained of).

In determining whether you can prove liability, you should look to the following doctrines most often and generally applied in most states.

A. The Prudent Man Test

This is applied in common law cases and may be used where no statutory duty is involved. The test is what a reasonably prudent person would do under the circumstances.

B. Doctrine of Res Ipsa Loquitur

This is the "but for" test and states in essence that "but for the negligent act of defendant, the accident would not have occurred." Negligence is inferred. To apply this doctrine, the following elements must be proved:

1. That the accident could not have occurred unless the defendant was negligent. Even though the plaintiff cannot prove the precise act of negligence, the happening of that particular type of accident is circumstantial evidence that the defendant was negligent.

2. That the defendant has exclusive control over the thing or condition that caused the injury.

3. That the plaintiff did absolutely nothing to contribute to the accident (such as a passenger on a train).

(See Chapter 10 on Evidence for detailed discussion of this doctrine, with examples.)

C. Doctrine of "Last Clear Chance"

This doctrine stands for the proposition that the contributory negligence of the plaintiff will not prevent his recovery, if it appears that the defendant, by the exercise of reasonable care and prudence, had the last clear chance to avoid the accident.

Some states now apply the "comparative negligence" rule in tort actions instead of the strict "contributory negligence" rule. Whether there was a last clear chance to avoid injury would be relevant to determining the comparative negligence of the parties in those states.

D. Doctrine of Negligence Per Se

Violation of a statute by the defendant may create *negligence per se* (by itself).

For this doctrine to operate, the statute which was violated must have been designed to prevent the type of injury the plaintiff suffered. In some jurisdictions proof of violation of the statute is treated as proof of negligence. In other states, proof of the violation of the statute is only some evidence of negligence.

Check your state case law to determine which rule your courts apply.

EXAMPLE

Mary, driving in excess of the legal speed limit, runs a red light and in so doing hits a pedestrian in the crosswalk who was crossing the street with the green light.

In this instance, Mary has violated the following statutes designed to protect this class of persons, that is, the pedestrian:

1. Driving in excess of the speed limit set by law;
2. Running through a red light in violation of the law;
3. Hitting an innocent bystander, a pedestrian.

This is a typical negligence *per se* factual situation. The act was in violation of a state statute. The statute sets forth the standard of care owed. You would look to the legislative intent to determine if the plaintiff was a member of the class of persons intended to be protected under the statute violated as described by courts in your state.

E. Cause

Liability for negligence must be based upon a casual connection between the defendant's act and the plaintiff's injury.

The cause of the injury may be primary, intervening, or concurrent. The defendant's liability depends on whether his acts were the proximate cause of the plaintiff's injury regardless of other cause.

1. Proximate cause is the cause of an injury or damage which is established by showing that the plaintiff's injury was not only the natural, but also the probable consequence of the primary negligent act of the defendant.

2. Intervening cause may or may not be the proximate cause of the injury to the plaintiff. If it supersedes the prior wrongful act or is an unforeseeable, independent act which destroys the causal connection between the negligent act of the defendant and the wrongful injury, the intervening cause becomes the proximate cause of the injury. Under this circumstance, damages would not be recoverable from the original wrongdoer, as his act would not have been the proximate cause of the injury.

EXAMPLE

The criminal act of a third party who shoots an accident victim at the scene, which causes injury not intended or foreseeable by the defendant driver who caused the minor accident.

3. Concurrent cause is the negligent act of two persons occurring at the same time and where the accident would not have happened absent the negligence of both parties. In this instance, both parties are liable, and the acts of both are deemed to be the proximate cause of the accident.

F. Doctrine of Contributory Negligence

This is a defense to a tort action based upon the negligence of the plaintiff. It is a common law doctrine. Negligence in this instance means that the plaintiff has failed to exercise that standard of care which a person of ordinary prudence would exercise for his own safety. This is the reasonable and prudent man test applied to the conduct of the plaintiff.

EXAMPLE

It has been our experience, and you will find, that a client will not always understand that simply because he was rear-ended while driving along the highway does not mean that the defendant is liable to him for his damages. It may have happened that in the defendant's rush to get to work, he changed lanes without looking through his rear-view mirror and did not see the car behind him changing lanes; or he may have suddenly decided to get off the freeway onto an off-ramp he almost missed, causing the vehicle behind him to swerve and hit him.

The defendant did have a duty to the plaintiff to have his car under control, but the plaintiff's own inattention and carelessness contributed to the cause of his damage. In a state which applied the doctrine of contributory negligence, the plaintiff could not recover. The result may be different in a state which applies the doctrine of comparative negligence.

G. Doctrine of Comparative Negligence

This doctrine determines the degree of liability of the plaintiff and how much he may recover based upon his contribution to the accident or injury. It is based on the doctrine of contributory negligence wherein the defendant may raise the plaintiff's contributory negligence as an affirmative.

EXAMPLE

In the automobile accident case described under contributory negligence, the jury may find (in a comparative negligence state) that the plaintiff was 50 percent wrong (or other percentage). In such case the plaintiff could recover only 50 percent of his damages. Check your state comparative negligence statute as to percentage limits of recovery.

H. Doctrine of Respondeat Superior (Imputed Negligence)

When two persons have some legal relationship to each other, one may have the duty to require the other to use care in regard to a third party. Examples are principal–agent, employer–employee, family-car owner–family driver.

Even though the principal employer or owner was not present, he may be held liable for the negligent acts of the agent, employee, or family driver under some circumstances where the doctrine of *respondeat* superior is applied. The negligence of the one is imputed to the other where the negligence was done within the scope of the agency, employment, or purpose.

EXAMPLE

Store owner is responsible for injury to a customer as a result of employee's failure to clean up a greasy substance on the floor where the employee knew or should have known that the substance was there where customers walked.

I. Doctrine of Assumption of Risk

If a plaintiff assumes the risk of injury by the defendant by the plaintiff's own actions and the plaintiff is injured, the defendant may invoke the doctrine of assumption of risk as a defense in states which apply the contributory negligence doctrine. In comparative negligence states, the assumption of risk may go only to the amount of recovery.

Under this doctrine, the plaintiff must have known and understood the danger and assumed the risk of said danger voluntarily.

EXAMPLE

The risk of death in going over Niagara Falls in a barrel when you cannot swim or the danger of slipping on the ice or breaking a leg when skiing down a slope and countless other such assumed risks of danger.

The significant limitation upon this defense of assumption of risk is that the plaintiff is not barred from recovery unless his choice is a free and voluntary one.

J. Doctrine of Strict Liability

Legal liability for harm may be imposed even where there is no proof of carelessness or fault (negligence) on the part of the person or company that caused the injury in certain cases. Examples are product liability cases, dangerous instrumentality cases (such as use of dynamite), or pet animal cases.

The theory is based on public policy and is prescribed by statute or ordinance in some instances.

For example, under the general common law rule the liability of a dog owner whose dog injures a person depends upon knowledge or notice of this dangerous tendency. In some jurisdictions, the law has been broadened by statute or ordinances to hold the owner of any dog (wild or domesticated) liable for the damages suffered by any person bitten by a dog while in a public place or lawfully in a private place, which includes the property or home of the owner. Such statutes or ordinances create "strict liability." Where strict liability is not imposed by statute or ordinance, the injured person may recover from a pet owner only if the owner had actual or constructive knowledge of the animal's tendencies for causing injury and had failed to warn the injured person.

Strict liability is based upon presumed knowledge of the tendencies of an animal to do harm. Liability of an owner may be established on the negligence theory if there is no statute or ordinance.

EXAMPLE

Say you own a German shepherd, who is a guard dog and you keep him locked up most of the time, but he gets out of the house while you are away because you left the door ajar when you left in a hurry. As a result, he injures your next-door neighbor. Your neighbor may recover on the theory of negligence if he can prove your lack of care.

Another area where the doctrine of strict liability is used is that of the ultrahazardous activity. Under this doctrine, liability is established for extrahazardous activities which may involve the escape of dangerous substances brought onto the land, a dangerous use of land or water, or the use of inherently dangerous instruments anywhere.

To determine the applicability of this doctrine is a question of law. The court determines whether the activity is ultrahazardous or whether an inherently dangerous instrument is being used.

In some states there are statutes defining such activities or instruments.

K. Automobile Guest Statutes

The occupant or guest statutes and the liability of the driver in these instances vary from state to state and are generally dependent upon whether or not the person was an invited guest, an occupant by sufferance, a trespasser, or a passenger for hire.

The law in most states, however, follows the general rule that the duty owed to such a guest is that of ordinary or reasonable care in the operation of the vehicle. However, in some states automobile guest statutes require that gross negligence on the part of the driver must be present to establish liability on the part of the driver.

Product Liability

In spite of increased government regulation of manufactured products and their labeling, injuries do result from the use of such products.

Whether or not an injured person can recover damages for his injuries depends on the facts in the case.

The basis of the lawsuit may be negligence, breach of warranty, or strict liability.

The law on this subject is in a state of flux.

In any case, the following facts must be proved to establish product liability:

1. The defendant manufactured or sold the product.
2. The product is defective or dangerous.
3. The defect was a hidden defect or the product was dangerous and had no WARNING labels. (Instructions may not constitute a warning.)
4. The product, because of the defect, caused injury or damage to plaintiff.
5. The plaintiff used the product in the way and in the manner for which it was intended or in a reasonably foreseeable manner. (Allegations or proof of this need to be made only if the manufacturer or seller claims, as an affirmative defense, that the product was not properly used.)

The defense of the manufacturer or seller may be:

1. Assumption of risk;
2. Unreasonable or unforeseeable use of the product;

3. Limited warranty (if the action is based on breach of warranty).

The *Student Edition, Restatement of the Law, Second Torts,* American Law Institute Publishers, gives the following examples of a manufacturer's liability for a defective product.

EXAMPLES

A manufactures a mattress. Through the carelessness of one of A's employees, a spring inside the mattress is not properly tied down. A sells the mattress to B, a dealer, who resells it to C. C sleeps on the mattress and is wounded in the back by the sharp point of a spring. The wound becomes infected, and C suffers serious illness. A is subject to liability to C.

or

The A motor company incorporates in its car wheels manufactured by the B wheel company. These wheels are constructed of defective material, as an inspection made by the A company before putting them on its car would have disclosed. The car is sold to C through the D company, an independent distributor. While C is driving the car the defective wheel collapses and the car swerves and collides with that of E, causing harm to C and E, and also to F and G, who are guests in the cars of C and E. The A motor company is subject to liability to C, E, F, and G.

PROFESSIONAL MALPRACTICE

To constitute professional malpractice, the conduct of the accused professional must be below the standard established by law for the protection of his patients or clients.

An unreasonable lack of skill in performing his professional duties or the display of illegal or immoral conduct which caused the injury or damage to the patient or client may be the basis of a cause of action for malpractice.

The standard of performance required in most states is the exercise of the degree of skill and learning ordinarily possessed and used by other members of the profession. This standard is proven by expert testimony at the hearing or trial.

A specialist is held to a higher standard of care than a general practitioner.

Malpractice cases against physicians have proliferated in the past. Malpractice suits against lawyers are becoming more common.

In medical malpractice suits, some states apply the "respectable minority rule" (choice of several recognized courses of treatment for the patient) or the "error in judgment rule" (made a wrong decision but otherwise followed professional standards).

The statute of limitations for bringing the action usually starts when the injury is reasonably discovered rather than at the time of the misconduct.

EXAMPLE

A sponge or surgical instrument was left in the patient's abdominal cavity during surgery. He suffered stomach pains after the surgery, but thought it was normal, until an X-ray was taken six months later, by another doctor, which revealed the foreign object. The action against the surgeon must be brought within the statutory limitation time from the date the new X-ray was interpreted by the new doctor.

An attorney may be liable to a client for malpractice even after he no longer represents the client (as where he damages a client by breach of his duty of confidentiality after he has completed his representation).

The attorney must perform for his client in accordance with the professional skills of the profession. He must also obey the ethical rules of the profession and the fiduciary duty he owes to a client. To be the basis of a malpractice suit, his failure in any of these areas must cause damages to the client. Otherwise, the remedy may be a complaint to the appropriate bar association for disciplinary action.

SECTION 2: PRACTICE

INITIAL STEPS

Before drafting a complaint or an answer in a tort case the legal assistant must understand the basic tort law applicable to the facts in the particular case. Getting all the facts and applying the theory of the case can be accomplished initially by using the following checklist. (Also read Chapter 6, "How to State a Cause of Action in a Civil Case," and Chapter 7, "Pretrial Practice and Procedure.")

I have found the following reminders to be most helpful in drafting a complaint or in preparing an answer to a complaint for personal injury and/or property damage claims.

SEVEN-POINT CHECKLIST TO ESTABLISH A PRIMA FACIE CASE

1. Was there a duty of care owed to the plaintiff by the defendant, which was violated?

2. Was the duty breached by the defendant the result of his failure to act (or not act) as a reasonable, prudent person?

3. Did the defendant violate a statute at the time he breached this duty of care?

4. Did plaintiff, in fact, sustain damages or injury as a result of the breach of duty?

5. Was the defendant's breach of duty the actual and proximate cause of the plaintiff's injury or damage?

6. Was the plaintiff in any way negligent, thereby contributing to the breach?

7. Are there any affirmative defenses to defendant's breach of duty, if owed?

DRAFTING A COMPLAINT IN A TORT ACTION

Let us now turn to specifics with a simple personal injury case and property damage claim to put it all together. (See Chapter 6, "How to State a Cause of Action in a Civil Case.")

It is well established that where there is concurrent injury to two separate properties, that is, personal injury and property damage, you can bring two separate causes of action for damage: complaint for personal injury or complaint for property damage.

In the alternative, the property damage claim can be an additional count within the complaint for personal injury.

In utilizing either approach, you should be aware of the statute of limitations governing the filing of these claims so as not blow the statute as to either. In most jurisdictions, the time for filing a claim for personal injury is shorter than the time for filing a claim for property damage. If the injured person died, most states have wrongful death statutes of limitations, which are even shorter than those for personal injury where death does not result.

Use the facts obtained in the answer to the questions in the preceding seven-point checklist. State those facts in separate paragraphs in the complaint.

(See Chapter 6, "How to State a Cause of Action in a Civil Case.") You should consult state statutes for the time restrictions in your state if the action is to be brought there.

ANSWERING A COMPLAINT IN A TORT ACTION

When a complaint filed against your client comes into the office you should immediately do the following:

1. Set up a file and index card, and if applicable obtain an extension of time in which to answer. Enter the same on your follow-up calendar. Place in the appropriate docket book.

2. Examine the complaint to determine if a routine answer, general denial, or affirmative defense is needed (see Section I of this chapter for some possible affirmative defenses).

3. Examine the proof of service to determine if proper service was made, and if not, whether you can file a motion to strike or a special demurrer or other similar type document.

4. If you find that you can file a simple answer, then draft such a document and attach it to the file and give it to your attorney.

5. If the complaint has more than one count, it is always best to determine the theory under which each count is being alleged, that is, common count, alter-ego, breach of contract, and so forth. This will aid you in stating your affirmative defenses. They may differ for each count. For example: Plaintiff's first cause of action is based on an alleged breach of warranty, the second is based on alleged negligence, and the third on alleged acts creating strict liability.

A useful, personal practice is to put notations of proposed answers in the margin of the complaint-pleading, next to each paragraph, as follows:

> Margin
> (deny)   Paragraph V
>
> (admit)   Paragraph VI

This type of notation makes it easier for your employer to review your work and make any additions, embellishments, or suggestions for your final draft of the answer.

PREPARATION FOR TRIAL

Thereafter, discuss with the lawyer the follow-up steps such as the schedule for sending out interrogatories, setting up depositions, developing requests for admissions, and the need or desire for a jury trial if the latter was not requested in the complaint.

1. Should you receive answers to a set of interrogatories propounded by you, review them by comparing the answers and studying the evasions and incomplete responses. Flag them for your attorney and discuss them, together with the possible need for a motion to produce or to compel further answers.

2. If you receive a set of interrogatories to be answered by your client, your attorney may want to object to some of the interrogatories propounded. Remember the time restriction for this type of action (Motion for Protective Order).

3. After or instead of the foregoing, consider requests for admissions. These requests for admissions may be based upon plaintiff's answers to your interrogatories, statements of witnesses or their testimony at a deposition, or information obtained as the result of a motion to produce documents or as a result of private investigation.

4. Should number 3 be implemented, the next step would be to move for an order that certain facts be admitted if that is the procedure in your court. Under some court rules, facts contained in a request for admissions are automatically admitted if they are not denied or objected to within a specified number of days (usually thirty).

5. If the plaintiff files a response to a request for admissions, review the responses of plaintiff, determine the need to request more admissions, and report your findings to your attorney. Here it may be possible to file a motion for summary judgment. If not, you are probably ready to have the case set for trial, if the plaintiff has not set it for trial.

6. If not already prepared and filed by the plaintiff, prepare and file an at-issue memorandum (or its equivalent in your court) with the court. In some states, this is a printed form and does not have to be signed by opposing counsel. Merely mail a copy to him.

7. In some states, after three or four weeks, the court will send out a document entitled Certificate of Eligibility to File Certificate of Readiness. This is a printed document wherein the court is advising all parties that the case is now on the civil active list and that the parties may now obtain a trial date. In

other states an order setting trial date and a date for a pretrial date and a date for a pretrial conference will be sent to you by the court.

8. In some states, you can now prepare for filing with the court your Certificate of Readiness, which is a printed form. In other states, you prepare your pretrial conference memorandum as required by the court and have your client available for settlement decision during the pretrial conference.

9. Notify the client of the trial date and settlement conference date by letter. This will prevent misunderstanding.

10. Notify all potential witnesses of the trial date.

Suggestion: Send out a copy of the letter to be returned to you, confirming the witnesses' appearance at the trial and setting a possible office conference prior to the date of the trial to review the facts of the case.

Complete your in-office trial preparation (see Chapters 8–12 and trial preparation forms at the end of this chapter.)

a. Review the file and determine what witnesses are to be subpoenaed;

b. Prepare the subpoenas and hold them in the file until needed;

c. Marshall all trial documents, photos, exhibits, and the like;

d. Start your trial brief (or briefs);

e. Draft your proposed jury instructions;

f. Draft appropriate motions, including notice of appeal, just in case;

g. Draft closing documents, arguments, and so forth.

For help in making the final trial preparation, three checklists follow. They are master trial checklist for office calendar, trial book outline, and instructions for preparing the trial book.

MASTER TRIAL CHECKLIST FOR OFFICE CALENDAR

Date

Event

Six weeks prior to trial

1. Confirm availability of witnesses for trial.
2. Determine and acquire all necessary evidence and documents.
3. Complete the taking of all oral depositions.

One month before trial	1. Review pleadings for any possible amendments (due to new facts found during discovery).
	2. Make decision in regard to additional pretrial discovery.
	3. Review any depositions.
Three weeks before trial	1. Complete all depositions analyses.
	2. Arrange for the appearance of witnesses, including making any hotel reservations needed.
Two weeks prior to trial	1. Complete the research of any legal questions (read carefully all pleadings to determine the legal questions involved in the lawsuit).
	2. Set the pretrial client conference for your attorney or complete the arrangements for pretrial client conferences.
One week prior to trial	1. Have the attorney complete preparation for direct and cross-examination of witnesses, including expert witnesses, if any.
	2. Docket call (if required by court rules).
	3. Organize trial exhibits (prepare the trial book, if necessary).
	4. Organize evidence in regard to attorney's fees, if applicable.
	5. For jury trial:
	a. Prepare motion in limine.
	b. Complete voir dire outline.
	c. Complete preparation of special issues.
	d. Prepare written stipulations.
	e. Draft your instructions to be requested.
Day before trial	1. Have your attorney meet with the client in preparation for testimony at the trial, unless it is routine and he instructs you to handle it.

TRIAL BOOK OUTLINE

I. Jury
   - A. *Voir dire* examination
   - B. Argument
   - C. Opening argument
   - D. Closing argument

II. Testimony
   - A. Witness list
   - B. Client's statement
   - C. Witnesses' statements

III. Evidence
   - A. Defendant's deposition
   - B. Plaintiff's deposition
   - C. Exhibit list
   - D. Instructions
   - E. Legal authorities and case decisions

IV. Pleadings
   - A. Plaintiff's original petition or complaint
   - B. Defendant's answer
   - C. Last-minute pleadings (*motion in limine*)

PREPARING THE TRIAL BOOK

Interrogatories. Paste each question on a blank sheet followed by the answer (if necessary for clarity). Otherwise arrange, as filed, in logical order.

Depositions. Prepare a deposition analysis or summary and put it into the book under Testimony.

Witness List. Set up the columns as follows: Name, Address and Telephone Number, Topic, and Time/Date for Testimony.

Prepare the witness list before the pretrial conference. Give one copy of the witness list to your attorney to take to the trial; keep one copy at the office for you or the secretary. Locate and schedule all witnesses (get assistance, if necessary). Fill in the list as each witness is scheduled.

Expert Witness Conference. Have the attorney organize the expert's testimony so that they buttress each other, cover gaps, and eliminate inconsistencies. Set and attend the expert witness conference with the attorney. Take notes at the conference to prepare a memo of the conference. The position of each expert should be summarized by you for the attorney. Background data on each expert must be itemized by you for the attorney. A memo of the expert-witness conference should be circulated among all the experts. Place the conference memo in the testimony section of the trial book.

Preparing and serving subpoenas. Prepare subpoenas or have them prepared. Use a standard form. Send to the process server or sheriff.

Exhibits list. Set up the columns as follows: Exhibit Number, Description, In/Out. The name of the case and your office file number (if any) should appear at the top. Prepare before the pretrial conference. Use In/Out for admission (in) or rejection (out). Use the same exhibit numbers throughout the pretrial and court hearings for easy cross-referencing.

Color coding (if used by your office).

Red: The client's testimony outline, deposition analysis, and interrogatories.

Yellow: The adverse party's deposition analysis, statement, and interrogatories.

Green. General trial matters such as outline of the case and *voir dire* opening argument.

Blue: Legal authorities relevant on evidentiary and substantial law points.

Purple: Procedural portions.

CLAIMS AGAINST GOVERNMENTAL ENTITIES

If the client's claim involves the federal government, read the special federal courts section in Chapter 5.

Although the Federal Tort Claims Act allows many federal claims to be filed directly in special courts, some federal claims require preliminary agency hearings. In any event, before you can file a lawsuit naming the federal government as a defendant, a formal petition or claim for damages must be presented within the prescribed time period to the appropriate federal agency for an administrative determination.

These petitions or claim forms can be obtained from the agency itself, and the filing procedures can be found in the United States Code creating the special court or the Administrative Act which created the agency involved.

State statutes usually regulate the procedures for making claims against the state, and waive sovereign immunity (recovery is usually limited in amount by those statutes).

If a claim is against a municipality or county or other local government entity, read any pertinent state statute and also the municipal or public authority charter and/or ordinances.

CLAIM AGAINST A MUNICIPALITY (LOS ANGELES, CALIFORNIA)

1. You have one hundred days in which to file a claim after the date of the accident or incident.
2. Thereafter, you have forty-five days' waiting period in which the claim is deemed rejected if you do not get a response.
3. You then have a six-month period in which you must file a lawsuit or be forever barred from bringing an action to prosecute the claim.

Note: All the above statutory limitations should be checked with your local state statutes so as to not blow a statute.

SPECIFIC STEP-BY-STEP PROCEDURE

The first step is to file the claim, which is usually a printed form that can be secured from the particular municipality. (See Figure 20.1.)

Figure 20.1. Claim against Public Entity

In the matter of the claim of _____, claimant, vs. CITY OF _____; COUNTY OF _____; DEPARTMENT OF HIGHWAYS; DEPARTMENT OF STREET MAINTENANCE AND REPAIR:

_____ hereby presents this claim to the City of _____; County of _____; Department of Highways; Department of Street Maintenance and Repair, pursuant to Section of the _____ Government Code.

1. The name and post office address of the claimant's attorney is: _____, Attorney at Law, _____, _____, _____.

2. All notices, letters, and documents regarding this claim are requested by claimant, _____, to be mailed to her attorney at the address set forth here.

3. On October 11, 19___, at or near the _____ block of Wilshire Boulevard, County of _____, State of _____, claimant received personal injuries under the following circumstances: On October 11, 19___, at approximately 8:15 P.M., claimant was exiting the premises of the _____ Restaurant, located in the City and County of _____, _____. Claimant descended some steps outside said _____ building and was heading in a direction toward the sidewalk located at or near the _____ block of Wilshire Boulevard in the City of _____, County of _____, State of _____. When claimant reached the end of the premises of the restaurant building and reached the sidewalk, claimant slipped and fell by virtue of a negligent and adjoining restaurant-building property. Claimant is informed and believes and upon such information and belief alleges that the City of _____, County of _____, Department of Highways and Streets and Department of Street Maintenance and Repair are responsible in some manner for the defective condition set forth above.

4. That as a proximate result of the negligence of the public entities here described, claimant slipped and fell, injuring her right hand and breaking a finger, and further, sustained cuts and bruises on her head and jaw. Claimant further sustained injuries to her shoulder, all of which have caused her great mental and physical injury and damage, and claimant is informed that said injuries will continue for a period of time presently unknown to claimant herein. As a further and proximate cause of the negligence of the above public entities here described, claimant suffered loss of earnings in an amount presently unknown to claimant.

5. So far as is known to claimant, _____, at the date of the filing of this claim, _____ has incurred damages as follows:
   a. General damages
   b. Special damages
   c. Loss of earnings

6. At the time of the presentation of this claim, _____ claims damages in the amount of $25,000, together with her medical damages and loss of earnings according to proof.

DATED: _____

_____
CLAIMANT

_____
Attorney for _____

Check applicable state code sections for appropriate procedures and law.

If the client is late in obtaining the services of your attorney, then obtain an application for leave to present a late claim form, as shown in Figure 20.2, which follows this discussion. This latter document should be accompanied by a notice of petition for relief from governmental restrictions and order that suit may be filed. A declaration in support thereof and a copy of the proposed claim should accompany the notice.

Your office will receive notification of the hearing on this request. If the petition is approved, prepare the order, file the original and copy with the court clerk, and serve a copy on the board of directors. If the board does not object, the judge will sign the original order and return a conformed copy within a two-week period. You thereafter have forty-five days in which to file your complaint.

Figure 20.2. Application for Leave to Present Late Claim

Claimant

_____
                              Claimant,

                                        APPLICATION FOR LEAVE TO
vs.   PRESENT LATE CLAIM ON
                                        BEHALF OF CLAIMANT

STATE OF _____, STATE
BOARD OF CONTROL,
                    Defendants.
_____

TO THE STATE BOARD OF CONTROL:

1. Application is hereby made for leave to present a late claim founded on a cause of action for personal injuries which accrued on July 16, 19__, and for which a claim was not presented within the 100-day period provided by Section 911.2 of

the Government Code. For additional circumstances relating to the cause of action, reference is made to the proposed claim attached to this application.

2. The failure to present this claim within the 100-day period specified by Section _____ of the Government Code was through mistake, inadvertence, surprise, and excusable neglect, and the State of _____ was not prejudiced by this failure, all as more particularly shown by the attached declaration of _____.

3. This application is being presented within a reasonable time after the accrual of this cause of action, as more particularly shown by the attached declaration of _____.

WHEREFORE, it is respectfully requested that this application be granted and that the attached proposed claim be received and acted on in accordance with Sections _____ of the government code.

DATED: _____

_____
Signature of Claimant

By _____
      Attorneys for Claimant

Practical suggestion: All the above documentation should be sent by certified or registered mail, return receipt requested.

MEDICAL MALPRACTICE CLAIM

The complaint in an action for medical malpractice must state facts which, if proved, would show both a breach of due care by the doctor and damage to the patient as the proximate result thereof. Medical malpractice is a tort.

The standard of care required of a physician is based upon the degree of learning and skills ordinarily possessed by other members of the profession in his field, as well as the use of ordinary care and diligence in applying and learning and the skills.

Since the level of learning and degree of skills are different for a general practitioner than they are for a specialist, the standard of care, therefore, for a medical specialist is higher. Should a general practitioner, for whatever reason, fail to consult with a specialist or refer the patient to a specialist upon determining that this is what the patient needs, this failure may constitute malpractice, if the general practitioner should have recognized the need for consultation with a specialist.

There are some other facts which may constitute a breach of the doctor's duty to a patient:

1. A physician may be considered negligent if he fails to hospitalize a patient where the standard of care indicates this to be necessary.
2. A physician may be considered to be in violation of his duty of care by his lack of diligence in attending his patient.
3. A physician may be considered in violation of his duty of care if he unjustifiably abandons or neglects his patient absent sufficient notice, excuse, or mutual agreement.
4. A physician may be considered to be in violation of his duty of care if he promises results which are not reasonably forthcoming as the result of the treatment prescribed or surgery performed.
5. A physician may be considered to be in violation of his duty of care if he fails to explain to and inform a patient as to the nature of proposed surgery and if he fails to obtain an informed, intelligent consent to said surgery. The exception to this rule, in some jurisdictions, is emergency surgery.

A plaintiff has no medical malpractice case unless he can establish that the doctor breached his duty of care and that the same was the proximate cause of the injury or death of the patient.

Note: In some states there is statutory provision for a preliminary hearing before the complaint can be filed in court. Check your state malpractice statute before proceeding with any malpractice claim. Also read the state case law involving similar cases. See Chapter 8, "Legal Research Tools."

MEDICAL MALPRACTICE DEFENSE

Both the attorney and the legal assistant may have to use a little psychology when working with the physician.

Generally speaking, as with the average layman, most doctors know very little about the law, the legal process, and/or the daily routine involved in court procedures. What they are fully aware of, however, is the time, and the fact that everything done in the legal process takes up too much of their time—time which they feel belongs to their patients.

Add to this fact that someone has filed a lawsuit against them, alleging misconduct or incompetence in their performance as doctors, and you have problems. Doctors, generally, do not understand how someone they have treated, perhaps for years and sometimes since childhood, could possibly sue them for anything. It is more of personal affront than, say, with an ordinary personal injury action where an individual has been allegedly injured by a stranger.

For these reasons alone, defending a physician in a medical malpractice suit is one of the more difficult tasks of your attorney; hence, you as his legal assistant should be aware of these emotional and psychological obstacles in order to aid your attorney in his dealings with a physician client.

Therefore, consider the following practical hints:

1. *Immediately* upon service of process upon the doctor he needs sympathy and an interpretation and explanation of the charge made in the legal language of the complaint.

2. Your attorney will explain the nature of the doctor's responsibility and liability, if any, to him.

3. You must explain the time restrictions, that is, twenty or thirty days in which to answer, as the case may be.

4. Explain why you need the doctor's help—hence some of his time— to get the facts from his point of view in order to answer the complaint and set forth affirmative defenses, if applicable.

5. Although your attorney will have discussed it with him, reiterate the role being played by your attorney and the doctor's insurance company (malpractice insurance carrier) to defend him against the action.

6. You do the above by explaining to the doctor that your attorney's expertise is medical malpractice (as is the insurance carrier's) and they are there to help him in every way they can.

7. Explain each step involved in defending the lawsuit, that is, the discovery process; what it is and what is involved, such as interrogatories; depositions, including his own; and the possibility of his records being subpoenaed for copying and inspection, and so forth.

If you do all the above at the beginning of the defense of the lawsuit, it has been our experience that the doctor will be much more cooperative when he is needed in each step of the discovery process and trial, should it come to that.

Although the plaintiff is the aggressive party, in most cases, the defendant in a medical malpractice suit may become the moving party and as such may immediately initiate the discovery process by sending out interrogatories and/or request for admission, or both concurrently. Bearing this in mind, consider the following tried and proven procedures:

1. When a complaint is received in your office, your attorney will tell you how he thinks it should be answered. He will often want you to review the complaint yourself to determine if he has overlooked anything.

EXAMPLE

A possible demurrer to a request for punitive damages. Should you discover this, advise your attorney and obtain permission to file a special demurrer to this allegation.

2. Or, the attorney may have noted on the complaint to go forward and file an answer alleging affirmative defenses.

EXAMPLE

A "good Samaritan" defense; or "contributory negligence."

EXAMPLE OF A CONTRIBUTORY NEGLIGENCE ANSWER

If, in fact, plaintiff sustained any injury and damage of any nature whatsoever by reason of anything done or omitted to be done by the defendant, which fact is not admitted, but is merely stated for the purpose of this defense, said injury and damage, if any, was approximately caused by the negligence of the plaintiff in failing to take proper and reasonable measure for their (his, her) own well being before and after the surgery as instructed to do by the defendant.

Note: It is vitally important in this type of lawsuit to include affirmative defenses. Hence, if your attorney, for whatever reason, overlooked to instruct you to allege affirmative defenses, bring this oversight to his attention if you have found any facts to support it.

3. Thereafter, or concurrently therewith, prepare and cause to be filed a set of interrogatories and requests for admission directed to the plaintiff. It is suggested that you mark these documents First Set of _____, since it has been our experience in this type of lawsuit that more than one set of inter-

rogatories and requests for admissions are required to obtain the information needed and wanted by your attorney.

4. Oftentimes, you will find that you have to compel answers to the interrogatories or requests for admissions, and since you are defending the action, upon the expiration of the statutory time within which plaintiff has to file said answers (twenty to thirty days), you should immediately prepare your motion to compel answers or compelling further answers (see Chapter 9, "Pretrial Discovery").

5. In the preceding connection, your duty in relation to answering the interrogatories served on the doctor is one of meticulous scrutiny, review, editing, and in some instances, rewriting. One major factor you should look for is the name or names of other doctors who may have worked with the patient, or may perhaps have been involved in the surgical procedure (or whatever the complaint is) to determine if there is a possible conflict of interest, that is, your office representing him as general counsel or otherwise.

6. Furthermore, check to see if in the interrogatories there was a request for information as to the finances of the doctor. If so, check the complaint to see if there was an allegation for punitive damages. If punitive damages were not pleaded, or pleaded incorrectly, then the doctor does not have to answer to the interrogatory as to his finances, since the request for punitive damages will not stand. If, initially, you had filed a demurrer to the allegation regarding punitive damages and said demurrer was overruled, this would allow the allegation on punitive damages to stand, having the effect of allowing the plaintiff to inquire into the financial stature of the doctor. The doctor would then have to answer the interrogatory.

7. Obtain copies of any and all medical reports by other doctors retained by the plaintiff in the possession or under the control of the plaintiff for your attorney and the insurance company (get copies from your doctor also for comparison).

8. Schedule (on notice) the taking of the deposition of the plaintiff.

9. Upon receipt of the notice of the Trial Setting Conference (TSC) and Mandatory Settlement Conference (MSC) or your state court's equivalent, notify the insurance company and the doctor. Especially notify the doctor, since unless she has signed a Consent to Settlement of the lawsuit, she does have to appear. You should consult with your attorney, however, to determine if he wants the doctor present at the Mandatory Settlement Conference. Then too, the doctor may want to be present just to be on top of what is going on

in the case. You will find that if attorneys' schedules permit, they like to be present.

10. Should the case go to trial, the step-by-step procedure is the same as with any other litigated matter.

OTHER TORTS

Along with an action based on negligence, there are four other basic tort actions which were not previously discussed. We generally answered the question, "What is a tort?" Now, let us discuss the *intentional tort,* which is one that causes a personal harm. It is a non-consentual relationship in which society does not have a stake. It is a relationship between individuals.

The intentional torts are those where the person being sued has done something which has caused harm to another person. For example:

Battery: when the defendant intentionally inflicts a harmful or offensive touching on someone. The key here is that it must be a voluntary action on the part of the defendant and it must have caused a harmful or offensive touching.

Another example: someone kissing you in public; or the boss patting his secretary on the "behind." In other words, any touching that is embarrassing can be offensive and will give rise to a tort dollar damage recovery.

Assault: assault is not and does not include physical contact. It is the creation of apprehension of harmful or intentional touching, merely frightening or creating fear. This is assaulting the plaintiff. Words alone do not create "fear." But, if you are blind, then the hearing of words may create "fear" and apprehension.

More important, the defendant must have the clear and apparent ability to carry out and commit the act and create the emotional fear. In other words, it must be immediate. The defendant cannot say, "I'm going to beat you up if you do that again." The defendant must say, "I am going to beat you up now, this minute, this second." **It must be immediate.**

Another type of intentional tort is called **false imprisonment.** In this area of tort law, the plaintiff has to know that he or she has been imprisoned and is being restrained intentionally by the defendant in a restricted area.

Example: (a) The defendant has placed the plaintiff in a room with locked doors and no means of exit; (b) Locked doors with a window open, gives the plaintiff a reasonable means of exiting the premises unless the defendant has threatened to harm a member of the family if the plaintiff leaves by that open window. This would constitute false imprisonment.

THE PRIVATE NUISANCE

A. Trespass;
B. Non-trespass.

These are unreasonable interferences and/or invasions of your property, those things which interfere with the peace and tranquility of the enjoyment of your property.

TORTS RELATING TO REAL AND PERSONAL PROPERTY

Conversion—the taking of a piece of property belonging to another. If taken permanently, one can sue for the full dollar value.

Now compare this to *trespass,* an example of which is joyriding. When you invade, but do not permanently deprive someone of personal property, this is a trespass. The loss, in this case, would be for damages to the property when the defendant was using the property. But, if the defendant takes the car and drives it across the state line or to a location where it is inconvenient or unreasonable, or you are unable to find it, then this is *conversion.*

HARM TO NON-PHYSICAL PROPERTY

This type of tort relates to one's reputation, emotional distress, embarrassment, etc.

A. Defamation of character

This occurs when someone communicates something defaming or embarrassing in the community, and it is heard by someone else and understood that way. These remarks do not have to be true or be read in the newspaper or heard on television. Defamation can take place in a classroom, a living room, a cafeteria, or by making a statement in front of others. It occurs in the setting up of a telephone call and asking for a reference as to your actions on your job.

For example, we all, in our lifetime, have had to get a reference from an employer. We all know that a potential employer will call the ex-employer and ask what kind of employee he or she was. The remarks that follow could be defamation. For example, your ex-employer could say that you are lazy; that you stole from the office; that you embezzled the petty cash. These are accusations which could conceivably cost you your new job; hence, they are defaming.

Another example of this would be that, while in the office, your boss walks up to you in the presence of other employees and says, "You are fired because you are incompetent and you are lazy and I have caught you in too many mathematical mistakes in your bookkeeping." This, too, is defamation of character.

In discussing defamation of character, be advised that it comes in two forms: (1) the form of writing, or (2) in the form of slander, which is oral. The defense to defamation of character is the defense of truth.

B. *Wrongful Invasion of Privacy*

You are entitled to certain private thoughts and papers and facts. Violation of these rights is the basis for a good cause of action from which you may recover.

C. *Right to Privacy*

The unauthorized use of a person's picture and likeness is an invasion of right to privacy.

You cannot present the plaintiff in a false light and hold that person up to public embarrassment.

Additionally, you cannot invade another person's physical solitude, or private conversations by bugging a personal telephone with electronic devices without permission. The violation of the statutes in this connection and the individual's right to privacy is the subject of a lawsuit from which the plaintiff could recover.

D. *Wrongful Causing of Emotional Distress*

This is best explained by way of example.

Seeing your child or mother or wife killed in front of you by a car or other deadly weapon.

Or being told that, because you are black, or Chinese, or a Jew, short or fat, you cannot enter this restaurant or join a health center, etc. Anything that causes you embarrassment or humiliation in public, causing you wrongful emotional distress, can be the basis of a lawsuit from which a plaintiff could recover.

E. *The Right to Rely on Things Said*

You have the right to rely on things said to you and not be unjustly harmed through misrepresentation. This occurs when someone provides you with a false, but material, misrepresentation of facts, which is known to be false but done with the intent to cause you to rely on it; you then rely on it to your injury.

Say you are going to buy my car and I tell you that the car has only 3,000 miles on it, when in fact I had eliminated three zeros. This is a material fact that is also false. The test, then, is: would you have bought the car if you had known that it had 300,000 miles on it instead of 3,000?

F. Disparagement

Disparagement is a little like defamation. False statements made to others about the plaintiff which cause injury to the plaintiff's business. An example of this is: a disgruntled customer standing out in front of a market, telling people not to go in because the food is bad; it is poisonous; they cheat you; the cashiers cheat you on your change; they have rats in the building, etc. This is disparagement upon which a plaintiff could file a lawsuit and recover.

G. Interference With Contracts

You have an existing contract and the defendant undertakes a course of action to cause injury to that contractual relationship. For example:

Defendant goes to the other party, the contractor, and says negative things about you, such as that you will not pay the bill, that you are hard to get along with, and such other remarks. And as a result, the defendant contractor withdraws from the contract. Under these conditions, a lawsuit can be filed to recover money damages.

H. Interference With Prospective Economic Advantage

Where someone wrongfully interferes with future business contracts or business.

EXAMPLE

This guy is a bum. Do not go into business with him." As a result of this, a potential investor changes his mind and does not go into business with the plaintiff.

I. Malicious Prosecution or Abuse of Process

Wrongfully filing a lawsuit against someone for which there was no justification in law or in fact. There is a growth area in the law, and the trend is now to punish persons who frivolously use the Court system and bog it down. A good example of this concerns inmates who are always filing frivolous lawsuits to get their sentences reduced or to complain about the food or to complain about the conditions in the prisons. Since they are allowed to file lawsuits without a filing fee, they have, in fact, bogged down the Court system so that those in the civilian world are unable to get their lawsuits heard in a timely manner.

SOME DEFENSES

A. CONSENT:

Where the plaintiff gives permission to the defendant to touch her. She cannot then sue for battery unless the defendant exceeds the permission given.

1. Actual or expressed consent:
2. Expressed or implied consent (what a reasonable person would assume that defendant had permission to touch her);
3. Implied by law (to save life or property).

All of the above are valid defenses and, as it relates to a female plaintiff, up to the part where she says "No." Then anything thereafter would be battery.

B. SELF-DEFENSE:

As a general rule, a plaintiff is privileged to use force to defend himself. But you cannot rise to deadly force unless you can reasonably conclude that it is necessary. For example, in California, the law was recently changed so that if you walked into your home and discovered a burglar, you could use force to defend yourself, provided that the defendant had in his hands a deadly weapon; or if the defendant was the size of, say, the Incredible Hulk, and you are five foot even, weighing 100 pounds. In those events, the plaintiff could use deadly force.

Consider another example: a 12-year-old weakling was coming through your window at night, and you were alone in bed. The only condition under which you could use deadly force is, if you could prove to the Court and sway the jury that you were in fear of your life. Then the question would be, how could a 12-year-old hurt you, unless of course you saw what appeared to be a deadly weapon.

Another self defense which would stand up in Court would be the defense of third persons. And here again, it would be a reasonable defense under the circumstances.

C. DEFENSE OF LAND:

You may not use deadly force to protect land or personal property. But you can use non-deadly force. (Please check your local criminal code to verify this law.)

D. THE SHOPKEEPER RULE:

This rule should speak for itself. For example, a person walking through a department store lifts a piece of jewelry and upon exiting the store is approached by the store detective inquiring about the jewelry which (it is apparent) has not been paid for. The defendant thereafter is locked in a room while the detective goes for authorities. This could be construed as false imprisonment.

As long as the "imprisonment" in the room is done in a reasonable manner, within a reasonable time, there is no defense against it. If, on the other hand, the detective leaves the suspect in the room for the rest of the day with no contact from anybody, then there is a possible lawsuit for false imprisonment. Once again, whether or not this defense can be used depends on the facts and circumstances.

CHAPTER 21

How to Assist in Collecting a Judgment

The laws governing the enforcement of money judgments are controlled by state statutes in the state where the money or property of the judgment debtor is located. This chapter addresses itself primarily to the procedures involved in the enforcement and collection of debts which have been reduced to judgment in the same state where the judgment debtor's property is located. The practice and procedure for the collection of judgments under "sister-state" reciprocal judgment statutes is also discussed.

At the outset, note that even in this area of the law the use of computers has invaded the attorney's practice of his profession and, hence, your duties as a paralegal.

The use of electronic support systems in this area of the law can be utilized effectively by you, in a small law firm and even more so in a large law firm, if the primary practice of your attorney is the collection of money judgments.

This type of law practice seeks to collect numerous money judgments in volume on behalf of the client (such as a large department store or medical association or other organization).

Additionally, this type of practice requires the preparation of complaints for money owed, open book accounts, and so forth, in volume. To this end, the computer or word processing system is a timesaver for the paralegal in charge of processing money collections and judgments, as the word processor, with its print-out attachment, conceivably has the capacity of putting out one hundred or more complaints a day, as compared to fifteen or twenty by a secretary who does it from scratch.

As you know, you only have to place a disk that has been programmed and customized into the computer, push a button, and retrieve the applicable print-out of hundreds of letters and envelopes as well as hundreds of complaints in a much faster, more efficient manner.

The complaints so printed out (if done with blank lines for the names and other personal data that might be missing) would thereafter require only the customizing of a court caption, the parties to the action, and the dates and monetary amounts due and owing which are involved in the contract or claim on behalf of the plaintiff–client.

MOST COMMON PROCEDURES USED TO ENFORCE MONEY JUDGMENTS

In securing satisfaction of a money judgment, the most commonly used vehicles to reach the property of the judgment debtor are:

1. Prejudgment attachment*, which is attachment of the alleged debtor's property before the trial where the debtor is expected to secrete or move his assets before the judgment can be obtained;

2. Garnishment;

3. Writ of execution (possession);

4. Such other remedies as may be provided in your state statutes and court rules.

STEP-BY-STEP PROCEDURE FOR PREJUDGMENT ATTACHMENT

PREJUDGMENT ATTACHMENT: PLAINTIFF STEP-BY-STEP PROCEDURE

This is the process of securing possession of property in controversy or of creating a security for the debt in controversy before the final judgment of the court on the merits of the case.

---

* As to prejudgment, this vehicle of law is in a state of flux as its constitutionality has been questioned: You should therefore check your local state code and court rules to see if it is still applicable in your state. In California, for example, the law governing civil judgments changed as of July 1, 1983. See §484, et seq of the Civil Code.

A. At the time of filing the complaint; or any time thereafter, the plaintiff may apply for an order and Writ of Attachment by filing an application for the Order and Writ:

B. This application, executed under oath, should include the following:

1. A statement setting forth facts which indicate the validity of the claim and that the debtor is likely to secrete or remove his property from the jurisdiction (check your state statute for necessary allegations)

2. A statement of the full amount owed or special payment

3. A statement that the Writ of Attachment is not sought for any other property than that upon which the attachment is based

4. A statement to the effect that the applicant has no knowledge, information, or belief that the claim is dischargeable in bankruptcy or that it has been discharged in bankruptcy

5. A full and clear description of the property to be attached, and that to the best of his knowledge the property is subject to attachment, that is, not homesteaded, and so forth

Note: The defendant must be served with the following documents at least twenty days prior to the date of a hearing on the request for issuance of an order and writ of attachment:*

1. A copy of the summons and complaint;

2. A notice of application and hearing; and

3. A copy of the application and any affidavits in support of the application.

4. Thereafter the court must first make a determination at the time of the hearing on the request for issuance of a writ of attachment that the defendant's assets exceed the amount necessary to satisfy the money judgment or secured by the attachment. When this has been accomplished the court will order a levy on the appropriate assets.

This package should be served on the defendant not less than five days before the date of the hearing (or other appropriate time restriction) on the Application, Request for Order, and Writ of Attachment.

---

* In California see Civil Code §684.00; 684.020 & 020(b); 030 as to service of enforcement money, judgment documents on debtor, creditor, and attorney, if applicable.

It should be noted, if applicable in your state, that you can obtain an *ex parte* hearing for issuance of a Writ of Attachment, provided you can show that it would cause great and irreparable harm to the plaintiff if the issuance was delayed until the matter could be heard on notice. Reasons for your fear must be stated in the petition for prejudgment Writ of Attachment.

Furthermore, do not forget that the plaintiff must file an undertaking bond to pay for any money damages the defendant may recover for wrongful attachment by the plaintiff in the action. The amount of this undertaking depends on the value of the property to be attached, which must not exceed the monetary jurisdiction of the court in which the action was filed. (You should check your local state statute and court rules for this procedure.)

STEP-BY-STEP PROCEDURE FOR COLLECTING A JUDGMENT DEBT

GARNISHMENT

"Garnishment" is a form of attachment which utilizes the appropriation of an individual's wages or credits held by third persons such as a bank or employer (under circumstances allowed by law).

The garnishment proceeding requires applying for a Writ of Garnishment from the court, or its equivalent in your state. You will serve the necessary papers on the judgment debtor's bank or employer as a warning or notice not to pay out monies or deliver property to the defendant which may be in their possession until further order of court.

In California, the Memorandum of Garnishee (or Garnishment), as it is called, served upon the third party (garnishee) is a document which is to be completed and returned to the court within a ten-day period and allows the garnishee to explain why he cannot comply, if that is the case. Absent that, the garnishee must list the property and/or monies due and owing to the judgment debtor. The judgment creditor (the plaintiff who won the money judgment) is the garnishor.

On the reverse side of this memorandum the garnishee will find, for his or its convenience, a list of the various exempt properties, if applicable.

Once again, remember that this document, and any accompanying document simultaneously served on the third party must be completed and returned according to the statutory time period in your state. Therefore, look to your applicable Civil Code section and be guided thereby, whether you represent a garnishee who was served or the judgment creditor.

In some states it is considered in violation of the law and in contempt of court for failure to comply with a garnishment proceeding. You should check your state statute and court rules for the applicability of this penalty or others.

WRIT OF EXECUTION

The Writ itself is normally prepared by the clerk of the court where the judgment was entered upon receipt of an Application for Writ of Execution prepared by you. This Application is delivered to the court with a nominal fee. The fee may vary from state to state, so check your rules of court.

It has always been our practice to prepare the original application and two copies. The original is for the court (sheriff). It is his authority to levy on the real or personal property wherever situated in his jurisdiction or a particular property, depending on state law. The second copy is for the attorney's file, and, as a courtesy, one is for the client.

Note: In some states one writ of execution is sufficient for all future levying. Other state court rules may require that a new application for a writ be prepared each time you require a new writ to be issued. Check your court rules for this procedure.

A copy of the writ of execution and levying instructions describing the property of the judgment debtor which is to be levied on and its location is delivered to the sheriff (or other levying officer).

Additionally, I have found it a good idea to call ahead to the levying officer's offices to get a "ball-park figure" as to the costs involved in levying on the property of the judgment–debtor, wherever situated.

Note: *Not more than one writ per county can be issued by the court clerk at one time.* I always liked to have them ready so that when the 180 days expires (time restriction in California), the next one is ready to be delivered to and issued by the court clerk and shot off to the next county without delay. (Check your state code and court rules for this procedure.)

Remember that the sale thereafter of the land (or other property) also has a statutory time limitation. You should check your state statute and court rules for this time restriction and procedures.

The writ of execution directs the sheriff to levy. The levy is the act of the sheriff in taking the judgment debtor's property into the custody of the sheriff pursuant to the writ of execution.

To levy on the property of the judgment–debtor.

1. Take actual physical possession of the property (such as a car or other moveable personal property); or

2. Serve a copy of the Writ on the judgment debtor–owner and post the property with a notice of levy, which usually contains a notice of the date of the sheriff's sale of the property.

ENFORCEMENT OF OUT-OF-STATE JUDGMENTS

The Uniform Reciprocal Enforcement of Support Act provides a method to enforce duties of support where the petitioning party and the respondent are in different but reciprocating jurisdictions.

If your state has adopted that Act, read the statute as accepted. Part III, Section II, of the Uniform Act covers the contents and filing of a petition under the act and covers the subject of venue.

All the fifty states and the District of Columbia are reciprocating states. Additionally, the following territories and foreign countries are reciprocating jurisdictions:

1. American Samoa

2. The Canadian provinces of: Alberta, British Columbia, Manitoba, New Brunswick, Northwest Territories, Ontario, Saskatchewan, and the Yukon

3. The Commonwealth of Australia

4. Guam

5. Puerto Rico

6. Republic of South Africa

7. The Virgin Islands.

This ability to reciprocate by foreign countries where applicable is based on the constitutional doctrine of "treaty supremacy" as provided in Article VI, Clause 2, of the United States Constitution.

There is also a Uniform Enforcement of Foreign Judgments Act (sister-state judgments), which is not reciprocal. Any state which adopts it can allow a judgment of a sister state to be registered and executed upon under the latest revision of that act (1964). The Act, when adopted by a state in its revised form, allows a sister-state judgment enforcement similar to the interdistrict enforcement of the judgment of the Federal District Courts (28 U.S.C. 1963).

The earlier version of the Uniform Enforcement of Foreign Judgments Act provided a summary procedure before the sister-state judgment could be enforced.

Check your own state statutes governing judgments and execution to find out which version, if any, your state has adopted.

The Uniform Act makes the right of the judgment creditor to bring an action in the sister state to enforce his judgment optional. He may proceed with the filing or registration of his judgment under the Uniform Act or proceed under other court procedure.

If a state has not adopted a version of the Uniform Enforcement of Foreign Judgments Act, the following is a typical state procedure before entering judgments obtained in other states.

The key is jurisdiction. In order for a sister state to acknowledge or have the power to hear and determine the matter or honor your state's judgment, it must have the jurisdiction of the person or the action and in some instances the property.

EXAMPLE

The judgment–debtor moved to New York to avoid the collection of the judgment. You can bring an action on the judgment obtained against him in California, by filing a lawsuit in the State of New York, which gives the New York court jurisdiction of a judgment–debtor and the case before the California Bar. The State of New York must give "full faith and credit" to the judgment obtained in California. Thereafter, you can obtain a writ of execution issued in New York and have it levied on any property, real or personal, belonging to the judgment debtor, in his possession or under his control to satisfy the judgment.

Under the Uniform Act here described, if it had been adopted in New York, the lawsuit would be unnecessary. The California judgment could be registered or filed with further legal action under the revised version of the act or ruled on in a summary procedure under the older version of the Uniform Act.

PROCEDURE FOR COLLECTION OF SISTER-STATE JUDGMENTS IN CALIFORNIA

The foregoing being true, consider the following California procedure as an example of what you may have to do in complying with your local state statute relating to collecting sister-state money judgments. The following procedure allows a judgment–creditor to apply for the entry of a judgment based upon a sister-state judgment by filing an application with the Superior Court (or other appropriate court in your state) for the county in which any judgment–debtor resides; or if no judgment–debtor is a resident, then any county in the state.

The application which must be executed under oath must include the following:

1. A statement that an action in this state on a sister-state judgment is not barred by the applicable statute of limitations;

2. A statement based on the applicant's information and belief that no stay of enforcement of the sister-state judgment is currently in effect in the sister state;

3. A statement that the amount remains unpaid under the sister-state judgment;

4. A statement that no action based on the sister-state judgment is currently pending in any court in this state and that no judgment based on the sister-state judgment has previously been entered in any proceeding in this state;

5. Where the judgment debtor is an individual, a statement setting forth the name and last known residence address of the judgment–debtor. Except for facts which are matters of public record in this state, the statements required by this paragraph may be made on the basis of the judgment–creditor's information and belief; and

6. A statement setting forth the name and address of the judgment creditor.

A properly authenticated copy of the sister-state judgment must be attached to the application.

Note: The normal closing paragraph follows, as in any application, and we suggest that it be under penalty of perjury, or if applicable in your state, have it notarized.

Another uniform act would aid in the collection in our state courts of judgments obtained by a foreign country. It is called the Uniform Foreign Money-Judgments Recognition Act.

"The Act states rules which have long been applied by the majority of courts in this country," according to the National Conference of Commissioners on Uniform State Laws. The act does not prescribe a uniform judgment enforcement procedure. It allows each state to use its own procedures or the procedures of the Uniform Enforcement of Foreign Judgments Act (sister states) if it has been adopted or the state wants to use it for judgments rendered in foreign countries as well as sister states in the United States.

The preceding discussion should give you some hope for collecting out-of-state or even out-of-country judgments where a country has a reciprocal provision, by treaty or otherwise.

CHAPTER 22

What You Should Know About Trademarks—Protectable Business Marks

Though there is both federal and state protection available to individuals relative to protecting their trademarks, most consideration is in and under the protection of federal law. Federal protection arises from the Trademark Act of 1946, as set forth in the United States Code, and commonly referred to as "the Lanham Act." This Act recognizes four protectable marks:

1. Trademark;
2. Service Mark;
3. Certification Mark;
4. Collective Mark.

It has been our experience that the ones most commonly used (and abused) are the service and trademarks.

DEFINITIONS AND EXPLANATIONS

A. TRADEMARK

A *trademark* is any mark, letter, or word (and the like) used to identify and distinguish goods of a particular person. The primary intent of a trademark is to protect—to prevent the confusion of the consuming public. IT MUST BE AFFIXED TO THE GOODS IN A COMMERCIAL SENSE.

A further purpose of a trademark is to identify and distinguish the goods of one from those of another.

It should be noted that a trademark may not be a word or phrase which is:

- Generic or common to the goods in question—for example, peas, carrots, etc.;
- Descriptive of the goods or contents (malted milk);
- Geographically denoting place of origin;
- Personal name of person or manufacturer;
- Color or shape of a container; or
- Scandalous or indecent or otherwise violative of public policy.

1. Trademark Limitations

a. Descriptive—not immune from protection;

b. Geographical; and

c. Personal names not normally protectable.

2. Protectable Trademarks

There are basically two protectable trademarks, and they are as follows:
  a. One which has become distinctive of applicant's goods; and
  b. One which has attained a secondary meaning. This secondary meaning is a protection to personal names and geographical designations which were not initially protectable under the Act, but, because of extensive use on the common market, became distinctive of the product.

3. Technical Trademarks

This is applicable where the surname is not primary, but merely a surname. The test here is whether a term would be immediately recognized as a surname without any other possible connotation.

The composition of a trademark may consist of the following:
  a. Letter, several letters, numbers, words, combinations of words, or even entire sentences;
  b. A picture or symbol or emblem (commonly called "logo"); and
  c. Any combination of permissible devices may be used.

4. Comparison

Recall that a *trademark* is any word, name, symbol, or device or any combination thereof adopted and used by a manufacturer or merchant to identify his goods and distinguish them from those manufactured or sold by others.

As distinguished from -

B. SERVICE MARK

·The Service Mark identifies and distinguishes a service performed.

This mark (service) is used in the sale or advertisement of services, the purpose of which is to identify the services of one person and in so doing, distinguish these services from those of another. This may include, but not necessarily be limited to, marks, names, symbols, titles, resignations, slogans, character names, and any distinctive and unique features of radio or other advertising used in commerce.

Collateral to the service mark we find the following:

C. CERTIFICATION MARK

The Certification Mark, such as the Good Housekeeping Seal of Approval, which is used by persons other than the owner of a trademark or service mark, to certify that the goods or services meet certain standards or have a certain regional origin. The person using a service mark or certification mark must exercise control over the use of this mark so that the certified standards may be met at all times. (This is protected under the Federal Protection Act of 1946, commonly called the Lanham Act.)

D. COLLECTIVE MARK

Then we have the *Collective Mark,* which is a trademark or service mark used by the members of a cooperative, an association or other collective group or organization; it includes marks to indicate membership in a union, association or other organization. (This type of trademark or service mark is also protected under the Federal Act, commonly called the Lanham Act.)

It should be noted that this *Collective Mark* is used primarily to indicate membership in an organization such as, for example, Third Degree Mason. But it may be used to identify the goods of individual members of the group. In this instance, the organization owns the collective mark and exercises control of its use by the members.

E. TRADE SECRET

A *trade secret,* as defined by *Black's Law Dictionary,* is a plan or process, tool, mechanism or compound, formula or process not patented, and known only to certain individuals and its owner; and those of his/her employees in whom it may be necessary to confide. Such a secret having a commercial value is not a property right, and the protection of which is based on the theories of fiduciary relationship and the breach of a trust or confidence.

Factors considered by the Court in determining protective or trade secrets may be the following:

1. Expenditure of money, time and labor in developing the trade secret;
2. The novelty of the secret;
3. Whether or not it is—in fact—a secret;
4. The conscious and continuing effort on the part of the owner to keep and/or maintain this secrecy of the product;
5. The value of the secret to the business entity;
6. The extent to which it may be isolated; and
7. The relationship between the parties having knowledge of the secret, i.e., employee-employer.

It should be noted that, though the law of trade secrets falls within the law of unfair competition, it gives much significance to the concept of fairness. Therefore, the relationship between the parties is carefully examined by the Court before any equitable remedy is made available.

An employer may protect his trade secret in one of two ways:

1. A written agreement between himself and his employee. (Though it has been our experience that oftentimes an employer will "protect" his secret in a verbal manner. In our opinion, this is ill-advised.)

2. By way of an implied promise on the part of the employee to the employer that he or she would not divulge the secret of his operation.

F. TRADE SECRETS AND FEDERAL PREEMPTION

Since the law controlling and governing trade secrets is still in a state of flux, it is suggested that you read or re-read some of the landmark cases involving patent law, license estoppel and the interpretations of the Court as to what other product may be considered a trade secret.

For example, some of these cases have held that an invention, design, process or even an idea may be a trade secret, and that these types of products may receive a license, which license may or may not be patentable; or that the object so licensed may not be patentable.

The cases referred to are as follows:

1. Sears/Campo Federal Preemption cases (three of them), as found in U.S.D.C.;

2. *The Winston Research Corp.* v. *Minnesota Mining & Mfg. Co.,* 9th Cir. (1965), 350 M.2d Fed. 2d 134;

3. *Servo Corp.* v. *General Electric Co.,* (4th Cir. 1964), 337 F.2d 716; and

4. *Lear, Inc.* v. *Adkins,* 395 U.S. 653895, Sup. Ct. 1902, the most famous of the four.

The decisions reached in these cases have caused attorneys to be cautious in advising the client in the area of trade secrets. As a result, state legislatures have been enacting and introducing legislation involving trade secret protection and disclosure, and providing for penalties of monetary fines and imprisonment to protect the owner of such trade secrets.

(You should check your local state code for appropriate state authority.)

DUTIES OF A LEGAL ASSISTANT IN THE PROTECTION SCENARIO

As a legal assistant working in an office whose specialty is copyright/patent law, your duties, generally, would be as follows:

1. To determine, through research, what name, symbol or trademark the client can place on its product. This procedure is similar to the one used in setting up a corporation and selecting a name for the corporation. In this instance, you must also submit several ideas for names, or trademarks, or symbols to your attorney after investigation as to their current use in the market place.

2. Once a name has been chosen, your job really becomes hectic as you must do further meticulous research as to a possible conflict or superior right in the use of the name so chosen, not only in this country, but on a worldwide basis if the client has an international company. In this connection, you not

only do research as to the use of the name, but also possible conflicts in trademark law in the various countries where the client's product is to be used.

3. The matter may necessitate conferences, negotiations and resulting agreements with third parties currently using the name or symbol, or one very similar to it (which would cause a conflict in the eyes of the public) to allow your attorney's client to use the name (or continue to use the name).

4. Once this has been accomplished, it is incumbent upon you to see that either of the marks is registered immediately. This is essential because registration under the Lanham Act is prima facie evidence of exclusive right to the use of the mark, and a strong presumption in favor of the validity of the fact that registration exists.

5. Finally, be prepared to file a lawsuit to protect the name, enjoining others from using a similar or identical name or symbol.

6. One other element which is a prerequisite to validity and ownership of the service or trademark is continued use in commerce for a period of five years after its registration. This makes the right to use a mark incontestable and the registration thereof conclusive rather than presumptive.

UNFAIR COMPETITION

DEFINITION

What is competition? The right of the individual to engage in private enterprise—and the collateral right of freewheeling competition between individuals.

Unfair competition NEED NOT actually involve competition between the parties and the parties NEED NOT be intentionally unfair. While there is such a thing as a "tortious unfair competition," this type of unfair competition may be the result of an innocent competitive act.

The remedy for unfair competition is an equitable one in the nature of injunctive relief, and in addition, money damages whenever incurred.

LEGAL REMEDY PITFALLS

Legal remedies in an action for unfair competition are inadequate for the following reasons:

1. Money damages arising from a business setting generally involve the loss of anticipated profits evolving from a speculative and unascertainable commodity; and

2. The conduct of the moving party, if continued, would create multiple lawsuits for which money damages would hardly provide adequate compensation.

Note: You, as a legal assistant, should look to your applicable state civil code sections to determine if these grounds are prevailing in your state.

DEVELOPING A COMPLAINT IN AN UNFAIR COMPETITION LAWSUIT (INJUNCTIVE RELIEF) BASED ON A "TRADE SECRET"

Practical Hints:

1. Remember to show that the plaintiff was harmed;

2. Remember to set forth that the plaintiff used every acceptable and reasonable means to protect his "trade secret";

3. Remember to spell out that the defendant had fiduciary knowledge of the "trade secret" and access thereto;

4. Remember to spell out that the defendant converted the same for his own use and benefit;

5. Remember to explicitly set forth that the defendant, in using and converting plaintiff's trade secret, *intended* to mislead and defraud the public;

6. Remember to allege that the defendant, in doing the acts above referenced, violated the fiduciary relationship as between employee and employer;

7. Remember to allege the "secret" converted by defendant was not of a nature or type which could be legitimately retained in the mind of a defendant, and therefore, could not be legally used by defendant for his own use and benefit.

DOCUMENTS REQUIRED TO ACCOMPANY AN UNFAIR COMPETITION COMPLAINT

1. Notice of Motion for Preliminary Injunction;

2. Memorandum of Points and Authorities in support of said Motion; and

3. Declaration of your attorney, and if applicable, Declaration of Affidavit by the client.

CHAPTER 23

Workers' Compensation

Here is a common misunderstanding: An employee who has been injured on the job is asked why he or she did not file a lawsuit against the employer. The answer most given is fear of job loss. The contrary is true. Whenever an employee is injured on the job, whether or not he or she is at fault, filing a claim against said "employer" is **not** against the employer. Rather, it is against the Workers' Compensation insurance carrier. Be it known that all employers by law have to carry insurance to protect the employee against mishaps.

Be it further known that, in Workers' Compensation claims, it is unimportant whether or not the employee was at fault. The law is clear in this regard. What may differ is the procedure for filing said claim against the insurance carrier of the employer.

A LEGAL CONFLICT

Another common misunderstanding: **you can receive state disability and Workers' Compensation payments simultaneously.** The procedure is that, upon injury, the employee, after the doctor has certified that the injury is work-related, should immediately apply for state disability to receive such sums that are due and owed as a result of employment. The application form for this state disability includes a question relative to whether or not the employee has received Workers' Compensation benefits.

At the time that the employee receives the first temporary disability check from the Worker's Compensation insurance carrier of the employer, then he or she must, under the law, advise the state disability office of such receipt. To do otherwise is fraud and can result in either a penalty or imprisonment.

Please be sure to check your local statutes to see whether or not this process is applicable.

In order to properly interview a client and complete the applicable claim form, then to follow the industrial claim to a successful conclusion, a legal assistant must know and have a full understanding of the Workers' Compensation laws in his or her particular state and how it operates. For example, states such as Louisiana, Alabama, New Mexico, Tennessee and Wyoming have what is called "Court-administered systems" in Workers' Compensation procedures. What this means is that all of the Workers' Compensation procedures are processed through the "Court" systems.

In the State of Wyoming, for example, the industrial accident procedure is encased in an "industrial accident fund," and the employer must be in good standing in order to qualify for joining "the fund."

After the legal assistant has prepared the original application, a filing fee must be paid to the district Court where the application is ultimately filed. In this instance, the employee is represented by a Court-appointed attorney or prosecuting attorney, if the injured employee lacks other representation. Your attorney should be aware that in the State of Wyoming, there are limitations as it relates to fees awarded to the attorney.

In the initial application, you as a legal assistant must be sure to include the following: (a) the need for applying for an award; and (b) you should stress the need for temporary and/or permanent disability. Because temporary and permanent disability claims are not automatic, they must be filed and requested by the employee (or the representative of the injured person).

Additionally, any and all claims, either by employee or employer, are made to the District Court in the county in which the injury occurred. If disputed, it is handled as a regular civil matter with appeal privileges to the Supreme Court of the State.

Though, like California, there is a Subsequent Injuries Fund procedure, there is no serious and willful application under the laws of Wyoming's Compensation Act.

Note, that the employee cannot sue his employer; and if the employee fails to file for disability, he has to pay for all hospitalization, doctors and other medical bills himself.

For our purposes, however, this chapter will be discussing the procedures of the Workers' Compensation practice in the State of California.

CALIFORNIA WORKERS' COMPENSATION

Because of the changes in California's Workers' Compensation laws, you as a legal assistant should be particularly aware of the deadlines and new restrictions involved. For example, as you know, in 1990 and 1991, the Governor signed into law new rules affecting Workers' Compensation. It would be your job to either be aware of these new changes or otherwise have a copy of the rules available to you in your office to refer to each time a Workers' Compensation claim comes in.

One of the new changes, which is mandatory, is the 30-day deadline for reporting an injury to an employer. Here, it could be construed or inferred that this could be a litigation avoidance claim or a litigation reduction claim. Both of these informal remedies involve primarily the insurance company, and could be considered as one of the "informal procedures" normally associated with the prosecution of a Workers' Compensation claim.

As to the litigation reduction procedure, the insurance company provides all of the benefits and pays temporary disability as determined by an informal rating procedure.

As opposed to the "litigation avoidance procedure," which is an "advisory service" also provided by the insurance carrier. This procedure is based upon the insurance carrier's medical only. That is to say, the insurance company will have one of its doctors evaluate the injury of the employee and, based on this medical report only, would advise the claimant as to what benefits, if any, he or she will be entitled to. REMEMBER, however, that this is an advisory service only.

In any and all events, the employer must receive written notice that the employee has been injured. This can normally be accomplished by the claimant (employee) securing a physician's Report and submitting it to his or her immediate supervisor. If, however, the 30 days have elapsed before the employee has had an opportunity to file this initial report with the employer, then and only then are you in a position to file the adjudication claim. (You are cautioned to check this procedure with your local state statutes.)

The next deadline you should be aware of is the five-working-day deadline for receipt by the employee of notification from the employer of potential benefits. Thereafter, if the employer has properly notified the employee of these potential benefits, then 14 working days after said notification, the employee is entitled to receive temporary disability and/or death benefits if the employee was killed in the line of duty; or he or she would be entitled to permanent disability.

This benefit is based upon either the termination of temporary disability and/or when it has been adjudged by a physician that the employee's condition has become permanent and stationary (which means that further treatment will neither improve the condition nor make it worse).

Once this fact has been determined, it is appropriate to start the inquiry and process for vocational rehabilitation. This type of rehabilitation is entered into between the employer and the employer's Workers' Compensation insurance carrier. This process or procedure will be discussed in detail later on in the chapter.

A. LAW GOVERNING

California Workers' Compensation is governed by the California Constitution, Article XV, Section 4. The basic statutory regulations in California are the California Labor Code, which pertains to rules regarding insurance requirements, and the Insurance Code.

These laws include the prerequisites and benefits payable to injured employees as far as medical treatment is concerned; temporary and permanent disability; life pensions; the Subsequent Injuries Fund; vocational rehabilitation and death benefits.

B. INSURANCE

Further, under California law, the employer has to have insurance. *The employer can be illegally uninsured.* This means that the employer has no Workers' Compensation insurance and is not permissibly self-insured and not legally uninsured. Employers can also be *permissibly self-insured.* This means that the employer has a certificate of permission from the director of industrial relations. And, the employer can be *legally uninsured.* This status primarily refers to state agencies, counties, cities and other local public entities.

C. JURISDICTION

1. Covered employment;
2. Injury arising out of and occurring in the course of employment.

D. VENUE

1. Application filed in the county where the employee or dependent resides on the date of filing; or
2. Cumulative trauma/disease claims where the last alleged injurious exposure occurred; or
3. At the WCAB office nearest to the residence on the date of filing.

E. COMPOSITION OF THE APPEALS BOARD

1. It is a seven-member board
   a. Five attorneys appointed by the Governor to serve four-year staggered terms;
   b. Two laymen.

   Judicial powers are vested and provided for in the *California Labor Code.*

2. *The Benefit Unit:* Monitors and insures that the employer(s) gives prompt payment of disability benefits, and/or *prompt* notice of non-payment on a claim to the employee.

3. *The Medical Bureau:*
   a. This division examines injured employees at the request of the Referee to determine the nature and extent of the industrial accident.
   b. It also evaluates the disability if requested.
   c. There are seven (7) physicians with offices in Sacramento, Oakland, Los Angeles and Long Beach.
   d. It maintains a panel of *Independent Medical Examiners* (IMEs) who are appointed upon recommendations of The Medical Advisory Committee.

4. *The Medical Advisory Committee*
   a. This is a seven-member committee of physicians in specialized areas of medicine and disease.
   b. It is their responsibility to review and approve panels of doctors when and if the injured employee, via attorney, requests a change of treating physician.
   c. These are appointed by the Administrative Director of the Division of Industrial Accidents.

5. *The Legal Staff*
   a. The WCAB maintains a staff of attorneys whose responsibility includes:
      1. Processing cases pending on reconsideration;
      2. Legal and factual research; and
      3. Preparation of legal memoranda for the Board.

6. *The Rating Bureau*—NOT TO BE CONFUSED WITH THE MEDICAL BUREAU—totally different function. These are 21 specialists, with the following responsibilities:

   a. Issuance of informal ratings in uncontested cases;

   b. Preparation of recommended ratings in contested cases;

   c. Preparation of pre-trial estimates prior to pre-trial hearings;

   d. Receiving C&Rs to determine their adequacy;

   e. Consultation services.

7. *Purpose of the Board*

   a. Guarantee support for employee and family while employee is unable to work;

   b. Provide medical support and treatment free of charge;

   c. Furnish money award for any permanent disability, or life pension if necessary;

   d. In case of death of injured employee, provide adequate compensation to family.

8. *The Hearing*

   a. It is an "*administrative-type*" proceeding *controlled by* and under the *supervision* of the WCAB;

   b. The procedures are governed by the rules and regulations of the *Government and Labor Code* of the State.

   KEY: Unlike personal injury cases, the employee can be <u>grossly</u> negligent, and still recover for injuries sustained.

   <u>However</u>, he or she cannot recover the pain and suffering as in a personal injury case.

   In industrial accident cases, <u>IT IS UNIMPORTANT</u> who is at fault. <u>IT IS ONLY IMPORTANT</u> that the injury occurred "during the course and scope of employment."

9. What is an industrial accident *or* disease?

   "<u>Any accident occurring on the job while in the course and scope of employment</u>."

   For example: If you are employed in a grocery store and it is your job to put away heavy bags of potatoes; or lift heavy slabs of meat; or boxes of canned goods from one place to another within the store, and in doing any of the above, you injure your back or sustain a severe strain or sprain of a muscle while performing said duties, necessitating medical treatment or hospitalization, this is an "on-the-job" injury entitling you to file an industrial accident claim, or Workers' Compensation claim.

10. <u>An industrial illness,</u> on the other hand . . .

"is any injury or disease which is caused or aggravated by a person's work or working conditions; and may include damage to artificial limbs, dentures, hearing aids, eyeglasses, etc., if incidental to the injury. *Examples:* chemical poisoning; stress or strain which may aggravate arthritis; latent diabetes, and psychological problems. These injuries are described as follows:

a. <u>Specific</u>: occurring as the result of one incident or exposure;

b. <u>Cumulative</u>: occurring repeatedly over an extensive period of traumatic activities, which combination causes a disability; and

c. <u>Occupational disease:</u> is one in which the cumulative effect of continuous exposure to the harmful elements of one's employment results in the disability, as in the stress and strain of your back and the chemical poisoning mentioned above.

11. *Against whom is such a claim filed?*

Contrary to popular belief, an individual claim is filed AGAINST the <u>Workers' Compensation insurance carrier</u> of your employer, not the employer personally, <u>unless he had no</u> Workers' Compensation insurance coverage. In California the laws require that all employers carry such insurance, <u>unless</u> they are certified to be:

a. Self-insured; or

b. A municipality or other subdivision; or

c. Some departmental entities of the State.

Practice and Procedure Before the Workers' Compensation Appeals Board (California Procedure)

The Industrial claim has three dimensions: the informal procedures; the formal procedures; and the appeal.

A. INFORMAL PROCEDURES (CONSENT OF BOTH PARTIES)

Voluntary provision of benefits.

B. FORMAL PROCEDURES

1. Filing the Workers' Compensation claim (Adjudication of Industrial Claim).

Who may file a claim? Answer: Anyone privy to the circumstances surrounding the injury, i.e., employer on behalf of the employee; employee on behalf of himself; medical provider (lien claimant); and, the legal representative of said employer. (If you as the legal assistant are preparing the claim on behalf of the employee, though you are allowed by law to do so, you should notify the Workers' Compensation Appeals Board **prior** to filing the formal application.)

What is included on the claim form? Answer: a short statement of the facts concerning how the injury occurred and on what date it occurred; a request for normal compensation benefits (temporary disability, permanent disability, medical and legal costs, etc.); and death benefits, if the employee died as a result of the injury.

Under the new rules, you may also include on this initial form a claim for serious and willful misconduct; and you may also include a request for vocational rehabilitation if you discern that the injury suffered by the employee will require it.

2. Death Benefits

The deadline for filing death benefits is one year after the date of death of the employee (or one year from the date of the accident); you should check the local state statute as to this ruling.

Children or spouses living within the home at the time of the incident are covered as it relates to the receipt of said death benefits.

Note: it is the responsibility of the spouse to inform you or your attorney that the injury suffered by the employee was the result of a work-related injury and therefore, death benefits are applicable. However, there are some exceptions and, as the legal assistant, it would be your responsibility to check the local labor code and/or the statutes as set forth in your local Workers' Compensation volumes.

Both of these formal documents (original application and Death Benefit application) have to be personally served on the employer and/or his insurance company, whichever is applicable in your state.

This should be served immediately upon your receipt, from the applicable Workers' Compensation Board, of the conformed copy. By conformed copy we mean a copy which includes the Board's number.

Thereafter you have 15 days, under the new rules, within which to contact the opposing parties in an attempt to resolve the matter.

During the interim period, however, you should have been receiving medical reports from the pertinent doctors—both your doctor and the insurance company doctors for comparison and resolution. Once you have received these medical reports and you have attempted to resolve the matter outside of litigation, you are now prepared to file a Declaration of Readiness to Proceed. This is a form which can be obtained from the Workers' Compensation Appeals Board when you are ready to present the claim to them for a hearing on the issues. If you have not already done so, you should procure and file with the Declaration all copies of the doctors' reports heretofore received by your offices so that the WCAB will have something with which to work and make a decision.

3. Filing the Answer to the Application

If you are on the receiving end of an Adjudication Claim, you have ten days after you are served with the Declaration of Readiness to file an answer. (In pre-January 1991, you had six days after service of the Declaration in which to file your answer.)

In your answer, you should deny the allegations in the Application and at the same time file any and all reports you have from doctors. (For those of you who are unfamiliar with this procedure, be advised that you can obtain a form copy of an answer from the Workers' Compensation Appeals Board.)

C. OTHER FORMAL PROCEDURES

1. The Subsequent Injuries Fund Benefit application:

    a. You can file a Subsequent Injuries Fund Petition when the employee has had a partial disability from any cause at the time he or she was injured on the job;

    b. When the degree of disability caused by a combination of previous disability and subsequent injury is greater than would have resulted from the subsequent injury alone.

    (See your labor code for this definition and explanation.)

    c. The application must show all the facts concerning the previous disability; and

    d. When the employee is entitled to benefits for a previous disability.

Note: The deadline for filing this Petition is the same as when filing the original application for normal benefits.

2. Petition for New and Further Disability Benefits

This Petition can be filed when the injury has caused a "new and further" disability. This occurs when the employee was able to return to work but is again temporarily or permanently disabled; or when the employee needs further medical treatment.

Deadline for filing a Petition for New and Further Disability occurs five years after date of injury where the benefits were already provided; or at the time the original application was filed on time; when the case was previously adjudicated; or one year after the last provision of benefits, even though five years from the date of injury; or if the employee did *not* file for benefits before.

The Petition should contain facts that show a new or further disability and/or if an original application had not been filed.

3. Petition for Serious and Willful Misconduct

The grounds for filing a Petition for Serious and Willful Misconduct arises when an employer or employee has caused an employee's injury by serious and willful misconduct. That is to say, there has been an intentional or reckless violation of a safety order; or an intentional act with knowledge that serious injury is a probable result of such an act.

The Petition should include the basis of the claim, i.e., violation of an established safety order; and facts supporting the claim. An example of this would be a correct citation of the subject safety order; the specific manner in which the employer violated the safety order; facts that the employer knew about the violation or the violation was obvious, and that the condition created a probability of serious injury.

It is vitally important that each theory relied on state the facts and allegations separately for each alleged theory of misconduct. Further, the employer's misconduct allegation must be filed within 12 months after injury. As previously noted, this Application may be included in the original claim for adjudication.

D. APPEAL PROCEDURES

1. Petition for Reconsideration.

To file a Petition for Reconsideration, the Workers' Compensation Appeals Board must have made an award, or a decision against the client. The decision must have exceeded the Board's or Workers' Compensation Judge's power; or the decision was procured by fraud; or the evidence did not justify the findings of fact; or the findings of fact did not support the decision; and, there has been newly-discovered evidence. As it relates to all of the above, please be sure to check your Workers' Compensation Appeals Board statutes, as well as the Labor Code.

If you, as the legal assistant, have been instructed to serve this document, note that you have 20 days within which to serve this Petition after the order, decision or award if you want to challenge it. If you determine that this is applicable, you have 25 days to mail the Petition if it occurs within the State of California. If you live outside the State of California, you have 30 days within which to mail it; and if the recipient lives out of the country, then you have 40 days. Note again, that you should check your local Workers' Compensation Board and the Labor Code applicable in your state for this procedure.

The deadline for filing an answer to this Petition, if personally served, is ten days after receipt. If served by mail within California you have 15 days; or 20 days if mailed outside of California; and/or 30 days if mailed outside of the United States.

2. The Petition for Writ of Review

This Petition can be filed after you have petitioned for reconsideration in order to seek and obtain a review in the Appellate Court, based on the following facts:

   a. The Workers' Compensation Board acted without or in excess of its power;

   b. The order, decision or award was procured by fraud;

   c. The order, decision or award was unreasonable;

   d. The order, decision or award was not supported by substantial evidence; and

   e. The findings of fact were made and the findings do not support the order, decision or award under review.

As to the deadline for filing this Petition, you have only 45 days after the Board files either an order denying reconsideration or order following the Petition for Reconsideration. You might want to check your Code of Civil Procedure regarding the deadline within which to file the Petition for Writ of Review. In any and all events, note that you have only 20 days after the Petition was served within which to file an answer; and ten days after answer has been served.

3. Petition to Reopen for Good Cause

This ability arises when you can show good cause to reopen the pro-ceedings in order to rescind, alter or amend a previous order, decision or award. In this connection, "good cause" means you have new evidence which was not previously available or reasonably obtainable; and the same was not presented to the Board; or that the law has been changed to support your position that could result in a change in the order, decision or award.

Please note that you cannot file a petition based on good cause to reopen to have issues of employment reconsidered once the Workers' Compensation Board has made its decision.

The deadline for filing a Petition to Reopen for Good Cause is five years from the date of the injury.

4. Miscellaneous Claims

Another claim which can be filed in today's society is a claim for stress. The prerequisite for filing such a claim by an employee is that he or she must have been employed by the employer for six months or more; or the injury must have been caused by sudden and extraordinary employment conditions, such as long hours or overwork or the conditions under which the employee worked. In ad-dition, the stress claim must be related to a physical injury. For example, an em-ployee who had been previously physically injured on the job came back to work before he or she was well enough to perform the duties required, and as a consequence, it became stressful for the employee to work in pain and/or dis-comfort. As the legal assistant, you should check your local labor codes to de-termine when this claim can be filed and if the injury sustained is applicable.

Another miscellaneous claim which can be filed would be one on behalf of minors and incompetents. In this instance, time does not run against a mi-nor or incompetent until a guardian ad litem or trustee has been appointed by the Workers' Compensation Appeals Board. This relates to any individual under the age of majority and/or any individual under the age of majority who is deemed to be incompetent by the Court for any physical or mental reasons. Here again, you should check with your local labor code and statutes to de-termine when such a claim is viable before the Court.

VOCATIONAL REHABILITATION

Nowhere in the area of law is there a more personalized suffering sustained by an entire family as is an industrial accident. The misery and pain inflicted upon the family of the injured employee when he or she becomes unemploy-able because of such an incident, cannot be measured in damages for "pain and suffering" as in the accepted personal injury case. In many cases, as a result of an industrial incident, these persons are maimed for life; or at the very least, unable to secure gainful employment in the same or similar job activity. In most cases, the adverse residual effects of an industrial incident will remain throughout a lifetime. That is why vocational rehabilitation is so very important.

In most states, this is considered a mandatory program which is entered into between the employee and employer, together with the Workers' Compensation insurance carrier and the state Department of Rehabilitation. Some attorneys, as a practical matter, will look to the Appeals Board to assist in setting up this rehabilitation or retraining program.

Under this program, the employee is entitled to receive temporary disability payments and advances against any permanent disability to which he/she may be entitled until the rehabilitation or job training program is completed. It is suggested that you look to your labor code for the exact procedure in applying for these benefits. In California, for example, the following procedure is in place:

1. Public agencies, the insurance carrier and the state Department of Rehabilitation are charged with the responsibility of formulating selected procedures and referral of individuals who may benefit by rehabilitation services or retraining programs.

2. The employer of said injured applicant and/or the insurance carrier for the employer is charged with the duty of notifying the employee of the availability of such rehabilitation or retraining program. Note that a rehabilitation plan and/or request for approval of said plan has a deadline which you as the legal assistant should calendar so that it will not be defeated because you let the statute go by. Under the new rules, the deadline to submit the plan after the employee and employer have agreed is 15 days.

3. The employee who is seeking rehabilitation is entitled to a "subsistence allowance" in an amount to sustain the employee, but not as a replacement of lost earnings.

4. Finally, of great importance to the success of the plan is the cooperation of the employee. A failure or refusal to cooperate or comply with the plan or program may cause his rights to a subsistence allowance to be terminated or suspended.

You should be aware that, although the benefits are not automatic, the injured employee, once advised by his doctor that his injury will incapacitate him for at least a year, can file a claim for Social Security disability benefits. Note, however, that these benefits, once applied for, do not commence until six months after the disability begins. It is therefore extremely important, once you find out that the disability will last beyond a year, that you file for the Social Security benefits.

THE COMPROMISE AND RELEASE

One vehicle used to dispose of a Workers' Compensation claim is by way of a settlement without a formal hearing. It is the Compromise and Release agreement which must be approved by the Workers' Compensation Appeals Board. This procedure is used to protect the applicant as to the amount of the settlement and attorney's fees requested. **Note:** this procedure may not be valid in your jurisdiction. Please consult your local rules.

Procedure: this document is usually prepared by the Workers' Compensation insurance company with a copy to the Appeals Board. All medical lien forms or reasonable medical expenses, or reasonable value of living expenses for the applicant's family are attached to the copy of the Compromise and Release mailed to the Appeals Board.

This form of settlement is a final disposition that forever closes the case. The applicant can never reopen a claim against the insurance carrier for this particular injury once the Compromise and Release has been approved by the Appeals Board.

This document is normally a form which can be obtained from the Workers' Compensation Appeals Board. To complete it, you do the following:

1. Insert the attorney's fees;
2. State the reason and purpose for the Compromise and Release;
3. Obtain a waiver from the Department of Unemployment as to its lien, if applicable;
4. Check all liens against the gross settlement figure to make sure they are accurate; and
5. Ensure that the applicant has signed and approved the Compromise and Release.

Thereafter, secure all signatures of the appropriate legal representatives for both parties; then submit the original document to the Appeals Board with copies to the proper legal representatives.

The Workers' Compensation Board thereafter will approve the Compromise and Release. However, if the judge, in his discretion, feels that the proposed settlement amount is not adequate, he can disapprove the same and/or amend it in any manner he sees fit, such as requiring that the applicant get more medical treatment, or determining that the settlement amount is excessive.

In any case, be sure to calendar the date you receive the order approving the Compromise and Release, so that you can advise your attorney as to whether or not the monies settled upon have been received or not received, so that he may take the proper action.

This is opposed to the Findings and Award, which is the decision, opinion and award of the judge who heard the matter before the Workers' Compensation Appeals Board. This disposition of the claim is far better for the applicant inasmuch as the Workers' Compensation Appeals Board retains jurisdiction of the case.

The judge, at his discretion, has decided upon a monetary award based on the evidence, which is testimony from witnesses, experts and medical reports of doctors. The judge can also order that the applicant receive future medical treatment; and/or lifetime medical treatment, and such other benefits as he deems necessary and appropriate.

On previous pages we have set forth the FORMAL PROCEDURES and how they are to be prepared, filed and to whom they should be delivered (such as original to the Court, copy to an attorney and copy for your files). Below we will list these procedure documents with their statute of limitations:

Document	*Statute*
Initial Application for Adjudication of Claim	One year from date of injury or last date of treatment
Answer	Based on common practice and procedure (see new rules for deadline)
Continuous Trauma (cumulative industrial)	May be filed at the time of initial application and based on a one-year disability and knowledge thereof that it is work-related
Death Benefits	One year from date of death
Industrial Diseases	One year from date of discovery
Minors-Incompetent Claims	Time does not begin to run against a minor or incompetent until a guardian ad litem or trustee has been appointed by the Board
New and Further Disability	Five years from date of injury
Petition for Commutation or Funds	Can be filed at any time after receipt of Findings and Award

Document	*Statute*
Petition for Reconsideration	May be filed within 20 days after receipt of Findings and Award (see code for new deadline date)
Petition to Reopen	Within five years of the date of the injury
Serious and Willful Application	One year from date of injury
Subsequent Injuries Fund Benefits	May be filed at the time of the initial application; and though in dispute, within five years of industrial injury
Writ of Review (Appeal)	30 days after denial of Petition for Reconsideration

A Hypothetical Case For You to Review Your Skills

For those of you who specialize in Workers' Compensation matters and/or are students of the Workers' Compensation field, you are aware that the two main mandates for circumstances of injury are those "arising out of employment" and those "in the course and scope of employment." In this connection, Workers' Compensation would be **the remedy** for an employee claiming intentional or negligent infliction of emotional distress. This is well documented in the case of *Livitsanous* v. *Superior Court* (1992) 1 C.4th 744, 7 C.R.2d 808. However, since certain employees are not covered specifically by Workers' Compensation for the above, it is imperative that you check with your local labor codes to determine the validity of the coverage.

All of this has been said to introduce you to the case which follows, which concerns itself with the course and scope of employment and whether or not the employee therein was covered by insurance at the time of his alleged injury. It would behoove you to check this case out to determine (1) your ability to recognize what is the underlying rule therein and (2) your ability to do the legal research required. Good luck.

Legal Research Problem. A Real Case. Find It.

Your client, Sam Jones, was employed by the Pill Drug Company as a salesman. His duties required him to call on doctors and hospitals to sell them supplies. He lived in Utopia, and his territory was the southeastern portion of the State of Bliss.

His employer's headquarters were in Big Town. On occasions he was required to go to the headquarters store of the company. He was to be in the headquarters store in Big Town on the first and fifteenth of each month, and at other times when in the area.

On Thursday, December 17, 1972, he left Utopia and worked accounts in various towns in his territory, then went to Little Town where he spent the night with his mother. On Friday morning, December 18, 1972, he called on accounts in various towns and then drove to the store in Big Town. He arrived at the store at about 2:00 or 2:30 p.m. He had some orders from doctors which he wrote up and left at the store. He obtained a purchase order from the store, and went to a gift store to pick up a gift, which was his personal business. He then drove back to Little Town and stayed overnight at his mother's home.

On Saturday, December 19, 1972, he left Little Town, drove to the store in Big Town, checked his mail file, waited on customers, talked with the President of the company about his car allowance, and made up an expense voucher for the week. He also picked up some items to deliver to customers, to save the customers freight bills.

On Saturday afternoon he returned to Little Town to get his personal things which were at his mother's home. He remembered he did not have a spare tire. He was unable to get the tire mounted at that time, and went back and visited with his mother for a while. At about 6:00 or 6:30 p.m., he returned to the service station to pick up his used tire. He then started west on U.S. Highway "A". He stopped at Dogtown for coffee, then went on to Ghost Town. When he arrived at Ghost Town he was tired so he stopped for another cup of coffee. He left Ghost Town; about three miles east of Utopia, his home, an accident occurred between his car and a semi-truck. The accident happened at about 10:30 p.m. on a Saturday night.

After leaving Big Town at about 1:00 p.m. that day, Sam Jones *had nothing further to do for his employer,* and had only to return to his home in Utopia. *He did not intend to perform any duties* in Little Town, did not make any solicitations or calls on customers, and *his usual hours of service* were Monday through Friday.

A claim for Workers' Compensation was filed for the injuries Sam sustained in the accident. The Workers' Compensation Court dismissed the claim. An appeal was taken to the District Court, and compensation was allowed. The employer has now appealed to the Supreme Court of the State of Bliss, asking that the claim be dismissed.

AFTERWORD

During the past 25 years, we have seen the growth of the paralegal movement rise from the welfare recipient being retrained in the basement of a law firm building, to the living room of someone's home where a school was being set up, to someone setting up a school in a garage just to make the quick, fast buck.

We have seen the established schools grow from 68 throughout the country to 500-plus in 1993. In this regard, we have seen the American Bar Association set down guidelines for the accreditation of these schools. We have seen various bar associations and paralegal associations attempt to provide a national code of ethics by which these graduated paralegals should be governed, once employed by an attorney or law firm.

And further during this period, we have seen the prediction of the United States Department of Labor come true, that the number of paralegals employed throughout the country would rise from 50,000 to about 250,000.

The Department also predicted that the paralegal position would become the number one position during the 1990s. We have seen this come true.

Now on the horizon is the question of licensing and/or certification of paralegals because of the various duties they now perform in the law office, outside the law office in legal clinics, as well as work done by independent paralegals operating from within their homes or their own offices.

The question therefore arises: what will the twenty-first century bring for the paralegal profession? Will its members become certified and/or licensed? Will the state legislatures and bar associations permit these educated and trained laypersons "to practice law" without infringing upon the attorney's profession?

Certainly there are innumerable ethical questions involved. What is more important is whether or not these ethical issues can be resolved for the benefit of the general public. It is established that the fees being charged by members of the organized bar have been placed out of the reach of the average citizen, resulting in the need for members of the paralegal profession to perform on their behalf.

It is the recommendation therefore of this author that the two entities come together and compromise their positions so that the general public, and the need for the delivery and access to legal assistants, can be reconciled.

It is hoped, therefore, that the contents of this book, and particularly the first few chapters dealing with paralegal ethics and in-house training programs, will assist the organized bar and the members of the paralegal community in reaching such a compromise.

At the very least, it is hoped that this Third Edition will assist the paralegal within the framework of a law office, as well as outside the law office, to make his or her job easier and protect the innocent bystander, the public, from harm.

THE AUTHOR

Index

A

Accord and satisfaction, 124

Action, 63. *See also* Cause of action; Chose in action; Federal court action; State court action; Tort action
in equity, 125
unlawful detainer, 218–19

Actus reus
defenses, 335–36
problems with, 334–36

Admissibility of evidence, 201–2

Affirmative defenses
in answer, 63, 67, 123–26, 129
in breach of contract actions, 375–76
F.R.C.P. and, 83–84
most common, 124–25
and motion to dismiss, 83–84
statute of limitations and, 84, 125

Alabama
court-administered worker's compensation system in, 512
federal judicial districts in, 74
Legal Services Corporation, 5
paralegal status in, 5
U.S. judicial circuit, 73

Alaska
federal judicial districts in, 74
no-fault divorce residence requirements in, 426
paralegal status in, 5
U.S. judicial circuit, 73

Alimony. *See also* Family law practice
Code of the Federal Regulations and, 431
enforcing court orders for, 433–34
Internal Revenue Code and, 431

Amended pleadings, 69–70
F.R.C.P. rules and, 86

American Jurisprudence Second (Am.Jr.2d) 157

American Law Report (A.L.R.), 153, 156

Annotated Case Reports: The "American Law Report," 153

Answer. *See also* Affirmative defenses; Counterclaim
to complaint, 63–64, 83–84
defenses in, 83–84
denial in, 127–28
filing and serving, 130–31
F.R.C.P. and, 83–84, 123, 126
steps in drafting, 126–30

Appeal
certiorari, 56
in criminal case, 356–57
in trial process, 241

Appellate courts
California superior courts, 56–57
Florida circuit court, 57
intermediate, 56
jurisdiction, 61, 79
New York Court of Appeals, 55
supreme court, 55–56

Arbitration. *See also* Mediation; Negotiation
and award, 124
compulsory, 81
filing for, 229
follow-up procedures, 230–34
initiating, 229
voluntary, 81

Arizona
community property plan in, 435
federal judicial districts in, 74
paralegal status in, 5
Unauthorized Practice of Law (UPL) Task Force, 5–6
U.S. judicial circuit, 73

Arkansas
federal judicial districts in, 74
paralegal status in, 5
U.S. judicial circuit in, 73

Articles of incorporation, 329–32

Aspen Computerized Law Index, 157

Assumption of risk, 124

Atlantic Reporter, 153

Attachment. *See* Prejudgment attachment

Attorneys, in paralegal training program, 18–23